Yale School of Architecture
RETROSPECTA 2005/2006

Retrospecta 2005/2006
Published by the Yale School of Architecture
Dean Robert A.M. Stern

Copyright © 2006
Yale School of Architecture.
All rights reserved.
ISBN 0-9772362-8-5
Cost $19.95

For information and copies of this book,
write, call, or visit us at:
180 York Street, New Haven, CT 06511
(203) 432-2288
www.architecture.yale.edu

Editors
Elisa Lui M.Arch.I 2007, Editor-in-Chief
Erica Schroeder M.Arch.I 2008, Coordination Editor
Leo Stevens M.Arch.I 2008, Coordination Editor
Pierce Reynoldson M.Arch.I 2008, Text Editor
Timothy Applebee M.Arch.I 2008, Image Editor

Editorial Assistants
Jamie Chan M.Arch.I 2008, Transcription
Ravi d'Cruz M.Arch.I 2008, Transcription
Jeff McBride M.Arch.I 2007, Proofreading
Jean Suh M.Arch.I 2007, Transcription
Adrienne Swiatocha M.Arch.I 2007, Proofreading

Editorial Consultants
Janet Ho
Allan William Martin
William West

Graphic Designers
Michael Gallagher M.F.A. 2007
Jiminie Ha M.F.A. 2007

Design Consultant
Pentagram, New York

YSOA Photographers
John Jacobson
Anton (Tom) Nikolaas Bosschaert
Adrienne Swiatocha

Printer
Finlay Printing, Bloomfield, CT

We would like to extend our most sincere gratitude to Dean Robert A.M. Stern, Michael Bierut (Pentagram Design, New York), Richard Kaplan (Finlay Printing), John Jacobson, Nina Rappaport, Monica Robinson, Dean Sakamoto, Carter Wiseman, Jean Sielaff, Richard DeFlumeri, Donna Wetmore, Kim Jones, Rosemary Suggs, Maria Huling, Marilyn Weiss, Robert Liston, Surry Schlabs, Jason Van Nest, Marc Guberman and Khai Fung.

Special thanks to all the faculty, staff, and students for their enthusiasm in and contributions to the 2005/2006 issue of Retrospecta.

We would also like to recognize the Rutherford Trowbridge Memorial Publication Fund and the Paul Rudolph Publication Fund, established by Claire and Maurits Edersheim, for their invaluable support.

✦✦✦ Contents

Letter from the Dean

Yale is a community of individuals. As we strive to recognize and respond to the wider world, we embrace diversity as key to the future of architecture. We welcome debate and foster difference because we believe that is the way of the world; as a result, for us all questions are open, without definitive answers. Architecture is never one thing. It is a constellation of possibilities.

An architect's task is to make environments responsibly. At a time in which virtually anything is technically possible, the ability to discern fad from idea is paramount. Each opportunity to design offers the prospect for reinvention – not for the sake of novelty, but for the sake of research leading towards a richer understanding of timeless issues of habitation, of culture, of place. To move forward, ours must be an architecture of multiplicity, building upon the past while embracing the present. An architecture that operates across time is the best one to knowingly confront the future.

Retrospecta 2005/2006 reflects a year's work, presenting the reader with a slice of life at the school. What lies between these covers is but a fragmentary representation of the creativity and critical inquiry that is pervasive in our studios, classrooms and laboratories. *Retrospecta* celebrates that dynamism of discourse which is the hallmark of a life well-spent in architecture.

Robert A.M. Stern
Dean & J.M. Hoppin Professor of Architecture

Letter from the Editors

This year the editorial staff of <u>Retrospecta</u> has selected the theme of identity. Identity is a concept for depicting the diversity of Yale's architectural program through a more comprehensive representation of project approaches, student backgrounds, faculty expertise, course offerings, school events and other educational resources.

In addition to the standard images and conversations which accompany the projects each year, we have provided the undergraduate institution of each student, and a title and description for each project. There are also more photos of the travel studios, events hosted by the school, and social activities among the students. As well, the inclusion of lectures, symposia, and works from a wide range of elective courses will help convey the array of ideas that are shaping our education and the development of the field.

We believe that the spirit of architecture has always been enriched by the diverse personalities that practice its craft. As this school's most pervasive means of public relations, it is as important for <u>Retrospecta</u> to represent Yale's identity as it is to represent the work that it fosters. Diverse and interesting people came here this year to learn, to teach, and to discuss the ideas of students; and it is the goal of this year's staff to document them. We hope that <u>Retrospecta</u> 2005/2006 proves to be not merely a record of the year's work, but also a supplement for anyone curious about what it is like to be at Yale.

Finally, we would also like to take this opportunity to extend our gratitude to our graphic designers for their incredible talents and professional guidance throughout the process.

Elisa Lui
Erica Schroeder
Leo Stevens
Pierce Reynoldson
Timothy Applebee

Enrolled Students
2005/2006

[* Leave of absence, 2005-2006]

Master of Architecture I

Third Year

Ashton Bennett Allan, B.A. Brown Univ. 2003
Eron Ashley, B.S. Univ. of Colorado, Boulder 2000
Seher Rai Aziz, B.A. Bennington College 2001
Scott Baltimore, B.E.D. North Carolina State Univ. 1999
Christopher E.M. Beardsley, B.A. Yale Univ. 2002
Benay Alena Betts, A.B. Brown Univ. 1998
Katherine Elisabeth Burke, B.Des. Univ. of Florida 2002
* Clint Field Burrus, B.A. Southwestern Univ. 2003
Matthew Mackenzie Byers, B.A. Colorado College 2002
Timothy S. Campbell, B.A. Williams College 2001
Angel Paolo Campos, B.A. Yale Univ. 2001
Joyce Jung-Hua Chang, B.A. Univ. of California, Berkeley 1999
* Nai Wee Chng, L.R.C.P. & S.I., M.B., B.CH, B.AO., Royal College of
Surgeons, Ireland 1993
Daniel Haeyoung Chung, M.S.E. Princeton Univ. 2000
Eren Ciraci, B.A. Istanbul Technical Univ. 2002
Dariel Luisa Cobb, B.A. Univ. of California, Berkeley 2000
Abigail Louise Coover, B.S. Univ. of Virginia 2001
Michele Naomi Darling, A.B. Princeton Univ. 1996
Mark Andrew Davis, B.A. Univ. of Washington 2002
Marina Bliss Dayton, B.A. Georgetown Univ. 1999
George Benedict de Brigard, A.B. Harvard Univ. 2001
Christopher Ryan Dial, B.Des. Univ. of Florida 2002
Melanie Domino, B.A. Barnard College 2000
Jennifer A. DuHamel, B.A. Univ. of Washington, 1998
* Rose M. Evans, B.A. Brooklyn College, CUNY. 2002
Brent Wayne Fleming, B.S. Clemson Univ. 2000
Aaron R. Fox, B.A. Wesleyan Univ. 2000
Adam Christian Ganser, B.A. Univ. of Wisconsin, Madison 1993
Armand Balthazar Graham, A.B. Princeton Univ. 2000
Russell Jon Greenberg, B.A. Yale Univ. 2002
Roy Foster Griffith, B.A. Columbia Univ. 1998
Drake Allen Hawthorne, B.A., B.S. Univ. of California, M.F.A.
Maryland Inst. College of Art 1996
Charlotte Frances Henderson, B.A. Auburn Univ. 1999
Nathan Patrick Hume, B.S. Ohio State Univ., Columbus 2003
Laura Ritchie Killam, B.F.A. Concordia Univ., Quebec 1996
Heather Lynn Kilmer, M.A. Ohio State Univ., Columbus 1995
Timothy Murphy Kirkby, B.Des. Univ. of Florida 2003
Ashley Brooke Klein, B.A. Emory Univ. 2001
Marisa Jocelyn Kurtzman, B.A. Wesleyan Univ. 1999
* Clarisse Marie Labro, B.A. Bard College 2002
Nicole Lambrou, B.A. Binghamton Univ., SUNY 1998
Michael Edward Lavery, B.F.A. Washington Univ., Mo. 1995
Heather Nicole Loeffler, B.A. Northwestern Univ. 1999
Andrew Lyon, A.B. Brown Univ. 2003
Mako Maeno, B.A. Barnard College 1998
Allan William Martin, B.A. Yale Univ. 2001
Shauna Lee McBay, B.A. Wesleyan Univ. 1996
Julia Mara McCarthy, B.A. Yale Univ. 1999
Frank Fuhan Nan, B.A. Columbia Univ. 2000
Susan Lynn Parapetti, B.S. Univ. of Michigan, Ann Arbor 2001
Abigail Dunlop Ransmeier, B.A. Yale Univ. 2000
Emily Y. Rhee, B.S. Univ. of Virginia 2002
Christopher J. Rountos, B.S. Northeastern Univ. 2002
Sara Elizabeth Rubenstein, B.A. Columbia Univ. 2002
Christopher Michael Rubino, B.A. Univ. of Pennsylvania, 2003
Frederick C. Scharmen, B.S. Univ. of Maryland, College Park 2001
Fred Gray Shealy, B.A. Clemson Univ. 2003
Meaghan K. Smialowski, B.A. Washington Univ. 2000
Louise Milliken Smith, B.A. Middlebury College 1998
Ross Charles Smith, B.A. Wesleyan Univ. 2000
Dawn Sowby, B.A. Arizona State Univ. 2002
William Langin West, B.A. Stanford Univ. 2003

Second Year

Joseph David Alguire, B.S. Univ. Illinois, Urbana-Champaign 2004
Sandra Arndt, M.S. Univ. of Wuerzburg 1999
E. Sean Bailey, B.A. Univ. of Toronto 2004
* Elizabeth Virginia Baldwin, B.A. Univ. of Florida 2004
Elizabeth Finnegan Barry, B.A. Oberlin College 1997
Gabrielle Eve Brainard, B.A. Yale Univ. 2001
* Gene Stroupe Cartwright, B.A. Yale Univ. 2004
Brook Giles Denison, B.Des. Univ. of Florida 1999
* Chiemeka Anayo Ejiochi, B.S.EE Princeton Univ. 2003
Harris Sittaa Ford, A.B. Princeton Univ. 2002
Khai Meng Fung, B.S. Univ. of Michigan, Ann Arbor 2002
Anya Alaine Grant, B.A. Wesleyan Univ. 2004
Marc Charles Guberman, A.B. Brown Univ. 2003
Sallie Rebecca Hambright, B.S. Clemson Univ. 2002
Greg Nathaniel Heasley, B.S. Univ. of Washington 2004
Janet Anne Ho, B.A. Stanford Univ. 2001
Sini Maria Sofi a Kamppari, B.S. Mass. Inst. of Technology 2002
Serra Kiziltan, B.Sc. Bartlett School of Arch. 2002
Alan Knox, B.A. Texas A&M Univ. 2003
Geoffrey R. Lawson, B.S. Univ. of Virginia 2004
Christopher Hsin-An Lee, B.A. Univ. of California, Berkeley 2001
Steve Sangwin Lee, B.S. Yonsei Univ. 2002

Young Jin Lee, B.S. Seoul National Univ. 2000
Elisa S.Y. Lui, B.A. Univ. of California, Berkeley 1999
Jeff McBride, B.A. Williams College 2002
Rustam-Marc Mehta, A.B. Brown Univ. 2002
Thomas Jason Moran, B.S. Univ. of Illinois, Urbana-Champaign 2001
Seung Hwan Namgoong, B.A. Univ. of California, Berkeley 2001
* Mieko Okamoto, B.A. Columbia Univ. 1996
Clinton Prior, B.S. Queensland Univ. of Technology 2002
* Johnathan S. Puff, B.A. Univ. of Chicago 2002
Mathew Dryden Razook, B.S. Univ. of Virginia 2002
Jacob Reidel, A.B. Brown Univ. 2002
Jeffrey S. Richards, B.A. Hamilton College 2003
Robert Samuel Roche Jr., A.B. Princeton Univ. 2002
Gregorio Santamaria, B.A. Wesleyan Univ. 2000
Neil Gregory Sondgeroth, B.S. Univ. of Illinois, Urbana-Champaign 2004
Kathryn Lee Stutts, B.S. Univ. of Virginia 2003
Ayumi Sugiyama, B.A. Univ. of California, Berkeley 2001
Jean H. Suh, B.S. Univ. of Virginia 2002
Adrienne Elizabeth Swiatocha, B.A. Univ. of Pennsylvania 2001
James Michael Tate, B.E.D. Texas A&M Univ. 2002
Audrey Vuong, B.A. Columbia Univ. 2002
Weston W. Walker, B.A. Cornell Univ. 2004
Kwok Yiu Vincent Wan, B.A. Univ. of Hong Kong 2003
Lindsay Michelle Weiss, B.A. Univ. of Pennsylvania 2001
Michael Jejon Yeung, B.A. Carleton Univ. 2004
Shelley Xiaolei Zhang, B.A. Univ. of Chicago 2002

First Year

Timothy John Applebee, B.A. Swarthmore College 2003
Claire Cole Axley, B.A. Univ. of California, Berkeley 2002
Moises Berrun, B.E.D. Texas A&M Univ. 2003
Anton Nikolaas Bosschaert, B.S., MS Delft Univ. of Technology 2005
Alexandra McCallum Burr, A.B. Middlebury College 2004
Alexander Stewart Butler, B.S. Univ. of Virginia 2002
Ji-eun Cha, M.E., B.A., B.S. Ewha Womans Univ. 2003
Jamie Alma Chan, A.B. Princeton Univ. 2003
* Roger Hsiahwei Chien, B.S. Univ. of Virginia 1995
Jonathon Matthew Cielo, B.S. Univ. of Virginia 2003
Minna Colakis, B.A. Barnard College 2003
Christopher Martin Corbett, B.S. Univ. of Cincinnati 2003
Michael Beaumont Crockett, B.E.D. Texas A&M Univ. 2003
Ravi Stephen d'Cruz, B.A. Yale Univ. 2003
Charles Thomas DiNatale, B.S. Georgia Inst of Technology 2002
Jennifer Jacqueline Dubon, B.A. Univ. of Pennsylvania 2004
Todd Griffith Fenton, B.S. Univ. of Virginia 2001
Garret James Gantner, B.S. Univ. of Wisconsin, Milwaukee 2002
Isidro Garcia, B.S. Mass. Inst. of Technology 2005
Jeff J. Geldart, B.Arch. Ryerson Polytechnical Univ. 2005
Gabrielle Ho, B.A. Univ. of California, Berkeley 2003
Mark C. Hoffman, B.A. Univ. of California, Berkeley 2001
Ireta S.H. Kraal, B.A. Oberlin College 2002
Whitney Meryl Kraus, B.S. Univ. of Michigan, Ann Arbor 2005
Michael Thomas Krop, B.S. Univ. of Virginia 2003
Joshua Wade Lewandowski, B.A. Univ. of Minnesota, Twin Cities 2005
Yichen Lu, B.A. Tsinghua Univ. 2000
Brent Caldbick Martin, B.F.A. Art Center of College of Design 1998
Nicholas W McDermott, B.A. Univ. of Pennsylvania 2002
Elizabeth Louise McDonald, B.A. Tufts Univ. 2001
Maria Claudia Melniciuc, B.A. Colgate Univ. 2005
Shaghayegh Meshkinpour, B.A. Univ. of California, Berkeley 2000
Lydia J.F.V. Miller, B.F.A. Queens Univ. 2004
Sara Murado-Arias, B.A. New York Univ. 2003
Hojin Nam, B.S. Ewha Womans Univ. 2002
Marc C. Newman, B.S. Cornell Univ. 2000
Stephen J. Nielson, B.S. Univ. of Virginia 2002
Nobuki Ogasahara, B.Arch. Waseda Univ. 2004
Garrett Thomas Omoto, B.S. Arizona State Univ. 2005
Cheon-Kang Park, B.S.M.E. Handong Univ.2005
Jason Pytko, B.F.A. Univ of Amherst 1999
Rachel Alexandra Reese, B.S. Univ. of Idaho 1993
Pierce Allen Reynoldson, B.S. Ohio State Univ. 2003
Nathan David Rich, B.A. Wesleyan Univ. 2002
David J. Riedel, B.A. Carleton College 2003
Roberto Attilio Rossi, A.B. Princeton Univ. 1984
Jeong Yeon Ryoo, B.E. Hongik Univ. 2002
Meredith Jaye Sattler, A.B. Vassar College 1995
Dylan M. Sauer, B.S. Univ. Cincinnati 2005
Erica Rachel Schroeder, B.S. Ohio State Univ. 2005
Benjamin Tully Smoot, B.S. Univ. of Virginia 2003
Leo Rowling Stevens IV, B.A. Yale Univ. 2005
Isaac John Strackbein, B.E.D. Univ of Colorado, Boulder 2003
Sohyun Sung, B.E. Korea Univ. 2005
Chiew Hong Tan, B.A. Nat'l Univ of Singapore 2005
Quang Vinh Truong, B.A. Dartmouth College 2001
Mark P. Van Brocklin, B.S. Univ. of Virginia 2000
Jessica Ann Varner, B.A. Univ. of Nebraska, Lincoln 2004
Christina Wu, B.A. Univ. of Pennsylvania 2004
Alberto Briseno Zamora, B.E.D. Texas A&M Univ. 2003

Master of Architecture II

Second Year

Namil Byun, M.E. Ajou Univ. 2000

Sung Ik Cho, M.S. Seoul National Univ. 1999

Mario Alexander Cruzate, B.Arch. Pratt Institute 2004

Michael Joseph Grogan, B.Arch. Univ. of Arkansas, Fayetteville 1995

Andrei S. Harwell, B.Arch. Carnegie Mellon Univ. 1998

Brian Dimitris Hopkins, B.Arch. Pratt Institute 2004

Sean A. Khorsandi, B.Arch. Cooper Union 2004

Christopher Ray Kitterman, B.Arch. Tulane Univ. 2004

Mayur Mehta, B.Arch. Kamla Raheja Vidyndi Inst. of Arch. & Engr. 2002

Frank Paul Melendez, B.Arch. Univ. of Arizona 1998

David Nam, B.Arch. Cornell Univ. 1996

Maxwell Riley Worrell, B.Arch. Oklahoma State Univ. 2001

First Year

Mohammed Mustafa Balila, B.Arch. Cornell Univ. 2005

Katherine Corsico, B.Arch. Cornell Univ. 2003

Jason B. deBoer, B.Arch. Univ. of Cincinnati 2005

Ayat Fadaifard, B.Arch. City College of New York, CUNY 2005

Jeremiah Joseph, B.Arch. Univ. of Kentucky 1997

Mustapha Mohamed Nouhad Jundi, B.Arch. American Univ., Beirut 2000

Soo-Hyun Kim, M.Arch. Korean National Univ. of Arts 2005

Yoo Jung Lee, M.E. Ewha Womans Univ. 2005

Karl Rajiv Mascarenhas, B.Arch. Academy in Architecture 2003

Timothy N. Newton, B.Arch. Univ. of British Columbia 1995

Carol Ann B. Ruiz, B.Arch. New York Inst. of Technology 2002

Allen Slamic, B.Arch. Kent State Univ. 2003

Joseph M Smith, B.Arch. Univ. of Notre Dame 2001

Maryjane Scime Starks, B.Arch. Pratt Institute 2005

Andrew James Steffen, B.Arch. Iowa State Univ. 2005

Julia Jee Hee Suh, B.Arch. Auckland Univ. 2004

Xinghua Zhao, B.Arch. Tsinghua Univ. 2003

Master of Environmental Design

Second Year

Joy Ruth Knoblauch, B.Arch. Cornell Univ. 2002

Frida Karin Rosenberg, B.S. Univ. of Texas 2000, M.Arch. Chalmers Univ. 2004

Leslie Ann Ryan, B.S. California Polytechnic, San Luis Obispo 1988

Sara K. Stevens, B.Arch. Rice Univ. 2002

First Year

McLain Clutter, B.Arch. Syracuse Univ. 2001

Gary Britt Eversole, M.Arch. Yale Univ. 2004

Enrique G. Ramirez, M.A. Univ. of California, Los Angeles 2005

Molly Wright Steenson, B.A. Univ. of Wisconsin, Madison 2003

Federica Vannucchi, M.A. Univ. degli Studi di Firenze 1999

Yale College
Bachelor of Arts in Architecture

Class of 2007

Design

Julie Andress, Silliman College

Henry Chan, Timothy Dwight College

Laura Cheung, Branford College

Elizabeth Friedlander, Morse College

Clay Hayles, Saybrook College

Seema Kairam, Silliman College

Marcus McLin, Ezra Stiles College

Christian Nakarado, Silliman College

Suchitra Paul, Silliman College

Ann (Lane) Rick, Morse College

David Sadighian, Calhoun College

Jillian Sala, Pierson College

Robin Swartout, Calhoun College

Luis Vasquez, Berkeley College

Mei-Lun Xue, Branford College

History, Theory, & Criticism

Aleksandr Bierig, Branford College

Elizabeth Bondaryk, Branford College

Chimaobi Izeogu, Trumbull College

Urban Studies

Erica Bergman, Berkeley College

Jared Enriquez, Ezra Stiles College

Daniel Fuchs, Calhoun College

Claire Matthews, Davenport College

Henry Ng, Pierson College

Maria Rizzolo, Trumbull College

Class of 2006

Design

Margo Angelopoulos, Branford College

Adrian Coleman, Jonathan Edwards College

Carl D'Apolito-Dworkin, Timothy Dwight College

Frances Edelman, Silliman College

Nathan Elchert, Silliman College

Peter Feigenbaum, Branford College

Chelsea Garunay, Saybrook College

Palmyra Geraki, Saybrook College

Columba Gonzalez-Quintanilla, Morse College

Katherine Lent, Morse College

Emily Nakashima, Davenport College

Christopher Ricca, Morse College

Andrea Sreshta, Jonathan Edwards College

Chibuzor Ugenyi, Morse College

Alice Warren, Morse College

Jeffrey Warren, Davenport College

Victoria Wolcott, Pierson College

Carlos Zedillo, Berkeley College

History, Theory, & Criticism

Tala Gharagozlou, Morse College

Samuel Kendrick, Calhoun College

Alice Phillips, Berkeley College

Jessica Shapiro, Timothy Dwight College

Gabriel Smedresman, Branford College

Amanda Webb, Branford College

Urban Studies

Jordan Barr, Davenport College

Leslie Cacciapaglia, Timothy Dwight College

Nicholas Friend, Calhoun College

Jeffrey Hamilton, Pierson College

Left to Right: (Standing) Brent Fleming, William West, Andrew Lyon, Fred Scharmen, Drake Hawthorne, Matthew Byers, David Nam, Mario Cruzate, Armand Graham, Christopher Kitterman, Andrei Harwell, Mayur Mehta, Michael Grogan, Meaghan Smialowski, Daniel Chung, Julia McCarthy, Charlotte Henderson, Katherine Burke, Michael Lavery, Dariel Cobb, Adam Ganser, Benay Betts, William Martin, Timothy Kirkby, Christopher Dial, Roy Griffith; (Forth Row) Mark Davis, Christopher Rountos, Christopher Beardsley, George de Brigard, Melanie Domino, Marisa Kurtzman; (Third Row) Scott Baltimore, Timothy Campbell, Mako Maeno, Sara Rubenstein, Frank Nan, Sung Ik Cho, Emily Rhee; (Second Row) Sean Khorsandi, Eron Ashley, Ross Smith, Gray Shealy, Paolo Campos, Max Worrell, Ashton Allan, Russell Greenberg, Jennifer DuHamel, Louise Smith, Marina Dayton, Laura Killam; (First Row) Leslie Ryan, Frida Rosenberg, Naomi Darling, Aaron Fox, Joy Knoblauch, Dawn Sowby, Heather Kilmer, Abigail Ransmeier, Joyce Chang, Susan Parapetti, Seher Aziz, Brian Hopkins, Sara Stevens.

Fellowships

William Wirt Winchester Travelling Fellowship
Christopher Ray Kitterman

The Gertraud A. Wood Traveling Fellowship, Awarded 2005
Frederick Casey Scharmen

The George Nelson Scholarship, Awarded 2005
Michele Naomi Darling

David M. Schwarz/Architectural Services Good Times Award
Frederick Casey Scharmen

The Fermin R. Ennis Memorial Fellowship
Sara Kathryn Stevens

Medals & Prizes

American Institute of Architects Henry Adams Medal
George de Brigard

American Institute of Architects Henry Adams Certificate
Abigail Ransmeier

The Alpha Rho Chi Medal
Christopher Beardsley

The William Edward Parsons Memorial Medal
Roy Griffith

The H.I. Feldman Prize
Russell Jon Greenberg
    Nominees
        Christopher E.M. Beardsley
        Katherine Elisabeth Burke
        Christopher Ryan Dial
        Melanie Domino
        Jennifer A. DuHamel
        Aaron R. Fox
        Adam Christian Ganser
        Russell Jon Greenberg
        Andrei Simon Harwell
        Jeremiah Joseph
        Mustapha Jundi
        Laura Ritchie Killam
        Christopher Kitterman
        Marisa Jocelyn Kurtzman
        Timothy Newton
        Susan Lynn Parapetti
        Frederick Casey Scharmen
        William West
        Maxwell Riley Worrell

The Wendy Elizabeth Blanning Prize, Awarded 2005
Andrew Lyon

The Sonia Albert Schimberg Prize
Meaghan Smialowski

The Janet Cain Sielaff Alumni Award
Fred Gray Shealy III

The Moulton Andrus Award
Abigail Louise Coover

The Drawing Prize
Nicole Lambrou

Gene Lewis Book Prize
Scott Baltimore

The David Taylor Memorial Prize
Sara Kathryn Stevens

Internships

Takenaka Corporation Summer Internship, Awarded 2005
Andrei Simon Harwell

The David M. Schwarz/Architectural Services Internship and Traveling Fellowship, Awarded 2005
Marisa Jocelyn Kurtzman

Scholarships

The Franklin U. Gregory Memorial Scholarship
Armand Balthazar Graham

The Charles O. Matcham Scholarship
Nathan Patrick Hume

The Everett Victor Meeks Fellowship
Leslie Ann Ryan

The Eero Saarinen Memorial Scholarship
David Nam

The Carroll L. V. Meeks Memorial Scholarship
Sean A. Khorsandi

The Samuel J. Fogelson Memorial Fund
Eron Ashley

The Christopher Tunnard Memorial Scholarship
Andrew Lyon

The Anne C.K. Garland Fund
Angel Paolo Campos

The Robert Allen Ward Scholarship Fund
Brent Wayne Fleming

The Kenneth A. Housholder Scholarship, Awarded 2004
Armand Balthazar Graham

The Henry Pfisterer Scholarship
Michele Naomi Darling

The James Gamble Rogers Scholarship, Awarded 2005
Eron Ashley
Angel Paolo Campos
Eren Ciraci
Abigail Louise Coover
Armand Balthazar Graham
Nathan Patrick Hume
Frank Fuhan Nam
Abigail Dunlop Ransmeier

The A. Whitney Murphy Scholarship
Timothy Murphy Kirkby

The Enid Storm Dwyer Scholarship
Abigail Louise Coover

The Herman D.J. Spiegel Scholarship
Allan William Martin

The Ulli Scharnberg Scholarship in memory of Carroll L. V. Meeks
Andrei Simon Harwell

The John W. Storrs Scholarship
Michael Joseph Grogan

The Harvey R. Russell Scholarship
Michele Naomi Darling

The Yen and Dolly Liang Scholarship
Julia Mara McCarthy

The Robert Leon Coombs Scholarship
Mario Alexander Cruzate

The Frederick T. Ahlson Scholarship
Ashton Bennett Allan

The David C. Morton II Scholarship
Frederick Casey Scharmen

The Stanley Tigerman Scholarship
Maxwell Riley Worrell

The Cesar Pelli Scholarship
Eren Ciraci

The Clarke Family Scholarship (Established 2006)
Ross Charles Smith

The Pickard Chilton Fellowship (Established 2006)
Adam Christian Ganser

The Dean's Scholarship (Established 2006)
Andrei Simon Harwell

Course Listing
2005/2006

Executive Officers

Richard Charles Levin, *B.A., B.LITT, PH.D., President of the University.*
Andrew David Hamilton, *B.SC., PH.D., F.R.S, Provost.*
Robert A.M. Stern, *B.A., M.ARCH., Dean.*
John D. Jacobson, *B.A., M.ARCH., Associate Dean.*
Peggy Deamer, *B.A., B.ARCH., M.A., PH.D., Assistant Dean.*
Keith A. Krumwiede, *B.A., M.ARCH. Assistant Dean.*

‒ ‒ ‒ ‒

Faculty Emeriti

Martin D. Gehner, *B.ARCH, M.ARCH, Professor Emeritus of Architectural Engineering.*
Walter DeSalles Harris, Jr., *B.ARCH., M.ARCH., PH.D., Professor Emeritus of City Planning.*
Alexander Purves, *B.A., M.ARCH., Professor Emeritus of Architecture.*
Herman David John Spiegel, *B.S.ARCH, M.ENG., Professor Emeritus of Architectural Engineering.*

‒ ‒ ‒ ‒

Professors

James W. Axley, *B.S., M.ARCH., M.S., PH.D., Professor.*
Thomas H. Beeby, *B.ARCH., M.ARCH., Professor (Adjunct).*
Deborah Berke, *B.F.A., B.ARCH., M.U.P., Professor (Adjunct).*
Kent C. Bloomer, *B.F.A., M.F.A., Professor (Adjunct).*
Turner Brooks, *B.A., M.ARCH., Professor (Adjunct).*
Peggy Deamer, *B.A., B.ARCH., M.A., PH.D., Associate Professor.*
Keller Easterling, *B.A., M.ARCH, Associate Professor.*
Mark Foster Gage, *B.ARCH., M.ARCH., Assistant Professor.*
Alexander D. Garvin, *B.A., M.ARCH., m.u.s., Professor (Adjunct).*
Mario Gooden, *B.S., M.ARCH, Associate Professor (Adjunct).*
Steven Harris, *B.A., B.F.A., M.ARCH., Professor (Adjunct).*
Dolores Hayden, *B.A., M.ARCH., Professor and Professor of American Studies.*
John D. Jacobson, *B.A., M.ARCH., Associate Dean and Professor (Adjunct).*
Fred H. Koetter, *B.ARCH., M.ARCH., Professor (Adjunct).*
Keith A. Krumwiede, *B.A., M.ARCH. Assistant Dean and Assistant Professor.*
Edward Mitchell, *B.A., M.ARCH., Assistant Professor (Adjunct).*
Eeva-Liisa Pelkonen, *M.ARCH., M.E.D., PH.D., Assistant Professor.*
Emmanuel Petit, *DIPL.ARCH.ETH., M.A., PH.D., Assistant Professor.*
Alan J. Plattus, *B.A., M.ARCH., Professor.*
Hilary Sample, *B.ARCH., M.ARCH., Assistant Professor.*
Joel Sanders, *B.A., M.ARCH, Associate Professor (Adjunct).*
Robert A.M. Stern, *B.A., M.ARCH., Dean and J.M. Hoppin Professor of Architecture.*

‒ ‒ ‒ ‒

Endowed Visiting Professorships & Fellowships

‒ ‒ ‒ ‒

Fall 2005

Leon Krier, *William B. and Charlotte Shepherd Davenport Visiting Professor of Architectural Design.*
Glenn Murcutt, *William Henry Bishop Visiting Professor of Architectural Design.*
Brigitte Shim, *Eero Saarinen Visiting Professor of Architectural Design.*
Peter Eisenman, *Louis I. Kahn Visiting Professor of Architectural Design.*
Jeanne Gang, *Louis I. Kahn Visiting Assistant Professor of Architectural Design.*
Kurt Forster, *Vincent Scully Visiting Professor of Architectural History.*

‒ ‒ ‒ ‒

Spring 2006

Greg Lynn, *William B. and Charlotte Shepherd Davenport Visiting Professor of Architectural Design.*
Demetri Porphyrios, *William B. and Charlotte Shepherd Davenport Visiting Professor of Architectural Design.*
Richard Rogers, *William B. and Charlotte Shepherd Davenport Visiting Professor of Architectural Design.*
Chris Wise, *William B. and Charlotte Shepherd Davenport Visiting Professor of Architectural Design.*
Will Bruder, *William Henry Bishop Visiting Professor of Architectural Design.*
Stefan Behnisch, *Eero Saarinen Visiting Professor of Architectural Design.*
Frank O. Gehry, *Louis I. Kahn Visiting Professor of Architectural Design.*
Sunil Bald, *Louis I. Kahn Visiting Assistant Professor of Architectural Design.*
Stuart Lipton, *Edward P. Bass Distinguished Visiting Architecture Fellow.*

‒ ‒ ‒ ‒

Affiliated Faculty

Karsten Harries, *B.A., P.HD, Mellon Professor of Philosophy (Department of Philosophy).*
Sandy Isenstadt, *B.A., M.ARCH, P.HD, Assistant Professor of the History of Art (Department of the History of Art).*
Vincent J. Scully, *Jr., B.A., M.A., P.HD, Sterling Professor Emeritus of the History of Art (Department of the History of Art).*

‒ ‒ ‒ ‒

Critics, Lecturers, & Instructors

Victor Agran, *B.A., M.ARCH., Critic.*
Thomas Auer, *B.SC., Lecturer.*
Diana Balmori, *B.A, M.A., PH.D., Critic*
Patrick Bellew, *B.SC., Lecturer.*
Phillip G. Bernstein, *B.A., M.ARCH., Lecturer.*
John P. Blood, *B.ARCH., M.ARCH., Critic.*
Karla Britton, *B.A., M.A., PH.D., Lecturer.*
Paul B. Brouard, *B.A., M.ARCH., Critic.*
Aran Chadwick, *B.Eng., M.S., Lecturer.*
Vincent Chang, *B.A., M.ARCH., Lecturer.*
David Chen, *B.A., M.ARCH., Lecturer.*
Peter Chow, *B.ARCH., M.ARCH., Lecturer.*

Fiona Cousins, *BA, M.S.e., Lecturer.*
Elizabeth Danze, *B.ARCH., M.ARCH., Lecturer.*
Peter de Bretteville, *B.A., M.ARCH., Critic.*
John C. Eberhart, *B.S., M.ARCH., Critic.*
Susan Farricielli, *B.F.A., m.i.d., Lecturer.*
Martin J. Finio, *B.ARCH., Critic.*
Bryan Fuermann, *B.A., M.A., PH.D., m.des.s., Lecturer.*
Deborah Gans, *B.A., M.ARCH., Critic.*
Kenneth Gibble, *B.ARCH.eng., Lecturer.*
Anne Gilbert, *B.A. B.S.C.E., M.S.C.E., Lecturer*
Philip Grausman, *B.A., M.F.A., Lecturer.*
Kimo Griggs, *B.A., M.ARCH., Lecturer.*
Sophia Gruzdys, *B.ARCH., M.ARCH., Critic.*
Stephen Harby, *B.A., M.ARCH., Lecturer.*
Erleen Hatfield, *B.S.a.s., M.S.civ.eng., Lecturer.*
Robert Haughney, *B.S., Lecturer.*
Mimi Hoang, *B.S., M.ARCH., Critic.*
Gavin Hogben, *B.A., M.A., dipl.arch., Critic.*
Adam Hopfner, *B.A., M.ARCH., Critic.*
Andrea Kahn, *B.A., M.ARCH., Critic.*
Gordon Kipping, *B.S., M.ARCH., Critic.*
George Knight, *B.A., M.ARCH., Critic.*
Andrew Kudless, *M.A., M.ARCH., Lecturer*
Amy Lelyveld, *B.A., M.ARCH., Critic.*
Timothy Macfarlane, *B.Sc MI.Struct.E. C.Eng. F.Cons.E., Lecturer.*
Dino Marcantonio, *B.A., M.ARCH., Lecturer.*
Bimal Mendis, *B.A., M.ARCH., Critic.*
Herbert S. Newman, *B.A., M.ARCH., Critic.*
Alan W. Organschi, *B.A., M.ARCH., Critic.*
Hideaki Ota, *B.ENG. (arch.), M.ENG. (arch.), M.ARCH., Lecturer.*
Paloma Pajares, *M.ARCH, Lecturer.*
S. Edward Parker, *B.S., M.ARCH., Lecturer.*
Ben Pell, *B.ARCH., M.ARCH., Critic.*
Craig Razza, *B.S.M.E., Lecturer.*
Kevin Rotheroe, *B.S., M.ARCH., m.des.s., d.des., Lecturer.*
Joshua Rowley, *B.F.A., M.F.A., Instructor.*
Sarah Sachs, *B.ENG., Lecturer.*
Dean Sakamoto, *B.ARCH., M.ARCH., M.E.D., Critic.*
Victoria Sambunaris, *B.A., M.F.A., Lecturer.*
David Shea, *BSAE., M.S. Lecturer.*
Robert Silman, *B.A., B.CIV.ENG., M.CIV.ENG., Lecturer.*
Edward M. Stanley, *B.S., B.S.c.e., M.S.str.e., Lecturer.*
Paul Stoller, *B.S., M.A., M.ARCH., Instructor.*
Lindsay S. Suter, *B.A., M.ARCH., Lecturer.*
Barry Svigals, *B.A., M.ARCH., Lecturer.*
Neil Thomas, *B.S., M.S., Lecturer.*
Jim Tinson, *B.ARCH., M.ARCH., Critic.*
Ingalill Wahlroos-Ritter, *B.A., M.ARCH., Lecturer.*
Michael Weinstock, *Dip.Arch., Lecturer.*
Claire Weisz, *B.ARCH., M.ARCH., Critic.*
Carter Wiseman, *B.A., M.A., Lecturer.*
Michael Young, *B.ARCH., M.ARCH., Critic.*
Claire Zimmerman, *B.A., M.ARCH., PH.D., Lecturer.*

‒ ‒ ‒ ‒

Administrative Staff

Richard DeFlumeri, *B.A., Senior Administrative Assistant, Lectures, Exhibitions, and Special Events.*
Sharon Sweet DeLuca, *B.A., Financial Aid Administrator.*
Vincent Guerrero, *B.S., Systems Administrator.*
Maria H. Huling, *Senior Administrative Assistant to Registrar/Admissions & Financial Aid Office*
Kim Jones, *B.S., M.B.A., Financial Administrator.*
Dana Keeton, *B.F.A., Exhibitions Administrator.*
Robert Liston, *B.S., Systems Administrator.*
Jean F. Sielaff, *B.A., Senior Administrative Assistant to Dean's Office; Alumni Affairs Administrator*
Daniel Staffieri, *Systems Administrator.*
Rosemary Suggs, *Senior Administrative Assistant to Financial Administrator.*
Marilyn Weiss, *A.S., Registrar and Admissions Administrator.*
Donna Wetmore, *B.S., Administrative Assistant.*

‒ ‒ ‒ ‒

Arts Library

Christine de Vallet, *B.A., M.L.S., Interim Director.*
Hannah Bennett, *B.A., M.A., M.L.S., Interim Assistant Director.*
Tanya Allen, *B.A., M.A., Library Services Assistant.*
Jennifer Aloi, *B.S., Administrative Assistant.*
Susan Brady, *B.A., M.A., M.L.S., Project Archivist.*
Beverly T. Lett, *B.A., M.DIV, Library Services Assistant.*
Jae Rossman, *B.A., M.L.S., Special Collections Librarian.*
Charles Summa, *B.A., M.A., Library Services Assistant.*
Fantasia Thorne, *B.A., Library Services Assistant.*
Christopher Zollo, *B.A., Library Services Assistant.*

‒ ‒ ‒ ‒

Visual Resources Collection

Katherine Haskins, *B.A., M.L.S., PH.D., Director and Project Director of Integrated Digital Image Resources.*
Tracy C. Bergstrom, *B.A., M.A., Visual Resources Support Specialist.*
Helen Chillman, *B.A., M.L.S., Slide Librarian.*
Sarah Coe, *B.A., M.F.A., Visual Resources Support Specialist.*
Maria Zapata, *A.S., Library Services Assistant.*

‒ ‒ ‒ ‒

Roll of Donors

[* in memoriam]

Friends
ASSA ABLOY
Autodesk
Sid R. Bass '65 BA
Leonor & Kent Bloomer '61 MFA
Hilda Ochoa-Brillembourg
James C. Childress
Carla Cicero
Laura Weir Clark & Fred W. Clarke, III
Peter H. Dominick, Jr. '63 BA
Elisha-Bolton Foundation
Warren Bryan Fuermann
David Hilder
The Home Depot
Rolf Fehlbaum
Judith T. Hunt
Elise Jaffe + Jeffrey Brown
Anne M. Kimberly
Elizabeth Lenahan
Bradley Nitkin '69 BA
Harley Osman
Cesar Pelli
Elizabeth B. & William K. Reilly '62 BA
Justine Amata Richardson '92 BA
Craig Robins
E. Kevin Roche
Joseph B. Rose '81 BA
Robert Rosenkranz '62 BA
Jeanne W. Ruesch
Robert M. Rubin '74 BA
Elaine Tillinghast
Betty L. Wagner
Anne C. Weisberg
Pei-Tse Wu '89 BA

1931
* William B. Cram

1933
Donal McLaughlin

1935
David Norton Yerkes

1938
Gardiner Angell

1939
Thomas J. Imbs

1940
Russell P. Morse

1941
Kenneth Gibbons
Peter K. Ogden

1942
H. Dickson McKenna

1944
Leon A. Miller

1947
David N. Cybul
Henry Kibel
Francis D. Lethbridge

1948
Raymond C. Giedraitis
Henry F. Miller
Eugene Nalle
Joseph Richmond Tamsky
Joseph T. Wilson

1949
Frank S. Alschuler
Theodore F. Babbitt
Jack Alan Bialosky, Sr.
Charles H. Brewer, Jr.
Russell C. Cecil
Elvia Fernandez
B. Fornonzini
Bruce P. Helmes
John Herron
George A. Hinds
William S. Kirkpatrick
Cyril K. Smith, Jr.
Edward A. Sovik
George D. Waltz

1950
R. Paige Donhauser
Henry E. Martens
* John L. O'Brien, Jr.
Roy M. Palhof
Herbert L. Seigle
Morris Simon
D. Jack West

1951
Stanley B. Brundage
Phelps H. Bultman
Frederick A. Craggs
Ross H. De Young
Nathaniel Firestone
Martha Cantwell Meeker
William H. Metcalf, Jr.

1952
Thomas C. Babbitt
Donald Z. Bailey
Frank C. Boyer, Jr.
Paul E. Buchli
James A. Evans
Dale L. Gibbs
* James Wilder Green
Morton Kass
Donald C. Mallow
Vincent M. Milone
Herbert M. Noyes, Jr.
Lawrence Frederick Nulty
James Elwell Palmer
Howard M. Y. Wong

1953
Duncan W. Buell
Andrew S. Cohen
Frank D. George
Milton Klein
Julian E. Kulski
Donald I. Perry
John V. Sheoris

1954
Mansfield M. Bascom
Charles G. Brickbauer
George R. Brunjes, Jr.
James H. Fitts
James D. Gibans
Brooks D. Kaufman
John F. Lee, Jr.
Roger L. Strassman

1955
Vica S. Emery
John L. Field
Duncan M. Graham
Thomas F. Graves
Hugh N. Jacobsen
Estelle T. Margolis
James Stewart Polshek
Jaquelin T. Robertson
Edwards F. Rullman
Sidney M. Sisk
Patricia V. Tetrault

1956
William B. Grindereng
Gerald E. Henniger
Walter D. Ramberg
Stanley B. Wright, Jr.

1957
Ernest L. Ames
Edwin William de Cossy
Charles Augustus Ferrari
James H. Handley, Jr.
Mark H. Hardenbergh
Clovis B. Heimsath
Lee Mogel
Richard A. Nininger
William L. Porter
Harold Roth
Howard W. Shoemaker
Richard Elliott Wagner

1958
Edwin G. Close II
Edward C. Collins II
Arthur H. Corwin
James S. Dudley
Jon Eric Ericson
Harold D. Fredenburgh
Alvin H. Holm, Jr.
J. Arvid Klein
Herbert P. McLaughlin
Allen Moore, Jr.
Gerald F. Oudens
Charles O. Perry
Jacques Richter
Malcolm Strachan
Harold F. VanDine, Jr.
Shirley L. Winter

1959
George J. Alfano
Frank C. Chapman
Thomas G. Green
Franklin D. Guidone
Louis P. Inserra
Robert Michael Kliment
Raymond S. Leahy
Eugene J. Lorincz
Franklin J. McNutt
Herbert S. Newman
David L. Niland
Earl A. Quenneville
Frederick A. Russell
Hans Ullrich Scharnberg
Bruce W. Sielaff
* John Jay Stonehill
Lee Anthony Syracuse
Terry G. Twitchell
Donald W. Velsey
Ralph J. Warburton
Carolyn H. Westerfield
Andrew C. Wheeler
Thomas E. Woodward

1960
James B. Baker
Thomas L. Bosworth
Richard Spofford Chafee
John K. Copelin
Geoffrey Edmands
Alexander Grinnell
John Hayes
David P. Jeffrey
Louis B. Joline
Julia H. Keydel
Renato la Ferla
James D. McNeely
Robert A. Mitchell
John J. Molloy
Ivan S. Poutiatine
Gertrude O. Seibels
Stanley Tigerman
Rodger A. Wilkin

1961
Donald J. Baerman
Paul B. Brouard
Robert W. Carington
Warren J. Cox
Francis W. Gencorelli
Charles T. Haddad
William J. Hawkins III
Lee H. Pomeroy
Jaquelin T. Robertson
W. Eugene Sage
Bradford P. Shaw
Roger P. Whitcomb

1962
James L. Alcorn
George E. Buchanan
Robert A. Cordingley
David W. Fix
Norman R. Foster
Richard A. Hansen
Tai Soo Kim
Keith R. Kroeger
James Morganstern
William S. Nichols
Leonard P. Perfido
Renato Rossi-Loureiro
Meredith M. Seikel
Donald R. Watson
Myles Weintraub

1963
Austin Church III
A. Robert Faesy, Jr.
John Ming-Yee Lee
John L. McGuerty
Ward Joseph Miles
F. Kempton Mooney
George Douglas Richmond
Louis H. Skidmore, Jr.
William A. Werner, Jr.
John V. Yanik

1964
Philip Allen
Lucinda L. Cisler
Peter Jeremy Hoppner
Charles D. Hosford
Augustus G. Kellogg
Judith A. Lawler
Charles L W. Leider
Robert J. Mittelstadt
Ramesh Baldevbhai Patel
Joan F. Stogis

1965
Michael J. Altschuler
Thomas Hall Beeby
Richard C. Fogelson
Peter L. Gluck
Norman E. Jackson, Jr.
Erik T. Jansson
Arthur A. Klipfel III
Isidoro Korngold
Charles G. Meyer, Jr.
Gary L. Michael
John I. Pearce, Jr.
Alexander Purves
Elliot A. Segal
W. Mason Smith III
Robert A.M. Stern
Frederick C. Terzo
Leonard M. Todd, Jr.
Jeremy A. Walsh
Arnold N. Wile

1966
Andrew Andersons
Samuel M. Busselle
Richard C. Carroll, Jr.
James Scott Cook
Joan C. Countryman
John J. Damico
Frank S. Grosso
Michael Hollander
Yousef Marzeki
Donald A. Metz, Jr.
Emily Nugent Mokriski
William F. Moore
Peter H. Nuelsen
William L. Riddle
Myron B. Silberman
Henry H. Smith-Miller
Lester R. Walker

1967

William H. Albinson
Edward A. Arens
Robert A. Bell
Jon A. Carr
David M. Childs
Gunter Dittmar
Charles M. Engberg
Alexander D. Garvin
Howard E. Goldstein
Glenn H. Gregg
Walter A. Hunt, Jr.
Eugene J. Lai
Simon Lazarus III
Chung Nung Lee
Wood A. Lockhart
Kenneth MacLean, Jr.
H. Fraser Mills
John W. Mullen III
Howard F. Phillips
A. Ramirez de Arellano
Theodore Paul Streibert
Darius Toraby
William H. Willis, Jr.
Robert M. Winick
– – – –

1968

Frederick S. Andreae
Gail H. Cooke
David M. Dickson
Richard M. Donnelly
John Fulop, Jr.
Christopher C. Glass
Nash R. Gubelman
John Holbrook, Jr.
Gerard Ives
Erno Kolodny-Nagy
* Robert H. Kuehn, Jr.
John M. Lucas
Louis Mackall
Peter C. Mayer
Peter Papademetriou
Hansell Merrill Pasco, Jr.
Franklin Satterthwaite
Donald R. Spivack
Salvatore F. Vasi
John J. Vosmek, Jr.
Thomas R. Welch, Jr.
James C. Whitney
– – – –

1969

Jeffrey K. Abrams
Stephen Harris Adolphus
Jane K. Cahn
James E. Caldwell, Jr.
Samuel R. Callaway, Jr.
Robert J. Cassidy
David B. Decker
Harvey R. Geiger
Edward J. Gotgart
William H. Grover
Eric R. Hansen, Jr.
Peter Andrew D Hentschel
Roderick C. Johnson
Raymond J. Kaskey, Jr.
Robert C. Kurzon
Jeffrey H. May
James W. Peoples
William B. Richardson
John H. Shoaff
Kermit D. Thompson
Peter C. Witter
– – – –

1970

Judith L. Aronson
Roland F. Bedford
Paul F. Bloom
Davis A. Buckley
F. Andrus Burr
Roc R. Caivano
Ralph E. Carlson
Charles Y. Dusenbury
Ronald C. Filson
George T. Hathorn
Peter Van W. Hoyt
John D. Jacobson
David C. Jamison
Jack Marshall
William J. Mitchell
Philip A. Monteleoni
Kathrin S. Moore
Ivey Lewis Nix, Jr.
James V. Righter
Steven G. Rockmore
Laurence A. Rosen
Daniel V. Scully
Robert F. Shannon
Pierre E. Strauch
Karen M. Votava
Peter Kurt Woerner
Jeremy Scott Wood
William L. Yuen
F. Anthony Zunino
– – – –

1971

John R. Benson
William A. Brenner
Jay Warren Bright
Rockwell J. Chin
Mark J. Ellis
Ronald L. Gonzalez
Anita Holland-Moritz
Robert L. Miller
Ray S. Oliver
H. Rodriguez-Camilloni
Susan St. John
Jeremiah W. Whitney
Peter J. Wood
– – – –

1972

Marc F. Appleton
Paul B. Bailey
Edward P. Bass
Frederick Bland
Stephen J. Blatt
Phillip M. Caldwell
Roberta Carlson Carnwath
Heather Willson Cass
William A. Davis, Jr.
Joseph A. Ford III
* David F. Gibson
Coleman A. Harwell II
William H. Maxfield
Barton Phelps
Jefferson B. Riley
Paul W. Scovill III
Richard C. Shepard, Jr.
Mark Simon
Henry B. Teague
Brinkley S. Thorne
Carl H. Wies
George Vincent Wright
Roger Hung Tuan Yee
– – – –

1973

Russell E. Bloodworth, Jr.
Arthur F. Duncan
Hobart Fairbank
J.P. Chadwick Floyd
Stephen R. Holt
James O. Kruhly
William M. Mack
Louise B. Meusel
Nancy Brooks Monroe
Robert S. Page
Karen Rheinlander-Gray
Steven C. Robinson
Michael J. Stanton
William A. Sterling
Kokseng Teng
Stephen C. Thomson
R. Jerome Wagner
John W. Whipple
Robert J. Yudell
– – – –

1974

Gordon M. Black
Hillary A. Brown
Philippe F. Campus
Sara E. Caples
Eric A. Chase
Andres M. Duany
William P. Durkee, IV
Eleftherios Pavlides
Thomas C. Payne
Patrick L. Pinnell
Elizabeth M. Plater-Zyberk
Barbara W. Ratner
Barbara J. Resnicow
David M. Schwarz
Richard A. Senechal
David S. Soleau
Joy A. Wulke
– – – –

1975

Tullio A. Bertoli
Martha A. Burns
S. Fiske Crowell, Jr.
Douglas J. Gardner
Karyn M. Gilvarg
Stephen A. Glassman
Susan E. Godshall
Margaret R. Goglia
Keith B. Gross
Susan L.M. Keeny
Edwin R. Kimsey, Jr.
Francis C. Klein
John D. Malick
Daniel B. Quinto
Larry W. Richards
Hervin A.R. Romney
Mana Sarabhai Brearley
Andrew K. Stevenson
J. David Waggonner III

1976

Benjamin M. Baker III
C. Douglas Ballon
S. Shalom Baranes
Henry H. Benedict III
Richard K. Charney
Robert S. Charney
Wen-Chi Chou
Stefani Danes
Barbara R. Feibelman
Carl M. Geupel
Anna Marie Howell
Daniel F. Kallenbach
James R. Kessler
Roy T. Lydon, Jr.
William A. McDonough
Eric Jay Oliner
Herschel L.D. Parnes
Adrienne K. Paskind
Richard H. Perlmutter
Carl J. Pucci, Jr.
Stuart N. Silk
John K. Spear
Herman D.J. Spiegel
Barbara Sundheimer-Extein
Philip B. Svigals
– – – –

1977

James David Barnes
Calvert S. Bowie
Louise M. Braverman
Peter D. Clark
Bradley B. Cruickshank
W.J. Patrick Curley
Barbara Fabiani
Paul W. Gurda
Stephen R. Hagan
Jonathan S. Kammel
Margo G. Leach
James Hirsch Liberman
Kevin P. Lichten
Randall T. Mudge
Davidson Norris
McKee Patterson
Paul J. Pugliese
Andrew K. Robinson
Charles B. Swanson
Cynthia Mitchell Tauxe
Alexander C. Twining
– – – –

1978

Frederic M. Ball, Jr.
Paul W. Bierman-Lytle
Judith M. Capen
Kenneth H. Colburn
James R. Deklewa
Lisa J. Gelfand
Ralph A. Giammatteo
Robert W. Grzywacz
Cynthia N. Hamilton
Kaspar A. Kraemer
John W. Kuipers, Jr.
William S. Mead
Yukihide Numaguchi
William Hall Paxson
David Spiker
M. Kirk Train
Margaret T. Weidlein
– – – –

1979

Steven W. Ansel
Jack Alan Bialosky, Jr.
James Leslie Bodnar
K. Daryl Carrington
Richard H. Clarke
Jeffrey P. Feingold
Bradford W. Fiske
Kevin E. Hart
Michael B. Lipkin
Gavin A. Macrae-Gibson
Audrey A. Matlock
Richard L. McElhiney
George R. Mitchell
Thomas N. Patch
Jon K. Pickard
Leonard M. Sussman
Miroslav P. Sykora
John T.C. Yuan
– – – –

1980

Jacob D. Albert
Turan Duda
J. Scott Finn
G. Peyton Hall
Stephen W. Harby
Edwin C. Heinle
Kenneth E. Hobgood
Linna Maria Hunt
Mariko Masuoka
Ann K. McCallum
Julia H. Miner
Claudio J. Noriega
Reese T. Owens
William A. Paquette
Beverly Field Pierz
Stephen Lee Porten
Paul Van Lent
David B. Zenner
Michael I. Zenreich
– – – –

1981

Cameron M. Armstrong
Hans Baldauf
Mark T. Binsted
Donald W. Blair
Richard L. Brown
Michael B. Cadwell
Douglass W. Cooper
Mark Denton
Eric W. Haesloop
Brian E. Healy
Mitchell A. Hirsch
T. Whitcomb Iglehart
Michael G. Kostow
Lawrence N. Lam
Mark Mascheroni
Jane Murphy
Daniel Rowen
Martin K. Shofner
Daniela Holt Voith
Spencer Warncke
Diane L. Wilk
– – – –

1982

John A. Boecker
Michael B. Burch
Domenic Carbone, Jr.
David P. Chen
J. Peter Devereaux
Bruce H. Donnally
Samuel E. Gardner
Raymond R. Glover
Kay Bea Jones
John E. Kaliski
Thomas A. Kligerman
Charles F. Lowrey, Jr.
Theodore John Mahl
R. Stephen McDaniel
Jay D. Measley
Paul W. Reiss
Janet S. Roseff
William H. Sherman
Constance A. Spencer
R. Anthony Terry
Margaret Liu
– – – –

1983

Maynard M. Ball
Anthony Stephen Barnes
Phillip G. Bernstein
Aaron A. Betsky
Carol J. Burns
Stuart E. Christenson
Charles D. Dilworth
William H. Gilliss
Frederick R. Groen
Anne Ridker Jaffe
Erica H. Ling
Elizabeth Ann Murrell
Gary Schilling
Brent Sherwood
Sonya R. Sofield
Robert J. Taylor
Michael R. Winstanley
– – – –

1984
Corvin G. Alstot
Michael S. Barratt
Roy G. Barris
Jeffrey Barsanti-Barber
Andrew D. Berman
Kenneth A. Boroson
Paul F. Carr, Jr.
Michael J. Chren
Marti M. Cowan
Michael R. Davis
Mark B. DuBois
Teresa Ann Dwan
James K. S. Griggs
Frederick R. Groen
Ruth Slobin Harris
Maria D. Kaltsas
Blair D. Kamin
Elizabeth M. Mahon
Michael L. Marshall
David Chase Martin
Timothy G. McKenna
Kenneth E. McKently
Scott Merrill
Jun Mitsui
Lawrence S. Ng
David L. Pearce
John R. Perkins
Ted Trussell Porter
Jill S. Riley
Jennifer C. Sage
Mary E. Stockton
Marion G. Weiss
Sherry L. Williamson

1985
Barbara A. Ball
Rasa Joana Bauza
Sanford M. Berger
William N. Bernstein
William Robert Bingham
Robert L. Bostwick
M. Virginia Chapman
Frank R. Cheney
Bruce Coldham
Bruce A. Davis
Michael Coleman Duddy
Jonathan M. Fishman
Charles R. Hasbrouck
Lucile S. Irwin
Andrew M. Koglin
Charles H. Loomis
Peter B. MacKeith
Chariss McAfee
Richard G. Munday
Joseph A. Pasquinelli
Mark D. Rylander
Roger O. Schickedantz
R. David Thompson

1986
Mark A. Armstrong
William Bartow Bialosky
Margaret J. Chambers
Robert E. Day
Owen P. Foley
David B. Greenbaum
David D. Harlan, Jr.
Richard W. Hayes
David J. Levitt
Jeffrey P. Miles
Nicholas L. Petschek
Warren Temple Smith
J. Gilbert Strickler
John B. Tittmann

1987
John P. Blood
Mary Buttrick Burnham
Soo Khian Chan
William D. Egan
Douglas A. Garofalo
R. Andrew Garthwaite
Elizabeth P. Gray
David B. Hotson
Andrew B. Knox
David G. Leary
Douglas S. Marshall
Timothy Day Mohr
Craig D. Newick
Amy K. Reichert
Winifred A. Stopps
Duncan Gregory Stroik
Andrea M. Swartz
Jennifer Tate
William L. Vandeventer
Lester Y. Yuen

1988
Atowarifagha I. Apiafi
Cary Suzanne Bernstein
Aubrey Leon Carter, Jr.
Richard M. Delaney
Allison Ewing
Natalie C. Gray-Miniutti
Charlotte Breed Handy
Drew H. Kepley
Ann Lisa Krsul
Oscar E. Mertz III
Kathryn B. Nesbitt
Ken Okamoto
Alan W. Organschi
Elaine M. Rene-Weissman
William Taggart Ruhl
Gilbert P. Schafer III
Alvaro Varela
Laura Weiss
Robert Duncan Young

1989
Larry G. Chang
Dale B. Cohen
Darin C. Cook
John DaSilva
Victor L. Deupi
Jennifer A. Huestis
Kevin S. Killen
Scott A. Kirkham
Frank Koumantaris
Maurice Stuart Lathers
Aari Blake Ludvigsen
Stephen D. Luoni
Christine W. Nichols
Giovanni Pagnotta
Juan Penabad
Rossana H. Santos-Wuest
Susan L. Seastone
Margaret Sherman Todd
Robert Ingram Tucker
Paul K. Watase
Claire Weisz
Randy Wilmot

1990
Lori B. Arrasmith Quill
Thomas Randal Bader
Charles S. Bergen
Stephen Brockman
Matt Bucy
Elizabeth Ann Danze
Stancliff C. Elmore, Jr.
William V. Fereshetian
Garrett S. Finney
Alison W. Horne-Rona
David E. Houston
Jack Hsu
Jeffrey E. Karer
David M. Levine
Marc D. L'Italien
Catherine Mercer
Deborah R. Robinson
Mildred I. Sung
Marie B. Wilkinson
Mark A. Yoes

1991
David M. Becker
John C. Gilmer
H. Randall Goya
Amy B. Janof
Amy Landesberg
Dominic L.C. LaPierre
Paul D. Mankins
Joseph W. Moore
Linda Stabler-Talty
Alexander M. Stuart
Lindsay S. Suter
Claire E. Theobald
Kevin Wilkes

1992
Andrew James Abraham
Hilary Buchanan
Kelly Jean Carlson-Reddig
Betty Y. Chen
Larry Greg Cohen
Timothy Craig Durfee
Frederick Adams Farrar, II
Morgan Browne Hare
Tae Sun Hong
Bruce Marshall Horton
Maitland Jones III
Deborah Aaronson Judelson
Douglas Neal Kozel
Shannon S. McDonald
Elias Messinas
Mark Robinson Sofield
Lynn Waskelis
Marion Converse Winkler

1993
Stephanie Anuszkiewicz
Christopher Richard Arelt
Gregory Miller Barnell
Sari Chang
Richard G. Grisaru
Louise Josephine Harpman
Doojin Hwang
Celia C. Imrey
Jordan J. Levin
Tara L. McCay
Craig Jeremy Moller
John Clark Riley
Gitta Robinson
Allen Douglas Ross
Scott J. Specht
Evan Michael Supcoff
Katherine D. Winter

1994
Brendan Russell Coburn
Mark C. Dixon
Pamela J. Fischer
Anne G. Haynes
Benjamin J. Horten
Paul W. Jackson
Mark R. Johnson
Thomas Allen Kamm, Jr.
William J. Massey
Eeva-Liisa Pelkonen
Edward B. Samuel
Craig N. Schultz
Albert J. Tinson, Jr.
Andrew C. Winters

1995
Andrew K. Anker
Carolyn Ann Foug
Allison Eden Karn
George Craig Knight
Aaron Matthew Lamport
J. William Lassetter
Jonathan Paul Siegel
Zon Sullenberger
Dana Elizabeth Tang
John Christopher Woell
Tom I. Zook II

1996
Jasmine Benyamin
John B. Clancy
John L. Culman
Don M. Dimster-Denk
Ching-Hua Ho
Russell S. Katz
Michael V. Knopoff
Joong-Seek Lee
Thomas A. Lumikko
Nancy Nienberg
Joseph P. Smith III
Dade G. Van Der Werf
Mai-Tse Wu

1997
Victor E. Agran
Milner Scott Ball
Gregory Joseph Goebel
Pankaj Vir Gupta
Jennifer Smith Lewis
Samuel Edward Parker III
Jeffery Ryan Povero
Rebecca Bearss Strader
Catherine Margaret Truman
William James Voulgaris
Shawn Michael Watts
Aicha Schleicher Woods

1998
Carl F. Bergamini, Jr.
Lana Berkovich
Holly M. Chacon
James Albert Cronenberg
Thalassa Alexandra Curtis
Melissa L. Delvecchio
Marjorie K. Dickstein
Glenn T. Fearon
Arianne Marie Groth
Edward B. Gulick
Kee-won A. Hong
Emily Sheya Kovner
Karl A. Krueger
Gregg A. Lewis
Martina Y. Lind
Ceu Guilhermina Martinez
Marc A. Roehrle
Elizabeth P. Rutherfurd
Justin B. Stein
Paul D. Stoller
Jennifer L. Taylor
Maureen R. Zell

1999
Kara Jeanette Bartelt
Elizabeth Marie Bester
Jonathan David Bolch
Kimberly Ann Brown
Katherine E. Cassidy
Eun Sun Chun
Celia K. Civello
Wael El-Dasher
Taeik Kim
Bruce D. Kinlin
Moshik Santo Mah
Lori Pavese Mazor
Ajit Pai
Jonah Arie Pregerson

2000
Benjamin Jon Bischoff
Bing Bu
Aristotelis Dimitrakopoulos
David Scott Drane
Oliver Edmund Freundlich
Anne Rachel Goulet
Timothy R. Hickman
Jason J. S. Hwang
Andrew Scott Mazor
Thomas Matthew Morbitzer
Ronald Michael Stelmarski
Lesli Sarah Stinger
Jennifer Lynn Tobias
Michael James Tower
Cheng-Hsun Wu

2001
Ghiora Aharoni
Paul J. Arougheti
Scott Garland Campbell
Yulee Carpenter
Juliana H. Chittick
Roland Sharpe Flores
Mark Foster Gage
Jeff Allan Goldstein
Hyunah Kook
David Blair Mabbott
Kenneth Gordon Masden II
Pamela Maree McGirr
Christopher M. Pizzi
Adam Joseph Ruedig
Matthew Joseph Seidel
Cyrus Subawalla
Elizabeth Weeks Tilney
Can M.A. Tiryaki
Jorge A. Zapata
Laura Louise Zaytoun

2002
Dana Heller Bettinger
Noah K. Biklen
Joshua D. Coleman
Pengzhan Du
Joseph P. Ferrucci
Alexander Haskell Jermyn
Sarah Marie Lavery
Ryan Scott Minney
Rashid Jamal Saxton
Jeffrey Paul Straesser
Robert A. Svetz
Martin Tomczyk
Kayin Tse

2003
Andrew William Benner
Marcos Diaz Gonzalez
Dana Kathleen Gulling
Jian Hei
Etienne Jean Jacques Kuhn
Youngsoo Kwon
Dongyeop Lee
Sangmin Lee
Sidney McCleary IV
Robert Court McClure
David Shmuel Paz
Nathan Bailey St. John
William L. Tims

2004
Graham W. Banks
Valerie Anne Casey
Christopher H. Cayten
Pu Chen
Stephen Yuen-Hoo Chien
Gary Britt Eversole
Zhigang Han
Matthew Michael Jogan
James C. Nelson III
Adam Sokol

2005
Ralph Colt Bagley IV
Daniel Adam Barber
Nora Ingrid Bergsten
Ceren Bige Bingol
Diala Salam Hanna
David Charles Hecht

FIRST TERM STUDIOS

[501a] Keller Easterling *(coordinator) with* John Blood, Mark Gage, Mimi Hoang, Gavin Hogben, *and* Ben Pell: *First-term students bring to the School a wide range of experience and background. Exercises introduce the complexity of architectural design by engaging problems that are limited in scale but not in the issues they provoke. Experiential, social, and material concerns are introduced together with formal and conceptual issues.*

The studio is comprised of one warm up and three major exercises. In the first project, **Skin,** *students are asked to explore the surface tension of a 100,000 cubic feet volume in its enclosure. The second project,* **Field|Multiple,** *employs the notion of field and site to organize a facility for bikes and motorcycle rentals at the site adjacent to New Haven train stations. In addition to discussing the notion of field and site, we will also investigate assembly techniques (load-bearing, skeletal, columnar, frame) that may become part of the organizational repertoire.*

Form|Informe *exercises two different intentions for making form. The first indulges in a fundamental obsession with geometry, while the second one refers to a number of strategies in art and architecture culture, including Bataille's speculations on "informe" that contains no geometric or mathematical scaffold. Students will design two versions of a shoe boutique with these alter egos in mind.*

The final project, **Animality|Spectacle|Diagram** *will use the contemporary discourse about diagram as a prompt. This discourse will nourish thoughts about program as space and activity over time. On the given site near Chelsea Piers in Manhattan, students design an arena for animal training and animal shows. The facility trains people and houses equestrian skills, but it also has a course for training dogs and dog owners with special needs.*

Skin &
Field/Multiple
501a

Whitney Kraus
University of Michigan at Ann Arbor
Overlap

The inspiration images are a translucent flower petal that provides the idea of variation produced by light and a microscopic view of sand that adds the geometry based on the organization of the molecules. The concept of castellated beams gives the hexagonal shape. The logic system dictates that as the number of layers increases in a panel, so does its structural role in the construction – single panels form roof, a pair of panels form floor and many panels form structural walls. It is in the intersection of panels and different sized hexagons that one experiences dynamic light.

Claire Axley
University of California at Berkeley
Field/Multiple

A mapping of density of use indicate the dynamism of Union Station as regulated by the train schedule. Shifts in use call for a flexible system to work in accordance with the site. The design begins by creating flat areas for stopping, contrasting with existing elevational shifts. Bike and motorcycle rental shops and cafe take form as a series of pods that run on tracks and engage the three groves. The movement of the pods allow for multiple uses of the groves and the potential for completely closing down elements of program during time of day or entire seasons.

Michael Fox What we're saying is that you're providing two very interesting problems: the tree and the pod. What we're asking is, what are the dynamics between them? Do they exist in some kind of tension? Does one have an effect on the other, or are they really sequestered? Have you ever been to Seiko Airport in Amsterdam? There is a project by West 8 where they were asked to provide a landscape for the airport. The problem is that it was changing so quickly. What they did was plant a row of Birch trees – and since they grow very quickly – it was a kind of landscape system. So that aspect of thinking of the tree as not fixed, but as organic over time is really provocative.

Keller Easterling You stretched the field of the train station in a way that is quite effective. With very little means, you stretched the site. You were all asked to have a dimension of time, which could be a throw away requirement or a profound discovery in your process. In this project, it ends up being a profound discovery.

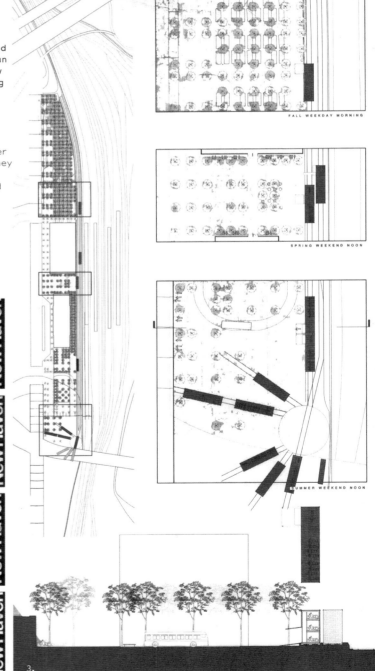

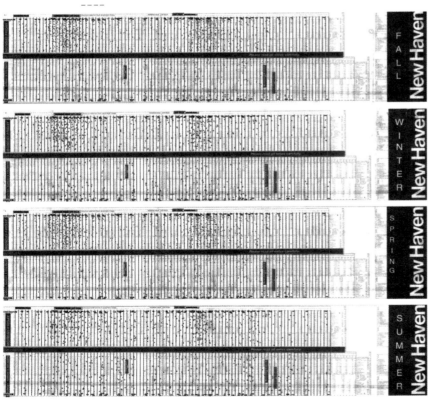

2.

3.

Jeff Geldart
Ryerson Polytechnical University,
Canada
Diluted Hierarchies

This project explored how architectural elements such as corridors, stairs, escalators, and doorways effect movement. The program of the bicycle rental facility was arranged in a way that attempted to dilute the hierarchies of the different modes of transportation. This was done through the integration of various ground treatments that would promote specific modes of circulation in specific patterns on the site at specific times of day, thus liberating areas of the site for multiple overlapping uses throughout the day.

Keller Easterling I am kind of intrigued when I look at the model because there are two habits of mind here — both of which are interesting. In the three dimensions, you have gone and ratified the transportation separations and there is no doubt these get separated — this is what we do in America. This is how we do it…this kind of reckless safety of chaos. When you look at a street in India and there are speeding vehicles at all different times, elephants, and someone squeezing into a car, but somehow there is this strange sense of safety and this heightened awareness in what's going on, and that's what I see here. That's really, really fascinating.

Gavin Hogben It kind of justifies the view that you're taking. Talking about in terms of India and when someone runs over the carriage chair, that's a riot now. There's something at stake in that…in this decentralization process. [laughter] I think that's where you need to put the pivot required. That's why I say that this acceleration and deceleration become a consequence at stake. There has to be something at stake.

Jennifer Dubon
University of Pennsylvania
Underlying Motivations

My site determination for the field project involved a two-hour study of the movement of people throughout the Union train station. I analyzed groups of people entering the main lobby area through different points. I roughly sketched their paths as well as their stopping points in order to understand the factors that influence people's travel distance to and from the station. The aim was to inform the layout of the program while also taking into consideration the concepts of a field.

Gabrielle Ho
University of California at Berkeley
Obese Retaliation for Fat Kids

This project injects a network of bike chambers across New Haven — chambers that form jewels of obese retaliation. Kids with obesity issues are encouraged by government agencies and insurance companies to bike and earn points for prize exchange (Apple iPods, Nike sport apparel, etc.) The concept behind this invention is to regard hierarchies of chambers as a 'field' of multiple orientations. Individually, these bike parks function as attractors within the construct [field], while the totality orients and directs fat kids for physical exercises.

Ben Pell I really enjoy the fact that you have gone into such detail and zoomed in scale on the bike and the nature of the bike and how people use the bike. It's really interesting. I wonder if you could have played that out a little more and thought about other ways in which the bike could be more of an interactive device with other pieces of program. So rather than only designing the storage, may be you could lock the bike into place horizontally instead of vertically, and people get on the bikes and its already part of a track. Or maybe there's a bike-up bar instead of a swim-up bar so that the bike actually becomes the key that activates all of the program — without a bike, you don't get to participate, which seems to be how you're setting it up.

Hojin Nam
Ewha Womans University, Korea
Program Field

Depending on the time and season, diverse groups of people use the station with different purpose. Each of them has the different waiting time and various ways to spend it. The site is programmed into three parts to meet these needs. Each part is turned on and off depending on the arrival of its user group; thus, creating the process of field generation.

| A: 1–1:30 pm | B: 1:30–2 pm | C: 2:15–2:45 pm | D: 3–3:30 pm |

7.

(1) Whitney Kraus
(2,3) Claire Axley
(4) Jeff Geldart
(5) Gabrielle Ho
(6) Hojin Nam
(7) Jennifer Dubon

Form/Informe
501a

Alexandra Burr
Middlebury College
Form

This project centers on the stiletto shoe in its varying heights and was generated from a module sized to a flat shoe. The module was then stretched in order to accommodate varying heights and architecturally represent the idea of the stiletto shoe as a device to elongate the leg, giving a sense of attenuation, height, and stretch. The resultant modules were nested together to fit as many as possible on the 40' wall and the surface was folded over itself and connected to form compartments with the best viewing angle.

Kent Bloomer I would carry on that notion of leaving the geometry behind and say that both your form and informe solutions have more similarity than dissimilarity. Both seem to be organized intuitively in terms of where you want to place them and what sort of densities you want to use. It's almost like a graphic or abstract expressionist composition rather than something that evolves out of something as rigorous as geometry. I think that similarity is added by the fact that they are both almost the same size and they are both long and a certain height, and they are both placed inside of a room.

[...]

Keller Easterling They both flirt with form and informe in interesting ways. I'm thinking that these sort of anthropometric series are like when they would design military uniforms and so on. They would try to do it by averaging sizes so that people could still look fierce in their hats. They were trying to get just the right individual dimension, but still have everyone in the same hat so that they were able to march together. Here, it's very significant because instead of coming up with the average, the module, you're actually blowing apart that idea by showing us all of the values at once and saying, 'With all those values, I could make it sturdy.' But the stretch is kind of an informe motive, playing with form material and trying to mess up the neat average of that.

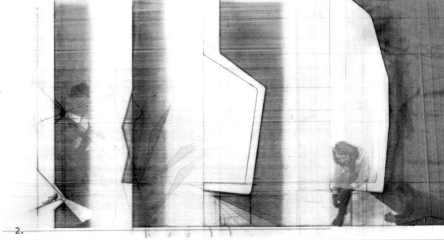

1.

Nobuki Ogasahara
Waseda University, Japan
Form: "Knit" Informe: "Strings"

Form: This woven shoe wall defines an entire geometric system that accommodates two different functions: shoe display and seating. Seating-shoe load distribution determines the geometry of this weaved wall. Informe: This string shoe wall informs the performative condition of the display. Strings work as structure to support display boards, mirrors, fitting seats, and walk-through openings.

2.

Stephen Nielson
University of Virginia
The Foot Fetish/The Shoe Pattern

Form: Through an analysis of shoe fabrication, a unit is derived which embodies the geometries that allow flat leather to bend, mold, and fasten. The connection methods of face-face, face-back, and overlap then mutate the pattern from the efficiency of its sheet. These mutations create pockets that shoes may be placed in or hung from. Informe: Foot as a prize proposes a spatial relationship between its toes and its admirers. Operations performed on this wall create spaces for shoe fitting and display. These spaces subsequently create gaps, creases, and holes through which the foot fetishist may admire his or her most relished extremity.

3.

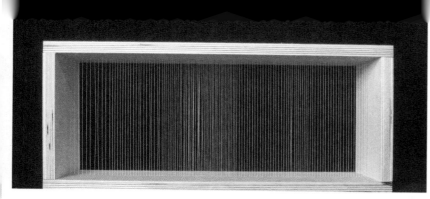

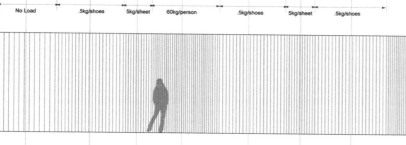

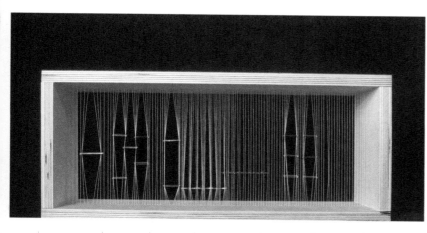

Andrew Benner This is a prototypical piece of a system, and could flatten or mutate…

Stephen Nielson Yes. It could go back depending on the programmatic needs. Certain liberties are taken and those I've found can usually be compensated and the system will re-evolve, regardless of what you do, as long as your means of connection are generally connecting the like-size sides. This side only connects to this side because they are of the same length.

Benner When you were working, did you ever set it on the floor? I mean, is there a way through this folding, you could create something that can be self-supporting? Because right now, there appears to me that you always need another wall. This actually isn't a wall. It's a way of cladding a wall.

Nielson I built it on the floor, which is probably why it's limp. But, maybe if there were two layers on either side, it probably would connect and give thickness and strength that way.
————

Ravi d'Cruz
Yale University
<u>Object/Objectification</u>
————

Form and informe spring from two sides of the one wall. Form is derived from the various quantitative characteristics of the athletic shoe: stability, cushioning, traction, and weight create parameters for movable informative display boxes. Informe is an unattainable idealization of the same shoe, consistent with the hero worship and deification of athlete-marketing strategies.
————

Garrett Omoto
Arizona State University
<u>Form/ Informe</u>
————

Both the form and informe walls are based upon the idea of the connection and how it relates to geometry, material thickness, and fastening. The form composition is composed of a single type of joint connecting panels of various sizes to provide horizontal surfaces for shoe display and seating. Similarly, the informe shoe wall is based upon a single type of connection which fold down and slide horizontally. The interest of the occupant is stimulated by the silhouette of the shoe attached to each platform.
————

Mimi Hoang I feel like in both projects you could be much more in touch with the thing you invent. In the form project, rather than relinquishing the invention of the details to considerations of program and ergonomics, you would invent a system that could be sequenced, like the sequence of how it gets assembled.

Keller Easterling When I look at the next one, Garrett [Omoto] has been making these for a while, so we've just been playing and learning a lot from them in the studio. What I'm wondering is [whether this is] another kind of rule set, in which more options become possible, that doesn't continually need to resolve itself into an orthogonal grid… Some of them would become more tetrahedral, even…

Mason White If you're interested in that, you might look at Buckminster Fuller's studies on synergetic and energetic geometry, in which there's an argument that tetrahedrons or other accumulative geometric forms generate a kind of synergy amongst them structurally and spatially. As this thing builds itself up in all directions, it's reinforcing the need for them to act as a collective over the individual.
————

SIDE VIEW

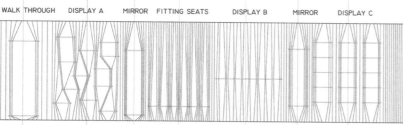

PLAN

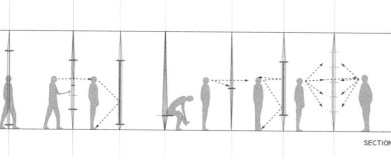

SIDE VIEW IN PERFORMANCE

SECTION

4.

5.

Animality/Spectacle/ Diagram

501a

Nobuki Ogasahara
Waseda University, Japan
<u>Spectacle Behind The Show</u>

Spectacle exists between spectators and participants. Socially, spectators receive service and participants provide service. But at another level, spectators are people who watch and participants are people who behave. To solve these two spectator-participant problems, my proposal adopts a mutual ramping system. Separating social relationships between spectators and participants, two ramps also define optical and physical connection.

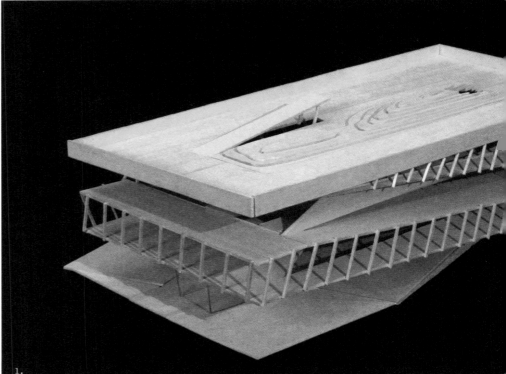

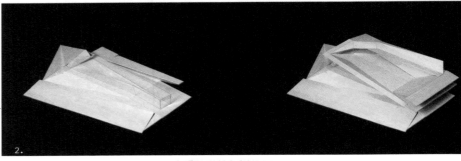

1.

Catherine Ingraham In this case, it seems as if the spectator and participation are one in the same. There is an oscillation of roles that — like the Panopticon, where the one who is watched is watching themselves — has internalized the spectacle in some way just as anyone who is on parade with the animal is a spectacle and a participant, and is watching themselves parading the animal. In a way I think it's always interesting to split a building. All these splits are extremely powerful moves, especially when they pass by each other in parallel. But I don't know whether the spectator and the participant is the opposition that you're really working with, and whether if you work that opposition in terms of animal/human that [you] wouldn't have to do something quite elaborate with what happens with that. Anything could be true about these separate two passages through the building. You could do any number of partitioning of these users and spaces, if you are actually thinking in terms of spectator and participations. Right now, it seems sort of generically realized.

Sunil Bald I echo your disappointment. It's the difference between the spectator and participant that we're having difficulty tracking. And if your perspectives

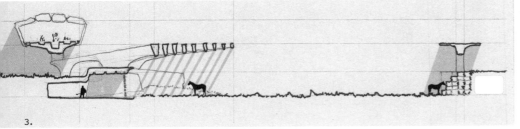

2.

3.

were using drawing conventions as sections through time, I would say that you've mastered the spatial sections, but what we're needing to see is how following someone, how their role changes through different moments in times through the building. I think that you could potentially get at that through the perspective.

[...]

Kurt Forster This almost calls for an animation. In a sense, all these transitions and separations could be made much more vivid. Since you prop up the entire building on this beveled [berm]…on this crystallized, reduced landscape? Why does it start with this razor sharp tray on the top? Why is it sawed off when, in fact, at that point, something like a fictionalized landscape begins to penetrate?

Ingraham But it doesn't, that's what I was trying to understand.

Forster It's a pretty irregular topography as opposed to…it looks likes the remnants of a fortification. In some way, it would not simply disappear from site if it hadn't been completely decapitated. The building in the end is confirmed as a pristine volume even if it is only through the edge of the roof as opposed to the face which seems to imply the entire site which gives rise to the ascent. The conclusion seems a bit schematic. You simply have to decide in the end what you want the building to reveal. Does it reveal landscape, or does it reveal finally having risen to its own height only itself?

Keller Easterling On one hand, it must remain sort of dreamy. And it must be part of this funny urbanism of animals. What they have to do in this building is climb up and down it. That's their form of urbanity. It's really in the city that this is something not dreamy. It doesn't rarify itself as a volume.

Nicholas McDermott
University of Pennsylvania
<u>Vertical Pier</u>

The idea for the Vertical Pier began with two observations about the context: the site itself being called Pier 63 while is not actually a pier in the traditional sense, and that big projects in New York are built vertically. The project can be thought of as one in a series of proposals that began with OMA's Parc de la Villette and continuing to FOA's Yokahama ferry terminal. A section of the latter project is stacked and manipulated to make the floor plates of the current proposal, giving height to the pier, a forum to animals and spectacle, and re-imagining the form that Koolhaas had tried to make horizontal.

Christopher Corbett
University of Cincinnati
Closed Loop Economy

Capitalism is based on the exchange of goods and services for currency. This project explores the possibility of creating a "working" landscape that utilizes inherent capital as a means to generate new experiences and programs. A closed loop economy is self-sustaining in which the by-product of this activity is the social capital gained by the participants. By introducing dogs and horses to an urban open space, a farm provides mutual benefits for both humans and animal. Manure becomes the main currency that an artificial ecosystem is based on. Vermi-composting, gardening, water collection and purification all become processes vital to the park.

Michael Kokora I like your project, but the next step is that things start to change. Certain things don't grow in certain seasons, but certain things do, which you haven't documented. What I want to see is how the operations of the site feed into one another, constantly devolving, moving, and reflecting some sort of environmental change. It's not really a closed loop, because you've got an estuary, saline, fresh water; you've got a lot of things coming into the system that you have to deal with. What I'm interested in is the way your landscape constantly changes, revitalizes, and refigures. What does it look like? It may have very different colors at different times of the year. That's something that you should try to document.
[…]
Emmanuel Petit So where are the places in which it still interfaces with metropolitan activities and processes? What other things give it energy? What is the critical value of this project? In what sense did you take the problem of the animal as an opportunity to be provocative with either architecture or other mediums? Let's assume your machine and your architecture functions perfectly, and does what you want it to do. What does it do to architecture? What does it bring to urbanism?
Chris Corbett I think it's interesting because it inserts the active landscape into what would be normally just a park. It becomes an opportunity for a community to start farming the land, which is a unique urban move.

Yichen Lu
Tsinghua University, China
Epidermis & Hypodermis

Through designing two interlaced systems, the project's goal is to reconsider the relationship between humanity, animality and nature. One of the systems is the steel lattice system, the 'epidermis', providing functions to human beings. The other is the landscape system for animals, which is called 'hypodermis'. Extending from outside to inside, the scale of the steel lattice system is increasing steadily. From east to west, the landscape system is growing under the steel system, stretching to the seaside, turning over as surface and finally becoming a rest space. Two interdependent systems embody a spectacle of integration within humanity and animality, which serves as the motif of the design.

5.

(1,2) Nobuki Ogasahara
(3) Christopher Corbett
23 (4) Nicholas McDermott   (5) Yichen Lu

[Overleaf]
(6) Bo Crockett
(7) Alberto Zamora   (8) Jessica Varner

Animality/Spectacle/Diagram
(continued)

6.

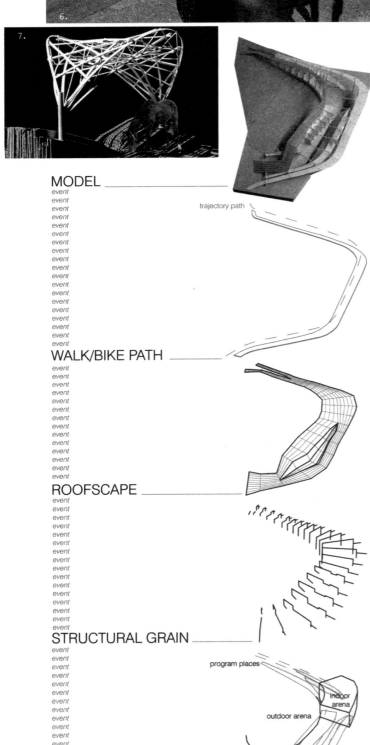

7.

MODEL _____

event
event
event
event
event
event
event
event
event
event
event
event
event
event
event
event
event
event
event

trajectory path

WALK/BIKE PATH _____

event
event
event
event
event
event
event
event
event
event
event
event
event
event
event
event

ROOFSCAPE _____

event
event
event
event
event
event
event
event
event
event
event
event
event
event
event
event
event

STRUCTURAL GRAIN _____

event
event
event
event
event
event
event
event
event
event
event
event
event
event
event
event
event
event

program places

indoor
arena

outdoor arena

trajectory paths

skin curtains

8. ARENA SPACE _____

Bo Crockett
Texas A&M University
Blinders

In this project, animality is amplified to become spectacle, superceding the absolute spectacle of New York City. It questions whether the average urban human has lost the ability to identify with the animal. The bulk of the building is a landscape where the horse and dog lead agrarian lives. Projected onto the façade facing the city are intimate real-time images of those animals. In this way, the actual life of the animal is translated into the digital imagery man understands. The building becomes a billboard for animality and underscores the idea that in today's society digital representation is reality.

Emmanuel Petit Your idea of the spectacle is very much concentrated in that graphic circle... use a decorated topography. I wonder if your project instead of being here is not the way you showed this. In order to make that believable and for that spectacle to happen, you would have to define the city square a little better than you have done because what you have is an island in the middle of the street. Is that the best spatial arrangement to make that kind of political sense of gathering happen?

Bo Crockett I was trying to create two different spectacles really, one relating to the city and all the people out here. You could close down and take over the streets down here if your having big movie stars arriving...and the flip side is the urban cowboy. Horses can go up pretty steep inclines, and they could do that in the city. That [idea] is pretty spectacular, I thought, for the middle of NYC, so there were two sides to it.

[...]

Petit You're interested in appropriating the spectacle and holding it back on its side. The thing that a couple of the comments are getting at is, 'Where are the people?' You make a big scene out of the animals, but the other half of the spectacle is the crowd. The crowd of one area is sealed under a roof, and the other is pushed along the street. I'm interested in where the people do come into contact with the animal; maybe you could talk about that.

Crockett Just seeing the animal can have an effect, but particularly for the opportunity for people to come out and ride the horses. Instead of being controlled by the specific path, the horse is allowed to have its own personality, allowing people's interaction with the true animal.

Gavin Hogben It's good to know that its an attempt to revamp spectacle rather than just meet the challenge directly. It is established that there are two types of spectacle, and I'm much more invested in those that occur inside the city rather than outside the city. The spectacle is a flattened screen recording some other event versus the event at hand. Those two are the things that can be abrasive of each other, in conflict, in contact...carve out one intruding on the other, beginning the process of your mediation. When that mediation starts to emerge, we're going to see a melding fusion...

Jessica Varner
University of Nebraska at Lincoln
Party and Parade

The building sets up a dialogue between the traditional event with the spontaneous event that finds itself occurring along paths of destination and paths of movement. The events are revealed through structure and skin at poignant moments and also at sometimes awkward moments such as specifically revealing hand washing in the bathrooms. The roles of spectator and spectacle are sometimes reversed to highlight the dichotomy between the two events. The outdoor arena finds itself responding to the larger urban context. The indoor area is contained within the fattening elbow of the building and situates itself against the urban fabric.

Albert Zamora
Texas A & M University
Making Do

The projective Diagram employed in this project inhabits the ad-hoc survivalist sensibility of the horse for which it was designed. This conceptual model proposes the architectural propagation of this sensibility manifest. Through the lens of Animality, human society and horse society are seen as equals commingling. By allowing the horse's needs to author the intervention, the Society of the Spectacle is ignored and thus called into self-consciousness without the relativistic intolerance of Guy Debord. The solution proposes a relationship that evolves over time through experiences and encounters, seeking pockets of terrain for both man and horse.

SECOND TERM STUDIOS

[502b] Alan Organschi *(coordinator), with* Turner Brooks, Peter de Bretteville, Mario Gooden, Amy Lelyveld, *and* Hilary Sample: *The second-term studio explores the theme of domestic architecture through the design and construction of dwelling space. During the first half of the term, a series of analysis and design projects explore the typological precedents, programmatic organization, formal composition, and construction methodology of individual and multiple-unit housing. This work forms the conceptual background for the work in the latter half of the term – the collaborative design and construction of the Building Project, an affordable house for a nonprofit developer in New Haven.*

Cohabitation
502b

Hojin Nam
Ewha Womans University, Korea
A House with the Experience Deck

In this project, two families live together in one household with parents, a disabled child, grandmother, and two children. A lift for the disabled child creates a deck that stops at every floor and landing. At each stop, the deck is programmed differently and divided into service core and main area by the structure line. Interwoven by the circulation stair, the program platform brings two family lives into one.

Peter de Bretteville You could make these drawings be more descriptive of changing spaces, even with the plans you have. There is a little more variety than what would immediately become apparent because the view is so overwhelming that you don't see that there are smaller and larger spaces. A lot of people have used cantilevered bays, and that would increase your spatial variety. The root of this is a very simple, elegant, and has a very clear idea of the stairs. I just admire the project that had an idea that can be systematically critiqued and expanded.

Erica Schroeder
Ohio State University
Cocoon Pods

The project investigates the active relationships between each possible occupant and the inhabitable space. Traditionally living areas are built with relationship of economic means and building systems; however, in terms of habitual living, economic means does not necessarily signify efficient and functional. Through the investigation of movement and regular body motion, a new way of living is created. Pods are created in order to enhance each dwelling room so that in the future prefabricated pods can be connected to any living shelter.

Yichen Lu
Tsinghua University, China
Space Occupation

The project takes a close look at how to establish a harmonized relationship between the elder couple and the family with a disabled child. A wall was used to divide the space in two while serving as a carrier of the interaction between the two. For example, with the movement of doors, the elderly couple could use the shared space to take care of the disabled child, while a double-height space was designed to accomplish a transformation from a mini-basketball playground to two living rooms. Thus, the project is no longer a simple design of dwelling, but in fact, is a stage.

Amy Lelyveld It's very productive…how you've modeled it and how you've drawn it and what I can understand of the thinking behind it. It seems to be at the brink of a very nice idea. But what I am wondering about is why, when there's so much force in the idea about the coming together, things are so much the same when they come together? Why do you only get a basketball court or why do you get the same volumes? In this model, the volumes are, more or less, the same because of the way they are disposed. The mechanism is provocative. I understand the concept of the wall, but I don't understand the material or workings of the wall… I like the way you displayed the information, but there's something opaque about the result when the thing comes together in its full flowering. When you directed it, at its most expansive moment, all these units are still the same, right?

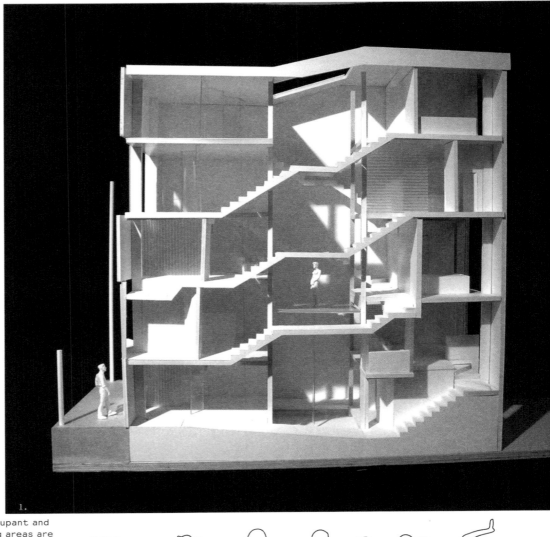

1.

2.

David Riedel
Carleton College
<u>Oblique Living</u>

In this two-family house, programs physically interweave and visually overlap. Layered gradients of shared visual space permeate expected boundaries to undo familiar levels of enclosure typical of an inner city infill dwelling. Boundary conditions between households dissolve at spot moments in passage. Programmatically wrapping around each other, two dwelling units cross paths frequently and obtain passing views of the other unit.

Bo Crockett
Texas A&M University
<u>Adaptive Territory</u>

The project responds to the restrictive nature of the site by adapting to the specific needs of the two families who inhabit the building and indulges in exploring the close proximity in which the two families are forced to live. Each unit has its own internal source of light and ventilation through a series of light shafts. The boundary between these shafts and the manipulation of the façades allow for interaction between both the families and the general public outside.

Alan Organschi I appreciate the kind of clarity of this. Not only the detail you brought into the model, because it really helps give a sense of the graining of it, but the organizational approach that you took, which is pretty rich. The notion that it's this nested section, two L's that interlock one another. Then you derive two common light wells from that, so you create this spatial complexity which has this great quality of bringing a lot of light at different times into the house. I also appreciate the functional gesture of thinking of that shared space, and how that might work as a laundry room. How something operates is a really interesting way to generate a design. One of the things I want to know more about is how deeply you understand the operation of those things, so you can take something like that and spread it through the building a little bit. How do you really push, within the design, the reading of those things either experientially or maybe even diagrammatically?

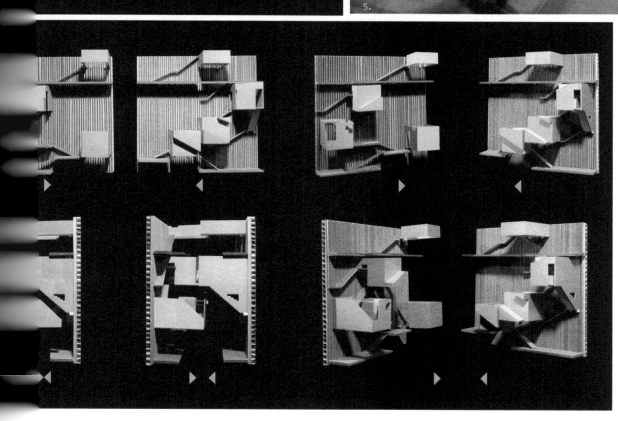

Refugee Housing
502b

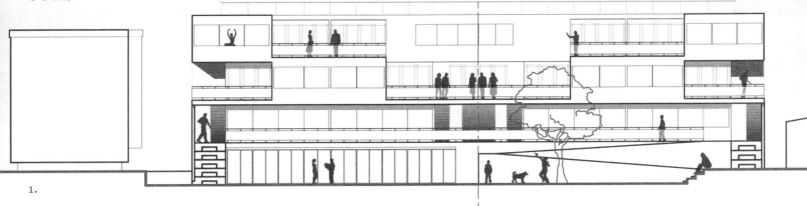

1.

Claudia Melniciuc
Colgate University
Linked Community for Those Displaced by Hurricane Katrina

The project proposes a system of connected dwelling units with the goal of creating a close-knit, supportive community. Every apartment shares an outdoor space with each of its two neighbors, such that the whole building is activated by a chain of one-to-one interactions. Newcomers are easily integrated, by getting essentially "plugged-in" to the chain.

2.

Christopher Corbett
University of Cincinnati
Refugee Housing

Leo Stevens
Yale University
Transplanting Type

This project is about transplanting typology – taking a foreign vernacular and releasing it into a field of a different type. Issues of language, style, and origin are brought into question with the introduction of this architectural outsider, paralleling the relocation hurricane refugees. More than any other type of design, the vernacular architecture of a region is tied to its people. It is reflective of their needs, comforts, and lifestyle.

Robert A.M. Stern I'm not sure I like the scale of the one story building on the street. I do like the bravura of it and the relation of the building to the site. What I like best about it is the handling of the spaces where you have a mat of building and then you carve through and create spaces. I think you've done that very, very well. The way you cross through the grain to create courtyards and tie it together as a unity and serve as a pathway system is quite ingenious. It's the kind of planning you have in near eastern cities and other cultures where they're basically patio houses, so I think that's very well done.

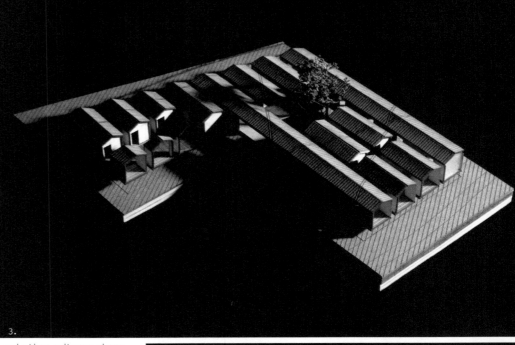

3.

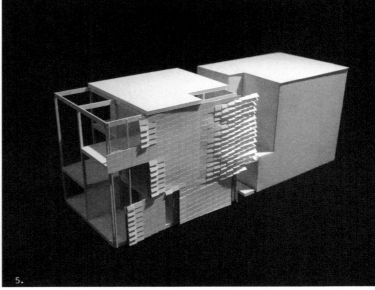

4.

5.

Jason Pytko
University of Amherst
<u>Visual Communities</u>

A series of individual buildings arranged about enclosed common areas, the project addresses all sides of its site. The front-to-back striation of privacy zones of a typical in-line house lot are modified through rotation and repetition of the buildings around the site. Each apartment is next to both a shared courtyard and private garden, and is visually connected with surrounding neighbors, even as each building is in a different orientation.

Ji-eun Cha
Ewha Womans University, Korea
<u>Penetration by Nature</u>

The floating mass makes the greenway along the canal street expand to the site. The green space penetrates into the house through the holes. Each Unit has its own light well which consists of a hole to the ground and an occupiable space. The space has access to the roof public space that is an event field only for the residents. The ground floor under the lifted mass is a community space for neighborhood as well as residents.

Claire Weisz I'm intrigued by that as an idea, not as a communal sense, but much more from the question 'how do you create a building where people are living in it temporarily, where you actually achieve an environment with distances, light, acoustic privacy, and something about autonomy?' At least from an architectural point of view, there is some sense of grandness without it only being about shape. I think the issues of proportion and use are the questions still on the table. At the same time, I like the idea that you are looking at some kind of porous building, something that has space in it, that it's not such a tight system.

Dylan Sauer
University of Cincinnati
<u>Patchwork Housing</u>

This project attempts to accommodate flexibility in transitioning between both introverted and extraverted tendencies that might be experienced by a post-traumatic refugee group. The site has been developed around a dispersed, horizontal organization in order to maximize the amount of outdoor space. Circulation space is dissolved into interconnected public courtyards that provide access to individual units.

Marc Newman
Cornell University
<u>More Party Wall</u>

The project targets a critical component of the row house: the party wall. The interstitial party wall room has three states of operation. The first is entirely closed – all units remain private. The second is partially open – neighboring units open moveable walls to gain access to the party wall room. The third is the fully open – all units are accessible to all party wall rooms circulating through the entire 10 unit system.

Stephen Nielson
University of Virginia
<u>Programmatic Infiltration</u>

Frequently, these FAR and setback regulations combined with efficient construction yield left-over ground condition that is labeled "public." By infesting the "public" space with public program, this project proposes a shift from residual to activated. This program must still address the street and back-lot as a gradient of privacy/security and publicity/availability, but also allowing the potential for an interrelationship amongst included elements.

Building Project
506b

Herbert Newman *(Building Project Coordinator)*
Paul Brouard *(Building Project Director)*
Adam Hopfner *(Building Project Instructor)*

with Alan Organschi, Turner Brooks, Peter de Bretteville,
Mario Gooden, Amy Lelyveld, *and* Hilary Sample:

Mission

Since 1967, the Yale School of Architecture has offered its
first-year students the opportunity to design and build a structure as an integral part of their graduate education. Unique
among architecture schools, this program is mandatory for a
ll members of the class. Undertaken in cooperation with
Neighborhood Housing Services, a local nonprofit developer,
the Building Project culminates in the construction of
a single family house in an impoverished neighborhood.

History

Charles W. Moore, who headed Yale's Department of Architecture (later the School of Architecture) from 1965 to 1971,
founded the First-Year Building Project in collaboration with
faculty member Kent Bloomer. Moore saw that getting out of
the studio and building something would have several benefits
for the students. As a believer in simple tectonics and basic
technologies, he hoped students would be inspired by the
mechanics of building. In the midst of the student unrest of the
1960s, he saw the project as a way for students to commit to
positive social action by building in disadvantaged communities.

Since then, the houses have allowed students to gain
the experience of working with a client and the opportunity to respond to the challenges of affordable housing and
urban infill. Students have shown great enthusiasm for these
projects focusing on community development and neighborhood improvement. Many of them arrive at school with
a desire to include such socially responsible work in their
future professional lives. Having the opportunity to participate in the design and construction of such building projects
often reinforces their conviction and inspiration to do so.

Client

Neighborhood Housing Services (NHS) is a non-profit developer based in New Haven. It has partnered with the Yale
Building Project since 1996 in constructing affordable housing
for first-time homebuyers. NHS's mission is to improve the
problem of urban blight by renovating existing buildings and
constructing new ones. Their projects not only benefit individual homeowners, but also help to rebuild entire neighborhoods.

Process

The studio competition, which determines the winning
design, was a highly structured and productive exercise that
occurs over a five-week period. The students began the competition by dividing themselves into six teams of ten based
on design interests and previous architectural experience.
The teams worked on the schematic design for three weeks.
At the end of April, the groups presented their project to a
jury composed of faculty members and representatives from
NHS. A winning design was chosen after the presentation
and the class immediately began to work together on the
construction documents. Since NHS supplements only part
of the construction of the house, students were responsible
for seeking donations for most of the building materials.

The project broke ground in May. The entire class
worked on the construction in shifts for a month and a half.
Thereafter, a group of fifteen students are chosen to finish
construction through the end of August.

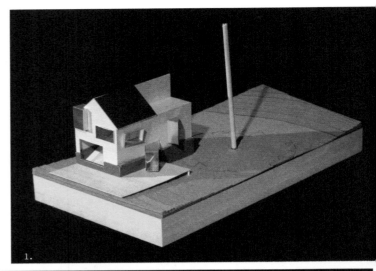

1.

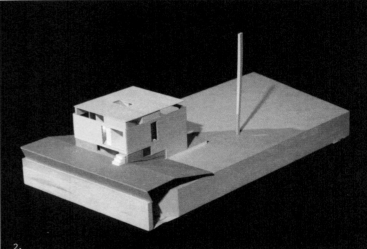

2.

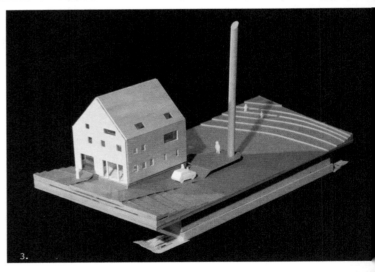

3.

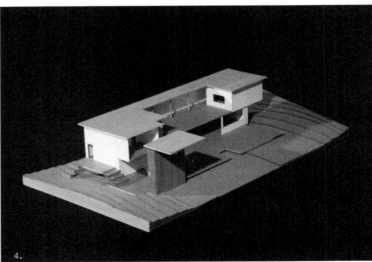

4.

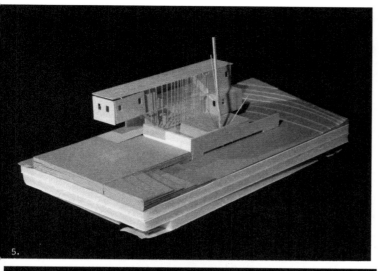

5.

9.

6.

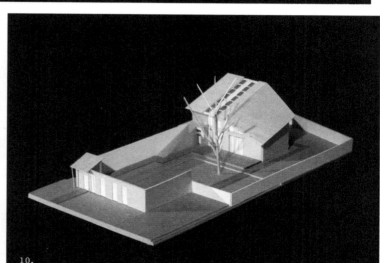

10.

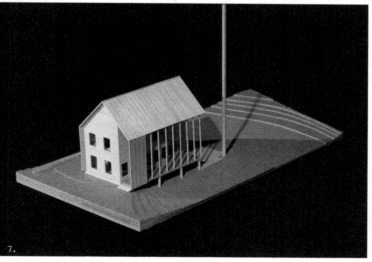

7.

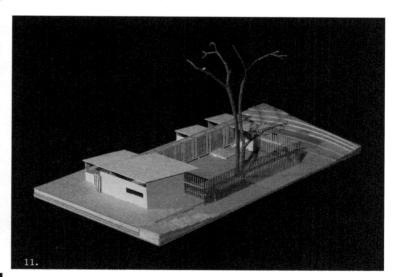

11.

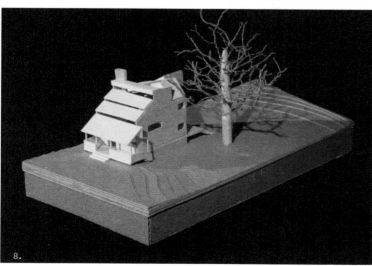

8.

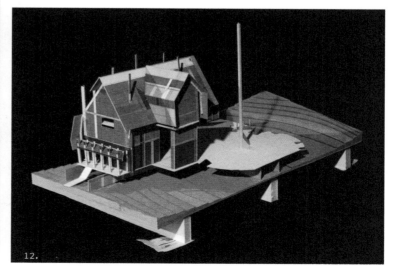

12.

(1) Quang Truong
(2) Christopher Corbett
31 (3) Alberto Zamora

(4) Todd Fenton
(5) Nathan Rich
(6) Leo Stevens

(7) Bo Crockett
(8) Isidro Garcia
(9) Isaac Strackbein

(10) Tom Bosschaert
(11) Sheri Meshkinpour
(12) Marc Newman

Team A - Banana

Timothy Applebee, Swarthmore College; **Moises
Berrun,** Texas A&M University; **Alexander Butler,**
University of Virginia; **Garrett Gantner,** University
of Milwaukee; **Isidro Garcia,** Massachusetts Institute
of Technology; **Joshua Lewandowski,** University of
Minnesota at Twin Cities; **Nobuki Ogasahara,** Waseda
University, Japan; **Jason Pytko,** University of Amherst;
Meredith Sattler, Vassar College

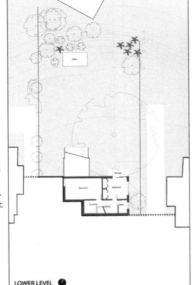

LOWER LEVEL

Charlie Lazor I like this house quite a lot. I
think it's far more simplified and direct. I think that
the view lines are in a sense not view lines, but view
fields. Sectionally, what I like in contrast to this one
is the development of this bedroom space. In the
previous project, they elected to gain ceiling height.
In this project, however, they decided to create yet
another living space. Now they did throw that back
up here, but what I find really compelling about this
for the design problem is that this could potentially
be a revenue generating space for the homeowner.
I find that, of all the design form ideas I've seen
today, [this is] one of the most compelling because
it does three things: it addresses the site issue, it
provides a positive non-architectural, financial benefit to the user, and then it has
this relationship to that tree space down
there. These spaces can potentially be
awkward. I now hail from Minneapolis, Minnesota, where the 'rambler' is a well-known
type. It's a builder's strategy, but in the
hands of a talented architect, you could
bring out the benefits of that.

Henry Dynia Providing an adjunct living
space…that was not part of the program,
and that's not something we required, and
for our purposes is not legal.

Mark Simon I like Charlie's [Lazor]
idea. What if the use was within the family
unit, extended family, where the extended
family watches the children while the mother is working.

Robert A.M. Stern You know, the room
down there is so far from the other two
rooms. Say the children are upstairs, and
there is a disturbance, or whatever, two
floors of stairs is a lot of separation to
have. And the children's laundry has to be
carried down. I mean, I guess I read plans
according to a different experience.

Lazor No. I think the master bedroom
is a hard sell for the program, but there's
a space down there that would really help
the person who buys this house. I do think
the Achilles' heal of this project is the
two bedrooms upstairs – maybe three up
one down.

Brigitte Shim This house raises an issue
here that is sort of in some of the others.
In Europe, they describe not square footage, which is a North American term, but
cubic volume. So your house, in terms of
cubic volume, your three-story dining room
is a pricey number – a volume of space
that is not actually occupiable. I look at

this project, and I almost think of it as two projects along this
line – this is the house and this is the other piece… I like the idea
in the initial site plan of turning the corner, an L-shaped condition around the big tree as an initial gesture. I think that works
very well. And like some of the others, you put the parking to the
side that's closest to the door so that you've taken advantage of
the breadth of the site. I think that the emphasis of the view to
the back around the tree works well, but I question the benefit of
that volume in relation to this L-shaped plan. Had there been a kind
of floor above this living room, it might have been a better plan,
might have resolved the turning of the corner in a better way. It
just seems awkward, for the gesture of the L, as a house design. It
doesn't take advantage of the things you've done to it. You have
more perimeter than the other projects do, so how you use that
perimeter to your advantage, internally, is kind of an imperative.

[…]

Lazor Is that elevation… Is its banal reading intentional?

Josh Lewandowski No, but it wasn't extravagant.

Lazor I thought there was a game going on here. Presenting a
very banal developer's façade, particularly this detail here – the
ultimate bad builder's detail – which I think, if handled well, could
be beautiful. You could start playing the context game that Dean
Stern is calling for, but do it in a way that talks about program,
technology and form-making.

Team B - Coconut

————

Alexandra Burr, Middlebury College; **Ji-eun Cha**, Ewha Woman's University, Korea; **Jeff Geldart**, Ryerson Polytechnical University, Canada; **Michael Krop**, University of Virginia; **Rachel Reese**, University of Idaho; **Dylan Sauer**, University of Cincinnati; **Erica Schroeder**, Ohio State University; **Sohyun Sung**, Korea University, Korea; **Mark Van Brocklin**, University of Virginia; **Alberto Zamora**, Texas A&M University

————

Robert A.M. Stern The model is different from the plan drawing, which is even more tortured in that re-entry arrowhead storage area. [The model] has fewer columns, so it's better than your drawing, I think. It's hard to see. Normally I hate plans like yours, but, actually, I think it's almost workable except for, like Charlie [Lazor] says, 'How do you furnish that porch?' You couldn't.

Charlie Lazor And the so-called front porch. I think that's a misuse of the term. I think that's a generous entry.

[...]

Lazor You have this envelope strategy and you have this interior, functionality, space planning strategy. They're two different things. What's frustrating about the project is that you hit on a building form... actually, I'm not sure that this has any typological relationship to the street. I think it's a barn, which is a great strategy. A barn is a large envelope with open space that is very flexible – a great typology to draw from. But all of the efficiencies of that, the economies, the directness, is upended and is smothered by this incredibly painful interior, where you take all of the expectation of going into this space and crowded it with all of this stuff – all these angles. At the end of the day, I think you crowded out occupation. I can't furnish this. I can't put chairs out there. My friends can't hang out here, or my kids. We've got this space that is a dining table, which, we know, people use very rarely. I'm trying to find a place for me in your project. So my question to you is what happened on the inside? How did you develop this strategy for the interior of the envelope, and why is it so counter to your envelope strategy?

Dylan Sauer I think we all were interested in the energy that exists in the contradictions between the inside and the exterior...

Lazor Wait a second. So this is a house for someone who is already financially stressed, and you're going to give them a domestic space of contradictions?

Rachel Reese We go back to the charged spaces where...the flexibility again. It keeps getting brought up. There's a space here where, regardless of who you are, you...this is a node for conversation or this is a node for options on both sides. So, hopefully it's charged by the circulation from a drop off to another place to sit...

Lazor Why is complexity...what was the word you used? Why is contradiction important? I think the contradiction is between the modern living and this rectangle shape which...a free plan wouldn't dictate a rectangle for the programming for a modern lifestyle. That's our take on...

Stern Do you really think that a modern lifestyle, whatever a modern lifestyle might mean, cannot function in a 30 by 60 foot rectangle? I think most people around the world would have to say, 'Oh, my God! I can't live in a modern way. I have to blow up my house.' I think there is a distinction between too much architecture and too much architecture babble and the real problem. I mean, when you start talking about nodes... Have you ever heard any person outside of this building talk about going home to their nodes? [laughter] Get over this! I mean it! It's ridiculous. There's nothing wrong with making a simple house. And the Galvalume outside... It's all nice to experiment, but if you take this iconic shape – and you do it very well – but to wrap it in a tin shed or a roofing material at best... Look how it looks on the street and what it would say to people. If you had taken the same thing, do it with clapboards or some highly manufactured clapboard look-alike material, which probably is cheaper than Galvalume, it would be another story and the proportions you have, which are a little quirky and weird, could come through. I think you have one wonderful move, which is the unusable backyard porch. With the angles, you make people look that way. Why can't they look all different ways? You are micromanaging people instead of giving people environments where they can find themselves in. It's a hard lesson, but it's basic.

————

Team C - Mango

Tom Bosschaert, Delft University of Technology, Netherlands; **Charles DiNatale,** Georgia Institute of Technology; **Jennifer Dubon,** University of Pennsylvania; **Mark Hoffman,** University of California at Berkeley; **Chiew Hong Tan,** National University of Singapore, Singapore; **Brent Martin,** Art Center of College of Design; **Nicholas McDermott,** University of Pennsylvania; **Elizabeth McDonald,** Tufts University; **Jeong Yeon Ryoo,** Hongik University, Korea; **Christina Wu,** University of Pennsylvania

----

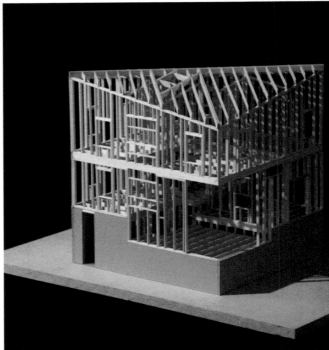

Team D - Papaya

Jonathon Cielo, University of Virginia; **Ireta Kraal,** Oberlin College; **Whitney Kraus,** University of Michigan at Ann Arbor; **Sheri Meschkinpour,** University of California at Berkeley; **Hojin Nam,** Ewha Woman's University, Korea; **Nathan Rich,** Wesleyan University; **David Riedel,** Carleton College; **Roberto Rossi,** Princeton University; **Isaac Strackbein,** University of Colorado; **Jessica Varner,** University of Nebraska
----

Robert A.M. Stern I would challenge the assumption that people who have windows on the side like this don't want to look at the street. It may not be the most beautiful street, but we know that after the Yale houses have been built, other houses have improved subsequently. But people like to look at streets. I think as a suburban generation that is often represented today and haven't grown up in cities, like to look at the street and see people. Aside from the safety argument — that's very important — I want to see the action. I want to know who is walking by...there's Mrs. Jones and her baby...

Jury [laughter]

Stern This kind of horse blinder thing...and if you're going to use the horse blinder, is it related in any way to environmental issues of the sun?

Nathan Rich There is an environmental justification in that they do shield from direct southern light, but at the same time, they are purposefully perforated. So that's what they do functionally. What they do conceptually and decoratively to us is they bring the site literally onto the house. What this ornament is, is a drawing of the Maple tree, and so it reinforces our conceptual idea. Another thing we noticed by exploring the site is that all of these houses had some form of décor on them. It was one of the things that Building Projects in the past have ignored and we wanted to address. The cowls were an opportunity to do this.

Charlie Lazor Now, it's beautiful, but it has to be more than beautiful, there has to be a reason for it. Brigitte [Shim] brought up the question of ventilation; is this the thing that reads as ventilation? Where the wall starts to separate, the air can come through and in this way read as a grill. This one, your street façade, is suffering in too many ways, and I think you have a lot of opportunities to make it remarkable.

Stern There are some nice things about your house. I like the fact that you have shown attention to the site — which I think is really commendable — and one assumes that the argument between the outside and inside, which you stated verbally, is at least represented here. In reality, it doesn't work as well as it could, or as well as I would like it to. For example, I would like to sit at this desk and look out to the garden. I don't really feel that the white wall of the powder room is the best relationship here. I think in a house like this, the whole wall could have been quite glossy, the south light is coming this way — Paul [Brouard] could help you figure it out — but in a way, you're thinking is maybe more abstract. I know less about landscape, but it is more believable than the house. These walls are not helping this cross reading, which is important in what you've done. When you get to the second floor, you are really coming to the stumble stuff. This bed is here so they can study their clothes in the closet, behind here [pointing to second floor plan] is the deck, which presumably looks out to the pretty garden, but there is no window in it. If I were in bed waiting for my tray of food to be brought up by my servant — because that's the only way you'll use such an arrangement — I would want to look into the garden. I want to see the space of this room extends across where I would see a table and two chairs, and I would have a fantasy that I was actually having breakfast outside.

Amy Lelyveld I want to come back to the issue of context. I guess I feel that there is a really big scale issue, especially when I look at these elevations compared to the other houses. It's not whether it's modern or historic, but it's the scale. It looks like an outbuilding or an accessory building. I almost wonder about the possibility of it being a public front. It doesn't mean you can't do all the stepping you do in terms of the gradation back in section. The idea that one could be moving this way and the grade is shifting the other seems to have some possibilities that add to your idea; it doesn't undermine it, it enhances it. I just think the kind of civic presence, what it says to the street is, 'I don't want to be here, screw you guys, I just want to be in my garden.'

Peter de Bretteville But that is only the very obvious step. I think you developed a tiny façade, as an elegant miniaturized...that is every bit as civic.

Lelyveld Right now it isn't.

de Bretteville Right now it isn't, but I wouldn't actually reverse the slope at all, it's a matter of re-looking the façade.

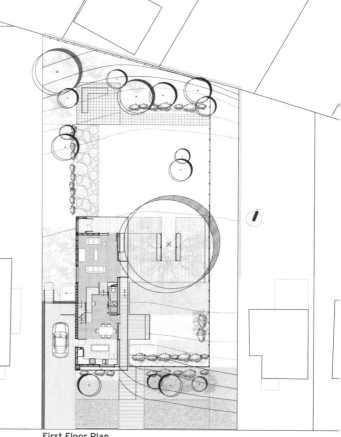

First Floor Plan
1/4" = 1'-0"

Team E - Strawberry
(Chosen Design)

Jamie Chan, Princeton University; Chris Corbett, University of Cincinnati; Minna Colakis, Barnard College, Greece; Bo Crockett, Texas A&M University; Ravi d'Cruz, Yale University; Todd Fenton, University of Virginia; Yichen Lu, Tsinghua Unviersity, China; Claudia Melniciuc, Colgate University; Sara Murado-Arias, New York University; Leo Stevens, Yale University

----

Robert A.M. Stern I think one of the things that this house has about its elevation, which is different from other houses we've seen today, is a discipline about geometry with the fenestration. The windows are relatively the same height and the proportions are coherent and might even be subjected to some discipline like the golden section or something like that that we never discuss anymore. It's not possible to have it anymore in this blob era. The discipline clearly comes into part with the rainscreen panelization. So my lesson, for anyone who might be interested, is that you have to have a discipline when you're making an elevation and sometimes the American traditional skin, shingles or whatever, does not carry within it an impulse. You have to develop your own inner sense of geometry. In this case, I hope that it was your inner sense of geometry, but in any case, the rain screen probably helped. What I also like about it, in your over-elaborate presentation of cabinetry, is what it does to the heights. You can see it beautifully in the perspective. It gives you a datum plane which starts at the upper floor and then carries through. The height of the living room is understood and measured. You measure it with your eyes and your hands if you have to. This is very well done in a sophisticated way.

Brigitte Shim For me, what I like about the house is that the skin would actually open up and accommodate other ways of ventilation. I also like the fact that there are actually two pieces. The west side is actually the wall and the roof. You're creating a dumber side. It allows and affords you to open up to the garden. That benefit is sideways, but also is stepping down into the garden. The project, I think, is really well grounded and [Team Strawberry] has actually seen and understood a relationship between the building and the site. For you guys, what I think has been the strength of the project is the skin and the building envelope. For the first time, I think I see a relationship between the skin and how you relate it to the site. And then to see this treatment of the elevation is wonderful because it's not a caricature. It's not about floor to ceiling glass, but it actually does orient you to the sidewall. I think you handled that quite well in terms of how the stepping works simultaneously. They're not two separate motions. They're actually the same project. I really appreciate that.

Henry Dynia It's not about how much we may like it. It's the fact that the people next door will have to look at that side [the metal side] directly…what does it mean? Have we thought about it?

Stern What happens just in case you get the commission? Do you have a plan B?

Mark Simon I think what really needs to happen is to find out who lives here and ask them about what it is about the side of the house that they value. What could they lose and what could they gain? What do they want? It's a negotiation.

Stern It's a very nice scheme. May be the next one will be nicer. But this is a question that when the clients ask, you can't go to the neighbor next door.

Peter de Bretteville Is it the issue that you want continuity? Are you married to dark metal? I don't believe that's the important idea. The important idea is this continuity. Continuity can be done in many different materials. It can be done in other ways. But really, I would hate to think that you're getting cornered by this big possibility of an alternative when it seems fairly obvious.

Claudia Melniciuc Can I stick my neck out? I think what is really important is truly the shell.

Stern How would you achieve the shell-like as an architect on the line?

Melniciuc It doesn't have to be metal – a continuous material.

Stern And what material would that be?

Melniciuc It could be shingles.

[uproar]

Stern Now, we can move on.

Alan Organschi Can I ask the client a question? Would you be willing to entertain a series of different solutions with the group if they present you with different options?

James Paley Well, I'm not sure if it were, say, shingles for the moment. I can't visualize it because it's not there. But I'm not sure how I would feel about having shingles on one side of the house and having three different textures on the other three sides.

[…]

Stern The house is very beautiful, and it's very well presented.

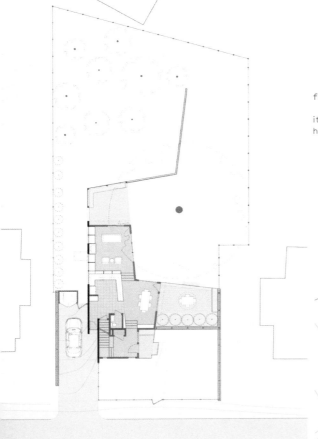

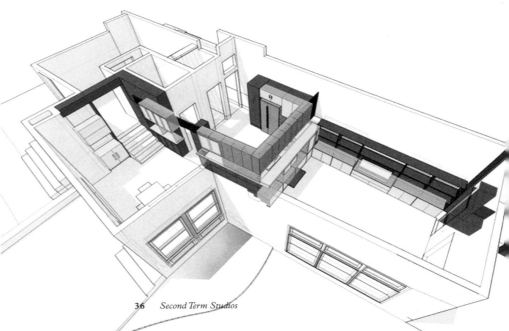

Team F - Watermelon

Claire Axley, University of California at Berkeley; Gabrielle Ho, University of California at Berkeley; Lydia Miller, Queens University; Marc Newman, Cornell University; Stephen Nielson, University of Virginia; Garrett Omoto, Arizona State University; Cheon-Kang Park, Handong University, Korea; Pierce Reynoldson, Ohio State University; Benjamin Smoot, University of Virginia; Quang Truong, Dartmouth College

----

Mark Simon I have to agree with Brigitte [Shim]. I think you've lost having a core that's not a core anymore…

Pierce Reynoldson …but it's not supposed to be a core…

Simon …those are islands, and they are not strong enough, or perceivable enough, to be read in this highly complex house.

Marc Newman This came up two weeks ago in mid-review. It really has to do with the issue of path, because the initial attempt was for us to actually delineate this diagram from a path…

Simon Then you're not talking about 'core.' You're talking about path…

Reynoldson That's because we're not talking about 'core.' I don't know where 'core' came from…

Benjamin Smoot We're not calling it a core. You [Mark Simon] keep calling it 'core' …

Simon Well…your word was 'core'.

Smoot No one said 'core'.

Reynoldson I used the word 'cluster', the word 'constellation'… I never said 'core'.

[laughter]

Simon Whatever it is, you're not defining it, you're not punctuating the…let's call it a spine. Do you want to call it a spine?

Reynoldson Not really.

[laughter]

Simon What do you want to call it?

Reynoldson If anything, it's a constellation because you walk around these pieces, you walk through these pieces…

Simon Then I guess what I hear Brigitte [Shim] saying, what I'm saying, is that a 'constellation' doesn't work, simply put, because you have a highly complex house and it gets lost in the complexity. You don't recognize it, it doesn't carry you through – it's not strong enough.

Peggy Deamer Could I just make a defense?

Simon Let me just finish, then you can defend. I just want to go on to two other subjects and then get back to this. I agree with Brigitte [Shim] that what bothers me is that you have a really wonderful set of spaces. I think this is a great idea, but it needs strengthening because it's not working yet. The circulation through the house is really quite marvelous, the site views are quite marvelous, but the central idea of the house just isn't there yet. This is something that architects have to work very hard on to get their ideas simplified so that they read.

[…]

Deamer I think it's right to defend that this is not a 'core' – that it's a series of elements, but I think it's also right to say that the series of elements is not reflected in the overall thing. So, I wanted to reframe the necessity, or the characterization, of these things as the things that can actually be made off-site. It seems to me that you [Team Watermelon] were actually trying to build up an argument of how you could do some special things that aren't on-site balloon frame construction. In some ways, this isn't just about identifying what appliances are, what 'cores' are. It's identifying certain pieces that can be made elsewhere. I want to defend that I don't think it's a 'core'. If it's a core, all of a sudden, we really can't make those things. But, where I do agree with the rest of the comments is that somehow we can't see that. For me, the problem is that you're putting all of your design energy into this divided house, part of which is contextual, part of which is abstract, part of which is pretending not to be there. It so overwhelms us that we can't actually go back to what I think is a very clear single proposition that is about the inside elements versus the outside elements, as opposed to the jazzy, wacko way that you are doing outside elements.

Newman I think that the idea of 'pretending not to be there' is actually quite poignant, because we did attack this constellation, these frameworks, from the start in a way that made it super easy to identify them. So we backed away and designed everything meticulously in hope that the density would be enough to identify it. I think that's where you're having issues.

Simon I think the density is there on the inside, but, as I said earlier, it's shy.

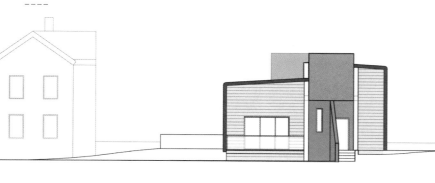

seat window bathroom pantry detail 1
SCALE 1/2" = 1'-0"

THIRD TERM STUDIOS

New Haven Community Courthouse [503a] *with* Keith Krumwiede *(coordinator)*, Peter de Bretteville, Martin Finio, Claire Weisz, *and* Davidson Norris *(lighting consultant): The studio concentrates on a medium-scale institutional building, focusing on the integration of program, site, composition, form in relation to structure, and methods of construction. Interior spaces are studied in detail. Large-scale models and drawings are developed to explore design issues.*

The program for this year's studio is a community courthouse located in downtown New Haven. As an alternative to traditional courts, community justice centers seek to reconnect the justice process with the communities that it serves. The **New Haven Community Court** *is modeled on other community justice projects in New York and Hartford. As such, the program and the principles it serves, builds upon both precedents.*

Peter de Bretteville
503a

Vincent Wan
University of Hong Kong, Hong Kong
Transparent and Animated Justice in an
Emerging Structural Field

By pushing the building to the site's periphery, room is freed up for an oasis at the back that is accessible to the public. By extending the green roof of the existing parking structure and allowing it to flow into the site, the landscape climbs up the building, penetrating and eroding it while the building protrudes into the landscape. The building is organized by a field of oscillating columns which respond to the site conditions, programmatic permutations, and structural requirements.

Peter de Bretteville The building is more complex than zoning activities. It also has to do with front to back, street to garden. It has this gradation – a whole layered effect, testing of ideas and layers of activities. It's a building with layered space.

Alexander Purves What I find important is not just the move into the garden but the garden comes together as a metaphor, as a reintegration of the building with the people of the community, and somehow the garden is standing before the community – would that be right? Then the question would be, would that be appropriate to justify that character?

Claire Weisz You're – I'll call it 'warping stretch' – not using it to your advantage spatially, other than attaching these spaces to the back of the wall. I wonder why you straightened it out here when what you want to show is expression, and want people to explore that thing? Why did you reverse that logic? It's making an ironic statement that I don't think you necessarily believe in.

Joeb Moore I can see a simple set of ideas getting inspired by the landscape corroding into the building, which is quite nice. And it comes up against your red core in your program diagram and your bay system, which is the Kafka-esque bureaucratic bar, which could have been played up more. It's a simple kind of provocation for you. This kind of field condition, which is your structure, your system of columns, starts a set of competing geometries, or competing symmetries. Therefore the landscape can be one kind of geometry and the building can be another kind. The erosion or collision or the kinds of deformation that were mentioned form these kinds of resultant conditions. And it could be driven by structure, it could be driven by program, or it could be driven in part by just the need of open space. You need to be clear about that because right now I can underline the entire project as just a field condition of a grid of numbers that lies underneath the building.

Sam Roche
Princeton University
A Community Courthouse for New Haven

A new courthouse servicing a dual program dispensing justice and providing social ser-

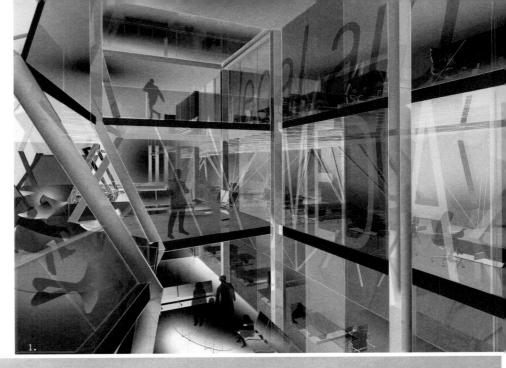

vices. The site was long, thin and varied with the downtown fabric on one short side and a wide perimeter road on the other. The design responded to the dual program and the varied site conditions. A tower makes a civic marker for the city while the more massive colonnaded block of the courtroom faces the ring road. The long façade ties them together with a colonnade.

Peggy Deamer What I think makes this a successful scheme is that the courtyards are incidental and not primary. What is interesting to me is that looking at it from this side, [you] started out really classically and then kind of Rossi-modern… I'm not a fan of a classicization of that, but I think there is a sensitivity to the elevations. The proper scale of objects of different buildings allows it to read both incidental and organized at the same time. From where I'm sitting, the way [the high piece] engages the higher building behind it is pretty interesting. To see that it works as you are coming down Chapel [Street] is quite great.

Craig Konyk The relationship of the massing and the organization of the plan is very straightforward. The resolution of the program is very comprehensible and understandable… Once you start addressing those volumes and masses with some kind of language of material and architecture, what's the process and what are your rules and where does it start and stop? And you then turn around the corner and you've got the really remarkable slab. I really don't know whether you just didn't get to it and you would have rendered that also with things like…pilasters?

[…]

Chris Genik I'm trying to understand your process. What is that language? I believe it is some kind of Doric, but I don't really know. It certainly doesn't follow the proportions. It's only the capitals… What are the rules you are using? Is it just purely compositional or is it something about the way the building develops in this proportion, this volume? You clearly have an initial good sense in how to organize those things, but you've also rendered it so that only

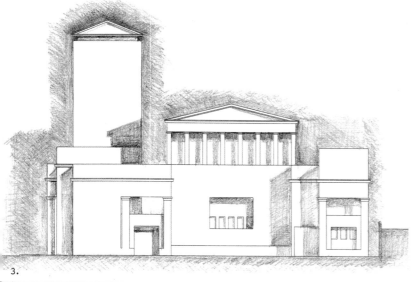

3.

The boundaries between these zones are breached only at specific programmatic points. The courtroom is centrally located in order to create a source from which each zone can emerge. Courtyards allow exterior spaces to become internalized and remain secure while also fulfilling reflective, healing, and gathering functions.

----

the character that you have articulated so well. It's not so much a planning issue as an articulation issue.

Keller Easterling I end up wondering whether there are any nighttime photos. I want the building somehow to glow. What you see in these renderings is that it's giving something back to the community — that somehow it's a vital institution. I actually don't buy the psychiatrist or fishbowl idea because what you do pretty successfully, I think, in the stairs and in the plaza, is to say, 'Look, you're camouflaged by all the rest of us. None of us are pure and there's a big crowd of people.' You can't tell who the criminal is and the whole purpose of this courtroom is to say you're going right back out there and we're all a part of it. You're picking up the other end of it and that the best protection of privacy is a crowd in some ways that I think you do very well. One almost wishes to see that kind of vitality in the plaza.

Joeb Moore One of the things I like about some of the ideas is this misalignment between what the individual and the group is and that there could be different sizes of groups from

5.

6.

the monumental plaza to the more job-training spaces, cafeteria spaces, filter spaces to the individual cell units which are off the conference desk on the second floor. That kind of indexing on this façade which faces the plaza and that maybe those lines, maybe there are more misalignments to them in the sense that they get pulled out... what is kind of fascinating about this is that if you look straight on it, you can't see through. In fact, you never see perfectly straight on. Even if you just shift an inch, there's some kind of discovery.

4.

those moments that you find precious are rendered. That great big slab of brick or stone is actually more powerful than the little porch on the top. So you need to be truer about all of those things you are trying to look at, not just the sort of favorite moments.

Michael Weinstock I think you are a true believer. [laughter] We've seen in Northern Europe and in England people really struggling to do what you are evidently interested in. If you have these great untreated surfaces, they may be completely overwhelmed by the classical detailing and the reworking of classicism that you want to do. In the worst case, they will make you look petty and trivial... So you really have to decide which way you are. Either you are kind of up to date with contemporary materials, where it is about mass and surface and the kind of qualities of light and a very, very muted reference to classicism, or you are a kind of full-blown classicist.

Geoffrey Lawson
University of Virginia
Distributing the security threshold

This project creates a framework to explore the relationship between security and civic space. By integrating social services into court facilities, security becomes a region of overlapping zones with increasing exclusion which are arranged across the site.

Jeff McBride
Williams College
Creating Community

Cloaked in perforated metal screens, it would appear that this building wants nothing to do with the community. Nothing is further from the truth. This courthouse fosters a community. Community development programs flank a central arcade and are separated by planes of concrete, creating varying degrees of privacy to the inhabitants while allowing for fractured visual access between spaces. In this main arcade, light from skylights emphasizes the the interior and activities within.

Alexander Purves I buy entirely your argument... I think a couple of questions come to mind about the architectural definition of that idea. One of them is the kind of monumentality, not just of the exterior stair, but of the interior itself. I think that there's a way in which you have organized the centers and the big stair in the middle that to me talks more about the large-scale public gesture than it does about the delicate interaction — the person-to-person — that you're describing as how you want the interior to operate. It's the whole processional quality about that space with these very large two-story masonry surfaces and then these stairs at the end of it. To me, that has a kind of large scale quality that is contrary to

Martin Finio

503a

Kathryn Stutts
University of Virginia
Network/Knot

The project is generated from an idea about the relationship between the lobby and the courtroom – the two most interconnected programs of the building. The lobby is a circulatory, divergent space, a network connecting the public to all the court services, and the courtroom is a convergent space, a central knot where all participants in court functions come together. I am interested in the interface between these two types of space, as well as the expression of the linear public circulation as it parallels Chapel Street.

Thomas Phifer I think there are a lot of really great things here and that's why I want to hear you say it. The program is fascinating – a federal courthouse is a very significant change to the typical court's program. One of the complications with actually achieving this kind of program, though, is in the discretion between the public amenities of the building – the things that are community based and the things which are court based. I think that it is important to create a dialogue between those things that allows someone who isn't on trial or someone who isn't in the penal system to engage in this building and to walk through it without being associated with all kinds of things. So what I was looking for was some stronger connection to the public, like a public walk-through among various program elements in casual basis so they can actually access these functions without necessarily parting to it... I guess what I am getting is that the root of that diagram begin a response to program.

Kathryn Stutts Program, but also very much Chapel Street. It's always been the two together.

Robert A.M. Stern Transparency is one thing, but how do you enter? People want the ease to enter. A canopy is a sheltering place. It's like a porch, and that kind of thing is not here. Although it is a spectacular diagonal geometry that you have here, it is actually quite overwhelming at the point of entrance, and a little threatening.

Mark Gage I wonder at what point this language became the new classical portico for courthouses. You know this sort of [Daniel] Libeskind-ing of surfaces, something which is certainly in the air. I think it is best used when

1.

it is used in conjunction with some ideas involving program and circulation, [instead] you are using it more as a placeholder than actually allowing it to participate in the difference that you are trying to create. I find it very problematic. You talked about binding together these ideas and edges, but really the language you are using isn't one of binding, but is one of adding. There is a very clear point where you can determine where that begins and this ends because with binding one would sort of imagine that this wouldn't be such a definite boundary, but would be bleeding into this in some sort of gradient. So the place of most intensity in terms of the fragmentation becomes the entrance, and that's where you pucker in and have your little pizzeria entry. But right now I think it's sort of ubiquitously used, and it is not reinforcing any of the ideas of the program behind it.

Billie Tsien I think there is a possibility of making your building more dark so that you could see the light. I mean, in a way, there is so much light that I don't know if the walls of light would be perceptible as walls of light... In many ways, the form of the building could be the same, but it can be clad in ways to make some places darker.

Gage That's a Thomas Aquinas argument that you need light to prove the existence of darkness and dark-

ness to prove the existence of light. That language of opacity verses transparency is something that you are taking for granted. In your project, things are either gray or they are glass. I

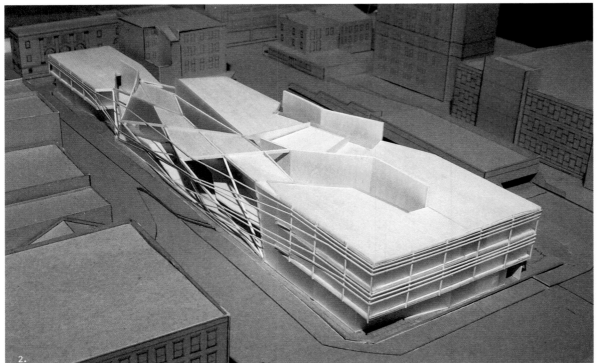

2.

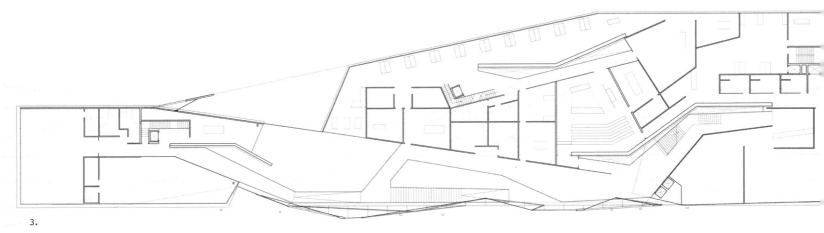

3.

think adding another layer of material intelligence that could reinforce your idea of entry or binding…so that the brightness means something and codes something, allowing people to know how to move through the building, like you enter into the dark space and move towards the light — like the poltergeist. Go to the light!

Harris Ford
Princeton University
COURTyard

This proposal for a community justice center explores a new courthouse type that focuses on prevention, reconciliation, and remediation rather than retribution and punishment. In response to its role as a new urban typology as well as an innovative judicial paradigm, and as both an organization strategy and a point of departure, the COURTyard justice center makes use of unconventional open spaces — lifted courtyards which provide places of repose above and gathering and waiting areas below.

[midterm review]

Keith Krumwiede …Particularly with this program, you can construct interesting sequences of access and disposal — accessing services facility. So how do I go to the court, I just don't go bang bang and that was it, then you are not circulating. I agree with Craig [Dykers] that it looks rather institutional. There are all these

big moves that are completely short-circuited by the access stair to the building. The cross-grains cut right into it when I imagine that the ramp has to be important because it certainly looks important. There's got to be something about moving up that [ramp] and accessing services in someway to construct the differential relationship with this court to the community versus a typical courthouse. It is not this kind of mean and immediate relationship. What I say by mean is being not generous. Your building suggests some kind of generosity, but it is always the promise without the realization.

Eeva-Liisa Pelkonen There is this kind of argument about languages — we all read Le Corbusier — that I am fascinated by. Is it accidental that these languages are used in your project? Did you look into Le Corbusier? In case you did look at Le Corbusier, what did you look at? What draws you to it? I mean, I would say obviously that kind of latent monumental-ism, kind of sculpturally dealing with certain kind of elements, even the kind of thickened wall, the plasticity of the wall that he expresses in the Brise Soleil. Of course, it is lost in here if you put glass in front of it. But those are the kind of latency there that could be explored. I would say to go all the way to look at Le Corbusier and to look at his work from the [19]40s and [19]50s. I think you can get a lot out of it.

Krumwiede I think that is a good suggestion for this kind of promenading experience of this kind of building.

Craig Dykers Not only that. If you look at Le Corbusier, the first thing Le Corbusier would do is to make that interior courtyard a public space. Forget about security. Find a way to get people — it's a community building — into this lovely space you've created.

Krumwiede Well, not necessarily. In La Tourette, the courtyard is inaccessible to the public.

Joseph Alguire
University of Illinois at Urbana-Champaign
Androgynous Architecture

This project attempts to resolve extreme typological variation through the processes of recombination and synthesis. The building is attenuated into three distinct appendages allowing such diverse programs as a daycare, jail cell, and coffee shop to coexist in a loose association. This hybrid of public, institutional, and commercial space finds itself triangulated between these poles of influence as an androgynous architecture.

Kurt Forster We see a lot of projects like this, say Rem [Koolhaas] or MVRDV, taking large aperture and punch it out according to program. You're not punching yours relative to program, but punching relative to structure. So you are stuck somewhere between coding room with aperture and having the façade looks like three floors. What is the conceptual rigor behind that?

Joseph Alguire The strategy was to bring the scale down.

Forster It seems like you've invested chiefly in making these monitors. The way you present it is literally a self-sufficient, uniformly enclosed piece that has been here put into the city seemingly for one dominant purpose — that is to monitor the city. The whole image is related to monitors, to things that arise, usually associated from things arising from something that's dark, and that they've got these big eyes, or big lights, through which you survey the city. This is a very powerful image, but I think it runs totally counter the idea of the program. This is tantamount to erecting a permanent structure of surveillance to scare the people so they never make it into the courthouse. Let's not forget that this country, by proportion to the population, has the largest prison population in the world. That's more than twice the population to the next country in Europe. So either the system is so much more efficient that it captures many more of the evil fish or it is so contrary to what is really happening in the society at large that it captures many more than what it would have to fish out of the problem. So you're building, in an almost vaguely scary way, is reminding us of this.

5.

Martin Finio I don't see it as a sinister thing. I don't thing it rejects itself that way. I think to his credit, he didn't over-orchestrate the experience of justice in the towers. The fact is that this is a social tower. I think it's not about surveillance. It is actually about transparency of the very public and very accessible space.

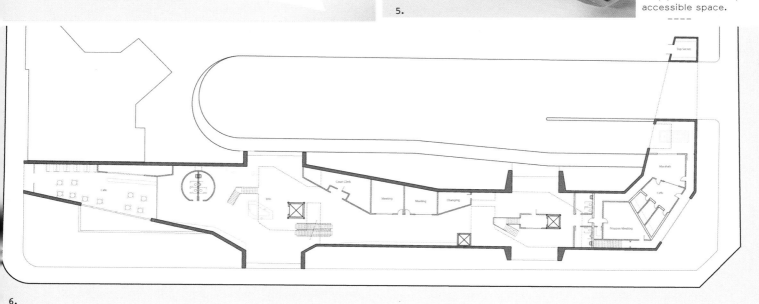

6.

Keith Krumwiede
503a

M. Jejon Yeung
Carleton University, Canada
Stratified Transparency

This Project establishes a civic front that faces an interior plaza extending the pedestrian network from Court Street and Orange Street. This move was to reinforce both a sequestered civic presence and allow for a receptiveness that would establish a new urban identity for the program. The community components of the courthouse program are situated along Chapel Street front, where it is readily accessible. The private court offices are pulled away from both Chapel Street and the entry plaza. This community-court gradient is organized via a striation of spaces that slip, merge and deflect in response to adjacencies that the program demands. The complexity of the program and its performance results in dense and layered circulation. Having spaces that orchestrate fluid movement and drift from program to program would create a court experience more representative of the community court model. These undulating walls control specific lighting conditions throughout the building, and are specifically tuned to moments and characters within the courtroom.

Davidson Norris Do you say that it would be difficult to find your way around this building?

Jejon Yeung You might. I try to imagine the spaces not in plan. As I built the model, I realized how complicated it was spatially. I had to make indicators of how you would go through spaces, but I like how through the transparency, you can still see where you might lead to next.

Norris The reason I bring it up is because I think one of the of the most Kafka-esque, literally, problems of municipal buildings is one's inability to understand where one has to go once in a building. That leads to enormous anxiety, even under the best of circumstances. If what you do is to develop a circulation system that creates, I think, these very beautiful spaces and very beautiful lighting opportunities, but what it creates primarily from the experience of the visitor is not knowing where they are going or how to get to where they are going or seeing where they want to go but not knowing how to get there. I think you have to question yourself as to whether or not that is a valid strategy.

Karen Fairbanks It looks to me that all the routes led you to the courtroom. I know what you're saying about the complexity of the layers, but I keep looking at the plan and thinking… no matter where I go in, I end up right around the courtroom, which is kind of interesting that it could be both so deeply protected and then so exposed to the public. I want to hear more about your ideas how these layer in this public sequence – how you register that relative to your ideas to this system and the way we understand how this works? There are some very amazing moments in the model and in the spatial sequence. I feel a bit disappointed that the section, I don't think, registers the promise of really the experience the model suggested because I think your movement really is limited to two layers of the space. There is a sense that the roof is very active and light comes down at a very active way, but I don't think you participate in that as well as you could. It might be

just a moment in section that I am seeing or the model that skews. You still striate in plan in layers. I think you are really talking about creating some new landscape for this whole system to be operated in. If it were more of a landscape, then we might come upon even odder relationships to some of these programs. You may find yourself somehow questioning where these grounds are and what your reference point is. How did you get yourself into this place at the beginning anyway?

Keith Krumwiede This is the first time I see multiple sections. For me, Karen's [Fairbanks] point really drives me to question the ground level and platform. Some of these can begin to take charge. I think maybe in addressing some of David's [Norris] concerns too about navigation and way-finding, you can use the ground to help control – to try to make it totally porous, but to say 'hold-on it is a court, there is all this stuff at the back of the house. I've got to keep that segregated; I've got to maintain security threshold,' and charging the ground can help you do that.

Marc Guberman
Brown University
Social Pillow

The community courthouse, as a building type, is a relatively new one. Thus, an opportunistic position to design the prototype emerges. Essentially, it is the handling of different, and at times directly opposed, constituencies. Hybrids of users, represented by those mandated to the facility versus those arriving on their own volition, comprise the mixture of staff and visitors. Each experience demands something unique.

This design takes the distinctions between user groups as its organizing principle in an attempt to provide for a choreographed experience, where each individual's priorities and idiosyncrasies can coexist. In this scheme,

float spaces provide a waiting area and refuge to the distressed. The clear delineation between the public amenities of the bar and the private functions of the tower is blurred in the courtroom. The bridge serves as the security checkpoint.

Claire Weisz Programmatically, I think it is very interesting. You have a kind of low service bar, and then you have a kind of judicial tower. In itself, it is a really interesting thing for a prototype.

Robert A.M. Stern Seeing partitions is a nightmare. This is the reason why when Mies developed the curtain wall for office buildings, he didn't do the biggest piece of glass that he could

1.

2.

order – that was the Skidmore Owings and Merrill way. Mies made five-foot modules because he knew that there were going to be partitions against the glass. You have fallen into the SOM trap.

Keith Krumwiede What is potentially prototypical in this are the elements that are particular to a community court versus any other court. It's that all of these other social services functions come to the courtroom. The courtroom, in a sense, is still a critical component, but it is reduced. It doesn't carry the same weight; it doesn't drive the overall building organization any longer. In your case I could see this building taking many forms. The principle being that the courtroom is always wrapped by the other services, and it is the definition of a type of interface between the public, the consumer of justice in this case, or the assistants. One is always faced with that opportunity first before having to interface with the courtroom. So it's that wall, it's the path along one side, it is the provider of services on the other side and it's the wall negotiation. So you can wrap this thing up, you can tie it in knots, but that condition could hold, that is about as close as I can get to a prototypical component.

[…]

3.

4.

Krumwiede What seems to me to sort of be the strength of this project is not so much that it is the street coming in. It's that you are actually opening up the building, this is actually one of the projects where I think letting the face be the section is kind of powerful because you are almost opening up…you are in a room without really being in an institution per say, and so there is a layering happening across which I think is quite good.

Peter de Bretteville The scheme is really intriguing to me. It seems to me that it has to play out on the first floor as a kind of loggia along that edge. That is very permeable, and has all the really normative, easily and directly accessible stuff in it. Then the argument would be that the exceptional elements, the courtroom and others, are liberated to be expressive of their own character, and their own programs. They could even be positioned in ways that are relatively arbitrary to the bar and could go anywhere.

Elisa Lui
University of California at Berkeley
<u>Tacit Security</u>

The biggest design challenge is to accommodate the different security levels demanded by the various programs. While some of the judicial programs such as the private offices and the prisoner zone require high security inspection, those that serve as interface with the public, like the courtroom and mediation office, require a medium-security access. Meanwhile, the social services are open to the general public. The aim of this design is to fulfill these needs through implicit means rather than creating opaque barriers between these different security zones. Visual transparency, circulation paths and light penetration become the tools to demarcate territories,

while paradoxically blurring their edges at the same time.

Karen Fairbanks It seems like really competing needs, which makes it more complicated. This idea that you want to find a way to meet the services of the administration so that there is a chance that those different institutions or those different people might come to some other conclusion about what might be the best for these criminals. On the other hand, your building really does still divide into two realms. There is a public realm, and clearly the idea of a public space is this skylight above a big staircase where you are open to move somewhat freely whereas on the other half of the building, there is this huge courthouse hanging above you. It is like the weight of this system sitting above you. The line between them seems fragile right now in the model and the way the elevations and the plan works. It is really just a wall. It seems to me that the wall, along with that edge has to do a lot of work to negotiate those things. The administration subscribes the plans around that line, and everything else about your architecture emphatically draws that line, so finding a way to get both of those things to read – both of the connections – is important. I think on the lowest level, you try to understand the perimeter and seeing this as one big volume. Perhaps, you want to do the same above. Really, that line keeps coming back. [You] read it on one side or the other – either person moving about with freedom or you are here in trial under this court. I see that as the biggest conflict here…

Chris Genik It seems like there is all kinds of potential. This program is written to turn the degrees of difference. In other words, it is not just community or judicial, but the interaction and the rub between the two programs. This rub must and should activate architecture in a way that is not so pre-determined and clear necessarily all of the time. There are moments where, for example, the structure is compressive and load-bearing, this may shift to a tensile system and actually propel you to understand both the architecture and your involvement with the way the program is articulated in a very different way. I am wondering where did you develop your thinking about this program. The architecture specifically is working for you to answer questions that you might have about the program. This kind of incredible moment of revelation that you have when you went to the previous site where suddenly the lock-up is a load. It's actually heavy and has weight and it has to be something, regarding to the larger structure. [That] doesn't just sandwich in quite so easily, but it has another kind of accountability and relationship to the architecture. There is an incredible narrative in this project that the architecture somehow needs to support or nullify – I am not sure which – but you actually have to make a stand for...

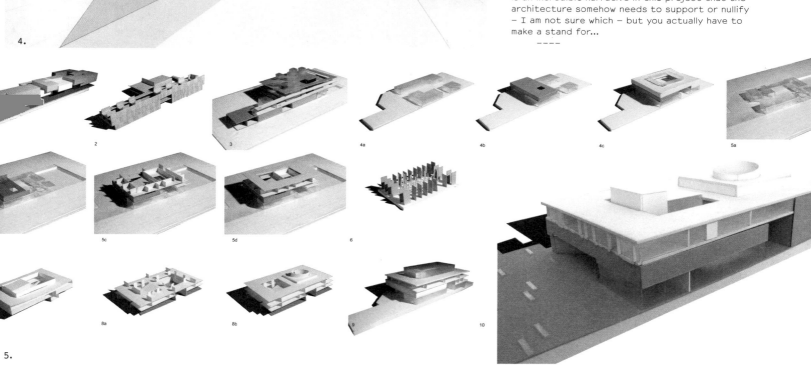

5.

(1,2) M. Jejon Yeung
(3,4) Marc Guberman
45   (5) Elisa Lui

Claire Weisz
503a

Christopher Lee
University of California at Berkeley
<u>Zig Zag</u>

This proposal addresses the issues of site by maintaining and defining a strong street edge while allowing the public to connect visually and physically back into the interior of the city block. The massing of the building is rendered in a masonry material and forms a bar in response to the long and attenuated site. A dogtrot opening relieves the pressure of the Chapel Street retail activity and allows people to pass through or into the building. In addressing the new program, the proposal seeks to gather, connect, and make more transparent the disparate functions of the Community Courthouse. In lieu of the double-loaded corridor, a spiraling movement of diagonal pathways carves voids through the bar building, revealing the inner workings of the social services and the courthouse.

Christopher Lee I see it more as being able to bring in light because the interest is always to get rid of the dark during the day in the double-loaded corridor.

Alexander Purves I think that this is a very thoughtful scheme. Why did you feel it was necessary to maintain the flat roof? And it obviously has to do with these various conditions...

Joeb Moore Well, maybe a different way to ask that question is, 'Why make it a conventional roof?' The cage is the skin that you've placed around...in other words, this construction type is quite different from the skin logic here. It begs the question of whether there can also be a kind of transparency, the same way you've produced this porosity and transparency. Could it also apply here? Which it does in your model by the way, quite nicely. Could you just quickly map us through the rest?

Lee Yes. Sure. So the idea was to serve both as a unifying element, tying together the social services and the court, but also using a low-tech version of perforated skins that we're seeing a lot of. So you would just be using regular bar grating...it has a low resolution pixel, so it gives you the opportunity to also create an identity or a prototype for the rest of the program... it could be through a logo, or pattern and color.

Keller Easterling One argument you could make, in a kind of

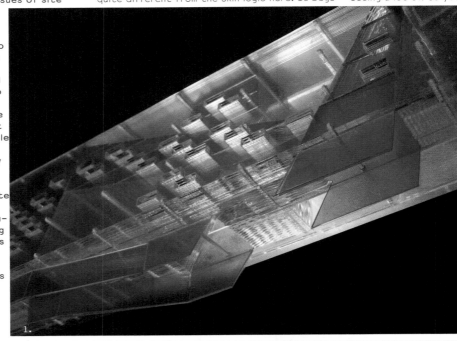

1.

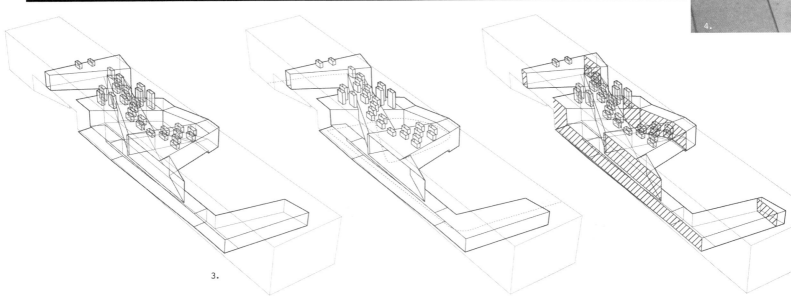

2.

4.

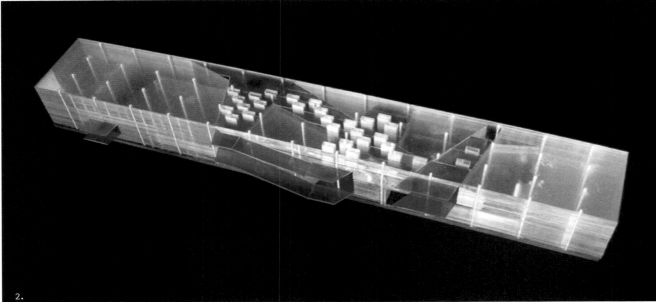

3.

Koolhaasian way, is that the bigger, the better and the more relentless. I don't know if this is necessarily true, maybe starting to get there that it is asking to be labyrinthine. And the only way that could be justified would be that if the building has its own internal organism. This is the whole argument about bigness, right? If it's big enough, then it's out of control, and it actually has something kind of wondrously anarchic, like an organism going on inside of it…like people who do that, Rem Koolhaas. It always seems so snide at first, but then there's always some kind of very incredibly pleasurable payoff. I think for yours it might be one of the surprise payoffs. Just when you're ready to say, 'Oh Koolhaas, you know, whatever.' Then suddenly you're delivered this incredible pleasure, and it's hard. I think for you it could be this back space, not just the parking lot. We find the double of something else back here, that it's almost like getting on a horse and falling off the other side. There's something else over here.

Moore It also reinforces the doubling that

COORDINATION work together. As a strategy, I understood the user to be a performer in the space, and when placed in the constructed social context of the community courthouse, the performer in conjunction with other performers in the building produces a spatial condition that is not necessarily the resultant of a formal move, but primarily because the collective performers and the activities within the courthouse produce an event. I have taken this approach as a means of exploiting the potential public nature of community justice. I have consciously attempted to both present order and deny order at the same time – a displacement of a placement.

Edward Mitchell I am asking for some clear definition. I think you are on to something, but it is missing at certain places in terms of your overall thesis. To me, no matter how friendly you get, there is still some kind of judgment being placed on whoever goes through the process, whether it is in the distance, or now outside the

spiraling up in the space, dumping into something where you recognize a certain arrangement of furniture that has a hierarchy of judgment and order. What gets weird and should become fun to play with are all the dumb stuff that are happening like the bathrooms, places of privacy and judgment and judging – who is a man and who is a woman and who goes into which space? Ideas of projection become representations of surfaces cast onto walls that tend to have representational quality of a civic institution, whether that's socialized job searching or health care. They are already minor courtroom facilities. I think the one thing you want to do is to re-examine and look to the specific architectural effects that counteract the idea of the open system…

Chris Genik What interests me is the interplay between this kind of invention, which you brought to the table, of a container and its presence anywhere in the plan. It just wanted to argue for more weight and more presence, more substance as opposed to the fragile ways you

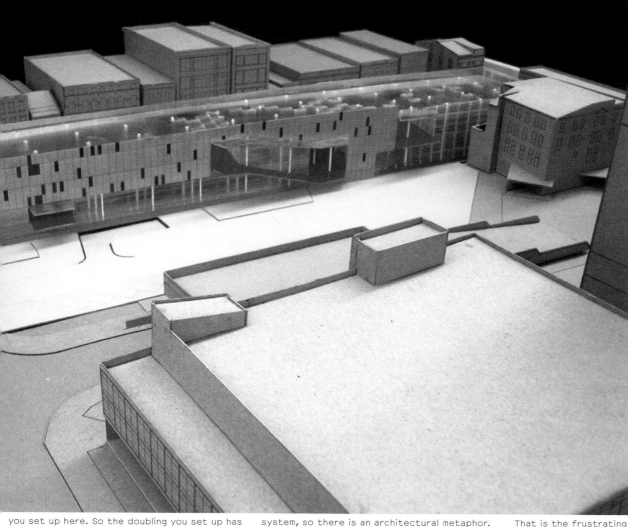

pointed out, particularly as a counterpart to the infrastructures of the building – about the rooms and so on and so forth, but are sort of arranged furniture-like large floor plate – because those are fundamentally two paradigms that you are playing off one another within this orbital field, that the structural bay and the objects are in the building. This contributes to a delightful interplay that has the potential, which actually is not really resolved. You don't really use them to tell the story of you going to the building either as an insider or an outsider to the system. How do you go from the figural container to just the courtroom or other functions of the building so that something extraordinary comes of it – either in the way that you mark or by having red tar going onto the site? There is something that you are always referencing ambiguously. You don't want to convince somehow. It is perplexing because they are really very interesting ideas. The project exists almost as a thesis that doesn't want to exert itself as a solution. That is the frustrating thing about it.

----

you set up here. So the doubling you set up has a way to kind of drive what we've been referring to as the labyrinth. So the labyrinth isn't just spatial. It's not just even the devices you've deployed, but even potentially programmatically; there's a kind of social matrix that gets produced by these two ends. So it's now being said that you could do that with the context as well, the street and the backyard.

J.M. Tate
Texas A&M University & Rural Studio
Active Infrastructure

This project seeks to engage architecture through ideas about infrastructural form and active organization. In designing the courthouse I saw the plan not so much as a plan, but instead as a map, where INDETERMINACY and

system, so there is an architectural metaphor. Traditional courtroom is configured based on the idea of boundary/edge. It is always very apparent where the threshold is when you come in and out, the whole ballet ritual of coming to the courtroom. If your thesis is going to make a building that is more or less open to spatial articulation and less with boundary and more with furniture to create an open flow of events, I still think you can maintain aspects of the courtroom. There are still certain points within that flow where boundary is determined. One would be the orchestration of the set of information that is projected onto a wall serving as representation of one of the witnesses, and then make the judgment toward them. This negates the traditional form of a courtroom, which your other one doesn't. It is interesting that the guilty people are walked through a kind of processing machine, move vertically through that staircase, which is really important. You are

Gabrielle Brainard
Yale University
New Haven Community Courthouse

The community court program asks us to produce two spatial conditions in close proximity. The judicial program needs to project authority, while the community service program needs to create a sense of comfort and accommodation. The service program is organized in a low, permeable bar that maximizes public accessibility. The judicial program wraps around and above the service program in a tower that frames a ground-level public space. The judicial program serves as the extroverted, urban face of the building, while the public program is focused toward the interior. This reading

Claire Weisz
(continued)

is reinforced by large cutouts which connect program vertically in the bar, while opening up the tower to views of the city.

Claire Weisz I think in this case, and we saw in other projects…of being the only community building all the way on State Street may be mishandling the opportunity to strengthen the nine square and to strengthen Orange street, which is habitable.

Keller Easterling I think the site of your building is really spot-on. In the general organization of the building, I like this kind of funny disconnection be-

tween this and this. While you are able to maintain the clarity of the parti in the first floor plan, although not so much on the second floor plan. The courtroom actually ends up being in a set of partitions – it is more within the realm of just drafting. Similarly, when you see the child care facility from here, I end up thinking that the plant-

6.

7.

ers that you have going forward would be with the skin, and figuring out the ways in which it either slums around or stretch around or gets torn and picked up. Here, you almost want to develop – as you are starting to do here – some ways that there is aperture. Like here, there is sheer ground. You know how to make aperture – like something is swollen and then torn broken. Here, this is less. It seems like a kind of modernist where something isn't part of the behavior of the skin. Here, what would be the repertory of that skin when the skin has become a wall that has a volume in it? Then I end up wondering somehow in the rules could there be a break here, so that [it] becomes open to the State Street side. You do the nicest move I have seen so far and that is to be able to see all the kids in there. Play around with that. Where it gets draped over, where it stretches, where it tears – I think you can have a pretty good time.

Joeb Moore I think what you can take home with that is to be aware of the representational object in your drawing and the apparatus or device you're going to conceptualize the skin. There are so many successful global moves like the general site and situational strategy – quite fascinating to Keller [Easterling]. It is very strong on that level. It is when we zoom in on the details, and even though we don't expect you to design all those details, we would hope that in discussion and in time you would discover that there are ways of drawing and representing or even working out a logic of drawing which could more deeply to imply your idea of the skin. It is that kind of misalignment of the skin that makes me curious about the grading of the image on the side. It ties back to a monastic tradition of the mystery of light.

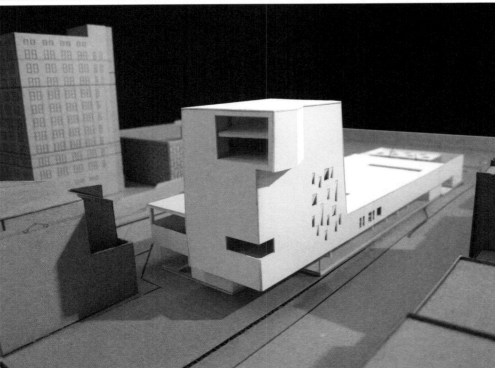

8.

FOURTH TERM STUDIOS

[504b] Edward Mitchell *(coordinator)*, *with* Peggy Deamer, Andrea Kahn, Emmanuel Petit, *and* Alan Plattus: *The studio, an introduction to the planning and architecture of cities, concerns two distinct scales of operation: that of neighborhood and that of the dwellings and the institutional and commercial building types that typically contribute to neighborhood. Issues of community, group form, and the public realm, as well as the formation of public space, blocks, streets, and squares are emphasized. The studio is organized to follow a distinct design methodology, which begins with the study of context and precedents. It postulates that new architecture can be made as a continuation and extension of normative urban structure and building typologies. This studio takes as its subject the fundamental of urban design, examining relations between how one represents, analyzes, constructs and projects the future design of an urban site. It posits the act of building in the city as an act of building city. The development of the greater New York metropolitan region reflects tensions between local and global economics, the changing role of technology in structuring urban form and constantly shifting urban demographic profiles. In recent years, commercial and residential developments have shot up in many riverfront locations near Manhattan – in Queen's, Brooklyn and along the so-called "Gold Coast" in New Jersey. In this context of extensive waterfront development activity, in and around New York City, the studio will analyze and propose urban design strategies for the waterfront of Red Hook, Brooklyn.*

Peggy Deamer
504b

Sandra Arndt, Rustam-Marc Mehta
& Lindsay Weiss
University of Wuerzburg, Germany,
Brown University
& University of Pennsylvania
In-ternal Fra-meworks: Highway
and Waterfront

————

Our urban strategy is to make the waterfront re-accessible to the public.
Red Hook is historically recognized as a
container port of prevalent value, but
recent demand for waterfront access
and decline of water-based manufacturing
has rendered this area of Red Hook to be
programmatically and spatially misused. We
identified the existing highway system to
the north as a new asset for the location
of the manufacturing industry. In order to
exploit that infrastructural advantage, we
propose to establish a logistic hub in close
proximity to the highway, causing a redefinition of the northern border of Red Hook.
On an urban scale, new arterial traffic

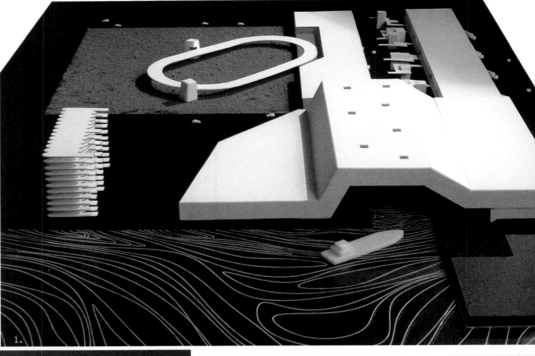

1.

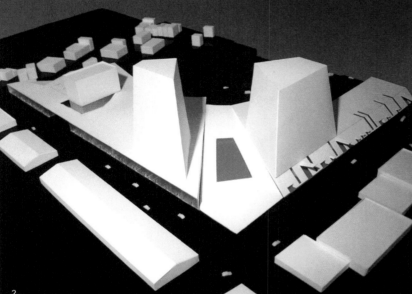

2.

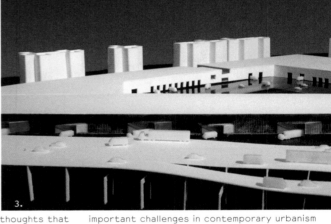

3.

routes are established to separate local from
regional vehicles as well as keeping Red Hook
connected to the adjacent neighborhood of
Carroll Gardens. The relocation of the industry
leaves the waterfront with new opportunities
for further development. We propose to break
the large scale blocks into a smaller scale,
consistent with the existing residential fabric,
by extending the streets running East/West
to meet the water's edge. This strategy does
not prescribe the nature of the potential
waterfront development; rather it begins to
establish public corridors which contain visual
and physical access to the ocean.

————

Robert Levit Some of us ask about the size
and what the architectural quality is. I think
Andrea [Kahn] made a remark about level and the
experience of the biggest building. Part of the
thrill of coming in contact with a building at this
scale is the strangeness of the contact. Under
ordinary circumstances you wouldn't have the
contact because you don't go to the factories,
and you are usually not allowed in for a variety of reasons. Part of the excitement is also
coming into contact with a piece of history,
but actually advocating the construction of a
building of this size. In this situation, you might
be making the argument of linking the other side
across the bridge and underneath the highway.
There are a lot of what-if's your scheme raises
and perhaps is unfair. The issue of the distribution of columns and the road of the circuitry
underneath is an interesting one. One of the

thoughts that
come into mind
with elevated
road is what
if you build
underneath of
them. If you got the stacking of the roads and
you build a building underneath the circuitry, you
can actually create a continuous urban fabric
granted that different jurisdictions would make
this combination of buildings difficult. To me,
the assumption that the enormously long truck
servicing facility along the edge would ultimately
block the connection and cut the neighborhood
into two is one that may not make sense.

Peggy Deamer I think in some way you all
have identified that this may work as a structure strategy, but hesitate as an architectural
strategy and I think that is exactly what they
have been struggling with – the idea of the
garage door that you were talking about. I think
they recognize these are small gestures that
could be conditioned. My question is 'are we
giving them advice on how to find architecture
within this strategy?' and I take this direction
of going under the harbor with columns not as
the way of doing more effective distribution. It
is a way of finding the moment where they could
do architecture, but it could really be the case
that this is a solution which architecture does
have a place. It is also a way to figure out where
exactly is it. Would it be occupying that roof?
Would it be making buildings on top of these?
Would it be making artificial landscape?

Alan Plattus ...I think another point to your
credit is that you didn't really put in your
argument about one of the problems with Red
Hook, which is that it is the result of the de-
segregated land-use planning and transportation planning at a radical level. One of the most

important challenges in contemporary urbanism
is try to put back together again the logic of
land-use planning and the logic of transportation planning. So the first question you should
ask yourself, regardless to what happens here, is
what goes next to a piece of highway that rips
the neighborhood in half. Do we spend a gazillion
dollars to do the Big Dig and sink it so we can
re-knit the neighborhood? Well, no, this isn't
Boston. I think your answer is very provocative and plausible in that respect, but the urban
design argument, which I think then leads to an
architectural argument, is that this is not Fort
Worth Alliance, Texas, which is where this stuff is
being done now which is in the middle of nowhere
with no connection to anything else out there.
That's the comparison. You would compare this in
Red Hook to what's going on in Fort Worth Alliance, Texas.

————

E. Sean Bailey, Jacob Reidel
& Shelley Zhang
University of Toronto, Canada,
Brown University & University of Chicago
The Royal Architects of the United States

————

Our site was the History of Twentieth Century
Architecture, from which we culled a collection
of types – the glass and steel high-rise, the
suburban bungalow, the public housing project,
the megastructure, etc. – that were subsequently redesigned and placed throughout Red
Hook to create a new self-contained urban
environment; simultaneously destination, departure point, and all places in-between. Our
methodology was Miniaturization – the pre-
ferred means through which despotic designers ranging from model railroad enthusiasts

to emperors (and lest we forget to mention, architects) envision, comprehend, and shape their world. In short, we built many obsessive, tiny paper and plastic models.

Robert Levit Your project proposes a tone of response which one can discuss and question it through. Each of the elements out of which you make your city are drawn from historical typologies and land-use strategies, and it reminds me of something that [Rafael] Moneo said in his essay on typology where he described the moment when typology becomes a self-conscious critical category in the practice of architecture. He suspects that it is also the moment when architects no longer participate in typology as a meaningful form of practice. The type is emptied out of its original content. The immersion within the logic, which produced the type, is economics. It is a form of social practice, land-use, and a whole array of somewhat instrumental and customary categories that cease to be things which one takes for granted. They begin to become things that one looks at as historical artifacts or perhaps acceptable to floatation and subconscious use. In your case, you have taken the form of public housing and made it into

a field. You reintroduced single-family [housing]. You have these hyper-dense tall buildings along the boulevard and then you preserve the historical forms of the Red Hook material. Each of the elements that you used, once upon a time, had a logic for its use and even a logic of mixture of relationship. In the way you all proposed it, it's much more of a textural commentary on what you treat as symbolic categories of urban form rather than a strategy through which to imagine some actual social, economical life of the city. I think it is compelling and beautifully done .You guys are obviously extremely bright and sophisticated commentators on architecture, but I am still curious what is it you want to make of this? What are we suppose to make of it as a strategy of urbanism?

Keith Krumwiede The perfect complacence of New York and not just Manhattan and the latest ubiquitous subdivision typology, which is a mix-dwelling type, mixed-use subdivision is what everyone is doing now. You don't just get single-family houses. Within single-family houses, you get apartment dwellings, you get a lifestyle center of shopping area, and you might possibly get some office space. On one hand, I applaud the project; I am not convinced that it is in

fact a real proposition about urbanism, but I think that it is, in fact, a brilliant description of historical conditions and temporary events in urbanism in the state of the cities in America. In fact, there is a kind of push towards a description of heterogeneity while still retaining segregation of income, of height in the areas, which are really now our cities, which are not places like Manhattan or Chicago.

Barbara Littenberg It is also making a both/and proposition. It is basically saying 'you can have all these things so people can choose to live here.' It doesn't say 'if you want

to live in a single-family house, you got to move to the suburban; if you want to live in the city, you got to live in a tower.' That, I think, is the most interesting part of your premise and I agree with that. It is a both/and, rather than an either/or [strategy]. The question I had a little bit is that of the garden patches. Where you are clipping things is a little bit simple-minded. Having made this as a theoretical proposition about these different things, you are lacking in a certain specification in terms of how you then in a clever way apply these things to the larger urban field.

Elizabeth Barry & Adrienne Swiatocha
Oberlin College & University of Pennsylvania
Red Hook ReMix

This project begins by identifying conditions of scale and programmatic adjacencies that are problematic to the site of Red Hook. It then attempts to resolve these conditions by rescaling and redistributing elements across the site in ways that enrich their value to the Red Hook community. Ideologically, the project asserts the attitude that green space and urban space are not mutually exclusive conditions, but rather have the ability to enhance each other in fundamental ways. Interventions

on the site are made through a restorative lens that conceives of "green space" as existing along a continuum, ranging from a direct experience of nature, to that which is more symbolic.

Keith Krumwiede I think this is about how do you begin to web geometry and ecology. Geometry represents a kind of human ecology in terms of what the systems are and how we understand them, which are not patches like wild habitat patches. All this is about wild life habitat and diversity. In fact, you can decrease the diversity so that one species can be healthy. It cannot have a lot of invasiveness. At other places, you can have species that thrive on diversity; so there is a gradient there.

Paul Lewis You are actually not doing much design. It is almost as if you have shifted to the developer mode. This is where the better real estate is – this is where you are going to span a bridge, and this is where the buildings are. It all sets in motion what I think is a brilliant move, which is the idea that you can now design the section that is where these two are going to interact and bring them together in a comfortable way and think about how it will produce imaginative programs, uses and space. It is the glow, right? What I am now really curious about is how you actually start to give that specificity. That would be the precise area where it is a blank right now. It will have to be actually designed for this project to be believable. I think you are really close. There are some fantastic possibilities, but I am looking for something that goes beyond the tag line of public. I think it does come back to the interesting intersection between massing, urban buildings, street and the idea about lifting that over an agrarian landscape. Now you have to specify that interesting fraction.

Julia Czerniak If you go back to your typology principles and think about patch dynamics: at the stra-

tegic level, if you look at any large park today, you will always find patches of private development and patches of semi-private space within the public landscape. In your homogeneity of the green, the gradient has to work the other way. It has to go not just from public to semi-public to private. It has to find pockets and patches of private in the green network.

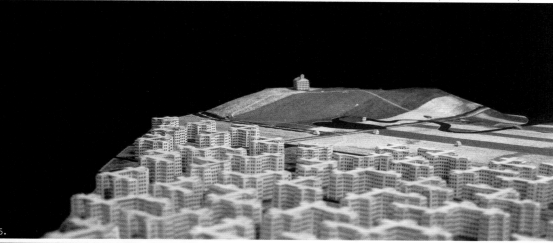

(1-3) Sandra Arndt, Rustam Mehta & Lindsay Weiss
(4-6) E. Sean Bailey, Jacob Reidel & Shelley Zhang
51 (7) Elizabeth Barry & Adrienne Swiatocha

Andrea Kahn
504b

Brook Denison & Greg Heasley
University of Florida
& University of Washington
<u>Gentrification: the Re-Cycling of Red Hook</u>

Our project challenges the negative assumptions associated with gentrification. Modern cities are inherently economic entities that rely on development to restructure their physical markets, thus creating new opportunities for private and public investment. Historically, its waterfront port and the import, export and storage of commodities have defined Red Hook. Through a choreographed sequence of street platting, infrastructure improvement, park reorganization and expansion, building densification and diversification, and new building type creation, we honor Red Hook's history as a neighborhood defined by the industrial marketplace, but update it for New York's role in the global electronic marketplace. By once again capitalizing on Red Hook's geography we now re-envision it to import, export, and store Manhattan's new commodity: people. This private re-investment and re-development is dictated through a symbiotic public partnership that allows for projects with more altruistic motivations: long-term environmental mitigation of the Gowanus canal, brownfield reclamation, sustainable water runoff and treatment, the creation of waterfront public park space linked to the greater New York waterfront greenway plan, and a re-connection and re-integration of Red Hook back into the fabric of Brooklyn while still maintaining it's distinctive character.

Julia Czerniak I think one way to argue this is to think about the project in the scale of reimbursement. I wouldn't underestimate the potential for making an argument for cleaning up the Gowanus. On one hand I like your sectional image, on the other I wonder why you have to keep the Gowanus when you have large tracks of green areas? You don't have to always keep it in its channel. You can also think about negotiating it more with the site that will speed up flow and have tidal change. You're talking about cycles of the city but the landscape is rather static. And if you think about it as something more temporal, there is a lot more cleaning you can do. So I think the ambition is there, and I think it is quite an interesting image with the golf course and the fountains, which could help the cleaning process, but I think there are lots of other scales you could work. So you could reconsider the path, the cover, and the static edge of the canal.

Alan Plattus I thought the idea of urbanizing lower Court Street was a brilliant idea. I find it plausible and also a pretty radical transformation. The street runs all the way back to downtown Brooklyn at the other end. It turns out, for better or for worse, the surrounding stuff like the Gowanus, which was your focus for a while, and Battery Park, which everybody is concerned about, have to some degree much importance. In fact, they might develop in a different way given the strength of what the corner is receiving. You could leave the crack that is on the park side there for the foreseeable future. Do what you've done like zoning changes and incentives for the development of the lower end of Court Street and the rest of it can probably take care of itself. The transformation would be so dramatic that the peripheral pieces of that would have an incentive to turn into something else.

Edward Mitchell You might want to think about your project ambition because I am not sure about the length of Court Street along the river. The way Brooklyn develops is that a lot of the

main streets are part of an old neighborhood fabric, and it's weird that Court Street cuts off by Hamilton but it has probably always been that way. I think there are ideas of continuity and ideas of break in the city in your big diagrams. I think you could make a bigger case of continuities and the environmental issue. Whether the streets are one of those things that needs to be continuous or not, I'm not yet convinced – again, more of the story, more concept behind that rather than just desire.

Czerniak I actually think you need both of them. I think you need Court Street and I think you need the park. And I think you can approach these large-scale projects without its economic and environmental sustainability at the same time. I think Court Street is going to enable the other. I don't think it's an either-or, and I think it's a big loss if it didn't become this green park. You don't build these things, these days, unless it's sustainable.
[…]

Paul Lewis It's as if all of the turns and the logic that you might want to use are now being kind of spread across too many different agendas and it's a little unclear on how that's actually going to work. It actually works better on plan.

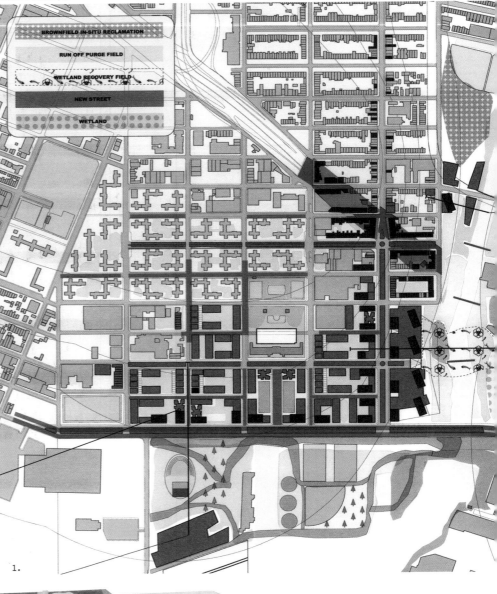

1.

2.

Robert Levit It's actually interesting. Going back to the comment in the beginning, the question of this edge versus that potential boulevard is critical in regards of the expectation of what might happen all along here. Even though I understand that there is something appealing about the normalization of the public housing by extending the middle or low rise housing further out, and if this does turn into a park at the end, then the idea that they would be low rise, and looking at the way they are oriented, would mean that these are very high-priced units. So you are not taking advantage of the implications of your park design. The question is interesting when in regards to scenarios and perhaps sequences of development, and the whole idea of phasing would be desirable.

Linda Pollak But I think you are showing, with this piece, the possibility that building and landscape can exist at the same time, or that you can have an institution or housing and the park at the same time. And you have so many sections up here and your diagram sections are really cool and great. From what you have you can get more mileage from what you've already accomplished, by being able to show on more complex plans as well.

[...]

Andrea Kahn You can push your strategy in the center of the fabric, where it is not actually inscribed yet but you were talking about retention time, which is actually an instance of what I would call greater exceptional literal crossway between architectural performance and landscape performance. And I think why that happens on the edge is the key question.

Anya Grant & Jeff McBride
Wesleyan University & Williams College
The Water's Edge

Waterfront development is happening all throughout the New York City region as places like Greenpoint/Williamsburg and Queens West are being transformed by these large-scale projects. Red Hook is vulnerable to these same forces – the waterfront is completely underutilized and development pressure is mounting. We proposed to control the forces of development along the waterfront by creating a framework of connections back into the city of Red Hook. Taking cues from huge projects like the abandoned Sugar Refinery, we zoned the waterfront for enormous buildings with wide-open public space along the water. These buildings and developments are strategically placed to respond to local infrastructure, commercial, and residential connections and encourage development in regions that are already poised for growth and improvement. Red Hook, often considered a backwater to Brooklyn, will develop an identity in the coming years – with our proposal, it will become a city intimately connected with the water's edge.

Barbara Littenberg Is this a self-sufficient gated community? Does it serve the people living in it? Does it have a grocery store in it? I mean, I was with you – your analysis was so good, and I'm so glad that you talked about loops and matrixes and grids instead of just an armature and a line, and it seemed so promising that it was going to go somewhere. And all of a sudden, you pick a site that is so peripheral, that after all that information you put it on the edge. It is where it is so remote from the existing neighborhood that you think it's a self-sufficient, utopian element, on the waterfront over the Battery tunnel. And it is somehow a piece of lower Manhattan that got thrown across and moved to this neighborhood, but I'm not sure why they would go there. The question is, will they in fact harness it as a development strategy for the neighborhood? Would they energize the neighborhood behind them or would they seem like one-off privileged buildings that are so particular in their architecture that they would have a funny straining effect on the rest of the neighborhood? You have to ask those questions about what you are trying to promote or signal to the rest of the neighborhood by the selection of that particular type and model at that particular point.

Alan Plattus It makes the analysis, which everybody admired, explicitly look like it is a set-up for the realization of a few large rather iconic buildings, rather than the buildings being somehow a validation or illustration or the next step in the logical analysis project.

Julia Czerniak I really really like this diagrammatical model where just by coding yellow, there is a status change of existing infrastructure and there are things that string along it. I think that is very smart, and it offers a lot of potential. And they are on the periphery because you were talking about getting people from the center to the edge. So the change of perception of transportation routes, waterfront, and development, which is precisely what is going on on this wall, is very strong. And when you get to the specific architectural events, which I guess

is where some of these questions are coming up, I think they do suggest the migration of the inside to the edge.

Littenberg To some level, I share the aspiration of this project which is to establish this as a viable neighborhood where things happen, but about the pull to the waterfront – all you have to do is to look at Manhattan neighborhoods. I mean, you don't go to the water. I live in Manhattan but I never go. I would rather go to the park to walk the dog than to go to the riverfront. It is a dimension.

Andrea Kahn I agree that going to the waterfront will have to add spectacle, but what is interesting to me about this project is that it performs one function of providing the spectacle, and then it adds – the other extreme if you will – the other node acknowledging that the waterfront can perform differently. These two things can be held simultaneously as a response to a neighborhood that is not homogenous.

[...]

Adam Yarinsky I like the ambition. I like the idea that you will have this string of icons around the periphery. Consequently, you are not going to completely script, but you are going to use these as catalysts. But what in my mind that you haven't quite developed is a diagrammatic logic of that sectional play out here. In fact, if you look at the difference between these two schemes, in one, you're using section as a way to produce density within a building that then becomes a spectacle in elevation, and then in the other, you're using the section as a way to produce density of infrastructure that you then can accumulate on stacked floor plates. So there are two very different ways of sections operating relative to primarily street and to the questions of the spectacle and the density. I think that is where the project is not, to me, making a convincing argument. And I think that would be a fantastic study that could take the planometric analysis and really make some propositions that are, right now, kind of between utopia and extremely pragmatic.

4.

(1,2) Brook Denison & Greg Heasley
(3,4) Anya Grant & Jeff McBride

Edward Mitchell
504b

Harris Ford, Sini Kamppari & J. M. Tate
Princeton University,
Massachusetts Institute of Technology
& Texas A&M University + Rural Studio.
Spot Urbanism

Spot Urbanism takes as its premise the belief that private interests and public amenities can and ought to be mutually beneficial at an urban scale, and seeks to spur neighborhood redevelopment through strategically distributed, localized "spot" interventions. Rather than resisting the large businesses and developments which have already established themselves in Red Hook, Spot Urbanism aims at turning these oft-maligned players into assets for the neighborhood, namely by attracting such private interests to underutilized sites where they will be hybridized with public and municipal programs. In turn, each 'spot' is tailored to local conditions to ensure distinct public spaces and smart growth.

Kate Orff I am from Brooklyn. I really question the idea – on one hand, nodal urbanism is what you are setting up and the idea that hybridity has to happen in section – because the most interesting part of this whole piece down here is that hinge between parks and the housing project. What happens is that on every Saturday and Sunday, there is this long line of street vendors, people and cars. You couldn't just walk down the street. It is an edge between two things, which happens on the urban field. I just wonder if in cloning these hybrid pieces of, what I would say would be a 'Spot Urbanism' – my interpretation of a spot urbanism, which happens on a line, the edge between pieces; I am trying to consolidate it in disperse parrot nodes around the field – is that really accomplishing what you set out to?
[...]
Robert Levit I think the two points about the hybridity in section and the interiorization within the block of the public spaces are really good. Distinct from the last project where you have only a single sponsor, which is IKEA, at the head of a very large and somewhat traditional Avalon green, there is something really disturbing about the iconography of an urbanism, which centers around a single sponsor like that. In your case, because you have distributed, you diffused this notion of sponsorship into a more plural setting, which I found to be more appealing. But on the other hand, the kind of excitement and fascination that come through in the architectural paradigm – blending inside and outside, drawing surfaces from the ground into the building – are all things which mix up private and public edges. It seems that the traditional kinds of sponsorship, whether they be Times Square or anywhere else, they still maintain a distinction between a publicly held property and privately held property.

Geoffrey Lawson & Clinton Prior
University of Virginia
& Queensland University, Australia
Collision City

The purpose of this project was threefold: (1) identify the precincts of Red Hook, their existing development patterns, and possible futures without intervention; (2) suggest a prototype for each precinct that could assist with infill development; and (3) propose a redevelopment scheme for the area of Red Hook that

1.

currently has no development pressure. This scheme brings together aspects of each existing precinct and creates a market for development through a public-private partnership, park construction, and brownfield mediation. This new Red Hook center is both highly urban in density and in infrastructure, but has the same amount of open space as more suburban areas of Red Hook. It also becomes a regional center as a collision between highly diverse areas without trying to overly smooth out difference.

Douglas Gauthier Your presentation is quite powerful. You are saying that you've got these

five corridors, but the project isn't about corridor one, two, three or four. It is about the relationship between corridors two and three, and between corridors four and five. It wasn't about these things you discovered, but about these things you discovered by ribbing them against one another. You found these existing conditions and within these existing conditions there is fraction. I expect to see a taxonomy of those conditions that would then play out in here in the same way that may be where we're asking for how the housing is being developed.

Keith Krumwiede It uses a void as a means of stitching as opposed to some places or even here where you are trying to hold the void through this hatch. There is no mutation, as oppose to working the type. If this were Douglas's [Gauthier] project, the taxonomy would begin to have a mutation, which is kind of what we are saying about the housing. If we squint, the way it is presented it is either/or. I think that is what we are interested in – the interstitial space.

YoungJin Lee & Seung Namgoong
Seoul National University, Korea &
University of California at Berkeley
Pier-scape Urbanism

We seek to revitalize Red Hook by maximizing its water exposure, extending its waterfront to Carrol Garden and turning it into amenity. This Pier-scape urbanism reconnects the city to the water in two ways. The first pier is an "Infrastructure Bridge Building,"

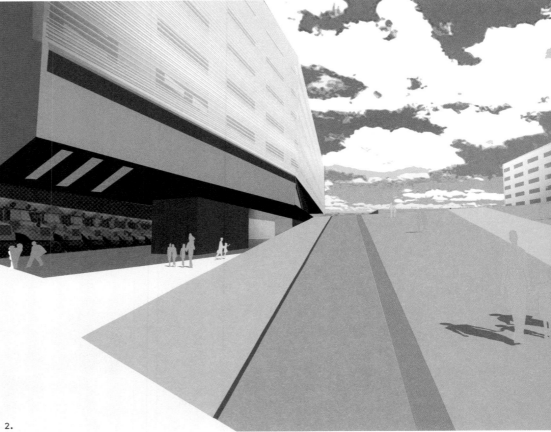

2.

which carries various public programs over the Gowanus expressway to reconnect with Carrol Garden. The second pier is built over the existing and developing fabric of Red Hook's waterfront. Several canals are created to bring deep water into the city, thus maximizing and extending the benefit of the waterfront to the heart of Red Hook. Green space and pedestrian promenade along the finger-shaped water edge are created to reinforce the connection with Brooklyn. This "extended city" blurs the boundary between the neighborhoods. Red Hook is now open and ready.

3.

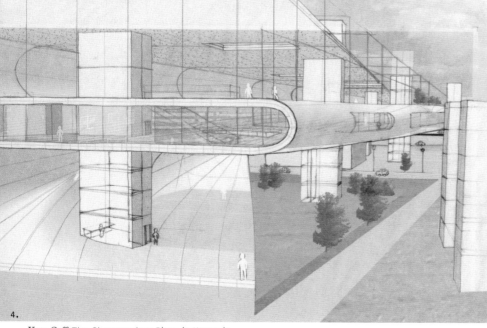

4.

has a more truth to it than some of these utopia images.

Douglas Gauthier Your diagram throughout the site is very clear, and it's very exciting, but then you don't extend what you get from the diagrams to your work. You don't give in. That diagram mentions to give in a great deal, has to compromise the mediation sites, the places where it is easy or sensible. Instead of that, you go towards the utopia superstructures level – let's make that articulation form instead of seeing whether that articulation could handle bushes and poles. I thought what was so beautiful about your presentation was the articulation lies over surfaces from grain to water. Here is your idea, but you somehow got fixated to the graphics of the ideas instead of working the idea through the site.

Kate Orff The Chongyechon River in Korea is a really interesting precedent for you. It was this situation where in the old Seoul, there was an elevated highway that was torn down and replaced with this long and linear walkway. The purpose was for real estate. They immediately changed the FAR [floor-area-ratio] from two-story buildings to ninety-story residential towers. Along those lines, I would do things differently in approaching this project. One is that I would be very careful about where the water is in terms of doing a new math analysis of where it was, where you could take out buildings, where there were brownfield sites that could get excavated or carved out… Be really incredibly precise about where the water is and what happens just immediately next to the water. Start with the Sanborn maps just to understand the nature of the property, the minutia. I think that would be in itself a project that would enable you to get out of this urban design mindset and

Neil Sondgeroth & Weston Walker
University of Illinois at Urbana-Champaign
& Cornell University
Carpark

We propose to intensify specific areas of Red Hook by introducing a new kind of public realm around, between, and within them: the CarPark. A vast system of interwoven surfaces and transient infrastructure, the CarPark allows for both recreational and auto-related uses to coexist within a highly flexible urban framework. Materials like TurfBlock, GrassPave, and gravel work in concert with objects such as potted trees, bollards, and light posts to mediate between expanses of asphalt and grassland. The resulting area can be claimed for anything from sporting events to camping, but also pro-

vides ample parking for both existing residents and those who will occupy the 3,000 new dwelling units within the undulating slab buildings.

Mario Gooden I am having some problems with the scale. This is a huge area and I think you are treating it as something much smaller than it is. I think you do the small size very well and maybe the big scale, but there is something missing in-between, for example between the big-box retail and the Red Hook Houses. I want to understand that condition. Perhaps you took the section at the wrong place. You took them at easy places, I think, where you could perhaps be more speculative, but not really asking the question… I really want to understand that condition between things at a larger scale.

Charlie Cannon I want to offer you what I hope you will see as constructive criticism because I want to be the proponent of the project, but I am not quite yet. The reason that I am not is precisely the problem of where the sections are cut. You said, 'How do you show the whole site?' I would argue that the thing you should do is not to worry about the whole site. If we go back and look at the use of haha, which creates these visual moments where there is an apparent continuity whether or not there is programmatic possibility. Your insistence that there must be programmatic possibility and even programmatic uncertainty is the thing that is doing you in. If you think about what the haha actually did, which is this landscape device that is basically the reverse fence, it controls views. If you look over your control ground, you look over your fields or someone else's field, they are all mine; my property extends forever. This is an incredibly careful section calibration that is making visual relationships between programmatic spaces that are actually quite in opposition to one another in terms of their uses. You guys missed that opportunity, and actually avoided it by saying that everything we're going to do, from my point-of-view, is the softest, most banal, easiest program because it is all recreational program. When the hardest program

5.

you have to figure out is security, is where you put the snow, is how these big-boxes are going to operate and how you are constructing places whether it is active drainage, active retention, which may be a social barrier at one point and a physical barrier at the other. Without doing that, it is a neutral field, but that is not really what you want.

(1,2) Harris Ford, Sini Kamppari & J. M. Tate
(3) Geoffrey Lawson & Clinton Prior
(4) YoungJin Lee & Seung Namgoong
(5) Neil Sondgeroth & Weston Walker

Emmanuel Petit

504b

Joseph Alguire & Khai Fung
University of Illinois at Urbana-Champaign
& University of Michigan at Ann Arbor
<u>Vacuum City</u>

Our project began as a thorough analysis of the immediate site, which recognized the scattered distribution of vacant lots that were being used for storage or parking. This became our generative concept to concentrate all urban infrastructure and services into a centralized urban node, removing the vacant lots in the neighborhood for potential development. The central node contains programmatic elements of public school, library, community center, and generous amounts of parking (municipal and public), distributed to emphasize particular connections back to the city.

Furthermore, the programmatic and physical isolation of Red Hook from the rest of Brooklyn prompted us to comparatively analyze the formal and organizational constitution of a series of autonomous island-structures. Certain attributes of the islands – social, artificial, and infrastructural, were reconsidered to work in favor of Red Hook. Thus, Vacuum City attempts to reconnect the segregated neighborhood by planning a major link between the central node and the adjacent highway and subway infrastructures, and the two other large vacant areas of Erie and Atlantic Basins via a cruise terminal, a park connection to the Brooklyn Greenbelt, and a mountain residential hybrid.

Alan Plattus Are you saying that there's actually a 'mountain pass' in the middle of the Alps there?

Khai Fung Yes, exactly. The sectional drawing here is cutting through this 'pass'.

1.

Joe Alguire The physical model is also showing the ramping through the pass, from grade at the street here up towards the center and down again.

Robert A.M. Stern What is this thing?

Alguire This thing is the central infrastructural core that we're talking about. The lavender slabs represent the parking, and the pink slabs is what we are proposing as the new public library to service the public housing, and the powder blue represents the community center below the library.

Stern How much parking do you have?

Fung Approximately 10,000 sf.

Kian Goh How does this address the initial premise of the islands you mentioned in the beginning? Are you proposing a vacuum that sucks everything up and creates a highly intense island in the center of Red Hook? Or are you trying to disperse people through the site?

Alguire I think we were using the islands as a study of how to re-establish a connection for Red Hook. Thus, we looked to islands to see how

2.

they were dealing with isolation.

Fung For example, the study of London's traffic ring suggests an infrastructure that restricts access to the city core, but our proposal is a reversal of this condition, since our proposal allows for complete access to the city.

Goh So, to undo the island.

Fred Koetter That parking garage…how does it service the community?

Alguire The idea is that it would serve both the community as well as provide municipal lots for public buses, storage, etc., which is what the Erie Basin area of the site is currently used for. The garage is conceived to service the school buses, parking for the neighborhood, the network of parks, and new residents.

Robert Levit When you propose something like this that violates or disrupts from the norm, then

you actually have to illustrate its operations. How big is this compared to the Beverly Center?

Keith Krumwiede Like ten times.

Stern Your geometry and that huge cutout at the corner, for whatever its virtues may be, is slightly hard to believe in relationship to your parking area. Although maybe you have a secret plan method?

Alguire Yes, we do, but you'll never know!

Stern Your vacuum urbanism basically sucks the life out of the city. It's like the biggest Hoover ever made.

Alguire Well, that was the design challenge. How do we deal with all the potentially dirty program in Red Hook? How do we use design to temper it?

Stern Well, the question is whether you did so as a team.

Alguire I think we did, but in a sublime way.

Levit Sublime and tempering are two different things. Is it sublime because it is inscrutable and huge? And whether or not it tempers as by mollifying the mess of traffic? Usually, you would temper traffic by building garages of ordinary dimensions and height behind the main streets to provide convenience or proximity. Here, it seems impossible to weigh the project in terms of practicality, I think it is the effect you are after.

Plattus It is hard to get past that, but when I look at the plans, you actually have four buildings, or four mountains with valleys. What you have done in coordinating the movement through the cruise terminal to the Erie Basin is that you have identified the under-utilized center of the city, you build here four things, creating artificial crossroads.

Koetter I think the large unexplained items in the city can be a really good thing. The description of 19th century train stations in London was that they were monstrous and bad for the city. They just belong to something that operates at a completely different scale. They are part of another reality. This core and the cruise terminal could be part of this other reality, which has to do with larger patterns of movement that may be part of this place. Then, you could say whether it is a good or bad thing for Red Hook.

Goh I like the fact that this is so large.

One thing is that you could have multiple blocks within one of the mountains. It is like a Koolhaas hyper-building, where it is so big that you have to think about it in other terms. There is this internal world that could be very different from the outside.

Levit Your drive towards sublime disruption of the scale of the city searches for its occasion. It has to serve some instrumental end. I don't think you've done that. That's the problem.

Krumwiede Building it will not necessarily mean people will come. Too much emphasis is placed on the absurdity of the project, or its gravitational pull. It wants to be like the sun, where everything revolves around it. Basically, the mountain as a diagram and as a focal point of activity should be tested more thoroughly, or you should remain strictly polemical.

Marc Guberman & Christopher Lee
Brown University
& University of California at Berkeley
Latenc[it]y

Latenc[it]y is a new Red Hook in which the preservation of the city's intrinsic characteristics are maintained in conjunction with vast development. The negotiation of this apparent conflict is at the heart of the project and a methodology born from an intense investigation of the city's vital characteristics produced the diagram for the urban plan. Latenc[it]y's agenda is to produce new typologies that allow for the free traversing of the city's current landscape to be coupled with vast growth, breaking down the dichotomy between waterfront and inland patterns. Mid-block towers that emerge from vacant lots and allow exterior public access to a second horizon as well as elevated loops that act as extensions of the street-grid at the water's edge create a smooth urban fabric, where the distinction between zones and blocks becomes less dominant.

Robert Levit I think that your staples, as Alan [Plattus] was calling it, are quite interesting. The idea of creating the loop, so when you drive to the end of the grid on a waterfront you actually can turn and loop back and that you do this with a piece of road infrastructure, which is also a building, and a piece of real estate in the city, is very provocative. Now there is a kind of typological invention combined with an infrastructural invention which I think makes a certain kind of sense.

Robert A.M. Stern You know it is not rocket science. You said you invented something. Whenever I hear somebody say they invented something, I say, 'My God, even if you are 90, I doubt you have invented something.' The way you invent things is by layering one idea on top of another – that is invention. You really meant innovative, and nobody has innovated anything since man has come out of the cave in architecture. In my opinion, they invented things.

Alan Plattus I am still interested in this different kind of infill strategy. I think there is a very tricky ratio for me of where it displaces itself as a sort of infill and where it displaces itself as Bambi meets Godzilla, the big foot

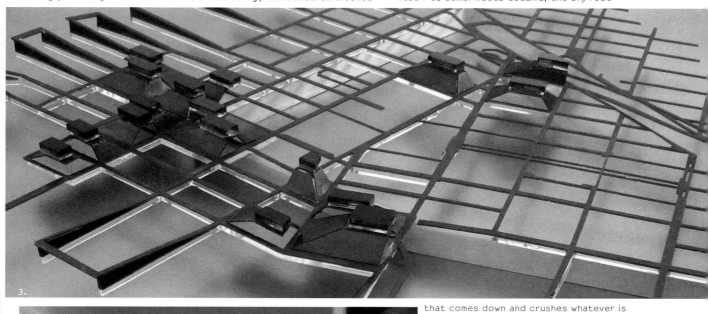

3.

4.

that comes down and crushes whatever is left of these poor little, semi-abandoned blocks. The infill block where you get a kind of ad-hoc savage type, a step-back type contrasting with the more conventional street front development, can potentially lead to some infill towers or larger pieces in the middle of the block. So it can be seen as either step up or spill down. What you are really doing is being opportunistic. That you are trying to find blocks where there is enough available real estate so you can have a different kind of infill strategy, other than replicating the existing typology.

Andrea Kahn The possibility of starting to re-orchestrate the relationship between interior block space and perimeter space or ground coverage and open area in a part of the city that is already so pot marked allows us to restate how people use or do not use that inner space. It is a potential kind of development that is not only infill building, but it is an infill building that produces new public terrain.

[…]

Fred Koetter I think when you speculate about things and use devices to illustrate it to yourselves, the nature of that speculation is a good thing – then new ideas come. Speculation lets you see things in a way that wasn't immediately apparent.

Alan Plattus
504b

Audrey Vuong, Vincent Wan
& M. Jejon Yeung
Columbia University,
University of Hong Kong, Hong Kong
& Carleton University, Canada
Production/ Consumption Demonstration

Red Hook is a place of production that is quickly becoming a place of consumption with the introduction of the cruise ship terminal, Ikea, restaurants, Fairway, and high-end residential housing. Our proposal is to sustain production within Red Hook while also addressing the new consumer culture. In order to re-engage production, we have analyzed two chain brands that will inevitably be introduced into Red Hook: Ikea and Fairway. Existing industries would be symbiotically orchestrated with Ikea and Fairway to create hybrid models as demonstrations of production and consumption. These parameters led to the development of new and unique urban typologies that were integrated with industrial ecology, renewable energy, and agriculture.

Paul Lewis There is a strange way in which you are almost evacuating space in order to make all kinds of stuff. It's a bizarre split personality again where in order to make a plaza full of undulating landscapes, you have actually erased the whole plaza first. Again, the sheer volume of work that's done and the level of invention at the architectural scale amaze me, but if you step back, I wonder how you would start to define how effective you are with each of these moves. Not the kind of access that has accumulated through all of the moves, but what happens with each one? The operating procedure is really an effective way of getting at what you want, and I worry that maybe it is too dependent on the exuberance of contradiction.

Robert Levit I can't help but remember what [Robert] Venturi said in '66 when he did the Copley Square competition. He said, 'The last thing an American city needs is more space,' and I think it is probably still true. Your work is remarkable, but yet in general the amount of built buildings in the space is

1.

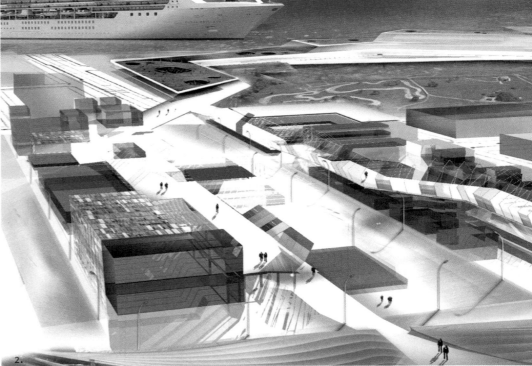

2.

3.

so tiny. You rely so much on your focus as form makers that I think you are persuaded that these are environments which are actually rich in social experience. They are rich as aesthetic objects, but if you try to imagine how long it takes to walk between buildings and how little there is to do around it, along any line of trajectory. I fear that I would feel agoraphobic.

Elisa Lui, Jeffrey Richards
& Kathryn Stutts
University of California at Berkeley,
Hamilton College, University of Virginia
<u>filter/infiltrate</u>

We have chosen to focus on the cleaning of the Gowanus Canal as a tool to revitalize the Red Hook community because we believe it offers the most potential. Given that the Gowanus is an active industrial corridor that is important to the community, we decide to adapt eco-industry as a development model and strategy

Keith Krumwiede What I think is incredibly admirable in this work is the fact that there is a learning curve here – a very steep one… They understand the complexity of the site, so to speak. We architects have always tried to engage in the quality of sites, and now there is an issue of the environment that is more and more pressing, particularly in a city like New York. To build architecture here, at the simple level, is to understand it. To my mind everything they've done is architecture because it springs from knowledge and information.

Robert Levit I think that it's a question of the representation of the landscape and the attention to the ecology… I think there is an underlying ethics that permeates this kind of work, and there is a sense of the ecological mix as a proper dedication.

Barbara Littenberg No, I don't think it's about ethics.

Levit I really do think that. Then I can take it as a symptomology where the fact that the fluvial diagram is dedicated to an instrumental remediation of the landscape. It is because of

which can produce the architecture.

Littenberg But you come from a program of landscape urbanism, right?

[laughter]

Levit So what? I think landscape urbanism frequently hides behind false ethics, behind the kind of scrupling which permits architects to proceed with their formal will.

Janet Ho, Ayumi Sugiyama & Jean Suh
Stanford University, University of
California at Berkeley, & University of Virginia
<u>Red Hook: Tourism, Development
and Recreation</u>

This project takes the existing conditions of Red Hook and reinvents the area as a unique destination for recreation, growth and tourism by offering programs that are otherwise unavailable in the urban environment of Manhattan and its vicinity. In this scheme, the desirable waterfront area is increased by creating a grand canal that runs through under-utilized areas of Red Hook and organizes it into three distinct areas. The first area consists of Van Brunt Street and its continued growth as a mixed-use district. The second consists of the transformation of the existing flat recreation fields into a naturalistic park. The third area consists of the existing Red Hook Houses, a public housing project, whose value will be increased by exposure to the new waterfront canal. This development leads to the creation of a "plug-in" scenario by which programs are connected to the expressway, mitigating the isolation of Red Hook from the rest of Brooklyn.

Robert A.M. Stern Earlier in the day there were some complaints about naively or arbitrarily segregating, and there was a call for a mixture of things. In that way you've gone way further than your classmates so far, at least from what I've seen, by using this mixed place to be versatile. Your formalism and – I hope not – your social engineering led you to stumble on the Red Hook Housing, but it is self-isolating anyway.

[...]

Paul Lewis You need to identify the different techniques you are using – is it cutting, is it addition, is it reprogramming, is it resurfacing? Then you would have a much clearer sense of what are the tactics being employed and not that it's the goal of the master plan or the master vision, but in fact what are the techniques, and are they useable, and are they effective?

Robert Levit But I also think that you have to be realistic about the character of the neighborhood and its relationship to history. They seem to have some of your concerns about history, and yet in reality, their proposition would never allow that.

Barbara Littenberg We keep talking about history, and when you talk about history, it goes back to intrinsically valuable fabric in the city. For example, a place like SOHO, which was an abandoned, no longer used area, became the most expensive area in the neighborhood. When you look at this stuff, some of it is going to happen more than others, or anywhere with a viable warehouse buildings, but with the demand of housing, it will.

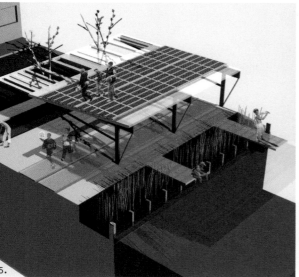

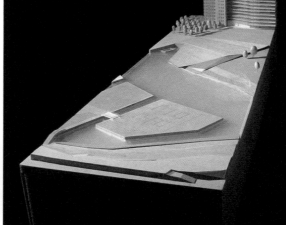

for the city/nature relationships. The concept of eco-industry is to invite series of interdependent programs to the site that can share their resources based on their relationship to the canal. We also envision the canal as the base of a green spine that connects the surrounding neighborhoods, creating both a physical and cultural network that optimizes local assets.

----

the idea that somehow you are dedicated to a proper ethical mission, and then you get into a tangle where you start to represent symbolically your ethics in places where it no longer even produces the instrumental complexity you want. And then the architecture is left out of the picture because you can't actually find the appropriate virtue

ADVANCED STUDIOS, FALL

Post-Professional *Helsinki* [509a] *with* Fred Koetter *&* Edward Mitchell; Leon Krier *Williamsburg, Virginia* [511a] *with* Jim Tinson; Glenn Murcutt *Elizabeth Mine, Stratford* [513a] *with* Amy Lelyveld; Brigitte Shim *Cities Center, Toronto* [515a] *with* Hilary Sample; Peter Eisenman *Criticality, Hamburg* [517a] *with* Michael Young; Jeanne Gang *National Labor History Museum, Chicago* [519a]; Alan Plattus *China Studio, Suzhou Creek* [521a]; Diana Balmori *&* Joel Sanders *Interface, Shanghai* [523a].

61

Post-Professional
Helsinki
509a

Fred Koetter & Edward Mitchell

Predicting the future of cites is an impossible yet necessary task. Our contemporary cities are structures of time as much as space. The dynamics of contemporary culture means that urban design must be adept at managing temporal structures, ordering movement, and prognosticating future trends without aid of specific programs or even clients and without the traditional zoning diagrams and spatial devices that architects historically rely on.

This year the studio will work in cooperation with the Helsinki University of Technology on plans for an area at the edge of Helsinki. The class will make a trip to Helsinki, conduct a workshop on the campus designed by Aalto, visit and analyze significant works of architect in and around the city, and make proposals to the city's planners and stakeholders.

Helsinki's regional population of over one million represents roughly 20% of the population of Finland. Like many other world cities, Helsinki has seen an increase in population at its older core, made up of mostly young singles and retirees and a loss of families requiring other services to the suburbs. The city's extensive plans for new housing are aimed at drawing the suburban populous back to the city, while maintaining affordable alternatives to the working populace of the city. The settlement patterns of the outer areas of the city are strongly associated with the Garden City movement in the early part of the 20th century and post war suburbanization; however, these concepts may be detrimental to the ecology and social structure of the city in the near future. The studio will look at developing more extreme urbanisms, valuing both the qualities and resources of the city and its surrounding environment.

Jeremiah Joseph & Mustapha Jundi
(H.I. Feldman Nominees)
University of Kentucky & American University of Beirut, Lebanon
<u>Extreme Landscapes</u>

The project is a study of methods for increasing urban density while simultaneously exploiting open fields for layers of ecological energy infrastructure and recreational activities. Sited at the Western edge of Helsinki, Finland, the project straddles existing lines of mass transportation to the North through large green fields and out into a shallow lagoon at the Southern edge. This ideal metropolitan snapshot allowed us to enhance density along the economic corridor of the highway and rail lines while also employing existing and new systems of energy production in a strategy that ties various qualities of public behavior with spatial production practices along the edge between the water and the marsh land. The project offers a perpetual state of overlap leading into a possible redefinition of a picturesque landscape.

Charles Waldheim This project has come an enormous distance since the midterm and I think it's a significant improvement. First of all, let me say why I think this is important work. This kind of work leads to an interest in new economies, transfers, flows of capital and material, which are increasingly the ways in which cities are characterized. You've identified this position geographically in the global flow of container ships and capital and intelligent workers and then you've proposed "well, why don't we look at models for what kind of urban territory or field could come from that?" So you've jettisoned quite a lot. You've gotten out of quite a lot of debris to take on something which is quite significant. You've proposed a very, very low density form of development which is a combination between agricultural and industrial use. It's looking at production economies, flows of capital, and trying to rewire them so that the waste material of one use becomes the supply chain of another. This is the Holy Grail of this kind of work. If you can harvest wind to generate energy to produce cooling to then get heating to then get ice harvesting to get tree farming... It would be nice for our audience to at least have a proposition where those things are being discussed. That's where I would be critical. There are moments when you are very smart, you understand the precedents, you've developed an extraordinary compliment of work, but there are moments

when I wish you would stop describing things in their phenomenal terms or their experiential terms and be just much more bloody-minded about capital, how big things are, how much it costs, questions of measure, unit, dimension, how many of this do we need to produce how many of that. And I think that one would need to imagine these places as much less dense. I don't think we can generate enough energy or capital or labor in one place any more to produce this level of urbanity. If you look at [Frank Lloyd] Wright's Broadacre City model, right? He built the model [19]34, [19]35 which was ten times denser than his proposal would have been. It was to illustrate its effects. And if I imagine your models in this way, they're effectively a ten times concentration in scale, I can somehow begin to image that they would operate. The thing that I would also be critical of in both cases is the references architecturally are just maybe a bit too obvious. And I know – maybe you've been spending your time on other things, and they're both very handsome, but we've seen that architecture before. We can locate it. The work of [Andrea] Branzi is quite present here. It's a significant precedent. I would rather you unpack that and say this is Branzi 1984. But having said that, I think that this line of work, the idea that you begin with infrastructure, you identify global flows of capital as they relate to environmental conditions, seems very promising.

[...]

Michael Weinstock Well, I'd like to say that I've been holding my breath during everything that you've said. First of all, I don't want to talk about that. It's kind of well established and there are comments and that's fine. The real kind of work that you've done that I think is really interesting here is where this should be addressed as a form of urbanism and as a form of architecture that could be inhabited. Now your system of approach will work really, really well. It's not that there are certain kinds of presumptions that you make. You start by doing an operative geometry for the radius and that kind of approach is a nice way of organizing a field condition. The simultaneities that are possible are not to do with over-lays, but when you have a system you have to look for energy transfers between them and potentially this has truly now provided a whole new way of urbanizing. It shouldn't be supplying energy for somewhere else, right? It will generate all its own energy and enough people can inhabit it. Also, the lagoon... I don't know this one, but most lagoons have kind of odd problems with salinity. There must be some ancient system that...

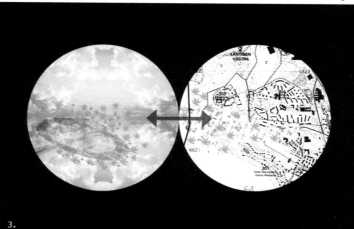

3.

Alan Plattus So you think the solution is making something attractive enough...

Weinstock We have to make an architecture.

Edward Mitchell I think that was a real ambition early on.

Richard Summers There's a question of how networked that system is or whether that happens locally or what the network of that energy is across that larger field.

Weinstock Well, I mean all over Europe, but particularly here, you do a crazy thing. You generate it [energy] in one place and then move it miles, hundreds of miles.

Mitchell If you look at the 19th century new technologies, they were always in places where new cultural practices were in place. I mean, the change was that in the 20th century it was a kind of negative. It's an attractor for a lot of other things and I think that's the ambition of these guys.

Plattus Nobody was clamoring to live in Sheffield in the 19th century.

Mitchell Not Sheffield. I'm talking about dams, hydroelectric plants, bridges, things like that.

Waldheim But not enough of us in the new economy can afford to live in Manhattan.

Plattus No. Right. Well, the crisis you describe is happening. The headlines around here are that they have decided that a good place to put a wind farm would be off the shore of Nantucket and, of course, Nantucket has one of the highest concentrations of ironically neo-liberal...

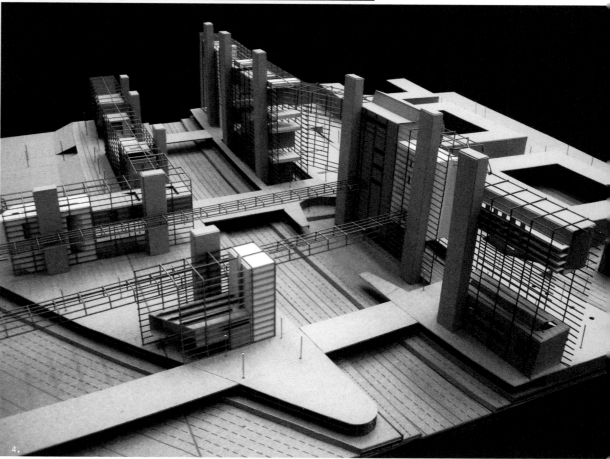

4.

Jeremiah Joseph It's an archipelago, this whole...

Weinstock There would be a saline differential between the open sea and this lagoon. Again, there are well established technologies that can work on that – the same can be said of the ice technology. It's kind of romantic or poetic – the ice house – and as an architect I kind of love that reference to an old style. The phase change condition between water and ice is also potential energy. I feel that you've done something quite remarkable, but what you've done is a very, very interesting question... My kind of big ambition for this kind of work would be how can people live and occupy this and not just treat it as a kind of landscape. The problem we have all over Europe, and you're going to have this, too, is people want these technologies, but they don't want them anywhere near where they live, they don't want them anywhere near where they want to go sailing or where they're recreating. That's the challenge. There aren't enough remote hillsides to put windmills on. There aren't enough remote places for energy resources.

Summers ...rich people...

Plattus ...rich people anywhere. And they don't want a wind farm out there.

Mitchell Ask Bob [Stern].

Katherine Corsico & Allen Slamic
Cornell University & Kent State University
<u>Insert City</u>

The automobile in Helsinki has created pockets of communities that are car dependent, isolated, and fragmented. With an estimated increase in car traffic, furthered sprawl results in an expanding isolation of amenities, surrounded by pavement, located at the city periphery. We are criticizing this current growth pattern of further isolation and disconnection. There must be a new typology that suspends the sub-urban automobile community and the urban tight-knit city. This hybrid

Post-Professional
(continued)

is intimately connected to the car, the city street, and its surrounding communities. We call it Insert City. Insert city is an accessible and livable urban fabric. It is an opportunistic infill that not only sustains its own density, but also provides resources to the surrounding communities. It takes the motorway and makes it part of the solution by allowing it to feed the city from below. A new sectional relationship is formed between the car, the city street, and the home.

Richard Summers [...] In the beginning, you want to make something very dense with a very different typology from what's there. It is all a very strong start. I think the trouble is if you are critical of the low density, suburban character of this environment, then what is the lifestyle that you are offering in its place? Questions of the housing typology and the landscape associated with it and what the network of the landscape is so that it's successful with the housing seems to me to be the primary issue. You're not giving what people will get in the center of the city – you don't want it to have the form of what's out there now – but I think that this is a type that is not particularly efficient. It's not yet providing a kind of open space that is beautiful or pastoral enough for the housing, so I think that the part where people live needed to be conceptualized as a richer landscape.

Eeva-Liisa Pelkonen It's frustrating that you feel that the space in-between is almost inhabitable.

Summers You could have it be a lot more dense in places because it's a very inefficient type and then it would have opened up places where... it depends on how much variety you have to have. What are the types of housing and types of open spaces that can be deployed and then, as Charles pointed out, how do you make the surface connected to or more expansive to other aspects of the landscape?

Brigitte Shim But I wonder whether the fact that the blocks are so close to each other might actually allow for a level of connection across.

Summers Right. So it becomes more extensive.

Shim Maybe it becomes a condition in which these guys [pointing to the model] get what some of these guys have but in a very different way so they become, let's say, courts at the upper level that may not be public but there may be swimming pools and amenities collectively, not individually, that shifts it away from a tower project to a more even fabric net condition which is actually really interesting. That the payback for being here as opposed to here is that there's kind of a whole grouping of things that by being up on top of the Ikea it supports a level of amenities that's different than if you're going incognito.

Edward Mitchell There was a point in there where it had a variety of space.

Shim But it would actually be rendered green, in a way it would be rendered green like this is green, but maybe a slightly different shade of green. One of the strengths of the project is not that the landscape is so great or the urban space is so great, but that you've actually taken on the full gamut and that we're not seeing a building, per se, but a prototype for a building proposition and a degree of density and a mixture of use that I think is what the nature of the studio calls for – that it's a test of the urban proposition through a kind of prototypical piece of it that starts to imagine a new city but looks carefully at the existing city to create its new density.

[...]

Summers It's a curious kind of city in miniature. If you were able to further develop this housing type with the big box below, the DNA of the center of the town, then you surround it with these larger recreational, structural things, it's your edge-of-town types. It's interesting because you go out of the city very quickly or out of that packed-in condition very quickly.

Fred Koetter The diagram came very early and it was extremely striking to me when I first saw it. If you look at this diagram below and you said here are these two neighborhoods and here's this place for the highway and what if that becomes the site no matter what its configuration? See what happens if you make it into a site and I think there's something very powerful about that. I would agree that in the section which has great potential, the upper layer is not as convincing as it ought to be, but I think that's okay. Your comment that the upper layer may be of this residential texture of the city and these outriggers are suburb – I'd never thought about that because I'd thought about being able to roam around all over that roofscape because it's a very opportunistic scheme. It takes that site between the two neighborhoods as an opportunity without doing anything to either one of them and giving them something in between that's useful.

Shim Throughout the day a lot of people talked about this connection between the two neighborhoods and there has been a lot of rhetoric about that. In a way, I feel that these guys have actually done it without making a lot of bridges or links physically but by the kind of fabric that would draw people there in a more city-making way as opposed to using cultural program or other things to do that.

5.

Joseph Smith & Andrew Steffen
University of Notre Dame & Iowa State University
Network City

In Network City, we are proposing a vision for a future Helsinki through a new planning logic. Using a new public transit network, this logic connects our disjointed site back to itself and to the greater city. The network allows for a specific urban fabric and density on the site centering about "Autobanks" which become the neighborhood foci and act as the catalysts for new growth. Each Autobank provides the means of transition from a car-dependent society to a district which provides spatial movement via networks of mass transit, parkland, and gallery.

Richard Summers The tension of the project is that one of the things about the car that is so corrosive over this traditional form of urbanism is that it is a technology that disperses itself across the landscape. If I didn't know your scheme was about corralling the cars, I would think it was a kind of mass transit scheme where you would have mass transit coming into those things and you would build all the density around mass transit because it brings people to one point. So you're trying to use the car like mass transit so everyone comes into one point. You have a captive audience so they're going to do their shopping and then they're going to go to their house. It's a clear and somewhat aggressive project to say that people are going to give up ready access to their automobile near to their place of work and in place of that we are going to give them what? They get the green piece? What am I getting?

Andrew Steffen Well, the trade off is a different lifestyle which we're hoping will facilitate all of those things. You work here, you live here, you play here. Because now in a suburban neighborhood you...

Joseph Smith A lot of people live in Chicago without a car or New York without a car.

Charles Waldheim It's a tax. So you're basically saying to compete in a global economy you're going to give up your automobile which means you've got to give them something else in exchange, right? Otherwise, people are going to hop over and go to the next...

Steffen It's a proximity to those things that they want to partake in.
Waldheim So what is it? Is it culture? Is it…
Smith Well, yes. We built a sports stadium here. This is an idea about how do we radically change a planning problem that we were given in Helsinki and still try to maintain a living situation that [people] like but also provides

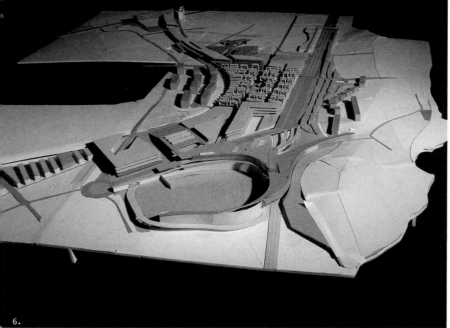

6.

alternatives which they may find…

Waldheim Let me delaminate two. Let me clear this up. I'm with you in a sense that you make such a strong rhetorical arguments about the automobile, but you have to give us some other alternative as a basis from which to evaluate that. I can delaminate the

7.

8.

car and talk about these transit oriented nodes that you build a big center around these Tapiola. You say we're going to build three of these. It's going to be a walking radius, right? And that will then provide these pockets within which market rate, whatever-the-type-of-the-day will fill in? Okay. There's a reasonable planning argument to be made there. It's not clear to me why the automobile is necessarily part of that conversation. It's a little bit socially deterministic. There's no causal relationship between removing roads and getting people out of their cars across political spectrums, across economic models. What's the advantage?

Edward Mitchell What you've done urbanistically is that you've replicated the density and scale of downtown. The big problem of parking in Helsinki and other Landschaft towns is that you usually don't own a car. You've got that but you've also got the opportunity to park in these big garages and these connections that are this fragmented street that actually doesn't exist all the way up…

Alan Plattus Is this the density of downtown Helsinki or is it more like the density of something like [Eliel] Saarinen's…

Fred Koetter I think it's somewhere between.

Plattus My problem, among others, is that if you took all of the buildings off of your road system and asked me to figure out where the logical location for nodes or public spaces might be, I wouldn't know what to do and I certainly wouldn't come up with the locations that you all generated. As an imprint, as a plan, it is rather strange to me. I mean the beauty, even if old fashioned, with [Eliel] Saarinen's scheme, is the combination of a kind of even romantic garden suburban fabric with moments of formality that generate public-ness. Today we're rather more skeptical of those kinds of compositional strategies – the c-word, as it is referred to – but we have other views like open green space, water, transportation systems, that might or might not generate, but it seems to me that for something that looks highly specific, I mean, every little piece is inflected. What does it all mean?

Closing Comments

Richard Summers I've been coming to these reviews for a couple of years and I was very impressed by the work today and how the students dealt with the very complex condition that these guys put on the table. In this case, you're working in a place certainly unlike the areas outside of Boston where [the studio] worked before… where the discussion was that there is no high architecture so you have a certain amount of freedom in the language. The built history of the place is fairly open game. In this case, you have a strong legacy of a kind of architecture – not just one, but several – and a very strong landscape tradition. I've been thinking about this because [Eliel] Saarinen has been coming up with people who are working on the history of urban design. People tend to speak about [Jose Luis] Sert in terms of how urban design started, but it turns out that [Eliel] Saarinen, when he went to Cranbrook, educated a lot of people who ended up doing what we call urban design now, so he was a very pivotal figure. Ed Bacon, who redesigned Philadelphia, studied with him. The [Charles and Ray] Eameses studied with him. So I'm looking at this plan and saying, should I understand that plan and what its ideas were? There are not too many other sites where you can say that there is a strong local culture, strong landscape tradition, and an architect that has also had a strong hand. And I typically don't choose sites that would be loaded in that way. So, good for you. There is a kind of modern tradition here, there is a form of modernist housing, there is a global overlay which has made it look outdated. All of those historical/cultural entities plus all of you contending with what it means to make something that exists at the scale of a regional plan, a neighborhood plan, and then the architecture, I deal with that in my teaching and it's a very difficult issue to achieve in one semester.

Leon Krier
Williamsburg, Virginia

511a

with Jim Tinson

In *The Long Emergence* we learn from J.H. Kunstler that the rapidly decreasing availability of fossil fuels will, within our lifetimes, result in a massive return to traditional forms of life, of urbanism, architecture, construction, agriculture. Despite the many fruitful experiences of New Urbanism, Williamsburg remains in the US the most inspiring myth of traditional architecture, it is less known for the exemplary quality of its urbanism. In fact Williamsburg is today not only a living environmental museum but also a laboratory for new traditional architecture as demonstrated by the recently completed building by Quinlan Terry.

The Colonial Williamsburg foundation represented by Cary Carson and Edward Chappell have assured us their enthusiastic support in monitoring parts of our course.

The goal of this studio is principally to make students understand and use the contrasting and interdependent relationship of "the vernacular" and "the classical" within the given language of Williamsburg traditional architecture and urbanism: what role this dialectic plays within the design of a single building in order to create meaning through contrast; contrast of uses, materials, forms, colors, and how it articulates the larger urban context into a readable, useable and enjoyable artifact.

The students will familiarize themselves with these essential planning and design issues through the available literature, through a trip to Williamsburg, through the study of significant examples of Williamsburg's buildings and architects. While in Williamsburg students will master-plan the area into 10-12 new blocks, forming a new quarter or hamlet within the city of Williamsburg. Each student will design an individual building and block and carefully relate it to its neighboring buildings and public spaces. Each individual will be influenced by the created context, and each building will have to play its meaningful role in the larger context of Colonial Williamsburg.

Opening Comment

Leon Krier We looked at this [Williamsburg]. The students, everyone, had to draw. They had to draw for the first time in their lives one of the buildings in order to understand grade elevations, construction, and materials. All of this material then had to be put into the computer so that it becomes a bank of knowledge, not only of style, but also of technique, which then becomes a common index that can be reused by everyone in the next phase, which was the problem phase. Once these records were made, we could do some brief exercises, which were to take a detail and to distort it. Distort it from the grotesque to the sublime, to be able to understand what is classical, to understand what is the nature of the classical as well as what is the best proportion of a column in a given situation. So they went from [having] very big fears to a sequence of extreme exercise, extreme architectural education, and mutation.

[...]

Peter Eisenman Leon [Krier], before we get started, I have two questions. What is the difference, to you, between the grotesque and the sublime? You said before that you were going to take a classical column and move it towards the grotesque or the sublime.

Krier There are many, many...

Eisenman I need a quick mission statement.

Krier Bulimia or anorexia would be a good [analogy].

[laugther]

Eisenman Oh. And the other would be: What's the difference between classical and vernacular?

Krier Yes. I think that architecture is mainly ninety percent vernacular. It is technology. It is techniques of building. It has no style. It is joining natural materials in a tectonic way. Concrete and steel displaced this because everything becomes style. When you use concrete there is no more vernacular.

Eisenman Why not use concrete instead of vernacular materials?

Krier No, it's not a natural material. It's nature, and we are not nature. We are cultural. We are fictitious whereas concrete is a form of blubber, which has no shape. It sticks together in forms that are completely un-tectonic and holds up for a while, but not for very long. It is a very fragile material. And very, well, nasty...

Eisenman What's the difference between bricks...bricks and mortar, mortar and concrete?

Krier Bricks? Oh, the cost. The energy cost. We should have Glenn Murcutt come up here. The energy cost to produce or create one brick is about 'x', and to produce reinforced concrete cost would be a factor of about seven at a minimum.

Eisenman But, just in terms of cost, [Demetri] Porphyrios' brick-and-mortar building at Princeton is the most expensive buildings ever built at Princeton. And I don't know what...

Krier We are conducted to an architecture, to brick buildings, of any style. All of our buildings are fake, even our industrial building, but that's the industrial condition. Nevertheless, we have the model of joining natural materials in a tectonic way – that is the overriding intellectual discipline. Now Architecture is [about] when you join these materials in an artful way.

Eisenman That's the artfulness of the vernacular? When vernacular becomes art, it's classical?

Krier Yes.

Susan Parapetti
(H.I. Feldman Nominee)
University of Michigan at Ann Arbor
Williamsburg

Pier Aureli Since we are speaking about the vernacular...and if I understand what vernacular means, which is using the local material without any monumental intention. Usually when you are in this situation, even starting from the old Egyptian times, you care about the stability of the wall. Because when you build the wall straight in an unstable situation, the wall can collapse. Then you make the wall in this way [motioning with his hands] and it will stand up.

Peter Eisenman Then you expect to see something behind it, Pier [Aureli], because I am not being disturbed by this funeral idea. I don't understand why it's not the same [symmetrical], but it is not the real rule of the architecture realm. That [pointing to elevation] is wrong as far as I know classical architecture.

Massimo Scolari We can't explain why this is wrong.

Aureli I just want to make one comment. I think that these are beautifully designed, this charming marriage of male and female symbols. I think there is, for my taste, a bit too much ornament. If you had just this [pointing to symbols] and the bare wall, it is much more powerful. If you look at this [entrance gate], this is beautifully designed.

David Schwarz You don't think the symbolism is a little much for such a small community?

Aureli I would have something very powerful here, and this is indeed powerful, and then come down and have something more informative.

1.

3.

Schwarz Let's just discuss something about the wall around Central Park, in particular the wall at 65th street and 5th Avenue. It is a very low wall. It is a masonry wall, but you're asking the wall to do too much work. All the work in Central Park is the pavements leading up to the wall, the wall itself, and then the layer of trees on the other side of the pavement. So there is quite a transition leading up to a pretty modest wall. It is a powerful transition from two very different conditions.

Jaquelin Robertson This is a simple fence with a formal gate. I find it to be very powerful and it's in the right place. That relationship is fine, I am much more worried about the museum and these two pieces and I don't think they work at all. They have the virtue of the same architect. So she

2.

has a great chance to design those two things together, but she has thought of them as apart I think – I don't mean to put words in your mouth. They look like they were not thought about as the same façade. If you thought of the facades as an urban façade, then it would be quite powerful.

Eisenman Do you see the building on the corner there, Leon [Krier]? It seems to me that would mark the entry to the place rather than … I mean for me, in a classical mode, that corner speaks to me.

Leon Krier I agree. I would make this [front façade] even simpler, more rural. Then right away, with this height, there is a pathway going right through the park – this is not a private park, this is the wood. I think it's beautifully designed, but I think now it would be much easier in the context for this building to be powerful – this [the wall] has to be quiet. So it's really about building up this context.

Aureli This is an entrance to a cemetery, yes? What is the meaning of the entrance? In my opinion, I think it is too vague. They need to be represented in the same way. The entrance to the cemetery is very important. I am thinking of Rossi's cemetery where you enter in

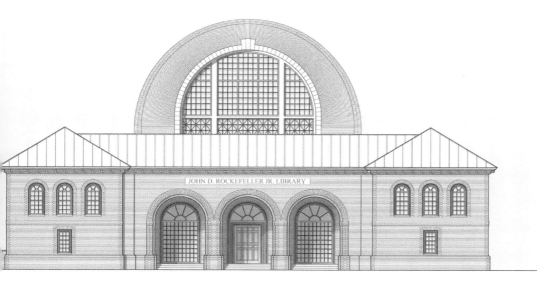

Leon Krier
(continued)

dialogue to the center, but then everything is being centered as though you were there at the moment.

Eisenman Because it looks like the wall around Rossi's cemetery, if you look at it. You know, I think Leon [Krier], I think precision in drawing, as you talked about yesterday, is important and I think she should be charged. That plan doesn't represent the dimension. We had a moment yesterday, so I just want to footnote that.

Schwarz If you [Susan Parapetti] were going on, the first thing you should do is to look at the governor's palace and the formal garden – which is behind it, I mean next to it – which is quite spectacular. Then you have the chance to ask, is it too far?

––––

Paolo Campos
Yale University
Colonial Williamsburg Foundation Office

––––

The objective of the studio was to understand the dialectic between the 'classical' and the 'vernacular'. Architecturally, the idea of a 'vernacular' language drove the proportions and composition of elements – for example, dormers are allowed to deviate in alignment from masonry openings in recognition of their different tectonic assemblies, the former being wood carpentry, the latter being brick and mortar. The window sizes and assemblies vary according to the functions of the spaces behind. The materials are in keeping with the local tradition of brick, stone, and slate for significant public buildings.

––––

Peter Eisenman The gable relationship to the windows below in Williamsburg are always aligned. Here the dormers on the left side are not aligned to the gables on the right side. To me that is breaking the rules, so that's number one. And he does the same thing on the back, so to me I don't get it. Number two, Colin Rowe, from whom I learned my classical education, always said that you cannot enter the void of the palazzo. You have a three part building: A, B, and C. You can only enter the A's and not the B's, and what he hated about the Gropius project was that you always entered the void in the binuclear house. To me this is a binuclear project dressed up in old drag. That doesn't even work as a binuclear project because you can't even stick that [pointing to model]. And I think this is where I get crazy, because there are rules of distribution and organization and that everything is clearly marked as poché. He said that you go through the courtyard, but you don't – you get off in the middle where you go to the offices undistinguished from the major space. You can't enter the void. You can't stick an 'L' onto a bar, you can't make the dormers not align, and if you look at the façade it has one, two, three, four, five, six, seven, eight, at least nine different window types on a simple façade. To me that's as bad as [Christian de] Portzamparcs' French Embassy in Berlin, which has fourteen different window types. So I don't see the difference between bad modern architecture – which is Portzamparc, which I can't stand – and bad neo-nitwit architecture that breaks every damn rule. And I say if these students learn something, it would be that they couldn't break so many rules gratuitously because otherwise anything goes. I want to make sure I say this, because I have nothing against beautiful classical architecture – I think it's great – but I think this is an example of a mistake similar to how we made mistakes yesterday. I want to point that out. [smiling]

David Schwarz What troubles me about this is that the elements [being] compared to each other are not right. This is way too big for this style of architecture. For me, you haven't taken the language you established for yourself and applied it to the building. But if you look at your lexicon, these kinds of groupings, this closeness of gables, is entirely wrong. One of the things most architects get wrong is a window. If you get the windows right, you're ninety percent there.

Robert A.M. Stern Can I offer my opinion? I think if you judge

4.

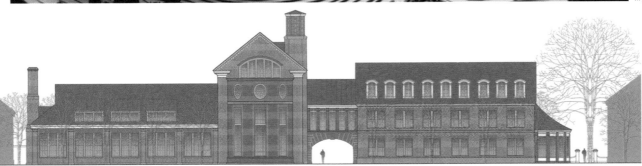

5.

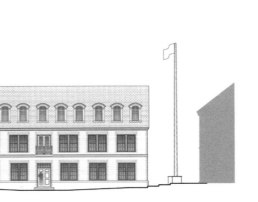

6.

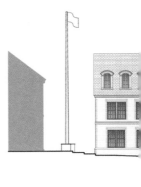

this building as an object building, or as a monumental building, it is a building in the vernacular. Now I do think the dormer windows should be right, and I think what Peter said about using the vocabulary in a more thoughtful way would be good. But I think it can be read as a building, a figural building, which has had additions in different times and it's a gateway to a stable yard. It is a perfectly reasonable compositional type and it has nothing, in my view, to do with the binuclear house. This has nothing to do with it.

Eisenman You cannot enter a palazzo…

Stern It's not a palazzo.

[laughter]

Stern It's an informal building. With all due respect, the problem with the contemporary moment for many architects, not you [Eisenman] necessarily, is that they can't do anything but palazzos.

Leon Krier And we do not want to compete and humiliate the monumentality of colonial Williamsburg. This is more like working in the context. I think this experience, entering into the courtyard, stepping into this space, getting off through the stair where you are on axis with the road, it's sublime… I don't mind them not aligning. No? Because why? Because this load bearing wall…

Eisenman All the models you showed us of Williamsburg all line up.

Krier It's not true.

Stern No they don't all align Peter [Eisenman], I'm sorry to say.

Krier But I remember now, forty years ago, we were at Princeton. We had a project, and you were raving that the windows were not aligned. Stop this. You don't need to see that they weren't aligned. And you were raving about the fact that they weren't aligned. You found it so sexy that they weren't aligned.

[laughter]

Eisenman If this is a vernacular building, it doesn't look like one – all right? I guess that's my thought.

Schwarz Stop one moment. American Architecture was crossbred after Williamsburg. Now you have this extraordinary infusion of Spanish colonial, Dutch Georgian architecture all again to crossbreed as you enter the nineteenth century. You would take all of those things and pull them together in an incredibly informal line up. You would have this kind of variety, you wouldn't do this [pointing at model], this of a different world. What it looks like is four buildings built at different times that had things added to them – which is very true of what happens now.

Eisenman Are you suggesting that it is all right to build a building in one time and make it look like it was built in four different time periods?

Schwarz Absolutely.

Eron Ashley
University of Colorado at Boulder
Williamsburg

Pier Aureli Where does this come from – all these joints? I mean it's a very bizarre, surreal piece of architecture. It could be…

Peter Eisenman Cynthia was saying that it looks like a code, I mean that thing there could be to gather the scolari. It doesn't look like any other project we've seen today.

Jaquelin Robertson I think the project somehow contradicts that of today through the recognition that we're probably going to have different programming for leisure time – if there is such a thing as leisure time. It may not include recreational mode, it may not include much of your way of tourism as we know it. I am wondering how you intend to heat this building?

[laughter]

Eron Ashley I would have said that there are a lot of chimneys. I mean – I don't know.

Robertson Hold on just a second – you wanted a vertical element.

Ashley Yes

Robertson Okay. Those of you [who] have seen [Arata] Isozaki's Disney building in Orlando – it's probably one of his best buildings, very simple. It's got this void in the middle of it, light to come in, whether it's appropriate for an office building I don't know, but it's incredibly powerful.

It also makes light in those trays of offices very interesting because it's quite straightforward, but when you arrive and leave, it's truly wonderful. When you make something this big, and it's coming down into a court in the middle of the hotel, you have to think about what is its purpose? Is it to bring light? Do you have a new rock garden idea? You just don't want to sit in that chimney because it will be disturbing.

Ashley No. It is a move through space definitely.

Robertson I'm trying to find out, why you spend that much effort and money on something that big symbolically? You spend the most money and time on a building if it is for the church government, the most powerful person, but it's a smokestack. It's so big. It brings so much attention to itself. You say that it's not just to have something vertical. When you look at this drawing in the context, this building is an object building, and I wonder if it's appropriate. Whether or not you like the architecture or not, it seems to me, in terms of the context of the town, the moves here are too big for the context of the town.

Krier I want to explain what Eron [Ashley] had to do. He worked for George Lucas in Star Wars, so it's interesting [that] the mies-en-scene and the theatrical side have come out.

[laughter]

Krier No, I mean, because this is a very low-key situation with some really strong perspectives.

David Schwarz My problem with it is the urbanism, not the architecture. I think it is the combination, too. It's about the scale of the thing compared to the scale of all of your neighbors – it's too big. I think the corner is too big for the town.

Krier You find in Italy this outer scale, and they are enormous when you see them in drawing, but when you walk through the town you don't even notice them – they become a part of the landscape. People just take it. It's scandalous for the outer scale with the rest. I think this is something that could be…

Schwarz All of your choices here are skewed to the axis in that it's unresolved in its relationships. Everything about the corner, and the way you deal with it, is void to the tower. Everything about it says 'look at me, look at me…' There is not one subtle gesture in the composition. And as I said, I'm not opposed to that. I mean it's just a private space and the courtyard space, but in a town that's just not correct.

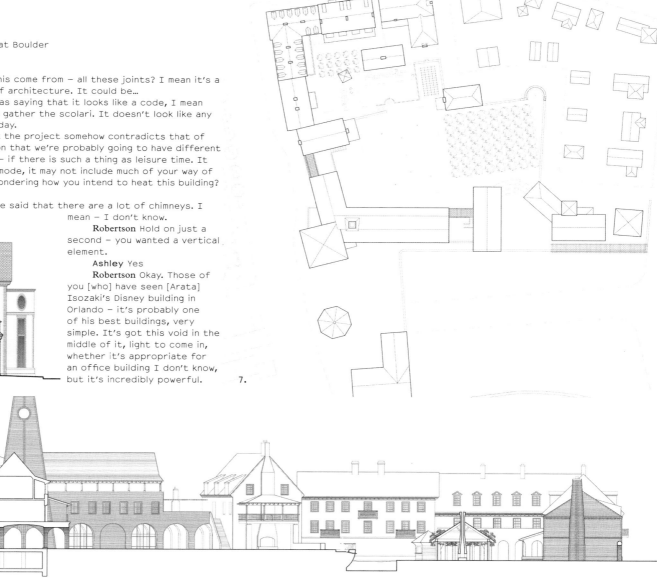

7.

8.

(4–6) Paolo Campos
(7, 8) Eron Ashley

Glenn Murcutt
Elizabeth Mine, Stratford
513a

with Amy Lelyveld

Stratford, Vermont's Elizabeth Mine was, in its time (1803-1958), the oldest large-scale mining operation in the country. Today this landscape of built and natural features is on the National Priorities list of Superfund sites. The abandoned mine buildings represent every step of a 150-year history of adaptation to changing technologies, markets and times. The site is located on the wooded rolling hills and ridges of Vermont's "Upper Valley".

The Elizabeth Mine is a valuable case study – an historical, environmental, recreational and cultural asset that demonstrates both the influence of the land on human activity and the impact of human activity on the land.

The work of the studio is to examine current re-use proposals for the site and to design a study center (K-12) for this rich yet degraded place.

Russell Greenberg
(H.I. Feldman Recipient)
Yale University
Elizabeth Mine Learning Center, Stratford, Vermont

This proposal for the Elizabeth Mine Learning Center condenses program around a concrete thermal chimney, penetrating eighty feet below ground to bedrock. This core acts as an immense structural lung and serves as a dramatic spatial metaphor for excavation. The building connects with the historically significant abandoned copper mines, utilizing the maze of existing tunnels as an earth duct to dampen yearly temperature swings.

Robert A.M. Stern When you're looking up and experiencing the money shot, are you underneath the building? I don't understand.

Kenneth Frampton I think you're a very gifted person, but one thing you have to watch is that you have the tendency to be too figurative in your thinking. So, in a way, this rock with a kind of figure with veins all over it, and its top all open… There's this moment in which architecture is not figurative – I risk offending people who believe it's an intrinsically figurative art – and it's a risk. You're very talented and this building is a very interesting building. Why do you need a rock there?

Russell Greenberg But I think it's the effect of it which is not necessarily a figure.

Will Bruder But it would be more mysterious than the concrete. The concrete, I think, is the dead end. There is so much rock-ness about this that you don't have to hit me over the head with a concrete rock for it to be there. I mean, I'm wanting this thing to be translucent. I'm wanting this thing to be another material in place of this color that we keep being told about by our friend here. I mean, the riff that he's taken us on all day… the whole surface wants to do that.

Greenberg You know what? When it's really dark, color goes away – becomes black and white. I think about this building as a dark monastery. It's cloistered, cool. It's about looking into that main space which is more lit than the exterior. Then the contrast to that is the landscape whose color is totally saturated.

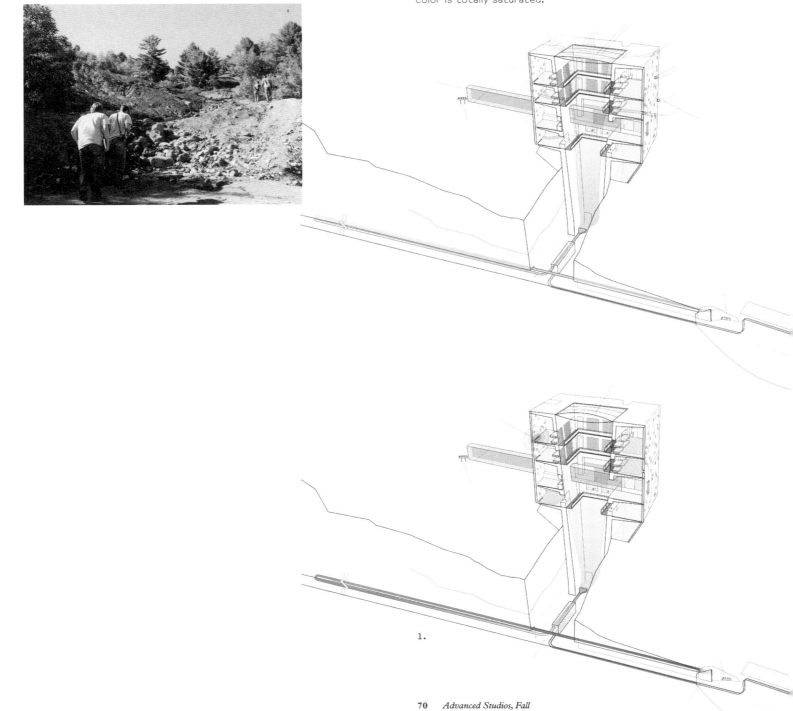

1.

Bruder The steel and glass part... you can get this laminated so that moirés out – so that it goes from the green spectrum to the red – just by walking by it. That sets up a whole other mysticism, but that's about materiality. I'd like to go back to public space. Take us into the entry and through the classrooms.

Tod Williams In the model I look up and see it as open, but in the section, unfortunately, I see a lid on the central shaft. I see the potential for the chimney-effect with air venting up the top, so maybe the lid could lift up quite a bit. One of the great things about Vermont is that in the summer the sun rises in one place and in the winter it rises in a very different place.

Frampton Coming back to my previous obsession...playful use of concrete? I mean, this question of figuration is a really serious issue. If you don't integrate that dimension of making things with the space of the building construction, what happens and it happened in this project, is that when you talk about it you talk about all sorts of stuff which inhibits the function of the scheme. If it had been a square plan – you probably started off with a square plan – you gain floor area all over the place which would give you greater freedom to sort out the sequence of a person coming in. Now, they have to go through three different stages crossing that light well. This is the problem of architects doing figurative sculptures instead of

2.

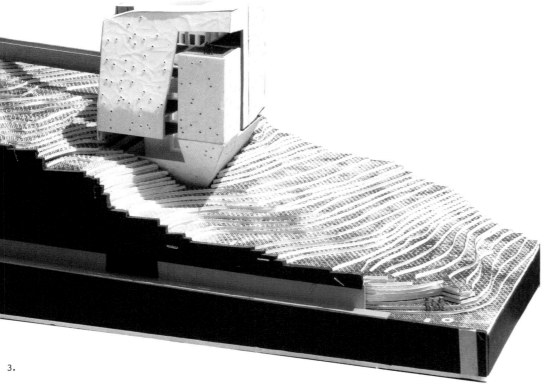

3.

doing architecture and what suffers is the architecture.

Greenberg Sorry.

Marion Weiss I have an inverted take on it. One begins with a sculptural premise and we use words that are going to kill you if you say them again in reviews. 'The thing mimics that...' You'll get nailed if you ever do that again because the whole notion of limitation about the transformation becomes the gray area. But in a sense you're inspired by the mesa, almost like a glacial erratic that's come out of here that somehow a respondent and contrast to this incredible landscape that you've discovered. You've done the one thing we've been praying for in the last five projects – densification and intensification through that densification – so I think it's a brilliant work. Having said that, there are a couple things you've touched on in terms of representation that I think if you were to represent what you're talking about with the same intensity that you're thinking and making rather evenly all the way around, a lot of interesting things... It's the representation of the intensification that I want to be amplified. But again, I think it's a brilliant work and we wouldn't have been able to have this conversation if it wasn't so ambitious.

Meaghan Smialowski
Washington University
The Disconnected Adventures of Copperas Brook

The project finds itself directly in the path of the site's primary water body, Copperas Brook. The siting of the main building continues an ongoing story of interruption, disruption, and redirection that one can uncover in the larger history of the site. Copperas Brook flows through the site, revealing a past of copper mining – a past of discovery, extraction, deposition, and, eventually, obsolescence. Moving forward, the site is redefined as an educational destination and the building serves to accommodate this program. In addition to providing sleeping, eating, and learning accommodations for visitors, the building imbeds itself into the landscape and redirects, controls, and filters that which flows in the path of Copperas Brook before it continues on its way.

Tod Williams It's a very beautiful presentation. I have very little to criticize except when I look at the model there, this winter piece feels not only small, but squashed in its size and section. It should be more substantial, more centered, more whole, and have more power than that and I don't understand why that's not the case. Of course it would be more economical to keep it compressed, but at the same time it would be more economical to shorten it and so on and so forth. It just feels that it doesn't have the commitment – a different kind of commitment to the time one would be in it. I'm not sure it's taking advantage of the south perspectives.

Glenn Murcutt I think the only thing that's necessary is for this roof to connect to that one.

Williams That would have brought that roof up a little bit.

Will Bruder The whole thing is wonderfully done. I like the way you've designed a building that talks about the slashing of the mines. You do all the drawings, you cut the salami, you cut the bread, bing bing bing bing, and this one is really crying for the long section to really understand every nuance. This scheme really makes sense because it gives you the sense that you're off the main public pathway. Nice tectonics and good ideas.

Brigitte Shim This project has really come a long way since the midterm. I remember how styled it was. For me, it's one of the projects that ties the scale of the site to the scale of the building – the rhythm of those pilasters is actually a really important part of the project. The two are not separate conversations but the same discussion. When we see a dividing wall between a composting toilet and a shower, it all starts to come together. I think you have an obligation, especially with a linear scheme, to show how we get to the parking lot and what happens out the other end. That dotted line is an abnegation of your control. You are responsible for that! It's part of your territory. It's not just any old path but a place that brings you to this critical moment. I think it would be great to think of this as a ruin. Imagine it 100 years from now. The program has changed, but this thing is still here as an infrastructure, as a memory of something. And I think to see it as a ruin that gets filled in and clad is not a timeline issue, but a building issue, about imagining a first order of construction and then the second crew comes in and they fill it in. It starts to create a construction logic that actually ties into a plate logic. That order of operations would start to inform the way you make things – what sits on top of something else, what sits next to it – and that infra-

Glenn Murcutt
(continued)

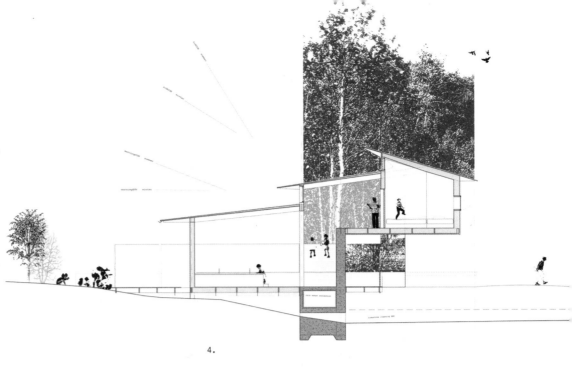

4.

structure then doesn't become so fussy. It actually is tough and rugged and the other pieces could be more finessed. You wouldn't use the same material to do two different things.

Kenneth Frampton I think it's a little misleading… the use of color. The misleading graphics about the color cuts out the possibility that the water that is collected would be visible. You seem to answer me by saying that it is visible, but I don't know where it's visible. I can imagine walking down a path and I look down and I see the water, you know, so the movement of the body and the movement of the water are running together. The building is a dam, isn't it? It'd be nice to see its damming function.

Williams There's a nice dam on Derby road which I've walked on top of. Maybe you have, too. It might be nice if all that's permanent is masonry. You give us a moment to look this way, but what about looking this way? You're kind of contained by the structure through here but I somehow feel that…

Frampton It is open, though.

Williams It is open, but this is a different kind of openness where one really opens out. I like the idea of looking at the treated and untreated water. What would this landscape look like 80 years down the pike when this program is gone? Would trees be growing out of it? Would the stream still go through?

Scott Baltimore
North Carolina State University
Coding the Site with a Path

This solution proposes programs in the spring, summer, and fall for approximately thirty students, where students would form a commitment or investment to the site through multiple visits. The daily program is orchestrated in a morning and afternoon program – a lesson plan would be formulated around the historic significance of the mine in the morning and the environmental effects of the mining process in the afternoon. This would be coupled with an understanding of the cleanup process.

The building is a hinge at the juncture of these two loops and serves as both a gateway to the site and as a device for viewing and understanding the site. The visitors arriving at the Elizabeth Mine Learning Center would most likely approach from South Strafford along Mine Road, entering the building along a slope overlooking the site. Visitors enter along a wall of displayed relics with the option to enter into the Elizabeth Mine information box or proceed along the historic path to the south and north cuts. A multipurpose room for eating, learning, and sharing is positioned along the hill, while the shared bedrooms are located behind a perforated Corten steel screen that provides privacy while also regulating its transparency to provide elevated views onto the site. The information box and vertical circulation are the programmatic links between the two programs.

Frederick Scharmen
University of Maryland at College Park
Elizabeth Mine

This project tries to operate in different scales and realms simultaneously, bridging the gap between land art and phytoremediation, architecture and education, the solar system and the microbiotic. The main building is organized along a single line from north to south, linking the built up area and its historic structures with the remaining forest wilderness, optimizing its exposure to air and sunlight, and following the edge of one of the toxic tailings piles remaining on the site. The living spaces reach up to exchange light and air, and the bathrooms are housed in service pylons, touching the ground to exchange water and waste. This exchange is the basis for one of three systems that format the larger landscape through remediation experiments. Outboard datalogging stations serve as camping structures and outdoor classrooms, their orientation and form linking them to the daily and yearly paths of the sun.

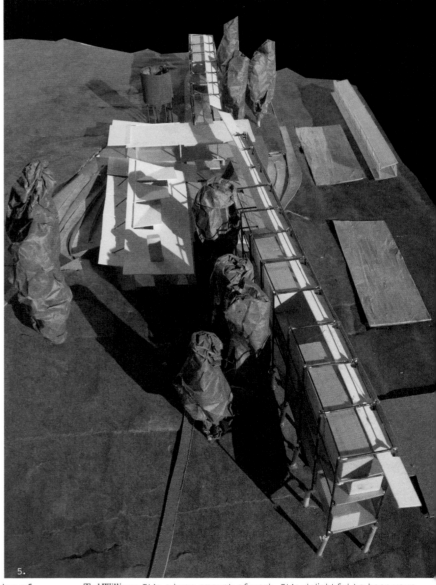

5.

Tod Williams It's a huge amount of work. It's delightful to hear your enthusiasm and your investment in connections that are solving this. It's great. I applaud you. I think the thing that I'm missing, if I'm missing anything, is to ask you whether you have really put yourself in the building – in the experience – as opposed to sort of looking at it and figuring it out intellectually. For some reason, I think that's something you still need to work on… how to be in there, how to reside in there. Maybe I'm making a mistake, but as I look down along this path through here, which I assume is a kind of free path. It isn't though.

Fred Scharmen What do you mean?

Williams Well, it's not very clear. You have a set of doors, a set of doors, another set of doors, and I'm saying that as you mature as an architect, I want you to be in that space and walk that space and see whether that's an experience you want — whether you're going to turn those into automatic doors or whether you plan another way around that — because I think that is a problem.

Scharmen It's true because they're one of the things that I never ended up building in any of the models.

Williams I sort of feel you are stuffing them into your work. I feel you're so keen on figuring everything out in such a great and ethical way that I just want you to spend the time and be in the space. Let your shoulders down and experience it. I think that will be a great pleasure for you.

Kenneth Frampton You know, one thing that is important is this issue of science fiction. It's very much industrial design and image that these sections have, partly coming out of this mode of construction. I think it's a very nice project and what you have to say about landscape is brilliant — the way the bridge building relates to the landscape, but also the way in which it relates to other landscape notions. It's just these SIP columns. They make me feel very uncomfortable. They make the whole thing feel like the moon lander itself. That, I think, is a pity. It probably needs to have some

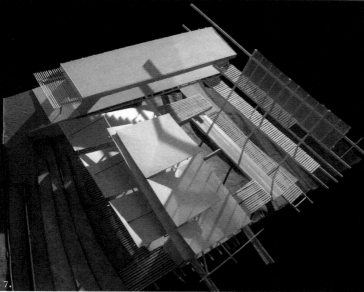

stiffening pieces going through… it needs to be framed, but…

Peggy Deamer I think that you're not coming down strong on what you think it is. SIPs are completely neutral. They're not moonscapes. SIPs are nothing, you know, and so… I'm more troubled by the fact that I can't get a fix on its imagery and its tectonic in order to do that. I wish it was as moonscapey as is being described because that would at least indicate that you have a position that I wouldn't disagree with. Your model, however, says something very different to me than what those renderings say so I don't think you're doing it. The reason I would make a claim for the moonscape is only to clarify or be consistent. I actually think that something that edges toward that talks about a larger notion of time. I appreciate that you're talking about a larger notion of geography and astronomy in some way, but you are also talking about a larger notion of time. So to me, you put into question the rightness of everybody else's scheme, which is so cute… so here and now.

Brigitte Shim In a way, there are a lot of things I appreciate about your project and a lot of things that frustrate me terribly. First of all, this is the first time that there has been a subtle depiction of the landscape. This is a site plan that has a sense of what is found and what you're adding to it, and this here is actually a timeline.

Frampton Right. Right.

Shim This notion of time… to see your piece as yet one piece that's part of a larger span of time is, for me, something that registers.

Patrick Bellew It also resonates with the time it took to build the tailings in the first place.

Shim For sure. And to see remediation as having a timeline to it is a strength of the project. I think also that notions of sustainability have

been touched upon and addressed in a variety of different ways. You've taken the full gamut on. The whole shooting match is in here which is a greater degree of difficulty and not always so easy to synthesize in the time period that we're talking about. So I appreciate the ambition of not just paying lip service to that but really trying to grapple with all the technical things that go with each one of those pieces. There's a lot to be commended and appreciated about it. When I get to the problem issues, like this ramp that I've been looking at this whole time, it's just so monumental. Here's this guy that's so sensitive and thinking about time and all these things and the amount of infrastructure that would be needed to create this — getting concrete trucks in there to build that sucker relative to all these other things that you're doing. I can't quite reconcile [it all].

Closing Comments

Amy Lelyveld We're going to be having a meeting of the Elizabeth Mine community members that are actively involved in the clean-up and design of the mine on January 12th, and I'd like to invite you, if you can, to come up or get materials to me so the community has the opportunity to see your work.

Will Bruder On that note, my suggestion would be to edit each of your presentations down to your four best story-telling images, pack them into a power-point, and choreograph it so that people can go on the journey with you. One disappointment for me today… Glenn [Murcutt]

is such a great storyteller, to hear him talk it's always this journey of words that is important to make things legible, and not many of you had that spirit of the journey in the words. We come in cold, from some other planet sometimes, and sit down here, just like your client might, and that community might. They don't think in terms of these images.

Glenn Murcutt Will, they all know this. I've told them about the ends of things. The arriving, the walking, the communicating, the sitting, the looking, the hearing, the smelling. When you begin your professional life, you have to keep those things in mind. You've got to be able to describe what it is like, arriving by car, coming towards the building, entering the building, knowing where you go. When you design around that question, you're likely to find that the scaling is right, that the experience is right, the changing of directions to be important, and to be observant. And how you relate to the mine is important. The whole area of waste management is very important. Water supply is very important. I really would have liked to have heard each of you talk about those issues in sequence. Then the questions the reviewers had would have would be reduced. But it's been a good effort. I know we've pushed you hard. That's how the studio is run.

----

(4) Megan Smialowski
(5-7) Scott Baltimore
73 (8) Fred Scharmen

Brigitte Shim
Cities Center, Toronto
515a

with Hilary Sample

Sustainable city building and the ever-expanding eco-logical footprint of our urban centers are pressing global concerns. Population growth, pollution, crime, suburban sprawl are some of the extreme problems that all cities world wide face. Currently, there is a critical gap between information and critical analysis of issues impacting our metropolitan areas around the world.

Cities Center

A Think Tank for Cities will have a physical presence in Toronto, the largest urban center in Canada. This new building will bring together global experts to study and monitor the health of our large metropolitan cities. Experts in finances, urban planning, housing, community relations, multiculturalism, policing, architecture and human rights from around the world will be housed in one facility to study the challenges facing ecologically sustainable urbanization.

This studio encourages energetic and speculative investigations into sustainable built form in the heart of a contemporary North American city. The objective of the studio is to enable each student to develop a critical engagement with program, the site and current construction methods simultaneously. This studio will investigate design at three fundamentally different scales the city, a building and tectonics in an integrated and synthetic manner.

The contemporary city of Toronto is the most multicultural and multilingual city in the world. 52% of Toronto's residents were born outside of Canada. Racial and ethnic diversity are woven into the social fabric of the city while its physical still reflects its antiquated British and American parentage. At the outset, each student is asked to reflect on the contemporary theories of public life and the everyday to provide a framework for inhabiting the complex global condition that is mandatory in Toronto.

Laura Killam
(H.I. Feldman Nominee)
Concordia University, Canada
Collector

The project has two primary objectives: to act both as a climate-machine and a social collector through the exploitation of rainwater.

The climate machine operates by using both horizontal and vertical surfaces to harness rainwater for cooling and non-potable water needs. This rainwater infrastructure works symbiotically with the mechanical systems of the building: as a cold-exchanger with the radiant cooling system, as an air-to-water heat exchanger with the air handling unit, and as a power generator to maintain flow.

These water elements organize social program by creating different zones of activity. The roof-level scholars' residences form a cloister around a collection pool, a publicly-accessible roof deck becomes an

elevated lake, water falling down the side of the building cools and activates the outdoor café and gallery space, and the sunken reservoir leads down to the library, computer lab and outdoor café which surround it.

Laura Killam In this climate it's good to go outside. If you want to go to the café, you have to go outside to get there.

Will Bruder That means you have to put a coat on. And then what do you do with that? And I'm not saying that in the summer you can't open it and make it a breezeway – that's still possible – but in the winter I think you really have got to account for that. If that was a really celebratory stair, that allows for the private side in the plan [as well as] the public side, so that the generosity of coming to the lecture hall…. You've got all the big parts in the right place – almost. But I mean it's just how you allocate that. If you're talking about stairs, why does the stair face the street and not the water? Why isn't that stair facing south so that it becomes the most wonderful place on campus on a sunny February day? You'd also limit the glare off of the waterfall which interferes with the computer terminal use.

Killam It's a good idea, but the problem I kept running into is that because it's quite far down for light to reach, my lightable library space isn't that large.

Bruder Well, you could have glass treads…

Kenneth Frampton I think you could get rid of that stair and it might even be better. When I asked you about this exhibition space, I think I was reacting to this strange arrangement and the relationship of that donut of protected core to the circulation again. I think it's a curious space.

Elisabetta Terragni What I appreciate about the scheme most is that the miniature scale of the project really relates to the larger structures in a way that is much more intelligible than trying to be a big project which could ultimately never stand up to the building across the street. Where you ran into trouble is that you made it so small and tight that you've got these little doors and bathrooms. I think it's a matter of understanding how many people are using the building.

Charles Waldheim There's this Toronto tradition of clear domestic Victorian campus fabric which I think you've gotten. And there's this type from the 1970s of rationalists like Diamond and Myers, super-structural things behind connecting them to old houses, and I wonder if the problem is that you want the water to fall too far. I feel like you could accomplish phenomenally what you want to in your courtyard without having to draw it sectionally.

Bruder I think connecting all the water is an ailment, not a plus. The pristine pool doesn't have to go anywhere, it just has to be up on that roof. When I look at this perspective, I want those to be meeting breakout spaces all around this pool. That is a great room up there, and talking to the Massey College fountain over in the courtyard. To give a sixty foot privilege to that pool… You don't have to cascade off the roof, it's just about the idea of water.

Frampton It's a beautiful project, but this question of editing is important – to know when to cool it to get the most out of the idea. In fact, you cheat a little bit in the model because the exhibition space is great, but we see here an open arcade.

Killam I guess how I chose to represent it is with the doors up.

Bruder On the domestic quality of it, you can't remove the stair because the stair needs to be on axis with the waterfall which needs to tie the cantilever together. I think there is a formality of axial picturesque views that takes it from being domestically scaled to institutionally scaled. So structure could be the thing that gives it a degree of monumentality instead of the water, because I agree that it's too porous and too residential in a lot of its spatial connections. The stair is tricky, the cantilever is too heroic. I think structure, when exposed, could end up giving what is primarily a domestic architecture a different scale and presence. I think the reason why the doors are up is because we need to see some structure.

Glenn Murcutt That stair outside in driving wind and snow could be extremely dangerous. I think that's the place where you could open up in the summer and close in the wintertime.

Marina Dayton
Georgetown University
Interstitial Spaces

Given the program of our building, a city center devoted to the cultivation of cross-disciplinary interaction and research, I chose to focus my project on the spaces in between destinations. It became of primary importance to create a space in which there would be maximum interface, encouraging the sort of impromptu and spontaneous gatherings that typically occur around water coolers, or as people pass each other in the hallways. These interstitial spaces define the architecture at both the scale of the site and that of the building.

The site strategy focuses on integrating the building into the existing network of pedestrian paths and open spaces on the University

2.

of Toronto Campus. I retained the existing buildings on the site and placed program within them, and pulled the main massing to the back of the site, creating a large public courtyard between the three structures which responds to the activity of the library across the street and establishes the city center as a node of community activity.

The building itself is conceived of as a series of de-laminated layers that lift up off of the ground, allowing a fluid flow of activities on the ground plane, while also linking the three structures together. The interstitial spaces of the building are established between these layers. A central green wall marks the main circulation and gathering space and a pedestrian path that cuts underneath the main structure allows people to view up into this atrium as they pass through the site. An occupy-able double façade lines the front of the building and a series of large, sliding pin-up doors open up the meeting rooms to this widened circulation space, borrowing space from it when necessary, and allowing the main façade of the building to register this changing activity.

Glenn Murcutt So that big stair is open to the sky? So water, rain, and snow comes down into this area?

Dayton Should I walk you through the rest of the plan? [laughter]

Dayton This side of the building was conceived of as the more public area, moving up to the meeting rooms, and the kitchen and dining space here.

Kenneth Frampton That's moving up through this green staircase, right?

Dayton They always have the means of moving up through elevators…

Frampton Yes, but why do they have to go to… I mean, they're in the middle of the plan, right? So they could walk up right into the point, can't they? Why do they have to go to the corner to go up?

Dayton The idea was to encourage people to walk up through the central space.

Frampton That's what I'm getting at. It's a little strange the way these central stairs are drawn, they're emphasized in this perspective because somehow they're united with the green wall, as you've shown in plan, but actually if I was to try to read this drawing when you weren't here, I would find it very difficult to know how to engage this stair because you

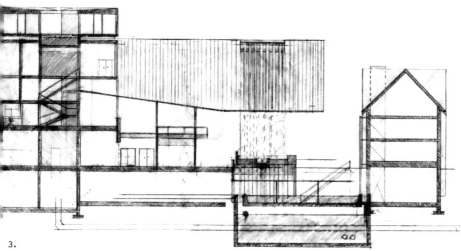

3.

Bruder This is the first one where I get the scale of the problem. I'm thinking of the museum in Frankfurt by [Stefan] Behnisch, years ago. It was this brilliant juxtaposition of the old and new, and that's a great project to look at when you're talking about how the two dance with each other. Those are important because again, city making is about spaces between, not just about object buildings, and to be a scholar in that regard is really a gift to the purpose and intention of the center.

Brigitte Shim
(continued)

don't find it on the ground floor. I think where my question is that you have a quite narrow stair accessed by a narrow bridge, so what is the primary purpose of circulation? It seems to be emphasized by the shaft in the middle and the greenery no less. It becomes very compressed and difficult to negotiate and then it gets underplayed in its representational role as a stair. The idea of having a green stair wall is a beautiful idea, but it's just so compressed there's no room to move. It's a public staircase.

Will Bruder It's further challenged by contemporary building codes. The grand stairs were pre-code, so to even think about the idea in the contemporary setting of a building process of approval and life-safety. It's even more challenging now to answer the charge. It's amazing that your diagram is so simple. It's about circulation and this recessed bar. The drawings are beautiful, the models too, so we're trying to dig in to find these roles. For me, that ramp going down, just to go to the back alleyway, and then giving me this totally inappropriate outdoor stair to get down in

flexible in terms of its public nature. This idea of opening and closing to the public is further explored with the façade system which changes its transparency through out the day, revealing and hiding the activities going on in the building. The operable vertical fins inside the double-façade made up of off the shelf perforated metal panels and transparent insulation panels close at night to prevent heat loss and opened during the day to provide different light qualities inside the building as well as to reflect sunlight to prevent over heating.

Eren Ciraci It's a building that opens and closes both at the scale of the site and at the scale of the façade detail.

Will Bruder Is this the radio station you don't include? I'm asking the question 'why not?' It even makes it more mysterious and right in the scale of the city. I'm just thinking, 'Do we need more spaces like that in a cold place like Toronto?' I looked at your site plan, I don't see landscape, I don't see occupation trappings. And so might that be the best thing you could do for your plaza?

4.

a grand way from the back alley to the ground floor is….

Keith Krumwiede I think it's a beautiful initial urban strategy. It's brilliant. To my mind, the cruciform in circulation is really an opportunity currently under-explored in your project. I look at this section and its hard to recognize that the stair could be the stair moving up, and perhaps even the stair moving down… It's hard to work in the transverse cross-axis along here, so you can then let this green extend. What you're not in control of yet is how to turn, architecturally and experientially, how to turn a body and actually have it turn the architecture… You don't have any transition laterally.

Bruder Let's get back to the urban gesture, with this comment, about how it's a brilliant move. My first blush, when I looked at your drawings, sectionally, I thought, wow, it's really cool. But when your model popped into the context model, and you get down, I really miss the… it's an empty lot. There's nothing as I approach around the edge of the library – it's a void. Would there be some landscape gesture, like a hedge that you can go through, that mimics your green wall behind? I'm looking for a false front, for a stage front, something that energizes and brings the street to me. [That] brings a whole degree of sensibility and then goes through these multiple layers to build the case.

Murcutt That entry is too carved up. To have a section of the ground around the building, just set away from the building, can have the most incredible difficulties bringing walls higher on existing buildings, in terms of waterproofing. It sounds so boring, but Louis Barragan said, 'Any work of architecture that's designed without surrounding in mind is, in my view, a mistake. And when serenity possesses joy, it is ultimate.' I think you're lacking the serenity here. Your entry door is part of another wall system. You get this wedge in the corner, and all of a sudden you feel as if this door is being jammed in the corner. This whole question of entry, the simplicity of it, is overcomplicated, and I am certain there's a very simple solution to this. It may be that the entry should have gone to one side or the other.

Eren Ciraci
Istanbul Technical University, Turkey
Open/Closed

The project explores the idea of open/closed as it relates to issues of sustainability, accessibility and identity. Private and public terraces, courtyards, meeting, dining and office spaces make the building

Glenn Murcutt I think it's a good question…

Kenneth Frampton A question with its own answer and now we can go look at plans!

Ciraci There's one entrance here and there's a separate entrance to the courtyard.

[…]

Bruder I think [your double façade] is bigger than that explanation. The top and bottom, that's where the wind blows in, the water blows in. Why would you go through the trouble and expense of having the north use this technology?

Murcutt Another problem is you've got no insulation for a phenomenally expensive wall.

Frampton To have the same fabric throughout the building also has – it's hard to know which comes first – but I think it has also affected your attitude toward planning the building because when I asked you several questions,

5.

you used the word 'could', 'could be', you know? I think that is regrettable in a way, and is actually an aspect of latter day minimalism.

Murcutt We have a saying in Australia about how 'less is more… or less.' It's the 'or less' [that] sometimes means you're leaving out a lot of things. For example, in your courtyard space you've shown the support system underneath it, but the heating of that during the summer would be phenomenal – if I'm understanding it correctly. I'm sure Toronto gets temperatures of twenty-eight, twenty-nine… thirty… thirty-five degrees Celsius. Thirty-five degrees Celsius with a glass roof and it doesn't appear to have shutters or ventilation.

Ciraci The courtyard will be open at the ground level, and there's also an opening here which helps the ventilation.

Murcutt But you need more than ventilation. In summertime, if it's 35 degrees, shade is the most critical element. To have that shade there is as important as to have thermal shedding. All I'm suggesting is that the roof has to be shaded. Now, you'd be better put louvers on top of the glass. You might also have something in the roof to get the water off. The weight in the winter with snow on it is considerable. Glass expands, a very important element, glass has a coefficient of expansion. So the joints become very important. Then you should start pitching the roof to move the water or snow. Then you should have a thermal detector in it, so that when the temperature inside is down to 20 C you have the louvers coming in to give you 21 C.

Bruder I think you fooled yourself and all of us, by your choice of rendering technique and presentation. Everyone reads a little bit different building. This rendering… it's so… I want it to work. Then I realize that part of what I love in it is that it is some pavilion. Your program is offices banged up against this stuff, right? And you're looking all the way

through the atrium, and we haven't even occupied it. That's not even the elevation we have. It'd be one thing if that's in the elevation. And so it could be seen as the wrong aesthetic tectonic, for the nature of this program and what it's about. You even tell us in your rendering of the system that there's a walkway against that louver system. That's really a cool idea, sort of like Koolhaas in Berlin, right? But then I look at your plan and can't even find where that is. We have the glass out here — why aren't the people out here and the books in here? We're not even going to the edge to make those activities.

Murcutt The scale works very well in that environment. He's worked

6.

out the scale fairly well. I think the real problem is the failure to realize what you're talking about, and how that might then develop in the façade that you've given. Your general strategies are interesting and I think your scale, one of the lowest of all we've seen, is not incongruous with the chapel, the carriage house, or Massey.

Elisabetta Terragni One of the problems I'm having with the project is that I'm attracted to it. I find it beautiful. I think that you have put your mind to how light passes into the building, how it might be reflected, how air moves through it, but you haven't actually thought about how people move through it. I look at the plans and I think, 'Gosh, somehow I can get up there through a mean stair or small elevator, come around here, and then I guess I'm outside and back into the circle.' I can't connect here. This shows a lot of potential for overlap, interlocking. I don't think you need to make a spectacle of circulation but it needs to work for people.

Closing Comments

Elisabetta Terragni I admire how you each approached the project in a different way, typologically — some starting to look at material. I would have loved to see some more in-depth material investigation. It seemed like many of you were really interested in it, and I imagine you were drawn to the project for some of those reasons as well. You're trying to look at the project from three different scales: the city, the building, and the tectonic. Sometimes getting to those is hard, but sometimes that shouldn't be the last thing. Sometimes that can start early, and really inform your project and your approach to the city. You have one more semester, so you've got a chance to do whatever you want before you have to make things really real.

Glenn Murcutt You've got to understand these issues in the same way that you understand driving a car, when you're changing gears and you don't even think about it, that it's so embedded into your thinking that it's no different then getting doors into a building, fire escapes out of a building, to get sunlight in during winter, out during summer, the whole environmental issue should be as integrated into your thinking as space, light, planning strategies, all those things should be no different. But at this stage, you haven't had it, and therefore it becomes the beginning of your learning, so you tend to look at it separately, as a typology perhaps.

Will Bruder Your question is form, skin, what comes first? What comes after? Where's the building, right? Again, this world we live in is increasingly about form. What happens with those cutting machines in the basement here, or your modeling capabilities is form, form, form, form. Well, form grows from that client and that program, from that context… This 'program genius' comment you made, that's a keeper — the genius of programming. Without that genius, the form can never become magic, profound, and memorable because there's this unbelievable disconnect. […] The other issue is that everybody puts parts together… but who makes magic? There's an idea in the process. There's an idea and everyone of those moves that seems so ordinary — like driving a car for Glenn [Murcutt] — there's an idea behind every one of those that builds into other ideas, that eventually the form is all of a sudden something that we've never seen.

Kenneth Frampton The idea can be many things. I think that what you have, to say more about this question of form, is that this question of having in one's mind material coming from the past, the recent past, that has a certain paradigmatic quality. For example, when Glenn [Murcutt] started to talk about the roof, and getting the snow off the roof, and the relationship of the glass to the snow load, and then the question of a sunscreen that could be adjusted or not, placed over the top of this, so you separate between the membrane that is emitting light but also the membrane that is melting snow. That is the kind of paradigm, in relation to atriums, that could be kept in one's head as a not unreasonable way of approaching the issue.

8.

(4–6) Marina Dayton
77 (7,8) Eren Ciraci

Peter Eisenman
Criticality, Hamburg
517a

with Michael Young

Alberti once said that a house is a small city, and a small city is a house. This meant that one could understand the design of a city through the design of its constituent parts and vice versa. As Palladio represented the ideal city of his time (in the Villa Rotonda) and Borromini and Rainaldi represented ideas of the baroque city of Sixtus V, so too have many architects, including Le Corbusier, attempted to represent an idea of the city in their individual buildings. The utopian visions of Ludwig Hilberseimer were a direct outgrowth of the siedlung block, just as the perimeter block represented neo-classical Berlin. But utopian visions of an ideal city died in 1939, and along with this demise, the failed totalizing plans like the Ville Radieuse for urban reconstruction. Instead, city visions became more modest, partial, and realistic, reflecting a new attitude about the problematic effects of previous urban visions. But something else also changed. Alberti's dictum, which had held for five centuries, was no longer valid. The individual no longer had the same relationship to the city; the building no longer prefigured an idea of the whole, thus the critical nature of architecture changed.

In formal terms it is no longer possible to conceive of the city as a continuity of repeatable and extendable prototypical architectural models. The idea of a city today can only be constructed by juxtaposed single fragments. While they cannot be reduced to a general principle, they contain conditions that are generalizable, discovered in the form itself. Thus it is the form of architecture that must be first recognized in the building of the city.

Rossi predicated a conception of the city not on a generic design but on the incremental elaboration of its parts. A new role for architecture, a new aspect of criticality, is a sense of itself as an architectural fragment. While having its own internal economy, it also gives one a sense of the city as a whole (a sense of the city in the logic of the architectural part.)

The studio will investigate an idea of criticality in architecture based on a different relationship of the individual architectural unit to the general idea of the city. It will use a competition project for a new 250,000-square-foot central library for Hamburg, Germany, as a test, or demonstration, case.

Opening Comment

Peter Eisenman In essence it [Pier Aureli's Ph.D. thesis for the Berlage Institute] was a discourse, Jeff Kipnis would say, against the idea of the part to the whole — that is, the building to the city. Alberti would say that a house is a small city and a city is a large house. It was an attack on that idea — that there is this relationship between a building and its context. Basically, this studio was an anti-contextual studio.

Number two, the idea was then how could architecture express itself differently if the terms of the relationship between a building and a city were changed. Pier [Aureli] cited in his thesis about seven or eight examples of projects that seem to do this. Schinkel was one, Ungers was another, Rossi was another, and so on. So the first third of the semester, the students investigated each of these examples. The first was Aldo Rossi. Then I gave them an interesting competition that we were working on for a new library for the city of Hamburg in the Dam Platz — which you can see here is the St. Petri Church. They were asked to investigate the architect, find out what it was that was operating internally that caused the author of the thesis to select the work. They were to use that research, in some way, to answer the program of the competition.

[...]

Another issue that arises in the [thesis] is this idea of the archipelago, coming out of Ungers' study of the green archipelago in his summer academy in the [19]70s. Since this project [had] a registry function, a housing function, and a library function, the whole notion of an archipelago — a cluster of objects — was one of the possible solutions to the project.

Katherine Burke & Christopher Dial
(H.I. Feldman Nominees)
University of Florida & University of Florida
<u>Hamburg Central Library</u>

The Green Archipelago, a proposal by Ungers and Koolhaas, provides the precedent for the understanding of the city as a field of fragments from which groupings can be made based on shared internal logics. The project develops a new architectural figure from fragments maintaining both the formal reading of the fragments as well as the whole figure. A process of differentiation overlays an original contextual figure with an anti-contextual normalized figure. Areas of difference, both additive and subtractive, become unstable, refragmenting the original figure. Refragmentation occurs both in plan and in section. In section, a void space is created as the difference between the additive figure and the subtractive figure. The figuration and refragmentation processes result in an internal logic between the building masses distinguishable from the city as a whole.

Leon Krier [rearranging the model's parts] If I put this like that, how can I know that this is not intentional or that this is not part of the scheme? You could present this scheme to us like that and there is no way that I could say, 'This is not the scheme as it should be.'

Massimo Scolari Yes, because geometrical figures in volume do not have memory, so you cannot tell where they come from. I am not a philosopher like [Jeffrey] Kipnis, but I think it was not very clear about the fragments. When you speak about Berlin, you speak about part of the city which has a sense and a meaning. There are buildings, the road, the façades…types in the sense of typos in Greek, which means something which is cast. So when you go there and you start to speak about fragment, you speak about fragment which is air, void, anonymous matter. This operation does not have any kind of significance in itself. Just like the fact that I decide to put this piece there or there. This is something that makes criticism very difficult — when you start to break away from any totalitarian rule from the very beginning. In general, I think this project is the most coherent of the projects we've seen today because even if I don't agree with the starting point, which is, 'I put that here and I cut a piece there and et cætera, et cætera.' What came out is an agglomeration of volumes, which are pure form without memory and, for that, everybody is very happy because there is no stylistic implication.

[...]

Jeffrey Kipnis Massimo [Scolari], I want to ask you a question. There was a conjecture at a time that the kind of memory you're talking about — [pointing at model] like this shift, or that shift, or the fact that I can see that was something that came apart — meant that you embodied a different kind of memory in the project through the abstraction of process. But in order to do that you had to have at least the implication of an ideal form, hence the geometry, so that shifts and shears and the kind of notational legacy of a process could restore a different kind of memory. So it wasn't against the cultural memory. It was the idea of exploring a different kind of memory. It would stop you from doing what Leon [Krier] did, which is arbitrarily rotating the figures in just any old way. Is that not a kind of memory? My problem with that is I think that kind of research is finished.

Scolari Any kind of memory we are speaking about, we should have.

Kipnis I see, but if I can read those shifts…

Scolari That kind of memory is a contradiction in terms.

Stan Allen [Baron] Haussmann would have been able to create a convincing narrative that says 'yes, you can't move this piece that way or that piece this way,' because he imagined a coherent logic of non-objective form. That's certainly a valid aspiration for a project, but it seems to me that – and I would like to connect this discussion to what Jeff [Kipnis] said earlier – this is the problem with having intelligent people on your jury, because Jeff [Kipnis] killed your project for me by pointing out the difference between this form and this form. You described the process of going from one to the other as normalizing a centered form. Sometimes the sidebars in a jury are interesting. While you were pointing at that fig-

ure three or four, different people said, 'It's a Chinese letter. It's a dog. It's a musical instrument.' In the space of three seconds, there were five or six different analogies.

Scolari Memories.

Allen [to Scolari] Well, I think it's figural. It has to do with figure, not necessarily cultural memory. The fact that the analogies suggested didn't fall into a kind of predictable cultural…

Scolari Yes, but how can you suggest the figure of a dog if you have never seen a dog?

Allen True, true, true. [to Burke & Dial] Two things happen when you normalize it. First, it is not simply quantitative. It's not that there is less information, it's that its information is of a fundamentally different order. Second of all, it becomes in the drawing right in front of us susceptible to being broken down into its subsidiary units, whereas the interesting thing about that figure is that it doesn't necessarily suggest an obvious syntax of how it could be broken down. I'm suggesting that there is a real lost opportunity in this project to triangulate between the abstraction of this language, which, as Jeff [Kipnis] has pointed out, has a long history in this century and a more culturally based memory that would be based on convention and historical memory that could be every bit as rich with it's figural associations without falling into those fragmented pieces.

2.

[…]

Guido Zuliani I want to try and connect what Jeffrey [Kipnis] said and what you're saying now because apart from the idea that you can do a gothic city from a church and I don't know that you can do anything like that. But I want to say something, because this marks an idea of, maybe, a kind of purgatory condition that these projects are in, in relation to the usual pure semiotics. Peter [Eisenman] has always worked where the problem was about a definition in many ways criticizing, transforming, modifying, any kind of possible operation on something that was a sort of ontology of the object – more founded in the ontological nature of the object. These projects, per se, are coming from a relation with the city, from a theoretical foundation of impossible general practice that has the city – in particular the European city – as a background. This relationship between the object and the city is something of an imbrication of one into the other. And these projects all fluctuate in between. They were not really the result of the usual analysis indicated or applied to an object to find a processional form or methodology. But on the other side, they are not dealing with the open space, they are not dealing with the city as a possible background that tells something about the nature of architecture. What Jeffrey [Kipnis] was saying about this other kind of narrative, this indexical narrative, belongs to this isolated object – it is a cultural, self-referential icon. And all these objects aren't dealing with the city, that's why they're all somehow conceptually and theoretically inconclusive. They are stuck in the middle ground in which they found themselves. They don't talk about the object and they don't talk about the city. That's why the problem of memory keeps coming into play. It's not there.

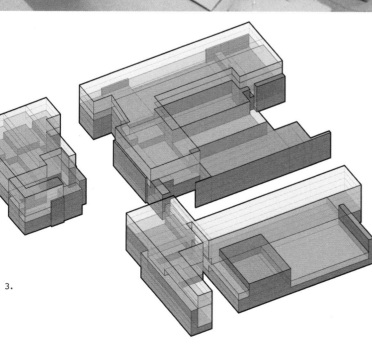

3.

Peter Eisenman
(continued)

Sung Ik Cho & Abigail Coover
Seoul National University, Korea
& University of Virginia
The Line

The goal of this project was to create non-contextual internal and external formal logics through the repetition of a contextual order. An initial formal analysis of Schinkel's Palace at Pariser Platz revealed alternating contextual banding to derive non-contextual logics. This banding emerged from extending the existing edge shifts of the site to create anomalous zones. For the Domplatz site, the same logic was applied. Three edge shifts were extended and repeated across the entire length of the site. Through their repetition the contextual nature of the edge shifts were negated. Two banded mats were created from the contextual edge alignments. The ABCBA rhythm of the horizontal mat based on Schinkel's logic was then offset by the second mat consisting of diagonal edge alignments. From the densest parts of the mat, a fragmentation emerged that formed a non-contextual archipelago across the site in both plan and section. A conceptual inversion in perception occurs in which the ground becomes the figure and the figure, in effect, becomes the ground. As a result, inversions of solid and void occur in both plan and section. Through the blurred relationship between inverted figure and ground, the non-contextual logics emerge.

Pier Aureli The thesis of the studio was to create an urban archipelago, whatever that means. I think that in order to create that you are dependent on some type of interior because the archipelago is always composed with a multiplicity of forms that you can inhabit. To rely on just one form puts the subject in a position where he or she is always at the exterior of that form and I think that can never become an archipelago. It will always be an object. In a way the ground, especially in that stage, could still be an archipelago because it could be in the inside of a form which this bar negates. Suddenly you are always outside which puts you in a very classic urban space.

Jeffrey Kipnis It's good to be reminded of that, because with the gap of the columns…let's say the gap of the columns hadn't been absorbed into that many buildings. But you have the archipelago masking itself as a bar, and that's because you heard some guy loves maps. And I didn't think it becomes thicker. It becomes a weaving…

Stanley Tigerman Or you accept the vulgarity of it and just make it a standardized bar.

Kipnis But how do you do that, though?

Greg Lynn What's today's standardized vulgar bar and where do you go buy one? Don't they have to design it?

Mark Wigley I think they're well on their way towards a dumb bar. No, I think they've contributed a whole series of dumb moves which I applaud.

Lynn [laughing]

Wigley I like the idea of the dumb bar articulating ground. I think, actually, you could win a competition with this.

Massimo Scolari Easy, easy, easy.

Wigley [to Cho & Coover] Get down there and photograph it. You know what I'm saying, right? You could win a museum in Guadalajara if you turn it up on its end, right? It's got that sort of quality. All the detailing would have to accentuate the dumbness which means, in the 'Gulliver' thing, it could be a dumb thing held down by an articulate ground. Archipelago? I don't know what the theory is. Isn't an archipelago – everything linked underneath the water, then it comes up – but the islands are actually connected? This would not be archipelago-like. If it's a dumb building with an articulate ground, this is not an archipelago. You can't go down, come back, and find the same dumbness somewhere else. It's its own.

Lynn Your project is ten years ago. Abandon the problem of facades. And curiously enough, guys like the instructor of this course were out there doing these crazy facades, thinking they couldn't do facades, all because they were deriving the earthwork onto the building. So take DAAP [Library] or something. I remember when Henry Cobb walked in and said, 'Hey, these are spectacular facades.' And everybody in there just wondered like 'what? facades?' But in fact, there was

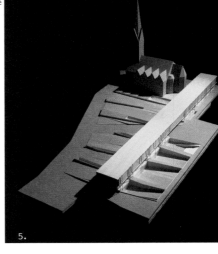

5.

internal logic_**inversion**

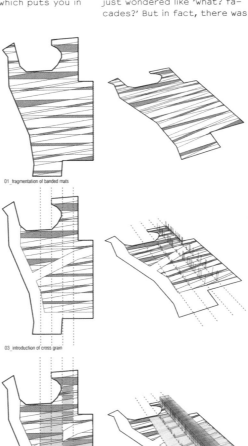

00_overlapped banded mats

01_fragmentation of banded mats

02_fragments cut by road

03_introduction of cross grain

04_displacement of ground by figure

05_first layer of solid/void inversion along fragments

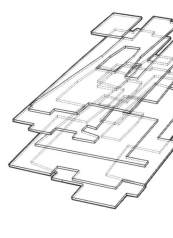

06_second layer of solid/void inversion along fragments

07_final inverted reading of fragmented bands

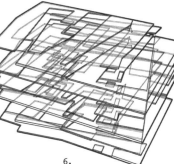

4.

6.

a way of connecting the earthwork to the building mass in a way that still kept the distinction between ground and building. They found a way to do facades. But this seems like a cop-out. It just seems like they don't know what a façade is. They don't understand the problem of façade. They don't understand the relation of structure to bar. And so it's kind of a caricature of what a dumb building would be, but it's not a dumb building.

Wigley That's right. But this jury could strip every intelligent thing out of it to make it truly dumb. Like one by one…

Lynn [laughing]
– – – –

Nathan Hume & Allan William Martin
Ohio State University & Yale University
<u>Registering Difference</u>
– – – –

This project uses the intersection of virtual and real orders to create a series of anti-contextual fragments on the site. The real order comes from the grid of the existing church and the virtual order comes from the grid of the former cathedral. The goal is not to register the grids, but extract only rhythms and alignments to create two frameworks to register difference. Internal architectural elements then exist between those frameworks. The three fragments imply several anti-contextual figures, but individually they register the difference between those figures by using the rhythms and alignments established by the two initial orders.

In addition to alignments and rhythms, shifting and inversion of solid and void also makes the whole appear as a part of a finite larger whole. Piranesi's Campo Marzio establishes operations of symmetrical separation (spacing) and radial distancing (spinning) to reveal hidden orders. It also registers historical information by the creation of figures that mediate the real present and virtual past. Koolhaas' Friedrichstrasse Housing Project at Checkpoint Charlie establishes a plinth of solid ground on the lower level wherein figures of void are distributed. In the interior, a grid becomes an armature against which difference can be registered.

– – – –

Jeffrey Kipnis It's a [Capgras] syndrome. If you see your mother, you say 'it's not my mother, but somebody impersonating my mother.' Everything you recognize, you absolutely recognize and the reason for that is that a nerve between the cognitive facilities and the affective facilities – the limbic system and the frontal lobe – which is broken. So you see something and you recognize it syntactically and semantically, but because you get no confirmation of the sensation you think it's not real. You don't detect that you got the right feeling. You read the missing of the feeling as a feeling. All day long that's what I've been looking for in the work. That would be a proposition of a linguistic based approach to architecture after indexicality. The reason you would erase all traces of the index is that you don't want to invite anyone into an objective frame of mind of reading the project. So you're taking away everything that would cause someone to stop and read the project, but you have to leave enough there to cause some other sensation.

Will Martin We were thinking that this project could be read as a rectangle with the corner removed, or an L-shape with an L-shape within

it, or a solid that's been sliced, but moments like that [pointing to board] would deny the idea that it's sliced or…

Kipnis Well, what's funny is that you haven't done it yet.

Sarah Whiting But it's a frustrated set of readings.

Martin …then you would see the other one and say, 'Oh, that can't be right.' But that was just a postulate.

Kipnis Yeah, but the worst thing you can do. You know, dat-dada-dat-dat [to the rhythm of shave and a hair cut] is not critical – leaving off the ending and possibly frustrating people. That's what the first project did this morning. So the answer, I think, is very interesting – the strategy of constantly creating expectation. It's just a tactic in these projects that I find odd.

Whiting I think this gets at the question of whether you turn the corner – and it's not that you expect a conclusion – but that there's enough there…

Kurt Forster But there should be more.

Whiting …that you're letting them feel something. It's the ability to get close to what you're talking about. It's suggesting that there's the possibility for these different narratives at play that don't frustrate.

[…]

Stan Allen Don't you think that the cuts are too easily subsumed into a conventional modernist language? The point that Jeff [Kipnis] is talking about in a conventional indexical project is that there is a sort of strangeness of the form that triggers the reading. You're provoked into trying to figure out the narrative of how the form got to look that way because the form doesn't look conventional. I think the problem here is that because your forms are very easily understood as the conventional forms of postwar modernist architecture, nobody is going to be provoked to try and figure out why they look that way. I would say there are two things at stake here. First of all, it's quantitative in a certain way. There's too little difference. Is it really consequential that this is very slightly wedge-shaped? In fact, somebody walking by might not even perceive that it's off. Again, that's the notational issue. If [Peter] Eisenman makes a very slight cut, he may also impose an orthogonal grid over there so you'll read that. But you don't set up any normal datum against which the very slight deviations you introduce can be read so that nobody is going to initiate that decoding mechanism that would say, 'Okay, there has been a complex transformation across the grade of this.' Now it seems to me that where this project really is promising is in the complexity. Again, I'm having, as I think many people are, a difficult time reconciling this with this. And this promises a high level of internal complexity within a fairly calm external envelope. If, in fact, you were straddling the line between a project of sensation and a project of indexicality, there may be some interesting play there that comes through the translucency of the glass plane, which we still don't understand how it's meant to be. We begin to get a hint of the internal complexity of this building and that would in turn provoke that decoding process that would motivate someone to think 'well, maybe I want to get inside that building…understand how these roofs work, what these different alignments are, how they're registered on the exterior.' And I think it could be an interesting proposition in terms of triangulating between a project of sensation and a project of the index.

– – – –

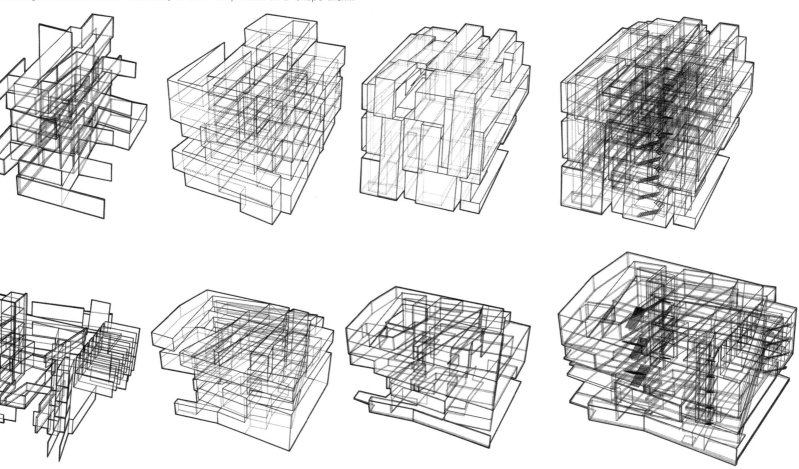

(4,5) Sung Ik Cho & Abigail Coover
(6) Nathan Hume & Allan William Martin

Jeanne Gang
National Labor History Museum, Chicago
519a

As the epicenter of some of the most important labor struggles in the industrial world, Chicago is the appropriate city for the new Labor History Museum, In fact, this museum building will be located on the site of the Haymarket Riot of 1886 in Chicago's West Loop district; the event that led to out familiar 8 hour workday. In addition to the potent content of the museum on an urban site in Chicago, the studio will focus on an approach to architecture that conceptualizes 'making'. This methodology becomes especially important for the design of a museum that addresses "work" because of architecture's inextricable tie to physical labor no matter how technological its design tools become. We will explore the materials of architecture from a number of vantage points including meaning, sustainability, assembly, and craft.

Marisa Kurtzman
(H.I. Feldman Nominee)
Wesleyan University
Museum of Labor History, Chicago

This design explores how museums can harmoniously contain distinct, unrelated program elements within a single volume. The program prioritizes two aspects of labor. Labor's past is preserved in the galleries, while its present condition is addressed through educational facilities.

1.

Because the people associated with these program elements have different goals and needs, I felt it was important to preserve their autonomy yet also encourage mutual awareness. Formally, this is expressed as a juxtaposition of solid spaces, those used according to specific agendas and set schedules, and voids, spaces that operate within Chicago's larger network of cultural attractions and rely more directly on contextual interaction to attract visitors. The result is a pinwheeled layering of solid educational facilities, which create a residual void that is activated as a continuous gallery surface. The program elements are intertwined but function independently.

2.

Fred Koetter I think the building is a combination of the process of arranging the different activities in such a way that they get a sense of legibility.

Ben Pell We've seen a number of projects that were using stacking in different ways to try to force that interaction between the living program and the exhibition program. The visitor can move through the building as if they are moving through this maze. Do you read that?

Julie Eizenberg Do you think you can explain the drawing on the far right?

Marisa Kurtzman I wanted to make people aware of who built the building and honor them at the same time. So this is an interior elevation showing how the building is wrapped with the names of all the workers who built it.

Stanley Tigerman Why didn't you say that in the very beginning? This is actually the most thorough and entirely consummate project that I've seen all day. The one thing I was going to criticize you for, you just took away. At the theoretic, symbolic, and the labor level, I felt bereft. I'm working on a couple of exhibitions abroad – the Intrepid on the Hudson River. How many people have lost their lives building buildings? Not just the American Indian working on a high-rise structure, but the worker working on one to two story buildings. You fall and you die. By embedding it all underneath inside that section, that's what I was looking for. I'm only surprised that you didn't say that at the beginning. That's what gives it a

poetic authority. I have nothing to say critically.

    Pell It's very nice to put everyone's names on the a wall, but it denies the complexity of production and the number of people and parts who play a part in a building. Whose names don't get to be put on there? If that could permeate this building, which is beautifully articulate, then you'd have something less sentimental and more about the complexity.

    Eizenberg The elevator, which is the universal access, is the back wall. How did you come to that conclusion? What's the way to get to the upper level if you're not a stair user?

    Michael Weinstock There's a precedent for that.

    [...]

    Hilary Sample How does this building respond to the environment of Chicago in that you preset the building on a sunny day? And it can probably be fairly simple things like double skins or...

Sunil Bald In this case, it seems like you've taken the educational component of the museum and have worked with the notion of 'how messy is labor?' It seems to me that you're taking the traditional program and encasing it within. It seems like the museum, to some degree, is just being thought of in terms of labor. Then, what about what is being displayed? How is it displayed?

3.

Abigail Ransmeier
Yale University
American Labor History Museum

Assembly of all types played a part in the labor movement, from unemployed masses assembling to wait for work, to lines of employees assembling mechanical parts in factories. As such, this museum can be seen as an assembly line; a continuous flow that displays gallery information while allowing opportunities to assemble, listen, discuss and learn. Gallery exhibits are organized in chronological order and follow a continuous ramp through the building from top to bottom. Organized in one line, the gallery is infinitely flexible, enabling the disassembly of gallery exhibitions while facilitating mass gatherings in areas over-looking the main assembly hall. The museum's private programs are housed in rectangular volumes inserted in the ramp system.

Jeanne Gang
(continued)

Michael Weinstock Skin has all kinds of reactions and all kinds of functions. There's a whole field of work out there dealing with skin. I feel that somebody has been talking to you about tables too much. Attempt to make something a little more than just wrapping the building. It would have been an opportunity to enrich the architecture.

Julie Eizenberg You talk about performance. You've got a suggestion about the safety net. If windows are open, you've got a connection to all the things that workers were deprived of.

Fred Koetter While I think this is an incredible [project], it seems to me that the complexity of this plan is related somehow to this perpetual change, which is related to the stiff box, which takes care of all kind of problems. I think this net structure could be explored more directly.

Ben Pell It's fine that you started out with a fabric and a model. I assume that you were attracted to all those possibilities of folding, etc. And then you realized that you had to give it rigidity, and then you made this leap into 2-D graphics. The things that you talked about in the beginning of the presentation – compression, extension, and aperture – all these things fell away at the end. It's this very non-linear development of the idea and obviously you lost a lot. Compression, aperture, and closure – all those things tended to fall away. You had a tectonic that was rich and had the potential to do all the things but, then you lost it at the end.

Hilary Sample There are many things that I like about your project, and I was thinking about the idea of the transparent building and, as new technologies present themselves, how do you represent it? There is a modern infatuation with the transparent building always being clean. Can this be self-cleaning?

Pell There's also a disconnect with the laser cutter. Here you have this building that is 6 feet tall. Even the way you are working with it – single pieces that are the final product is this flat, non-tectonic product, which is impossible to build. And here you

about people coming to the museum. This is about the sons and daughters of laborers, and the laborers themselves. Not everyone is in white collar industry, and you would feel that there's an egalitarian quality to it. There's a sense of pride and exuberance to it that I think is really commendable.

Sunil Bald Actually, this whole aspect of taking the whole assembly line, which is this linear model, kind of denies or attempts to deny the history of its own making, right? It's a non-self referential system. When you take something like that and begin to coil it back onto itself. Then there are these opportunities to have this self referential system. To that notion of self reflection, it takes on a level of efficiency. I think that's a really strong idea which you begin to get on in your project. When you have this idea that focuses more on the process than the product, then what are the residual effects? How does that create an ultimate system? I guess there's a layering of different system than there are these redundancies. It's those disruptions that make me rethink the process of product and labor and their formal meaning.

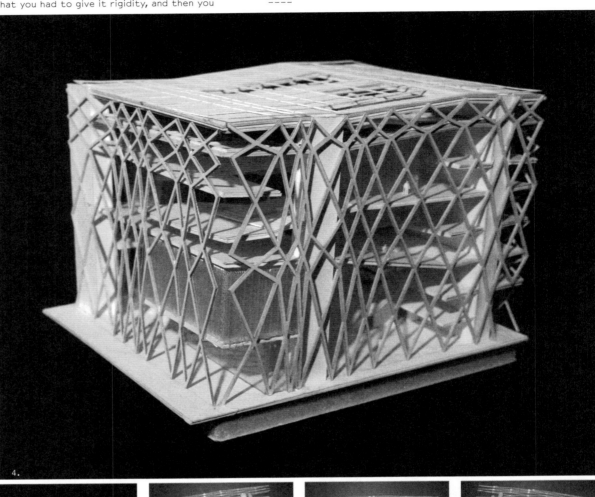

4.

5.

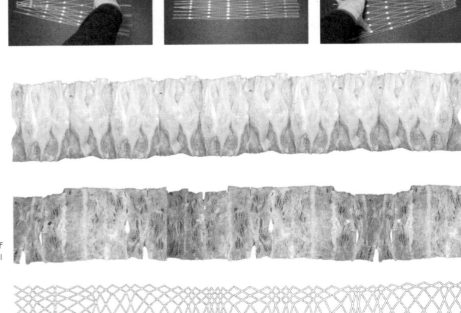

6.

have this project that is trying to express the notion of construction and people assembly. I realize this is a small scale model, but I think it reflects in the final design of the piece. There's an irony in the fact that the image that you selected was robbed from the Internet.

Eizenberg There's this ingenuity about the workforce, about American industry, about employers and laborers which you somehow captured in your section. I feel an emotional connection between employers and laborers that I want to applaud you for because this is

Melanie Domino
Barnard College
Chicago Labor History Museum
————

This project is centered on an exploration of the wall. The intent is to explore different potentials of the museum wall as well as contest the conventional idea of such a wall as a pristine, neutral surface. This approach to the wall is especially topical for a labor museum in which the process of constructing the building becomes part of the story of labor. The act of bending is used to shape the museum walls and create a variety of apertures, displays, and means of circulation that multiply the number of functions normally associated with the wall and modify the visitors' interaction with the wall.

————

Michael Weinstock Most buildings have a kind of redundancy. Redundancy was the word used to shed labor. The steel industry in Britain is almost stripped of older craft skills. People used to follow their fathers. Unions were always involved. So that kind of concept of redundancy might be a useful way to think of a material strategy. When you have a material strategy, you should try to work with it.

Stanley Tigerman I think unions are also becoming defunct because of their general unwillingness to educate. They remain because of the rampant free-based capitalist economy that always was there. And so it's not just about material. It's a labor museum. That's a loaded word.

Weinstock Yeah, I agree. What I found very interesting this morning is the educational component of the museum. And, at least in the European history of the unionism, one of the major functions of the unions was to educate. There's this kind of weird cross-over of things that get stripped away and get reformed and reworked.

Tigerman But she's loaded it up even more by locating it in one of the most devastating sites in the country, where a lot death occurred. The unions attempt to change things. And then, even later, when materials were prefabricated, unions reluctantly hire goons to beat up and kill the other non-union labor workers.

Weinstock So, basically, redundancy is a good material strategy.

Eizenberg There's basically a lack of conviction about the materiality of it. There's reason, but we're not sure why.

Sunil Bald Well, it seems like the plan...

Fred Koetter That model and the drawing...there's a relationship between the places and the building that's produced, which is an incredibly attractive thing. I think you should think about that as a way of looking at spaces.

[...]

Eizenberg No, I don't think you'd question the cost if it had more consequence.

Ben Pell What's interesting here is that this stair puts you into two spaces...let it be stupid. What is the minimum radius? You begin to show it there, but I'd like to see much more of it.

Bald It could come out of a single material and a single move

Eizenberg There's an issue about it being too detached and too intimidating basically from a public perspective and that doesn't give the right message about the idea of labor on the site. It's so closed, abstract, there's no idea of connection or where or who we are.

[...]

Eizenberg Translucent is not clear. There's nothing that lets you see in.

Jeanne Gang Compared to that rendering, that should have translated.

Weinstock I want to defend translucency...

Eizenberg I don't have a problem with translucency in itself, but this is used unilaterally. There is no related to and there is no sense that you should be in context. It's like I'm here, you're there.

Weinstock That's pretty much the union position.

Eizenberg [laughter] It is. That's the problem.

Tigerman Even though I'm decrying the rectilinearity of the core and the toilets, another approach could have taken that replicated it on the inside as some kind of cloister. In the interstitial spaces, the two rectilinear things work out only on the soft corner, so the inside and outside would be ambiguous twice. That would be interesting because that is implicit. It answers the question of section. If you had started there, then the opposition of pieces could have been a challenge for you. I think it's great. I don't remember anything I did as a student that was worth pursuing, and that's worth pursuing.

————

7.

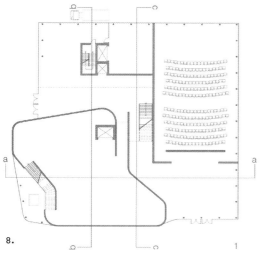

8.

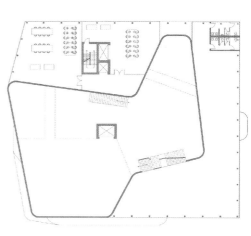

1

2

3

Alan Plattus
China Studio, Suzhou Creek
521a

This studio will be the sixth year of a three-way collaboration between architecture students and faculty at Hong Kong University and Tongji University in Shanghai. This year's studio will follow several past studios in its focus on the Suzhou Creek, an urban corridor that is experiencing rapid redevelopment as older industries are relocated, working class neighborhoods and warehouse districts replaced by new high-rise residential and commercial development, and the Creek itself purged of industrial waste and pollution as its banks are reclaimed for public open space. In particular, the 2005 studio will study a very interesting area just to the east of a major highway crossing the Creek, where several older industrial buildings have been reused as art galleries, studio space and related retail, forming the core of one of several emergent arts districts in China's most dynamic cultural center. The studio will consider the development of several adjacent blocks where traditional low-rise high density housing and historic warehouses survive at the moment, and consider possible redevelopment options in the light of emergent trends in Shanghai development, including the phenomenon of Soho-like arts areas, preservation-based commercial and residential projects, and the development of new public spaces.

Christopher Beardsley & Andrei Harwell
(H.I. Feldman Nominees)
Yale University & Carnegie Mellon University
NoSu: The City That Works

The new Chinese dream is to move to the city, live in high-rise luxury housing, and lead the lifestyle of the wealthy West. This massive urban migration is leading to serious urban unemployment, a problem the government has not adequately planned for. We propose a hybrid development strategy as a model to best develop Shanghai in the near future, marrying the benefits of the formal sector with the social need to manage the informal one. Utilizing derelict land on the banks of the Suzhou creek, we propose a free market version of the traditional Danwei, or work unit. Anchored by a film studio and a school of design, a new urban fabric provides mixed income housing, retail and light industrial incubator space, organized around an improved network of public areas.

Tony Atkin How much of this can you legislate? [How much] do you want it to be an attractor that just brings people on its own accord? Or is it legislated? Do we, say, put a piece of Harbin [China] — that if they want to come to Shanghai, they have to live here? Do you qualify?

1.

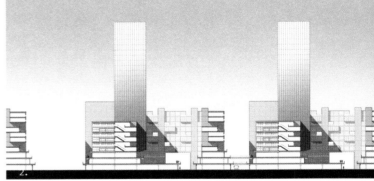

2.

Andrei Harwell If you wanted to come here, you can apply. We want to take advantage of the fact that there still aren't some…

Atkin I think you are on a slippery slope there.

Harwell But it is possible to do something that is not completely necessary…

Alan Plattus Well…

Gary McDonough This is sort of fascinating that the American groups are solving the problem of China by a more authoritarian structure. Do we have any indication that the Chinese are asking for more authoritarian structures? It is really a strong statement that says, 'Let's go back to this kind of totalitarian regime.'

Plattus It's a carrot on a stick.

Atkin Is it?

Plattus Well, according to what was suggested, you need a stick to keep the wealthy classes out of what looks like a fairly desirable new development. The carrot for the migrants is that they can apply and get accepted – they get a unit here and they get access to the school and to the training facility, but your point is well taken. These guys had this discussion with critics all along. To what extent is this social engineering of a not-so-friendly kind?

Christopher Beardsley I don't think we are talking about a totalitarian regime here. What we are talking about is that the Chinese government is already building housing for these people moving to the city, and is subsidizing it, and is building towers and putting people in. What we are saying is that they should be building a better fabric that doesn't just put people in these towers…

[…]

Plattus People would get an apartment and then all their cousins from the countryside would move in.

Diana Balmori Yes, absolutely. That's the pattern in China.

Plattus It is the pattern in American cities as well. If I take you to Fair Haven – we are all dancing around this issue – the answer there is no different than it is in any other country, regulated or not. Usually what it

takes is a catastrophic fire where some building that was zoned for three units turns out to have fifty people in it, and I am afraid to say that it is the same in Western areas as in Eastern areas. It is the question of whether anyone has the guts or the resources to regulate it.

Atkin Well, it is nice to say that the wealthy people who live in the towers would subsidize everything, but they probably wouldn't under the condition that [they] are free not to. The condition is driving…

Plattus The waterfront is meant to be a gentrified, consumerist scene.

[…]

Keller Easterling I am thinking of a few things. I am trying to use Queens as a good example for why this would work and why it would have a kind of vitality. At the same time, I am at war with myself because I am wondering if the class-consciousness in China is even fiercer right at this moment than it is in America. In Queens, there is a mixture of a lot of different kinds of migrations in one place, and there is a kind of tolerance that goes with that. Would there be the same tolerance between the tenants? Another war I am having is the sensitive… that the sidewalk in the sky – not so much the sky – but the double, triple plinth is somehow going to intensify and provide more opportunities for those people who are in the informal economy. I am not quite sure. For me, it lets the air out of it a little bit. Certainly, when one thinks of the words we use in housing projects of the last century, there is a different condition. I would rather see everything on one floor and see more like a stall condition off of that street than seeing it kind of diluted in that way. I don't know how to reconcile my sense of…

Plattus I think the real issue here is, for me, the image of believability and how all this stuff does or does not flow into it. The model is too much about the architecture. What we focus on in that model is the architecture, for better or for worse. But one knows from experience in these cities that things happen. You rarely look up to the architecture anymore. It is really a much more close focus operation and I think that one of the things that is potentially jarring, but interesting, is the co-existence of that kind of very 'nice' waterfront development, where everything is perfectly comfortable, with immediately adjacent streets, and where people are making lots of small things on the street.

Easterling I think it is part of our work to think of any of these things – it may sound cliché – could roll in any direction. If I look at it in one way,

it looks like a good place for organized crime. If I look at it in another way, it looks like a place that can have the vitality of the Kowloon Walled City, or something like it. It could have a kind of self-surveillance that is what I was thinking about. How do we control those subtleties of affect and behavior in something like this?

Timothy Kirkby & Fred Gray Shealy
University of Florida & Clemson University
Junghu Intermodal Transit Hub + Garden Residences

Building upon the need for transit systems along the dense housing in Shanghai, this project stresses the contemporary desire to simultaneously remain local and global. This design is the terminus for a high speed rail line that will link Beijing to Shanghai. Our program anticipates a new influx of business travelers and tourists and seeks to accommodate and distribute them upon arrival at the edge of the city center. Inverting the usually expansive and horizontal urban train station and frontispiece hotel typology, the train station is inserted vertically and surgically over the existing Tibet Road. The road system is decongested and collated. It separates systems of transit and movement onto different levels adjacent to the train station so that the various flows can be read as a transparent section from the street. The main hotel program is placed directly above the train platforms, allowing passengers to access their rooms immediately after disembarking the train. Multi-modal BRT, ferry, and subway lines converge at the station, allowing for rapid and citywide interconnectivity. Adjacent to the station are residential structures that reference the traditional fabric in a high-rise structure. At the center of these structures are

Alan Plattus
(continued)

traditional Chinese gardens that exist on multiple levels, focusing attention visually, culturally, and socially to the inner core of the communities housed within. A few of the hotel rooms are dispersed among these communities to create an emphasis on cultural/ecological tourism, allowing both incoming travelers and residents to intermingle.

Adam Yarinsky A position of a high-rise tower was to bring in light and air. Either you have to radically transform the notion of that, other than a kind of reiteration, or you have to think about the programming of these different items. Perhaps, you have light industrial on a lower level – a kind of multi-level programming – because obviously the housing on the bottom is the least satisfactory.

Alan Plattus I think that there is another answer that you all have been flirting with, but I think it is still uncooked except for this version, which becomes more circumstantial side by side when you put two of these together like this. They acknowledge each other's presence by losing some of their autonomous characteristics in response to the concerns that Adam has voiced. I think in the next go around of this, I can easily imagine you achieving a certain density, but only at a certain cost.

Edward Mitchell It is interesting. I think you guys have done tremendous amounts of work, and I am lucky enough to see these things. A couple of bigger questions began to rise because the nature of the presentation says two things: everything would be pretty much as you thought it always was, and you ensure it through as much technology as you can get in there. I think the question, probably in general across the studio, is 'how is thing going to change?' rather than 'how much do we have to pump into this thing in order to preserve its status quo?'

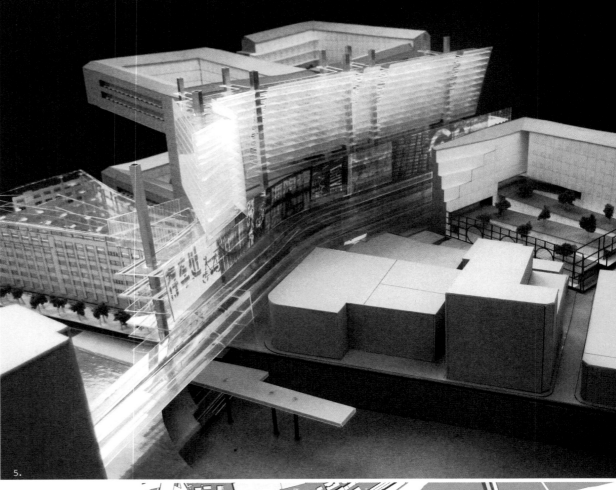

5.

Leslie Lu Getting back to the high-rise question – I can see that particular proposition somewhere close to the water. Right now, the base doesn't seem to engage the creek at all.

Gray Shealy Not formally, but if you remember walking along the site, the creek front of this side is very dense and congested. There is a wall that is about six feet tall. There is a road that is basically the width of the building that put the existing local road underneath.

Tony Atkin I have to say I really agree with Keller [Easterling]. These have taken on a kind of fortress look – bunkers – whereas those models are about the possibilities of opening down to the city area. You have to think about the sun and [how] surfaces reflect. The guy that lives back there has a terrible apartment, especially in a case where you don't actually suggest densities. I would take some density out of it, do something really terrific, and really accomplish something big.

[...]

Joel Sanders I think what is strong for me about your proposal is the kind of relationship between housing and the emerging of apartments and hotels. I appreciate it. What surprises me at the end of the day is why break the project up into orthodox housing here. I think there is something about your programmatic thinking that isn't following through. I think if you had done so, to me, it would not be one, two, three buildings. What it would say to me is that it could be conceived as one project with a menu of different typologies that can co-exist in one community, which I think would also answer many questions one had about light and air.

Plattus Whether they merge or not, they begin to understand that they are part of the same system, which I think is what Joel [Sanders] is talking about.

6.

Sanders It should be really one system. The person who might be elected to be in this room might still want the possibility, not only to get into that garden, but, even at a smaller scale, to have a garden like this. Nevertheless, I think there is still a black and white notion applied to the short-term and the long-term. Is there a way of taking the traditional Chinese garden but updating it and transforming it?

[...]

Plattus I think the confusion in this case is that I think their intention has always been not so much to create a signifier of China as much as a signifier of refuge — a kind of escape, at least a temporary escape — from the chaos of the cities around them. I think the lingering question here for me is — actually, for all the questions at the architectural level — still urbanism. I am not sure exactly what you guys think about this. When I look at the site plan, I think there is a question which we have back and forth discussion on: is this the harbinger of a comprehensive redevelopment of the neighborhood which would sweep away all in its path with a few exceptions, or is there something apparent in typology that you studied in that it is self-limiting? I think it is the potential of this, as something self-limiting or at least self-regulating, that has always interested me, but I still don't know the answer.

Mitchell That's what I meant. What I wanted to ask is what is the limit of the modern project? We are just doing it as limited in terms of language, which is not interesting to me. Even light and air are not thematically a limitation to it, which isn't interesting to me. What is more interesting to me is where you see that limit of solving all the problems through technology.

Michael Grogan & Sean Khorsandi
University of Arkansas at Fayetteville & Cooper Union
Delirious Shanghai

Situated along the Suzhou Creek, a tripartite strategy of mixed use, street-defining buildings wrap the perimeter of the site, transitioning between the primary roads and the site interior. Pinpointing five uses that respond to contemporary issues in China, programmatic zones within the interior were developed, incorporating new and existing structures which relate to each other while maintaining autonomy. The interior zone is intertwined with a raised public esplanade along the Creek's edge. This much needed urban space is envisioned as part of a larger system that will snake along the creek, responding to China's emergent middle class social condition.

Joel Sanders It would seem from your intentions and your diagrams that you're interested in creating a vital urban place in which different constituencies, living, working, all meet and sort of overlap. I want to see how that's manifested in the architecture. On the one hand, I think we've seen it already, right? One could imagine, even more like a traditional city, that constituencies wouldn't be relegated to separate structures, but they could truly mix and interlock within the same building. But instead, you're proposing something that feels very much like traditional models. Housing blocks, right? [It's] almost a kind of community college. I'm very much reminded, as a New Yorker, of the World Trade Center and the West Side Highway in which there is this giant modernist block and there is a community college raised on a plinth. Each of them is oriented around its own public space. I guess I'm puzzled why these typologies, which are so closely put together, are the place to begin. But if we are, it seems like the burden of the merging and mixing is on these sort of public plazas and public spaces to be the kind of insinuating fabric which would allow that all to come together. And that's what I keep on looking for and I'm not looking just in plan, but, particularly, in sections that could express how

all these guys interlock with that surface. And I wonder how the surface migrates and merges and flows through and that's what I would expect, but instead, I look at what you've drawn [and] they seem, again, to be separated. Even your representation itself...

Sean Khorsandi That was a tough thing, actually, in doing this drawing, delineating...

Sanders But the diagram is all about articulating difference and in that way it feels like the traditional model of the city, but I would imagine those pieces in different zones. It's as if you cut and pasted and pulled

them all together, but they're still just next to each other. There isn't that next step architecturally.

Diana Balmori I like the public place, but instead of being a river here, it is, again, a separate piece that just sits there and in a certain way the edge condition is much more effective than these planned spaces, again, separated from the building. So as public spaces, I think they're not the best way to go. The second thing I wanted to point out was that you started with a very interesting story about water, so I thought that in some way you were going to show me how this whole urban development was going to deal with that issue without simply being able to use it as water.

Robert A.M. Stern As Joel [Sanders] pointed out, there's a lack of connectivity to the rest of the city which is endemic and revealed in your drawings — it's a problem, but also, there's so much space — public spaces. I realize it's a very big city, but still, you have to always ask the question about how much space can any part of the city absorb, especially when it's at an edge. In Central Park, in the middle, surrounded by people coming from hundreds of directions, literally. This is an edge.

Keller Easterling I'm wondering if there is some kind of unique urban design document that you can invent that has to do with paradoxes of size. There could be something that you do to that esplanade to overcome the problem of the flood wall. It could be in [reality] actually very tiny, but it would be in perception gigantic. It's like so many parts of a city where everyone remembers that small, tiny little thing. That tiny little thing is the epicenter of something that organizes a gigantic area, and you would do a drawing like that, but it would be your invented urban design drawing, which would almost be like when they show the United States shrunk [down] if we had a rail line...it would be something like that...that would satisfy your sense of some sort of relative scale, but it wouldn't actually be that.

7.

Alan Plattus There are several things that people have said that point to a strategy which is that the representations you all have made are at one level incredibly detailed and convincing, but become increasingly isolated from the original connections that you had envisioned. I think to see this, as with the first Hong Kong group, as part of a network that extends along the creek, addresses some of the issues of where the people are coming from. This is not just a space for the neighborhood behind it. It's got to become a city-scaled space. Western urban designers have learned over time to compress their spaces more and more. Tony's [Atkin] comments also suggest that if you ripped about thirty percent of the overhanging deck off, you would have a step-back condition where you expose some of the spaces underneath, but at the same time, have the generosity of that edge. From my understanding of the generosity of the edge, as it passes through your kind of inner-block fantasy, the whole point is that there is this continuous public space that participates in the unpredictability of each of the pieces of the city it touches along the way and this just happens to be one little snapshot of it. There's probably a missing representation that I wish I had thought of earlier in between the sheer formalism of the block exterior and the literalism of your particular site, which suggests that along the way there are all these other events that might take place.

Sanders Despite the criticism, there is an enormous amount of work and development, and it's incredible. I feel like you know...like you have designed every one of these housing projects. Quite a lot of work.

Diana Balmori &
Joel Sanders
Interface, Shanghai
523a

A book could be written about how architects have re-solved the limit where a building meets the sky. This studio is going to look at a defining line which has received very little attention: the boundary where building and land, architecture and landscape meet.

We will begin by analyzing specific examples of how significant buildings have engaged the landscape. Then we will apply our research to a current project slated to be built in Shanghai, a scenario that will provide a lens for examining these issues. The program is a park with a theater located in a very urban well-established section of the city, the French Quarter. The city's program asks for 80% of the land to be a park and 20% to be a theater that will stage London plays and Broadway musicals in Shanghai. The client, Le Sheng Li, is a well-known developer who has previously built the Shanghai Grand Theatre and the Pearl TV Tower, the icon of modern Shanghai.

But why choose this program to investigate the intersection of land and building? Typically, theaters tend to be conceived of as freestanding objects whose opaque walls shelter a series of interiorized functions – auditorium, stage and back-of-the-house facilities – spaces that are indifferent to their surroundings. This project offers a fresh opportunity to rethink these conventions. Our goal will be to design convincing proposals that allow for rich spatial and programmatic overlaps between theater and park while at the same time coming to terms with those programmatic and technical requirements that resist material and spatial continuity.

Christopher Kitterman & Maxwell Worrell
(H.I. Feldman Nominees)
Tulane University & Oklahoma State University
Datum

This project examines the relationship between architecture and landscape. Sited in the dense, ultra-urban setting of Shanghai, the program brief required our studio to engage two seemingly different programs – a Broadway style theater within an urban park. Using a principle derived from our trip to China documenting and analyzing the gardens of Suzhou, we focused on the concept of datum. Our response to the Shanghai site offers a potential unrealized in the Chinese gardens: architecture can now exist above and below the horizontal ground plane of the cityscape connected by a series of threaded pathways that move between these two zones making both earth and tree habitable. Programmatically, the mass of the theater resides below the horizontal datum of the ground plane, while the lighting studio and public amenities reside in the tree canopy.

Charles Waldheim Compared to where it was at midterm, it has gotten so much clearer. One of its strengths is the idea of being above and below the canopy of the trees… the way that they organize the plan and the structure is very clear and strong. And as you develop the building project it has become even more strong and fully evident, so that is great. There is a bit of a question in my mind about the course for the trees question. That is to say, do you have a central clearing or not? I feel strongly in both ways. But I wonder if there is some merit to breaking the opening in the middle of the site and giving somewhat of a different experience there because the different realms in the canopy, below ground and on the ground, are quite distinct, but there is a lot to of each of them. And no matter how much variety there is within, it is an enormous site. I guess I am talking myself into the idea that there is some kind of void in the middle and some differentiation in there in terms of hierarchy. What I appreciate is the fact that you develop this kind of fly space and given it a prominence and scale that has some other image attached to it and that you get people hovering in that kind of landscape space. For me, the question where the glazing goes is to be discussed, but if there is anything to be criticized, it is that you so greatly exaggerate the vertical sectional separation; I wonder if you may not be overstating that.

Kent Smith I'm a huge supporter of the project because you've actually dealt with the trees as an architect. I mean, they are beautiful. They are operating as buildings almost… above the action of the landscape. And then the relationship of how you move from the project down and carving in to the ground, I actually think, is great because it clarifies the ground plane, how one moves from one to the other and come up above it. I also really like the certain notion of reinvestigating [the history of] Shanghai. Now you are participating in that discussion which goes beyond the particular site. The potential is great. I love the way it begins to skirt over other conditions and it is never just a pure extrusion above the ground plane. All of those potentials are encoded within slivers and shifts that are barely missing each other and I find that is a lot of what Shanghai is about. Just producing the potential of inhabitation without going in to every little thing and leaving it open for inhabitation to emerge through it's use is amazing. This is a very, very strong project. I want to congratulate them.

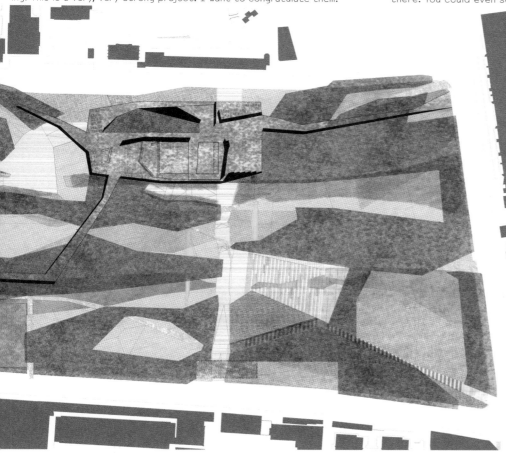

Valerie Smith I love the idea of this carving. To be able to go deep into this underground plaza linked throughout and come out on the other side and up to see this incredible view of the city is here so amusingly rendered. The only thing I may be just a little bit confused about is that because it is so strongly about carving down and coming up, I am wondering if that is then obscured a little bit by this canopy of trees, or maybe it is just something that has to be worked out in the model.

Joseph Rosa I like how you thought about how architecture occupies the landscape and how it works spatially and how you describe getting into this space is rethinking the procession into a theater. This is where you could actually construct a theory. The experience is part of the arrival there. You could even see down the road where the line of trees in the future will form a well in the site.

Waldheim The canopy has this interesting effect of contextualizing the building. It is huge and yet somehow it is completely in the context. And you've also resolved the edges using the fabric of the trees as if they were building fabric.

Fred Bland So yes, yes, yes, yes, and yes. Why? Let me just add as an old urbanist who has over the course of a 40 year career now removed – literally torn down because they were hurting cities so much – a second layer of a city. Let me just put a warning out there. I think it's wonderful what you've done, but getting this experiential quality which this is about is wonderful and I think it is a unique way of seeing Shanghai, but all who are designing cities have to be very careful about making a second layer because it almost never works. It dilutes the energy that we want in a city. Very few cities have that energy. That said, it might be said that Shanghai has both the energy and the density that requires it, so if that's true, I would have liked to have seen a plugging in of that second level into activities that are more natural, even maybe flying it across the street.

Matthew Byers & Ross Smith
Colorado College & Wesleyan University
Pathways

This project evolved from a visit to the ancient Chinese gardens in Suzhou, China, where we observed that they function today not only as a garden environment, but also one that could conceivably support retail. Our site in Shanghai was situated in the middle of a vibrant retail district. We felt that while Shanghai needed a large green space, we did not want to remove the existing retail fabric. Therefore, our project became a synthesis between theater spaces, shopping and parkscape, with shopping along

3.

the perimeter of the site, and a park experience in the core. The pathways that navigated between these elements became the focus of our project, as evidenced in our sections.

Anuradha Mathur You actually seem to enjoy the site. Even though you give us the partition, you keep all the program, but you keep it simplistic. The bigness of it is almost like a camouflage scheme and it all becomes part of the landscape. I am wondering if there is the possibility of improvising in starting to have those kinds of events that are open-ended, and you create those grounds where the light hits harder and you can let street carts to come and go. You have created a place where people are sublimely walking through it – a large open territory which can be appropriated. So despite all the programs that are fit in, there is still a lot of possibility on the surface. I enjoy the project if I see that possibility, but not just as a formal possibility.

Fred Bland I wonder why the bamboo does not slice all the way across to connect the public space. It just seems like there is not yet – maybe it's just

Diana Balmori &
Joel Sanders
(continued)

4.

the scale of the model – but there's not a kind of multiplicity in how you might move in the site. A site this big needs to have an idea of two parts: one commercial and the other cultural. It just seems like it needs some counter moves to help me through. But the plaza is interesting because it suggests that it does work both ways. I can imagine how I can move in this direction or that. And the rest of the park is much more linear and directed without that multiplicity.

Joseph Rosa Looking at the theater, people can pass it without even noticing. So in a certain way, it is a sum of a lot of things. When I am looking at the scheme, there are two buildings and there is the landscape. They are not occupiable moves, but they are buildings demarcating the landscape for which there is a garden and vast parking between it. In some of the other schemes I think they were pushing the notion of what the amphitheater could be. I see you have created a lot of interesting kinds of theaters, but when I look at the larger building here it is just a conventional thing. I'm seeing an interesting building but a normative theater type.

Alan Plattus What I admire is that having gone to the step to say let's not abandon the street, saying that we can strengthen the park by holding some of the street edge – keep it's activity. You would then be able to allow yourself to continue to be a little bit conventional in that respect, like saying what happens to those restaurants now when they back up into the park. And there is a lot of precedent of that in this neighborhood in Shanghai because a lot of those old villa compounds have been turned into entertainment restaurant areas and one of the lovely things about them is that you can eat in the garden. So rather than layering the whole back of the restaurant with flower market, you find a lighter place for the flower market, but many of the restaurants would have a street front and a garden side. You would take that urban convention of street to garden very seriously in that respect. I do think you have to get through this front-back issue. I think you can't back into the garden.

Charles Waldheim Would you go so far as to suggest looking at the extent of the fabric? I can't stop from wondering about doubling the existing buildings framing the entrance to the theater complex. Why couldn't this fabric on the other side also begin to embrace partially considered selection of the curated elements of the built fabric that is there.

Plattus Sure. I would say that. In fact, the world of French concessions have these big wall compounds, but now they are opening up – they are becoming small hotels, they are becoming restaurants. There is a whole other layer of urban experience that penetrates the walls.

Waldheim Like the Yale campus.

Plattus Exactly. At it's best, if you can actually do that. But here you could imagine doing a pump roll of two different kinds, one of which would be along the street in a conventional sense and one of which would cut across the watch through these mid-block experiences, since these blocks are so enormous.

Kent Smith There is something here which I think is quite beautiful. You pick out the very large conditions that we have already mentioned, but I really want to talk about the details of the project. When you look at this diagram you start to understand how the terrace condition starts to operate with the theater, like the scale, and how might you even start to inhabit this. Then you begin to move out of this notion of theater just being a theater and potentially having multiple scenarios. And then the conflation that I find very fascinating about Shanghai is how the public can also operate privately in particular moments. Then the inversion of that as the day or the week unfolds. It would be very fascinating for me to see how to engage and bring people through the project. The landscape itself can actually move up and inhabit the entrance itself so you break down the scale between the city and this huge wall.

Joel Sanders Looking at the development of the scheme – these are some of the earlier models and it was really about a giant shopping center – so the fact that you kept your basic sensibility about the site, but at the same time really radically rethought it, deserves much credit.

5.

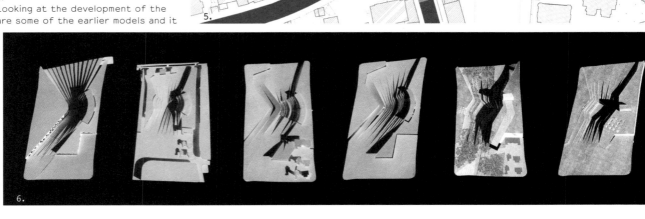

6.

Naomi Darling & Frank Nan
Princeton University & Columbia University
Parallax

Our scheme explores the theme of reciprocity of view-framing between architectural and landscape elements, and of spectatorship between the performers, theater audience, and park users. By reinterpreting an element of the classical Chinese garden: the double-corridor/garden wall, we device a series of architectural and landscape walls that intersect and overlap to define various programmatic components and to choreograph non-axial routes to engage the user. Movement through the park and theater complex produces its own theatrical experience, as serendipitous views, both static and cinematic, constantly conceal and reveal the various park and building elements through the layers of architectural and landscape screens.

Fred Bland I'm wondering, in the development of the theater, you ganged the stage houses in the back and you put the lobbies separate from one another and spaced out in the park, which is a perfectly plausible diagram. But the opposite is also plausible, where you create an excess of energy that the lobbies create and compile the stage houses with that. I was just wondering if you really thought through that or if it was more of a form-making exercise.

Naomi Darling The reason we decided to go with the stages together was really intrigued by this idea of connecting with the outside and creating a larger theater space that all three spaces can tie into. Ultimately, that seemed more interesting to us than a lobby space.

Joseph Rosa I was just looking at your earlier study models. There is just something visceral that I really like about the topography gone natural, or constructed natural. I like the idea of this building, sunken and inserted under the landscape, the other kind of folded-in of gradings. What I like about that is this kind of visceral push to the landscape where the building effects it. I kind of like the existing building. What is interesting is that maybe no one would address those buildings. There are some things that you just can't really cover up with trees. I'm not sure of

some of these elements and this idea of transparency with this layering, which is very strong, but if you think about the buildings that have been successful in that way or landscapes that play with it, you have a very big landscape. I just think visually the axes or some elements have to be grounded. Some of them are going to be vistas in the landscape and that kind of vista is different from a building that is transparent. Thinking about a building that has been tattooed or etched is still about the container. And you notice those containers that Herzog & de Meuron do are very normative. It's the banality of the container that's etched. So you have these complex forms with that — it doesn't dissolve the building as much. It makes you more aware of it instead of allowing it to actually disappear on the simpler gestures. It's all about the view you see but which you can never get to. And that's kind of what you are trying to do here and that's great, but you almost have to edit yourself back a little bit to allow all of this strength to come forward.

Alan Plattus You've made this very elaborate, remarkable viewing mechanism and it almost doesn't matter — something totally banal, twisted, and turning into something quite wonderful because of the fracturing of the view. And I think in a way the energy is, in your case, all in the side of making the machine — the viewing machine. And then it becomes the landscape. I don't think that is right or wrong, but I think you should be aware of the difference between that and what you see in the classical garden, which is both the making of a machine, but then the equally careful, if not more careful, composition of the view in all scales. I wonder if there is not something fundamentally honored about your position as opposed to the classical position where the emphasis all falls to the side of the mechanism, which is a kind of an autonomous machine for viewing and is self-referential. What you are viewing from other parts of the viewing machine is other parts of the viewing machine. And that might be, whether you intend it or not, the statement about where we find ourselves as opposed to making the seen or seeing. In that respect, the empty space in all these cones of vision becomes kind of a symbol. It's always kind of anticipated, but never a realized performance on that stage because it is about the theatricality of it more than it is about the literal theater of the performance center.

Anuradha Mathur I'm struggling with whether if, in fact, you found a way of seeing and you could go anywhere and see things, you should have more control of those moments and more release of transparencies. I don't actually feel it as a cone of vision. It's about moving through these containers.

Rosa I just think there is something about the points that could be more controlled and allow the gesture of what you are making with this building in this landscape aware of that sandwich between each other.

Bland You are saying something different that is derived from the classical Chinese experience and it is made very modern by you. You're saying let's take it and prescribe the paths and reveal along the way a series of special revelations, if you may. I think the thing is incredibly rich.

Ali Rahim Landscape operates temporarily. The project isn't going to end up like that. How many years is it going to get the level of foliage in your renderings? How will it begin to shift? Maybe in one year you have a particular set of views and five years it shifts and in fifteen years it is completely different, and that's how your architecture begins to operate within them. As opposed to a final landscape, you can begin to understand the potential condition that may shift how one begins to operate in lieu of the architecture. I'm just wondering how you will begin to negotiate shifting terrains and things changing through time. You begin to understand how the architecture might be able to alleviate all the potential movements which can lock in light, but also operate the section — particular ways of moving through and in the whole, really responding to the relationship between the interior and exterior as well as through the project.

7.

8.

ADVANCED STUDIOS, SPRING

Greg Lynn *Giant Robot, Indio* [512b] *with* Mark Gage; Demetri Porphyrios *King's Cross Central, London* [514b] *with* George Knight; Richard Rogers, Chris Wise, *&* Stuart Lipton *Some Unheard-of Machine, Stratford City* [516b] *with* Paul Stoller; Will Bruder *Live/Art, New Haven* [518b] *with* John Eberhart; Stefan Behnisch *Palast der Republick, Berlin* [520b] *with* Ben Pell; Frank O. Gehry *Music Center Studio, Los Angeles* [522b] *with* Gordon Kipping; Sunil Bald *The World Social Forum, Sao Paolo* [524b]; Keith Krumwiede *Edgemere/Edgeville, New York City* [526b] *with* Patrick Bellow, Jonathan Falkingham *(Urban Splash Development, and* James Axley; *Thesis* [599b] *with* Keith Krumwiede *(coordinator) and* faculty.

Greg Lynn
Giant Robot, Indio
512b

with Mark Gage

The studio will be organized around the urban and architectural transformation from the management of sound within a spatial chamber to the diffusion of sound in a dynamic and immersive atmosphere. Previously, in the 70s, there was believed to be a shift from music pavilions that were monuments to mechanisms. This has been argued as a shift from a mechanical to an electronic paradigm.

Instead of a concert hall, we will be designing a permanent architectural focal point for a summer festival. Our studio will begin with the giant robot as a paradigm, or more appropriately as a mascot. Instead of abandoning monumentality and form in favor of movement and electronic mechanism, each student will attempt to combine spatial focus and intensity with mechanical and/or electronic pyrotechnics. The brief will ask for the creation of a permanent focus with architectural qualities and merits commensurate with a monument. The annual cycle of use will vary drastically as once, maybe three times a year hundreds of thousands of people will converge on it. We will define an architectural problem that is neither monument nor gizmo, but something else that can incorporate both positions. They may or may not move, but they will certainly be robots.

Not that great concert halls have ever been designed this way anyway, but nonetheless, the derivation of the design will be through neither acoustic nor functional criteria. Instead, we will begin by looking at a half a dozen canonical precedents beginning with Garnier and from this analysis each student will pose their architectural ambitions for a giant musical robot. The spatial, structural, volumetric, figurative, urban, landscape and material ambitions of each student will be stated very early in the studio and in relationship to a canon of architectural precedents.

Fred Scharmen
(H.I. Feldman Nominee)
University of Maryland
<u>Giant Robot: Crystal Voltron / Indio, California</u>

The project is based on research into technology, motion, and aesthetics, drawing on diverse sources: the mood manipulations of set design and 19th century Romantic painting, the formal methods of graffiti art, and the bio-technical fetishization of Japanese animation. The brief for the project asked for a transformable concert facility for a yearly festival, the major goal being the integration of spectacular motion into music performance. Giant Robot: Crystal Voltron is a series of low metallic hills that use a language of cracks and fissures to expand and unfold into a media tower with two stages, pulsing with sleek menace.

Sylvia Lavin I am just going to put this in terms of opinion. I am completely uninterested in linking the formal problems of problematic fundamental sets of issues in terms of the performance and the origins of the robotic. If you think of the relationship between architecture and machine, one of the discourses – it's not the only one, but it is in

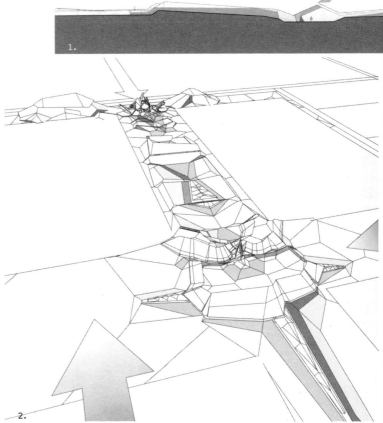

my opinion the most appropriate for an architecture program, a design program, not an engineering program – is the one of the aesthetics of the machine age. I don't really think there has been a direct confrontation with the third machine age in architectural terms. There has been a secondary one, and you guys are doing it in terms of with the integration of media, but to try to work with the new status of the machine, to move away from equating movement with the 19th century to new forms of machine that mimic biological behavior and have a whole different formal oncology, not morphology, but the formal oncology. Somehow I feel that we'll be spending all day figuring out where the joints are and whether they are working and whether they understand the difference between an automaton and a robot. I don't think we can get to whether they have done their job, which is to imagine a new way of understanding the relationship between architecture and contemporary technology and the culture it produces.

Fred Scharmen Do you think there is always nostalgia for other robot cultures, too?

Lavin The question you got asked before by Peter [Arnell]… what is the state of contemporary robot culture? What is the broad nature of contemporary robotic culture? It is still relevant.

Peter Arnell It's the weirdest thing. Maybe we find out that that culture has a certain limit in scale. It's possible, right? Maybe we find that thing is a kit of parts – that it's disposable. There are a whole lot of things to find out. I think at any given moment of time when any true transformation took place in any built environment, it took place because of a great understanding of how the material could be structured, whether it be the pyramids or the Eiffel Tower. It was a great representation of that movement of time, so I don't know whether to remove it would be necessarily right. But when we start moving big things like this, I guess the question is what message are we giving? What message is being heard in this project? I'm curious about that. Don't you think there is an obligation in a funny way to understand moving parts that aren't in architecture today? Since it is a stage and the links in my mind between performance and performances as a building involved in a performance, it's unlike someone showing up. It has two areas. One is a destination. The other is what happens when it's not a destination and doesn't have a zip code. I guess that other part of the question is really important. I don't want someone to figure out the joints and the engineering or any of that, but I think there is a bigger question. It almost seems like borrowing a language, an attitude, or a culture too soon without some knowledge. But the biological thing and where it came from and the cloning of attitude, sensory, experience, movement, all of this into robots is a big topic. So cloning a building into robots hasn't been done yet and that's the subject that is interesting.

Jeffrey Kipnis In Scientific American this month, this is the latest thing of robot engineering introduced by the top Japanese robot engineer. It's all about why robot engineering is so compelled to erase the consequenc-

Nathan Hume
Ohio State University
Reconfigurable Spaces

The project creates a porous enclosure capable of creating outdoor rooms for musical performances. The rooms exist separately as performance spaces while maintaining a larger relationship across the polo fields to create an overall complex with pockets of food, beverage, and restrooms buried in the landscape between the stage structures. The skeletal structure creates views through the stage to the mountainscapes while providing reconfigurable spaces for micromesh pillows containing lighting, sound, and projection equipment. The enclosure above the crowd allows for the unfurling of fabric across the field. The pulsing movement of the structure creates a wave effect as the fabric billows over the crowd. At night embedded lights within the fabric enhance the site as it becomes illuminated by these pulsing fields of lights.

Jeffrey Kipnis I'll tell you from my point of view on this project, not as a critic, but as a theorist. This is the most interesting image I've seen all day. These forms and those motions are entirely different than any of the

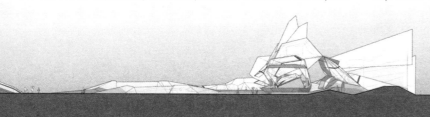

other motions we've seen all day long. This thing is falling and has a different kind of motion and these forms have a different... I'm very interested in it.

Greg Lynn You know what's funny? We went to the [Hollywood] Bowl while it was off-season. Everybody went there and there was an incredible technical zone. It's the coolest thing we got to look at. It's proto-robotical. We got there and there was an empty metal ring — none of the lighting. It was totally dull. The medium that we work in — which I am getting more and more frustrated in — doesn't let you get the stuff in it when you are designing it. I think if you just get it up with the lighting and the sound rig and the technical stuff, it gets much more interesting, but it lacks the level of tectonic stuff.

Peter Arnell I think when you were speaking you were referring to using the software as a real tool to study, develop, advance, rule, be in it, go around it... Another thing is the seduction of a presentation. They are two separate things, right? I mean, I assume that you guys know how to operate software. Then there are great artists that operate software and then there are technicians. When you speak of this [technology] to develop and understand it is another thing...

Hernan Alonso-Diaz Before we turn around, I love this project — not in terms of the way the studio has been framed, but in more conventional terms.

4.

This project has a lot of interesting operations with the change of the scale, elements, articulation — there is a whole series of changing aspects. I think it is working really well at this level, but not in terms of the raw move-

es of the present engineering world. I don't think you represent a wrong ethic, I just want to understand that we're discussing an ethic that is at least open to debate.

Neil Thomas But isn't it true in saying that they are doing that because they spent the first twenty years to get to that point — to deal with the thing they now want to erase?

Lynn Let me get you guys on the same page because the debate is wrong. We don't know what a moving stage looks like, so we don't know how to simulate one.
----

ment. This one to me is way more sophisticated than any of the ones we've seen today. I just want to say this because the conversation has been more general and I just wanted to point this one out before we turn out. It's not so much discovery and not really that new, but it's very interesting in the technical control. It solves many of the problems in the studio.

Sylvia Lavin But to be fair, Hernan [Alonso-Diaz], you have to admit, especially coming from you, if you call that one familiar [pointing to another project], then this one is very familiar.

Alonzo-Diaz This is true, but this one for me is very well done and that one has a lack of sophistication.

Greg Lynn
(continued)

Lynn That's because all you see in architecture is an interesting massing. I think that I'm the same way. We've got to get past that because too much of this is just stopping at the massing. We have to get past the massing.

Kipnis Are you kidding me? Every SCI-Arc installation in every gallery in the world is brick bark at best. You build a frame, you shrink-wrap it, you put roses in it, and it's done. It's not true that...it's been warped through so many times at representation scale and at its first modeling scale that it is tedious...

Lynn Look. I think if you show that image to the Tolett Brothers [pointing to perspective], they're going to see Coachella [Valley Music Festival] in a way that they don't see other things.

Kipnis If all you want to do is satisfy a client with an exciting image, you shouldn't be at Yale with us talking about your work.

Lynn No, no. It's not about satisfying the client. No. I'm just saying that that's an indication that you're talking to a broader cultural sphere. I think Hernan [Alonso-Diaz] is right. Once you start to build this architecturally, it's much more frustrating than some of the others.

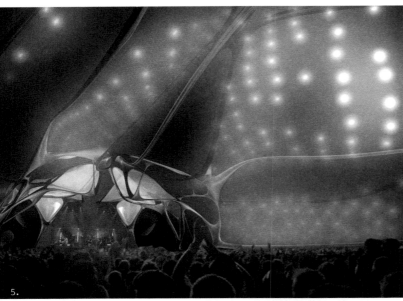

5.

Armand Graham
Princeton University
Giant Robot

The studio begins with the giant robot as a paradigm. The robot will be a permanent architectural focal point for the Coachella Music Festival in Palm Spring, CA. The architectural problem is that it is neither monument nor gizmo, but something else that can incorporate several positions. The proposed robot exploits the spatial and animate qualities of the fiddlehead fern. The fiddlehead elements are used for shading, spectacle, and to transform the structure from polo to Coachella configurations. The aesthetic ambition is alien and futuristic.

Andrew Zago There is a question of how long these [stages] will last? Will they last for the next thirty years?

Armand Graham I think it lasts as long as the evolution of the festival. Right now, with the site, they will need to create a new venue somewhere else in ...

Greg Lynn Don't be lame, Armand [Graham]. Answer the question as best as you can. Don't be a student. Be an architect.

Graham Yes, I see it as disposable.

Lynn Thank you.

[laughter]

Frank Gehry There is kind of a faceless quality about the imagery. I know the computer smoothes over a lot of stuff and they clearly don't have enough time to design all of the joints, but this is at a scale where there would be joints. There would be connections that would inform it and maybe take it to a point where Jeff [Kipnis] eluded to – where it would become more real as a built thing rather than a plastic toy. I just don't know where you guys go with that. But I think when Jeff [Kipnis] raised the issue...will it be something that's included?

Lise Anne Couture I want to pick up a little bit about motion graphics. Even though there is a spectacular quality to some of these images, there is kind of deadness with the project and the absence of the temporal. The way you represent your projects, you are using it as a representational tool and not really something where you are stopping along in the process and analyzing it. It's very open and closed. I don't know why one wouldn't consider the intermediately stages or think of the permanence between open and closed. Maybe there is something that goes so slow that there is constant change. What are the kinds of spatial effects and how will they vary over the course of time?

Sylvia Lavin I have to defend the plastic toy. The plastic toy is a new kind of reality that totally suppresses the joint. If you go back to the Italian design of the [19]60's, a huge amount of Italian engineering went into the suppression of the joint through plastic.

Gordon Kipping Not at this scale.

6.

Lavin I understand that, but I don't want to push it back in the direction of a mechanical, known model of motion. I think the models of motion that are here are not adequate, but I wouldn't push them that way. I would try to push them in another kind of way. We are not being sold on these kinds of motility yet. I am also really surprised that the site was not taken advantage of. Right now, we have two issues. What is the relationship between the potential movements of the object and the performance itself – not beforehand, but how does it work after the performance? The other thing is the spectacle of the crowd and making the crowd dance and choreographing it in a different kind of way. On some levels one would be putting them on some kind of train track. That would be the easiest and the dumbest way to do it.

Hernan Alonso-Diaz To pick up on that, it seems like you can divide the argument that you two are doing two parks, but there is a lack of understanding with the evolution of a [stadium] species. If you track the Rolling Stones tour over the last ten years, their aesthetic is much simpler while they keep having bigger and bigger screens. You would expect them to reconfigure the stages with the experience. They are going out of their way to incorporate their audience. They build the stage so that they can be right in the middle of the audience. How does reconfiguration change the experience of the audience? You would almost have a musician at every stage – at opposite sides of the stage – where every part of the audience has something. These are the issues that all of you need to show and represent.

Frank Nan
Columbia University
Giant Robot

The main theme explored in this project, a design for band shells and event tents for the Coachella Music Festival, is the potential of transformation between a two-dimensional surface to a volumetric enclosure. Taking inspiration from paper folding, I worked mostly in physical models to study the possibilities offered when ground

surfaces might transform into walls, or when walls could become canopies, ceilings, and etc. The final scheme is a tent structure whose skin, supported by a series of vertebrae-like arches, can extend in multiple positions to create different types of enclosure. Depending on the time of the day and the type and size of the performance, the structure can function as private tent, and semi-open canopy, or a giant backdrop for a large scale performance.

Jeffrey Kipnis My criticism is short and simple. This studio is to architecture what the comet was to dinosaurs. On the other hand, when the comet wiped the dinosaurs out, a new species emerged and I think you may be at the beginning of it.

Anand Devarajan One of the most interesting things about this, besides the fact that your dealing with the spatial conditions around the site, is that you have actually tried to multiply the different types of configurations. It allows you to take advantage of the current events along with all of the different people coming together in one space. It seems like it has this plurality that Coachella [Valley Music Festival] seems to have rather than being one overarching typology.

Peter Arnell The economics of this says that you want to invite in sponsors, so it seems that the things that are constantly moving go away. And if you're looking to book concerts, the artists tend to go to where they have the better facilities, or the facilities that allow them a greater

trip, so to speak. So if you're at this one [pointing to one part of the model] and if you're three miles away from the other one, you'll probably book this one because there is a whole host of audio visual things that are happening that allow you to incorporate your after-story into it. It seems like that if it is turned over to the stage designer or the performer as an object that complements the performance, I think it's a very successful project.

Devarajan I am just thinking it's interesting to finally see something that has a different quality that allows for anyone who comes to install the show. There is an identity around the site that allows flexibility.

Arnell I am just saying that if the site becomes a tool, like a mike or a speaker or another tool in this equation for this project, then maybe it finds a rightful place in the building of the stadium, arena, or stage if in fact it is given to somebody as a tool. I can imagine that people would want to view it up here [pointing to model]. I am just saying if you begin to see it as a landscape instead of an object...

Peter Frankfurt One of the things that I find interesting here is by having the palm – looking at a thing with identity – palm trees could definitely be an interesting icon. When they're down, it's an enclosed place and, certainly for geriatrics, for high-rollers, that's a good place to be. It's cool, it's very theatrical, and when it opens up it turns into something else completely. That is a form of architecture. It transcends space design. There is a space that becomes something else.

Frank Gehry Well, is it really worth it? Are you getting enough bang for the buck in what you're doing? I like the way it looks and everything, but couldn't you do it with lights and sheets and tent-like structures and really make it even more ephemeral, quicker, and cheaper?

Sylvia Lavin Well, it's a little disappointing when you say that when you go like this [opening up her hands], and now I have a projection screen, it's a very conservative and banal idea about how one might incorporate media with surface or how you would treat a surface. I think your surface is very interesting – the way you can think of this as becoming ephemeral by virtue of the entire fastening through the motion or the orientation of all the light sources or thinking of how you could use technology to embed these with a form of intelligence so that there's a way to disperse

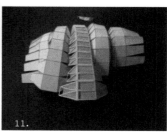

image or effect or any other combinations. I think that potential of your project is completely downplayed.

Demetri Porphyrios
King's Cross Central, London
514b

with George Knight

King's Cross Central presents a most exciting and significant development and regeneration opportunity in the United Kingdom and Europe. Redevelopment of KXC also offers opportunities to enhance the townscape and public realm with quality buildings.

Buildings are about people; and the intent of the studio will be to create lasting places with a sense of place and belonging. The studio will address the design of the Granary site at KXC (a most remarkable Industrial Heritage Site) with the view of designing a Fine Arts School of international importance.

Students will visit the KXC site in London, England, will meet with the developers and study their current proposals as well as visit other relevant buildings in London.

William West
(H.I. Feldman Nominee)
Stanford University
A School of the Arts at King's Cross Central

On this disused industrial site, I interpreted the mandate of historic preservation broadly. While I maintained much in the usual manner of adaptive re-use, I also removed existing structures in favor of a new roof inspired by the train-shed builders of the Industrial Revolution and an adaptation of the bottle kilns that were once a ubiquitous feature of the English industrial landscape. In addition, the drawings were experiments at digitally recovering nineteenth-century engraving techniques. In this way, the scope of preservation is limited neither to the site that is given nor to the structures that happen to have survived on it.

Darin Cook It seems that it wants to happen more – that rectangular opening. This is the one place where you're connecting vertically. You're really making a punch through the roof...

Chris Wise Just to see the arch coming through. Just to get that connectivity.

Robert A.M. Stern It just seems to me that in a city like London or New York, where big spaces are so hard to come by, and here's this opportunity to really create a space which would be complimentary to the new parts and the old parts of the buildings at the same time... It's a very thought-out scheme.

Charles Gwathmey Here's the thing that I find. Keeping all the front buildings, the little shoulder epaulets, everything, is fabulous. Plus, the plan that you've put in there is fabulous. And then stripping off the façade on the inside and glazing that, and then having this extraordinary field of columns, and this roof, this is one of the most elegant schemes I've seen on this particular project. It's not just beautifully presented, it is unbelievably clear. You should be commended.

Stern It does show that at Yale it is possible to have a nice plan. [laughter] Demetri's [Porphyrios] going to pay for this one.

1.

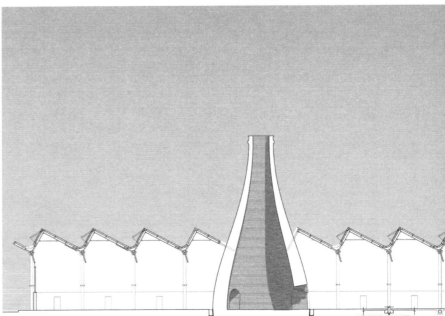

2.

Gwathmey Make yourself do the figure-ground drawing of the larger site. It would be very beautiful.

Alan Plattus One of the things we speculated about at midterm was whether these objets réaction créatif, the necessary little... the capers in this. They are exactly what Le Corbusier meant by inscrutable things that he would occasionally drop into his schemes in order for the rationality of the rest of it to be measured against the poetry or the gratuitous quality of these things. So the question that lingers over that is you have three of them...identical. Are they an archeological operation for demonstration purposes? Do they then become honorific spaces, like conference rooms? Or do they have a kind of ordinary, everyday use that's related thematically to what they once had, and is it in fact that the artisans that are going to be building this would have found reconstructing last weeks brick box easy by comparison following them? They are extravagant. And yet – I would say to your credit, but also to further the puzzle – they are necessary. The scheme would be fine without them, but it's much more with them. So what are the limits of that investigation? Again,

I'm recapitulating. We wondered out-loud, at mid-term, whether anything else would do as well. Exactly, do you turn it into something punctual, or is that completely beside the point? Do they have to be like the thing that [Arata] Isozaki stuck in the courtyard at Orlando like a cult temple that had fallen abandoned? We don't know anymore.

Paul Finch The great thing about this is that the use of those kilns in his project sets off the residences. Why this scheme is powerful, as opposed to simply very elegantly and beautifully presented, is because it has a historical and metaphorical meaning to the scheme. London was an industrial city in which the making of things, in which the burning of things, brick and everything else, the absolute fundamental part of a large city, of which, of course, the railroad tracks were in themselves a remnant. So what I think this scheme is capturing is a kind of refined version of those, in a way. The other great thing about it, the conjunction of these things, however modestly used – it's pretty modest compared to their historic use – actually coincides with the great contemporary industry of London today, which is education. And London as a series of schools and universities, with this extraordinary influx of students from all over the world, in conjunction with this industrial use, I think makes this a powerful metaphor in what we said before is going to be a rather ordinary commercial part of London, and will make it both strange and attractive, and somehow very recognizant of its own history.

Andrei Harwell
Carnegie Mellon
University
KXC Art Institute

This design retains the Granary building and one existing transit shed. These buildings face a new busy public plaza directly adjacent to a hip new shopping district and house gallery and retail – the most public program. Behind them, a square organizes semi-public functions: auditorium, library and faculty offices. A large new structure at the north of the site houses industrial-scale production workshops which are connected to an exterior work yard. Rising above the workshops, a tower houses studios and classrooms. The

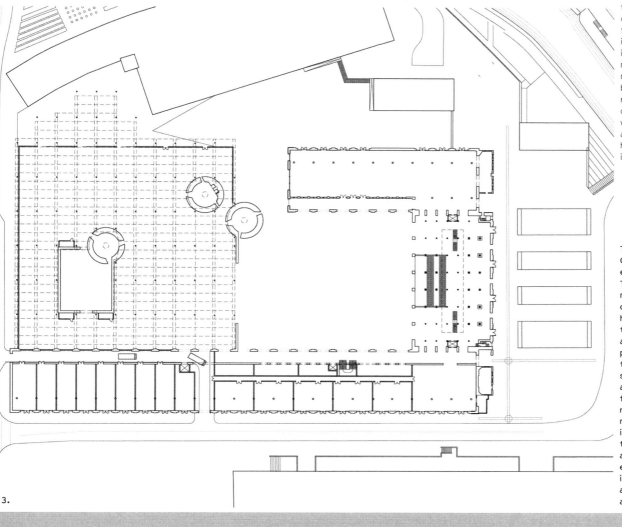

3.

Demetri Porphyrios
(continued)

tower faces north, giving occupants access to northern light. All the buildings are linked by a 30' tall gantry crane designed to move large pieces of art within the site.

Jaquelin Robertson This is the first one that has talked about what the opening looks like and that's worth discussing.

Robert A.M. Stern On another review that I was on, upstairs in Will Bruder's, every guest from Tod Williams to so-and-so, said Yale students didn't know how to make an entrance other than a stair. So I guess it goes to show it's a Yale problem, not a studio problem.

Andrei Harwell It's not the monumental hole. It's that to create a hole in that building, you have to make something so big that you lose…

Paul Finch It's Alice in Wonderland. It's into the rabbit hole. I see this huge space.

Robertson It's very monumental. You think that's playful?

Harwell Playful isn't the right word. It's supposed to be sophisticated. I mean, I don't know what word to use exactly.

Robertson It's pretty monumental, I think.

Stern Trendy.

Harwell Trendy!

Stern Trendy is the word you should use.

Deborah Berke It looks like you're trying too hard, like the opening credits on that movie, Matrix.

Finch I think one of the really good things about this is, in London, we've got a huge museum of modern art, Tate Modern. The only problem with it is that we haven't got any artists that know how to use this huge space like that. We actually need an art school to train people to do art at a sufficient scale to occupy a gallery. And this has an effect of raising the scale of your game because you're not only making large pieces and needing these jigs to carry them around, but this is actually upping the scale of what you're doing by having the tall building. I think it's great.

Berke I think this is wonderful, and you've done such an extraordinary amount of work. We can talk about all the little bits and pieces, but I think Charlie's [Gwathmey] question gets to what exactly is your relationship between making an architecture of this place and this time, verses referring to old things? And where you totally floored me, and I couldn't quite believe you said it, was that you pulled the inside floors off in order to reveal the arches, and then opposite to them, you've just copied them in order to make the other side of that space. You did say that, right?

Harwell Yes, I did say that.

Berke That's appalling to me!

Finch Why?

Stern Why?

Charles Gwathmey Yes, why?

Finch Why?

Berke Because if you're going to show us the original ones…

Stern But why is it appalling?

Finch If it's good enough to keep the originals, why not do it again?

Berke Because if you could do it again, why not tear down the whole thing and make exactly what you want? In other words, is he going to show us a history museum?

Harwell They are doing that exactly on the site. They're tearing down the old building…

Finch So, why is it appalling?

Berke Okay, see this wall here? That's a brand new wall that is made to exactly imitate what this wall looks like when you pull the floors away from it.

Finch And that shocks you?

Berke It appalls me. That's why I use the word.

M.J. Long I think you could put arches in the wall, but it would have to be different. It would absolutely have to be different.

Berke Exactly.

Long It could be made in a different way.

Stern This is the modernist argument. There is another argument.

Alan Plattus So it's when you ask the brick what it wants to be, and it says, 'different from that brick over there?' [laughter and applause]

Stern The history of architecture is filled, all through history, with people reproducing elements, from one part of a building on another part of a building, to complete an idea or whatever. What is so appalling about it?

Finch Did it give you what you wanted?

Harwell I think that this would be an amazing space.

Finch So it's what you wanted to do?

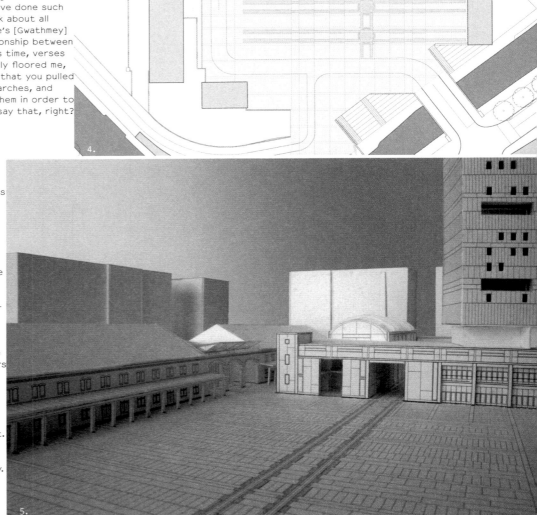

Harwell It is.

Long I think the power is with a new timber roof. And so, when you come in, you don't want to come into something that announces itself as a little thing. You want to come into something that's part of this great building and that's why it's not just 'let's be different.' It's 'let's maintain the sense of I'm in a big thing,' at the same time enjoying the fact that I can use arches to create the canopy.

Ashton Allan
Brown University
Constructed Ground

The existing Kings Cross Granary and the surrounding area have many levels of constructed ground that include two train stations, a canal, and the tube. Many of these levels are reminders of the site's history as an industrial area. This project uses the existing granary complex for artist studios, administration and gallery space. Under the central courtyard, a new ground is constructed for the art school's production workshops and theaters. The architecture of the underground evokes a sense of the subterranean and can be experienced by the public from a cryptoporticus on the canal level.

Paul Finch This, I think, is a tremendously practical proposition... I think the only thing missing out of this is you haven't actually quite pushed how useful this black space is. You could put an auditorium in there; you could put a fantastic conference facility in there. You might extend it and put some parking in there, which could be very useful, or for studios like the ones next door, with all those people huddled around a village of screens. The last thing that they want is daylight. They could all go down. You could bury them all down there, while the other architects that do like natural light could do natural light stuff on top. This thing is absolutely heroic and what I like about this scheme is, I think with a little twist, it's absolutely and completely practical. Now I'd just work out how deep you need to go, not on the basis of your Piranesi thing, but how deep do you need to go to get the deepest use, say, a steep-rake auditorium 1500 feet below...

Robert A.M. Stern I don't think you'd like that. I don't think you'd like all those floors and things in there.

Demetri Porphyrios I think Paul [Finch] actually has got it. You have to focus on something simple. It's like one story. Everything else is like fragile mishandled used things

to say anything. I think it's absolutely fantastically practical, and the issue of 'oh, well, you have to go through the basement to the canal,' it's neither here nor there. If the canal was ten stories below, would we say 'ah, that would have been the right thing?' Ideally here, you should really go as much as you could actually go. You go for ten, fifteen, one hundred stories. You go until you come out the other side of the earth. [laughter] It is one of the few schemes that has actually looked, at least provisionally, not fully, I understand, at other issues about sustainability and this and that. And the references are absolutely fantastically drawn.

Tom Beeby The poetics are amazing. To water it down by making uses for it... I think it's actually an incredibly powerful image and it's presented in a perfect kind of way. The whole scheme and the way it was presented and the ideas are terrific. I wouldn't let anyone talk you into watering it down.

Porphyrios I've been thinking about what is gained...

Jaquelin Robertson What I would say is you gain a lot of reasons of how it was thereby connecting to that. That's what a cryptoportico floor level is. It's below grade, but you can see out from it. That's one of its geniuses. You could then take the bottom row of bureau stuff that you talked about, if you wanted to, and put it under that, but that would have been the major cryptoportico level. And if it was seen, it would have been equally beautiful. The light coming in through the holes in the garden, it would have

been wonderful. And you would have seen and said, 'yep, of course, easy.' And that would be better than going down three hundred feet.

[...]

Alan Plattus I know it's futile to argue with Demetri [Porphyrios] on this one, but...

[laughter]

Stern But it's worthwhile.

[laughter]

Plattus He says it's one story. Yeah, most basements are one story. But I think that typologically, fundamentally, no matter how beautiful it is – and I couldn't agree more, it's beautiful – that it is relative to everything above it in space. And there's a reason why major public uses rarely, with the exception of certain kinds of things which programmatically go there, don't find themselves at that level. There's also reasons why our fascination with the semi-underground architecture is just that...the whole point of the grotto is to have something to connect it to in a discursive way. And I guess what one is looking for is something other than an escalator or a purely vertical well that can engage that set of spaces and make them more than simply what is under the courtyard.

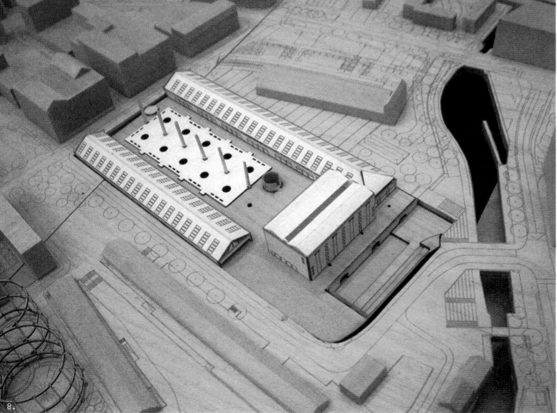

for symbol, and may or may not exist, et cætera. But I think, it's one of my favorite things, and I'm glad that Paul [Finch] said that before I had

Richard Rogers, Chris Wise, & Stuart Lipton
Some Unheard-of Machine, Stratford City
516b

with Paul Stoller

The design and building of contemporary urban environments presents the ultimate challenge:

How do we design a new city quarter so that it stays relevant for many generations past its initial structure, as the world develops around and within it?

The students' test-bed for this living experiment is Stratford City in east London, England, a 72-hectare (178 acre) railway lands site.

Stratford City will become a new mixed-use metropolitan hub large enough to generate its own critical mass. Critically, it must be linked back into the existing hinterland. It has fast transport connections to London, and will soon connect to Paris and Brussels in less than 2½ hours via the new Channel Tunnel high speed train link.

Students are invited to assess and challenge today's view of urban priorities, design, construction and manufacturing processes. From there they are to develop a clear understanding of their design intentions, showing how they will develop solutions to meet not just the initial needs of the project but also, importantly, a future proofing strategy. For the purposes of this studio we will take that to mean a minimum of 100 years (5 generations).

Students should explore key system thinking in areas such as IT and coms, new manufacturing, user-driven and community-driven design, integrated transport, economies of scale, renewable energy use and supply, resource provision, and physical reworking in response to lifestyle changes, and show how their design examples connect into them.

Adam Ganser & Russell Greenberg
(H.I. Feldman Nominees)
University of Wisconsin & Yale University
Some Unheard-of Machine

Alexander Garvin Which major pieces of the structures for the Olympics remain after it's all over?

Russell Greenberg It gets whittled down to 25,000 square feet. These grass berms stay and bring it down to grade. Just this side of the stadium stays and you can then watch games or concerts. The aquatics stays, but these two arenas are slated to be moved somewhere else.

Robert A.M. Stern So where are those two ladies from [the BBC comedy] Absolutely Fabulous sitting?

Greenberg They're sitting in the media tower at the east end of the main park.

Diana Balmori You seem to have filled everything except for that slot and I don't know if that was your intention for that slot to forever remain the Central Park of the town, but it doesn't seem to be connected to a function of the area.

Greenberg Effectively, that thing is packed with program. Although it looks like a park, it's a mall.

Stern Is there a section that explains this?

Peter Rees This is a great axis of considerable width. What's happening in it? Is it just green space? Occasionally there are these cut-outs from it, but what happens on this green mall?

Greenberg I think it's a time issue and a rendering issue, but we're seeing it as an interesting landscape, something that's dynamic and has undulations to it.

Malcolm Smith I think the amount of landscape is unrelenting. Go to your grid. If you look at the original master plan, one in six of those would come out. You would have a conventional grid with some open space. The trouble with this space is what is a great conceptual idea – an urban park – is not terribly usable because there are a whole range of social backgrounds that require different sorts of open spaces. I'm not saying it's not a good idea, I'm just saying let the rest of the place absorb the humanity.

Balmori What I wanted to finish saying is that the approach to infrastructure is very, very good. The neighborhoods as you've laid them out, vis-a-vis the infrastructure… I don't see a relationship. I do see a relationship with the railroad. I see a relationship with the park. I don't see a relationship between the infrastructure and the different neighborhoods. I don't understand why you've laid them out as you have.

Stern How do people move from the north villages to the south villages?

Greenberg Through the shopping or on the top.

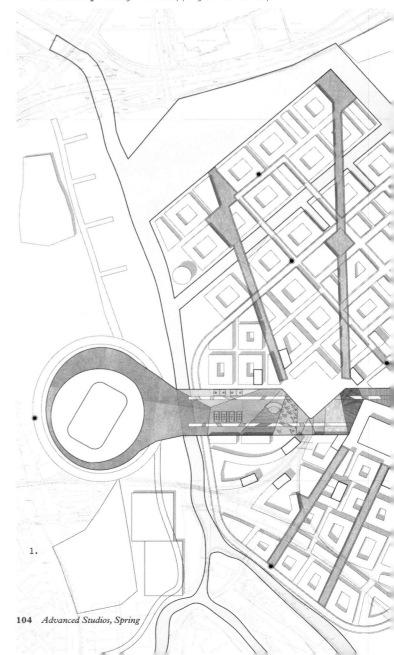

1.

Stern I guess it's the graphics. You made it look like a landing field rather than any kind of park. That's part of the problem. Your plan drawings don't seem to show any concern for the movement on top of this thing.

Alan Plattus You know that if you made a few strategic connections between, for example, those plazas that poke out and get very close to each other…if you started to connect those to each other, not by a mall, but by open-air, real-world urban connections, I think suddenly the plan becomes quite rich in terms of the potential for interactions. The other thing I wonder if you have considered is whether the green could also invade laterally in the same way the plazas invade the green. In other words, could that whole edge get activated in a variety of ways?

Stern I want to ask one more question about this. What about the shopping? Is it even nice shopping and is it the best place for shopping?

Greenberg It's a mall.

Stern And what would happen if somebody said, 'We don't want that shopping'? Could we, for example, lower the grass down to the roof of the Chunnel and just call it a day? What would you do with the dirt?

Greenberg The dirt?

Stern If the shopping turned out to be a bad idea, which it might be. If it doesn't survive…

John Gattuso First of all, I think that this model is very good about explaining the complexity of the section that's going on and I commend you for that. In fact, all of these drawings are very helpful. I, too, am looking at this great swath of space which is almost the Mall of Washington, DC in its size. It just wants to have these cross-sections and cut-throughs that start to break it up in scale, maybe even blur the lines where some of the green starts to seep north and south. I think it will end up making it a much more interesting space. I wonder what the quality of that retail experience would be? It's a shame to take retail which could be wonderful at animating the street levels of these buildings and sticking it underneath this green mall. Maybe there's another program use. Maybe it's meeting space, a convention center, or something that wants to be a big enclosed box and not something that would be ultimately entering the street. The biggest observations from the sections you've done is that this cut is so deep – I mean, it's mammoth – that my first thought is why can't you just keep that Chunnel buried and just do something with ventilation. It's yet another intrusion into this neighborhood which is already surrounded by these big barriers. You start to address that by covering over that. To me, some solution of the nature you're proposing is warranted to not further subdivide the space.

Demetri Porphyrios I think it's quite an excellent scheme. There are a few things I do love and you don't talk about them. I'm not sure if I'm putting words in your mouth or not. You've taken a very typical, well-known-in-England block and you've actually elaborated it – or it looks like you've elaborated it – and you've actually given it different dimensions, different sizing, different courts, different this, different that. What I find absolutely ingenious – I'm not sure if you're aware of it or not – is this: look at the way they're taking a small block, long blocks, limited blocks, and the way all of these things move together. From a distance, they're tightly laid in, not compositionally, but trying to elbow each other as if they were trying to suck into this mother. This is quite spectacular – the way all of that stuff collides and hits in that space. I have to congratulate you for all the work you've done on these blocks.

2.

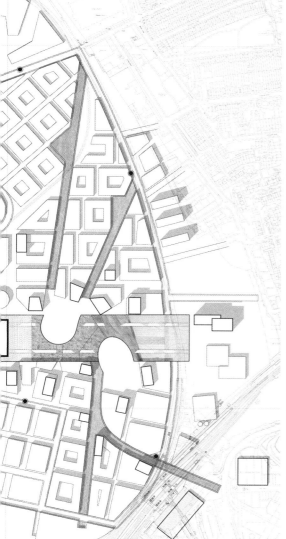

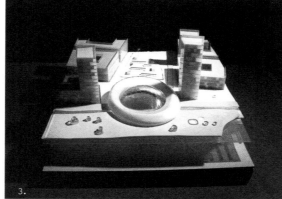

3.

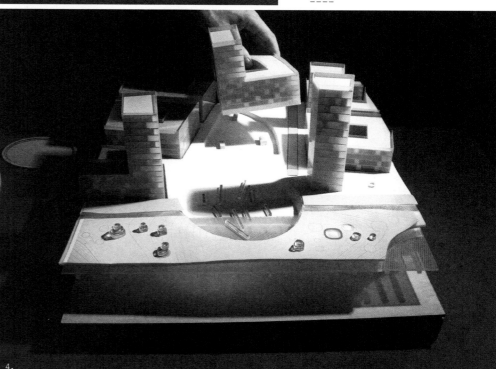

4.

Rogers, Wise, & Lipton
(continued)

Mario Cruzate & Andrew Steffen
Pratt Institute & Iowa State
University
<u>Catchment City</u>

Catchment City proposes that for a large new development to be successful, it must be a value to the entire region and based on a network
of resilient urban catchments – smaller units of decentralized communities, ecologies, and energy infrastructures.
Phasing for the larger development becomes
particularly easy as it is built up via self-sustaining catchments one at a time. The majority
of residents that work within their catchment
receive energy and resources from that same
catchment (from social resources to gray
water to local produce to recycling) and can
be self-supporting while providing a resilience
between the centers when shared resources
are required. Catchment City also posits
its existence on being a regional landmark,
extending its network of catchments to the
surrounding context and eventually to the
entire surrounding region.

Nick Johnson They're the first people to talk
about intimate places and the scale in relationship to their particular neighborhoods. They've
thought about the relationship between the existing neighborhood with the new community and
how that would act as an intimate place, dealt
with through landscape. They've thought about
the topography of the site and you've also
taken us through the strategic plan. I'd also like
to mention the Tower of Shame. You know, the
idea that you put all of your recycling up and
you show just what people do consume. It shows
that you're thinking about some challenging and
not necessarily straightforward paths to a solution. You've given it some life and character, so
there's not an awful lot we can have a go at.

Paul Finch I agree with that. I think that al-
though that is the case in diagram, what happens over 100 years…
it goes in phases. I think you've dealt with it as much as anybody
could. You could easily say, 'Well, what would happen to these
buildings?' If you've over-engineered them a little bit, they'll have
multiple uses. The problem with Stratford is not what you've done
because it's the other way around. If that existed and what you
were proposing was this, then I think we might have a bit of a
problem. I completely take the point 'well, why don't we have more
of what happens over there,' but this comes back to the point of
how the new influences the old. This is a new condition but actually
it looks very traditional because it's blocks and streets and stuff
like that and I don't see anything wrong with it whatsoever. So I
congratulate you on what you've done so far. What's more, we do
get a sense of what that might be like. Water – you're quite right
– is a very big deal, partly because we have a drought and partly
because we've got a flood plane. We've got this completely schizo-
phrenic attitude toward it, you know. We don't know whether to
be frightened of it because it's coming up, or frightened because
not enough of it is coming down. All of that recycling stuff is right
on the button, so I say well done.

Diana Balmori The plan looks very professional. You're creating small pieces by changing the direction of the grids and it's
believable. I want to praise you for how you have dealt with open
space – how you haven't been afraid of actually designing open
spaces. I need to praise you for it. The water use and collection through one whole neighborhood is very believable and I think
that's unusual. I really think that the open spaces are believable and well
distinguished in your plans. Now, the contours of that park, on the other
hand, seem to make that park like a barrier. You need some more work there
changing the edge.

Chris Wise To me, these two diagrams are the reason you've been able
to do all this. You're the first two to draw diagrams clearly enough – both
anchor diagrams – which are a series of communities linked both inside and
outside the South End. Richard [Rogers], if he were here, would be absolutely delighted because they're lifted straight out of his book. So, you
know, it shows that you can learn something by reading.

Alexander Garvin I want to commend you on the quality of your visual
presentation. I can follow what you're doing and therefore I am able to
make real comments about it. It's clear and understandable. Your diagrams
are relevant. You're starting in an area that I know very well, and that's
an Olympic Village. While I commend you to the skies for doing an Olympic
Village that doesn't look anything different from the rest of Stratford,
which is most important for the re-use – because we're mostly talking
about white elephants – but I know that the first stage will never look
like that. You've haven't thought about moving the athletes to any of the
competition sites. Leaving that aside, this might be the right way to go.
I'm not sure that's 4,500 apartments. That's what you need at the minimum
before you get the referees and all. But if that's the first stage, then
it's the first time anybody has mentioned really anything about accommo-
dating the Olympics. The second stage is how do you absorb what is built

and then how do you grow over time. You're drawings are very interesting, if not confusing. That one looks like Paris and the axis down Champs
Elysees, but it turns out it's not. This one makes me think of New York or
Philadelphia—actually Chicago, because of the squares—but it doesn't work
that way. And when I got to this, which is so beautiful, so interesting, so
complex – and I share Diana's [Balmori] view entirely about this – but I
don't know why anything is where it is and I have a problem with that. Presumably there are monuments, destinations, and land-uses, and they would

reflect all of those squares. I think it's an arbitrary position. This one
has a lot of variance, but I don't know why.

Christopher Beardsley & Ashley Klein
Yale University & Emory University
<u>A 100 YEAR PLAN</u>

Stratford City is expected to experience rapid growth as a result of
its adjacency to the site of the 2012 Olympic Games. Currently, the
Olympic Park Proposal serves to enforce the separation of Stratford
City. The current Olympic Plan is wasteful and more than half of the
buildings and infrastructure will not have a life after the Olympics. In
addition, the current proposal does not maximize its potential as an
economic generator for the future. The current plan for Stratford
city has a relatively low density. If the given building footprints were
used, the same square footage of Stratford could be achieved at
seven stories, keeping the overall FAR the same.

Stuart Lipton You're not going from anywhere to anywhere. It's an
island. It's insular. I don't want to knock your plan, but it does not follow
through. The grid that you propose, despite your point about flexibility,
is inflexible. You could have said, 'We will have sixty percent of this on a

grid.' The reality is that life is changing constantly. Perhaps some of the blocks should be inside out. The last point is that one wants these lines. I look at a majority of these plans in English terms, where there is plenty of delight, plenty of theater, and think you should take this grid and invest it with twenty-first century delight. Whether it's a high rise building, waterfall, theater... there's something there that makes this place feel alive. This has a lot of potential for us, as well.

Alexander Garvin There are two things that you are doing which the previous schemes did not. First of all, you have public realm hierarchy. You have a private courtyard, semi-private used in common by the people, and you have a series of passageways that you might call streets and squares and finally the big open space around the waterfront. You avoid one thing about the main open space and that is this set of white elephants. You're not going to have an Olympic stadium in use every day. Your reuse of this in temporal terms got me thinking about how you deal with a place in terms of a century. How do you support them? The key to that is in your basic block structure. First of all, the floor plate in your apartment house and office building are the same. The double loaded corridor scheme that you have at under sixty feet is fine for the apartment houses, but I don't think office buildings have the same situation. Since you have a multipurpose block, why don't you figure out the demand for apartment houses? What if the developer builds your six stories? You've got a height here where the efficiency of using an elevator comes into question. Above four stories, you have a problem. You might say anyone who builds an office building can build thirty stories or fifty stories and then you get to the impact Diana [Balmori] was raising in the last case. You begin to get variety in three dimensions. The second thing that is that the key to this goes back to what Stuart [Lipton] was saying earlier. You have places here, but there are no destinations. These red things, I suspect, are destinations of some sort...railroad stations. My instinct would be that on this route, you have large numbers of people coming out. On the next iteration, I would urge you to take the non-residential, non-office, non-block thing that you've solved and include destinations. Then the public realm is going to change because it will have to adjust to those destinations. You actually did what Peggy [Deamer] and I were looking for. We can't see the railroad anymore, but we know where the water is and the public realm has something to do with both of them.

Peter Rees Okay. The approach of 'let's build a new Turin. Let's

7.

forget about Stratford because it's put it on the edge of the map.' That's fine. You can do that, but if you are, just a few miles from here a Riverside apartment is going to cost twice as much as one that faces away from the river on the same piece of land. So we've got some wonderful blue edges

here. We've got an island in between the two branches of the river. It's not the River Thames. It's grey and brown, but if we set up edges along these, bring it right out along the water – maybe overhang the water a little bit – you've doubled the value. If you can create the edges and still utilize your concept with your hierarchy of spaces and if you could animate these spaces and explain how they feel, do it. I think you could make it together. Just one more point in terms of presentation of material – forget the research. That's for academics. Leave it to them. It's the flare – the sex appeal – that we want. You don't even have to draw it. Just cut a picture out of a magazine to give us some sex appeal to turn us on to it.

Diana Balmori First of all, I'd like to respond to something Peter [Rees] said. For God's sake, leave some public space open along the edge of the river. But still there's something to do with the relentlessness of it – I don't object to it. There are pieces of many cities that have these six story places that are put on whole blocks that can be very nice if we know that the core and the street are well designed. What I would have liked is a sort of Nolli Plan – that you actually design one portion, particularly the center, and then I would like you to react when that relentless pattern hits the river. When it hits the park, something happens to it. It's transformed by what it hits. It needs to react to what's around it. I think these spaces could be quite interesting, but I want to see what happens at the ground floor.

Chris Wise I'd like to stick up for you along the lines of the things you've done in terms of planning. I think you're really onto something, whether or not the variation of streets works. Conceptually, the idea – certainly an office plan of eighteen meters is a bit wide. Some of the best places in London started out as brick works that were turned into an office and are now apartments. They're certainly sustainable to live in. You're really onto something.

Will Bruder
Live/Art, New Haven
518b

with John Eberhart

The focus of this studio will be the reconnection of New Haven's city core to the waterfront through the urban development of pedestrian movement patterns. The program will include infill community art parks, attainable urban housing and a new contemporary art museum. The studio will engage issues of site analysis, architectural programming, urban and architectural design.

The problem will culminate with the design of a contemporary art museum/ 'kunsthalle' (museum without permanent collections) and art school of approximately 50,000 square feet, an adjacent mid-density condominium project of 40 units attainable housing, including 10 artist studio/residences, and a series of small art park community spaces.

The first weeks of the studio will involve an intensive group site analysis of New Haven from the Yale campus east beneath the Interstate to the harbor's edge, case studies of relevant museum and housing projects, and the development of an urban master plan. Following, the studio will travel to Amsterdam and Rotterdam for a week of research and analysis of art museums and housing (especially the East Islands of Amsterdam).

Finally, the studio will engage in the development of individual designs for LIVE/ART New Haven that will include: contextual appropriateness and conceptual clarity from the macro to the micro, tectonic refinement of structure, materiality, details and light as well as multi-faceted approaches to sustainability.

This studio will challenge the student to invent, test, and apply new skills and ideas about the relationship of architecture and community.

Jennifer DuHamel
(H.I. Feldman Nominee)
University of Washington
Kunsthal New Haven

It's possible to visit New Haven and never realize it has a waterfront. Currently the waterfront is separated from the city by regional train tracks, a US interstate highway, and a local interchange. Between the train tracks and the interstate is the manufacturing and commercial zone of Long Wharf. IKEA's newly opened store in Long Wharf is now one of its most trafficked in the U.S. New Haven is cut off from its waterfront by the train tracks, I-95 and I-34. Long Wharf, the neighborhood in between these regional connectors, is a low-scale manufacturing and commercial zone. The studio challenge is use a kunsthal, an art museum with no permanent collection, to connect New Haven to it's waterfront while also encouraging private residential development in Long Wharf. The formal strategy of the project is to build tall with the art program to react to the scale/speed of the highway but also to respond to Marcel Breuer's Pirelli Building, the only other tall building in the area. Go low with the public program to connect with the pedestrian scale of the street and to inspire similar private market development. Separate art from public program. Pull the public & administrative functions to the street, thereby activating the sidewalk and encouraging similar pedestrian-scale development. Use this program to enclose the sculpture garden, and within the garden, locate a regionally scaled building just for art. The building then is a cube containing art set

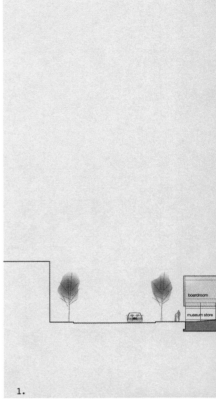

1.

within a sculpture garden that is wrapped by two levels of public program in an inexpensive, flexible structure. The sculpture garden is raised one level, covering parking below. This affords garden access to the administrative, school and library functions as well as allowing it to be easily secured. Connecting New Haven to its waterfront is accomplished by invigorating the main pedestrian and vehicular access routes with the public program of the museum and hopefully encouraging a similar private market reaction throughout the neighborhood.

Julie Eizenberg Where is the nicest place to be?

Jennifer DuHamel For me, I would probably like to be in the discovery center, where it's quiet. I hope people would also come hang out in the garden.

Eizenberg I think the sculpture garden would actually be a very nice place to be. Why don't you have a café?

Tod Williams It says you go up to the street and I think that's at least correct.

Steve Christer You have the street and you have the garden. You're not activating this as strong as you could.

DuHamel The thing that is looking out over the garden is where the private administration…

Stefan Behnisch I look at this place with the four tables and it's not exactly the place I would want to be. I would like to feel more atmosphere.

Ben Pell Every level could be a different experience. Obviously, the nature of the experience is going to depend on what's on display. More of those kind of renderings during the design production process could help you design those spaces.

Louise Harpman I also admire the strategy of the New Haven Green as a void within the center and you making this void an active space. The question is, as a garden space, is there an idea about an object as a perimeter? You have a whole series of perimeters. That's a real gift to everyone who works here – they have access to the garden space. There's a real opportunity that I think is there for one more level of design, which is to understand that as a course membrane and that as an active membrane. That ground plane, which is a totally constructed plane, needs to affect the plane.

Behnisch If there's a sculpture garden, it would be great if you could

2.

look at the drawing and you don't have to explain that it's a sculpture garden and not a parking lot. You know, that what's wrong with stealing some sculptures off the [Inter]net. It's a garden and a garden is not a football lawn. I think it's a very good scheme, don't get me wrong. I think the best way to present the scheme is that you don't have to tell us about it – that all the materials speak for themselves.

Will Bruder I think it's terrific in that virtually every space in the building does seem interesting. You could actually be a pedestrian moving through the whole thing, because it's extremely gentle. It would be kind of fun to see you reverse and think of that as an automobile entrance.

John McCullough The urban design strategy is so clear to me. You've taken this thing on and you've dealt with this right upfront. I think it's a

Joyce Chang
University of California at Berkeley
Kunsthal New Haven

Due to freeways that make it accessible to other neighborhoods, Long Wharf has long been one of New Haven's most underdeveloped neighborhoods. My project anticipates growth in Long Wharf by providing transit hubs, canals, and a light rail system. Most importantly, a long boardwalk will connect downtown New Haven to the Long Wharf waterfront. Kunstal New Haven, a destination that shelters art and provides waterfront access to the public, will be situated at the end of the boardwalk. The boardwalk runs through the main building of the Kun-

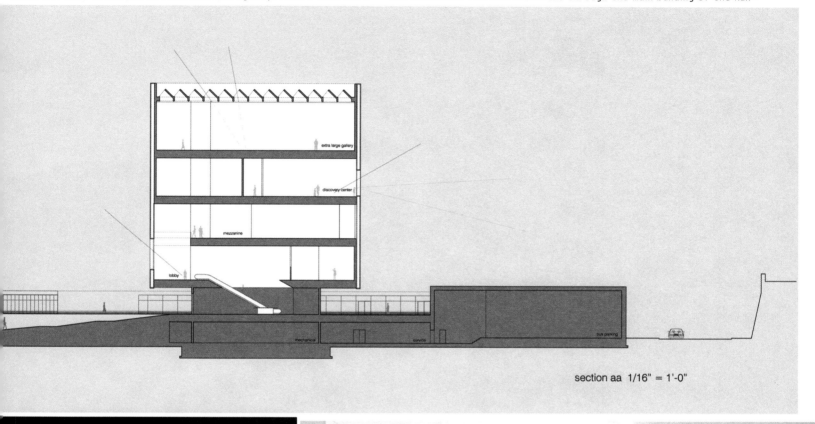

section aa 1/16" = 1'-0"

3.

very mature work. I think it's a powerful building and it's a fabulous

stal and leads visitors directly to the waterfront without having to enter the galleries. The separation between galleries and the everything else is crucial to enhancing the idea that Kunstal New Haven is a true public realm that people can freely enter to enjoy its functions, waterfront views, and separation from New Haven's busy downtown.

----

gateway to the city.

Marilou Knode What would be interesting is the integration of green spaces. There are so many artists working with landscape design. Every one [museum] has this discovery center, which is a very specific term. That's actually the place where they drop all the kids. It's going to be very loud. So discovery is not the place to use. It's not a place that has four little lonesome tables. If you could actually work with the artists so that you can... There's the interpenetration and I think it could be very productive. I would love to go to work every day where I have a view of the Green on the other side. I would work even longer hours. Some might quibble with some of the openness, but I think that would be up to us to solve.

Tod Williams I remember your midterm scheme. It was a little more bold. Increasingly, it's getting timid. Maybe it's too timid. I personally like the inside wall right there. I feel that when I look at it, I wonder what this thing is made of? What does it accrue to? And it occurs to me that there are many, too many, materials. It feels that it's trying to please too many people. It feels that it is trying to become something smaller in scale than what it actually is. I urge you to think about what supports the structure. I mean, it doesn't necessarily have to be wooden piers. The idea of putting something under the water is actually a moral responsibility as to what the water's edge becomes. It means you need to almost design the underbelly of the building, too. It just appears that

Will Bruder
(continued)

piers are pretty big buildings if they're on piers. They are massive buildings. I like it, but it could be more like – stop trying so hard.

Marilou Knode Just a couple of observations. [The first thing is that] the north side is going to have natural light that wants to be captured. The second thing is that you need accessible public space. You're not going to force people to go up and outside. The third thing that I have to say is that this almost makes me think of La Jolla. It makes me want to have a plexi bottom so that you can actually see the water underneath. It would be interesting to somehow connect [across] this water.

Steve Christer You may want to consider what it's like to walk up that south ramp. Sorry, let me back up. I think it's a wonderful scheme. I really enjoy it, but there are a few things that trouble me. One is that south wall, because sun does shine here and it's nice to look out of windows. That's why we don't like this mirrored glass. I'd like to know how you feel about it.

Joyce Chang When I built this model, the major difference was that there's another ramp that goes from this mid level to the back. I think there are just too many landings.

Christer The sun goes through that and it makes everything inside very hot, which isn't nice. That troubles me. I really start to question [whether] there is a reason why we have a slate wall here. I actually think that they're doing three different things. Why three things? I think I've got the answer. It seems to me that this one sits on the ground, right? What I'm getting at is that there is an emotional relationship with the site of the building. This is your anchor into your site. You've got this one here that deals with the air thing. My last question is what's this one? Does this one float?

Chang That one does not float. That's administration, so that actually has a wall anchoring straight down.

Christer The sea goes up and down, doesn't it? It occurred to me that if it went up and down, maybe it could be another place to come into the building. Then you go in another way and you've got anoth-

you're renovating the pier rather than designing a new structure.

Behnisch I like it, but there are many moves per square foot. Usually piers are pretty big buildings if they're on piers. They are massive buildings. I like it, but it could be more like – stop trying so hard.

the quality of the shoreline. Would you redesign the core as well? I think in your case, you would have to. Also, the idea that there's a whole other commerce and I think that the Yale Boat Club is over there. There is actually water traffic here. How does one participate in that? I think there are opportunities for other types of urban commerce. It's all about water. What's the quality of light in this reflective type of environment? One of the most effective examples is that I encourage you to go to is the [Fairmount] Water Works in Philadelphia. I don't know if a space like that exists in New York or New Haven, but I think that you'd enjoy and appreciate that in terms of materiality because it's a collage that doesn't have specificity. Then you would want to test that.

4.

5.

er way that it relates to the site. You've got this thing that says, 'I'm here.' I think you could take all those things so much further. That thing that Tod [Williams] is talking about walking on the coast…that's really important. That's where everyone wants to walk.

Louise Harpman I feel that in this case you should have different answers…that you should know

6.

Michael Grogan
University of Arkansas
Re-inhabiting Pirelli

The dismal industrial site, bounded by highways and rail lines, is punctuated by the now-vacant Armstrong/Pirelli building by Marcel Breuer. Originally envisioned as a gateway to New Haven, the forlorn structure becomes the site for this project. Breuer's building, clad in deep precast concrete panels, is actually a steel-framed structure. Selective exposure of this contradiction was one aim with this proposal. Two parameters were established for the reoccupation. The existing structural frame was to remain intact, and the volume of the original warehouse wing, recently demolished, would be re-envisioned as a podium for the sculpture garden.

Tod Williams Well, this is an extraordinary effort. I have a couple of questions. One is that you didn't ever cut a section through the auditorium which, I think, is really poor and it seems like a compressed, squashed piece. It seems like an odd thing to put in the center. The other thing that [I question] is the way it makes a transition… the skin being pulled off at this point and this point, and the way you respect the Breuer [building]. There is so much that is interesting about your project. It doesn't seem

likely that there would be artists living up there in these rather contained, separated buildings. I find that it either has to be much better integrated into your concept…[more about] the process than just being applied. The basic balcony seems to be unclear relative to the museum or residential space.

Michael Grogan I think that stems from the initial study that we talked about today. My idea was that the residential boundary becomes a wall that integrates into the buildings. The Breuer building is much larger than the building.

Behnisch I like…how you gut the building, but residential is totally different. I'm actually intrigued by your sketch models where you took the Breuer apart. It's great. I like it very much.

Steve Christer Architecture is incredibly challenging and I know that you have to work doubly hard at what you're doing because you're not doing it on your own. It's also important that you take it on because that's what works about what it actually is. I really enjoy that you have the programmatic boundary. It really feels that the guts of this building are coming out and turning into something else. You go through the program and think 'oh God, I cannot…' When you're on that train, you've got to run fast and really enjoy it. It's like at the last moment. You're very, very close.

Behnisch I think he was probably thinking about the final review.

Ben Pell I'm drawn to the aesthetic of your model and to your process, but what makes me uncomfortable is where you get that incredible respect for technique. For me, I'm concerned that it's a little bit

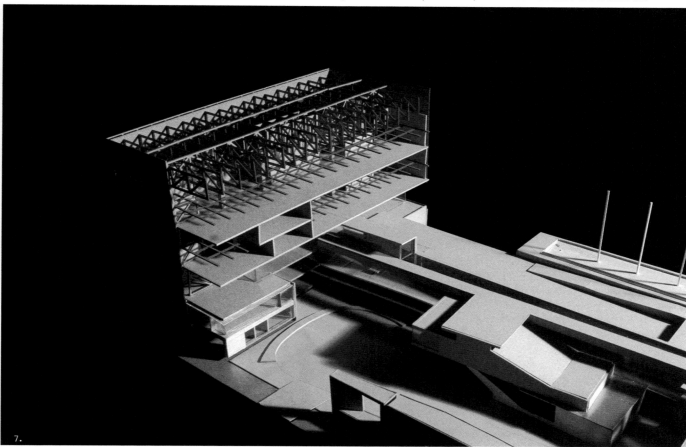

7.

of a stylization. It's almost like a nervous tick. It just kind of happens. So I'm not going to ram you with that, but I wish that I heard from you that there was some intentionality behind the hyperarticulation. I look at it and all I really see is Thom Mayne. Everything that everyone has been projecting onto this justifies it for me, but I'd really rather hear it from you.

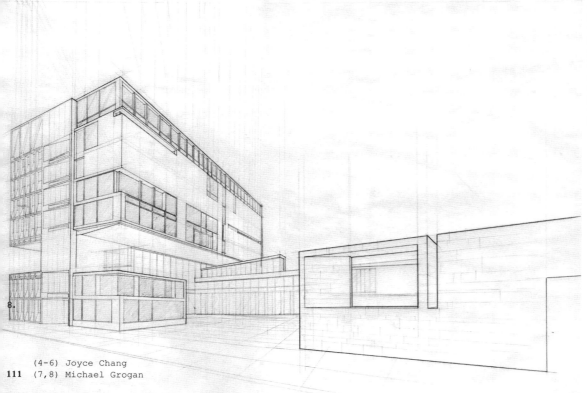

8.

Stefan Behnisch
Palast der Republik, Berlin
520b

with Ben Pell

The reunification of East and West Germany into a single political state on October 3, 1990 heralded a significant shift in global politics. The following year, the Soviet Union collapsed into more than a dozen separate countries, ending an era dominated by anxiety, uncertainty, and territorial one-up-manship known as the Cold War. In the two decades since *glasnost*, many traces of the Iron Curtain have receded into history, leaving few reminders of an era that directly impacted every nation in the world for nearly a half-century.

One of these remaining fragments is the Palast der Republik, erected in Berlin in 1976. At the time it was built, the Palast was a showcase of cutting-edge East German architecture, hosting cultural events, arts and crafts fairs, in addition to serving its parliamentary functions.

The building – left derelict and scheduled for demolition – still stands today on Unter den Linden, the prominent East-West axis of the city, comparable to the Champs-Elysees of Paris. Over the past several years, a guerilla arts program has appropriated the site for concerts, installations, and talks under the banner Volks Palast (People's Palace), restoring some of the cultural, if not physical grandeur to the original building.

Embracing the political and cultural complexities of the site, this studio will engage in the design of a new building to host a Museum to the Cold War. This museum will operate in multiple ways, providing gallery and event spaces, which will document and present the history and reach of the Cold War, while continuing to provide space for cultural performance and public appropriation on the site.

The studio will focus on issues of sustainability, adaptive reuse, and the retro-fitting of structure and program on this hotly contested and powerfully weighted site.

Christopher Kitterman & Maxwell Worrell
(H.I. Feldman Nominees)
Tulane University & Oklahoma State University
Three Museums | Three Experiences

Understanding the role of the institution as a container of vast quantities of information, the museum adapts to provide layered experiences of the Cold War by creating three unique 'museums.' Through research and analysis of the Cold War, the importance of multiple readings and overlapping conditions became apparent. In order to respond to these conditions, the museum allows for varied experiences that convey different types and scales of information both simultaneously and independently. Within the framework of the different museum experiences are seven intensities that serve to organize the museum both programmatically and architecturally. Each of the intensities contains a research component, cinema, and public amenities that respond to adjacent experiences.

Peter Eisenman Could I ask you a question? Since you talk about all this responding to the site – which I'm happy that you all are wanting to

1.

respond to the site – the question I have is how come your building doesn't respond to the other buildings that are around the site? That is, they seem all rectilinear and orthogonal and your building isn't. So how come you're interested in responding to the site so much except in your building?

[…]

Eisenman To make a long story short, I don't see any octagonal buildings. It's not just one edge. It's all the edges. I mean, it seems to be designed to make a figural building in a context of orthogonal buildings, in other words, to go against the context, which I love, but since you're telling me that you're going with the context, I don't know how to interpret…

[…]

Neil Thomas What I think he is saying, is he not, is that the buildings around it are orthogonal but the generators you're talking about, these angles, are not ninety degrees. There's a whole series of geometries going on and that building begins to discuss those geometries. So the form isn't necessarily orthogonal in relation to those buildings. It's more those ideas you're talking about – the site, and the edge of the river.

Marion Weiss You decided that contextual would be the exact heights of all those blocks, which is unbelievably strong, and that you kept.

2.

3.

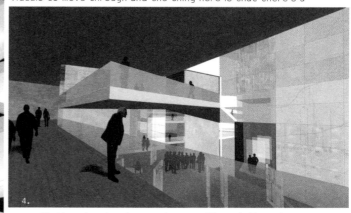

4.

Chris Kitterman The idea for the landscape is that for the Palast, this is a huge parking lot. We feel that the Schinkel with the Lustgarten – I guess when we say formal, this kind of symmetry – that it's contained on three sides. One with the dome, one with the Altes, and this kind of landscape move, and we just felt that it petered out on this side over here. And so a way to kind of make this a space, we thought that we could define this edge not with a building, but with landscape, so one edge is landscape that you don't really move through, one side is landscape that you move through.

Selldorf Point taken. But how do you move through these trees and walk through those trees?

Kitterman Well, maybe we should move to the boards.

Eisenman You asked us to come here. [laughter]

Kitterman There's a spacing that allows individuals to move through and the thing here is that there's a curve that's not welcoming you to move through those trees.

Keith Krumwiede You modeled your trees in a similar manner that you modeled the site's trees and you get this completely different reading. I think that the site model is correct and they're drawn over here…

Eisenman I just wanted to say that if you hadn't said a word and had said, 'Hey guys, do you like our building?' We would have all said, 'Yeah.' Let us figure out what it's doing, right? The minute you tell us what it's doing, it ain't right? I like the building, but your explanation really put you in a hole.

Kitterman Can we erase all that from the…thing?

Robert A.M. Stern No. That's the part we take and put in Retrospecta.

Abigail Ransmeier & Nicole Lambrou
Yale University & Binghamton University, SUNY
Cold War Museum

This museum proposal involves demolishing the former Palast der Republik and leaving a landscaped void in its place. The result is a linear park linking the open space in front of the Berlin Television Tower with the formal landscape already framed by the Berliner Dome and Schinkle's Altes Museum. While the Cold War is often understood as a conflict between US and Soviet spheres of influence, this history museum rejects the simple juxtaposition of Democracy vs. Communism, conversely highlighting the Cold War's global effects. A cluster of undulating towers represent five vertical galleries, each displaying Cold War material from a geographically distinct point of view. As these galleries move vertically through space and chronologically through time, they merge to create overlapping zones used for circulation and shared exhibitions.

Peter Eisenman Could you tell me what those diagrams are? They

Annabelle Selldorf But I understand Peter's [Eisenman] question, because it's obvious that the orthogonal nature of those places around it sets up a precedent that you can't just forget. So what I don't fully understand it what…an allée, for example, that's something that I understand as formal. But a bunch of trees in a grid – is that a formal organization of, I don't know, is that a forest? I just don't know. What is it and what does it do?

fascinate me and I say to myself, 'Wow, would I like to see that building as opposed to this building.'

Abigail Ransmeier It is that [building].

Eisenman What? No it's not.

Ransmeier It's all the overlaps that happen in this building, but we failed, I guess.

Eisenman No. But what's wrong with that building? Why did you change

Stefan Behnisch
(continued)

from that building? Because that building doesn't seem to have five separate elevators. It seems to coalesce and it has this play of hard edged forms with circular forms and deep cuts and it seems, formally, more articulated than this [referring to model].

Annabelle Selldorf It seems more thematic in a sense and so you might as well stick with it. [...] And it's not so hard to go back to it because now you have gone through and you have figured out that you don't need five elevators. That's evident. I don't think that's a big deal. Just take it out. I love this. I think it's a very interesting idea to have this and I happen to think that you don't have to make it cohesive, but you have to make it possible. [...]

Mario Gooden But I think one would also want to be flexible, which is why I'm troubled by your really wanting to hold on to these five towers and treating each continent with equal weight. You have two continents, Africa and the Middle East, that you put together. But you're treating each continent with equal weight, whereas the relationship between this continent and that continent or this country and that country may not be the same all the time. So, as a curator, how do you allow that kind of flexibility in terms of understanding the information thematically or linearly?

Ransmeier It's funny that you are talking about this, because North America is so much a part of the Cold War, when you take her out it's like a whole cultural commentary.

Krumwiede Sometimes, when it's political, you have to start dealing with a project politically and architecturally. You kind of want to be like the Senate. Everybody gets two senators regardless of how many people they have. It's all equal representation. You've gone down the road where you want to

that you go to Nebraska? And it's just a question. I'm not coming down on either side. But you can't be across from Schinkel and just go... [hand gesture] like that, I don't think. And if you're going to go like that, you have to tell me why. Maybe Stefan [Behnisch] can tell us something about this... why it didn't seem to be in the... I'm very excited about both projects, right, but I wouldn't say both projects are contextual... And I'm not interested in contextualism, either, so that we know. So the question is how does one thumb one's nose at Schinkel just a priori? How does that begin?

Henry Cobb I think you're [Eisenman] starting from the questionable assumption that if you don't pay attention to Schinkel then you're thumbing your nose at Schinkel. I don't think that's true. These projects are not thumbing their nose at Schinkel. They're saying 'something else is going on here.'

Stefan Behnisch The situation of the site...the only historical context I could see there is the Palast der Republik.

Eisenman I didn't mean something... I was too strong. You wouldn't know that Schinkel was across the street is what I was saying. And you, Stefan [Behnisch], don't think that does anything to an architect?

Behnisch ...No, because, well, I'm from over there [laughter] and I know about forty-five Schinkels in Germany and I'm – even though he was probably a great architect – I'm not impressed by the individual Schinkel buildings.

Eisenman No, but his urbanistic strategies are stunning.

Behnisch Some.

Eisenman Oh, the two...we can talk about this another time.

Robert A.M. Stern No, no! This is a good time.

[laughter]

Stern Bring it on. Let's do this.

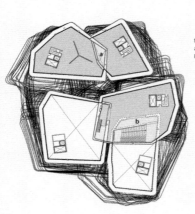

floor 11 [1950] — — — — —
a. decolonization of africa +mid-east
b. theater [the formation of nato]

floor 3 [1980] — — — — —
a. iran contra affair
b. unrest in eastern europe
c. cafe + reading room

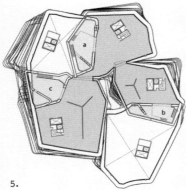

5.

be very curatorial with this thing. You don't leave much freedom, so somewhere down the road your really want to take on that task. Look for those swells where the geographic difference is not the prime focus of the Cold War.

Adrian DiCastri I like that as a generating idea, a kind of neutrality to geography, as a starting point, but, in a sense, it's a form of political correctness and you're trying to remove value. I think that with the kind of absolute fundamental importance of the continental identity, rather than letting that idea be the generating idea that can then be inflected. You don't have to keep it pure all the way up on every floor and I think that's the power of those diagrams. You start with an idea as a kind of poetic and then you allow it to inflect as you move up through the building.

Eisenman Let me ask a general student question. We've now seen two projects. This is a really wildly contested site project, as you know. It's located across from one of the great buildings of the world and one of the great spaces of the world—the [Karl Friedrich] Schinkel Altes Museum – and yet both projects that we've seen – and I want to know if it's the critic, I want to know if it's...we could be in La-La Land. We could be in Nebraska! This thing would equally work as well there, you know? And it's really exciting. I'm not saying it's not. What I want to find out from the student corps here is why, when you're given a site like this, so loaded,

6.

Behnisch What I think...what the trap is a little bit for all us is, or was, is discovering the complexity of what we thought was just a simple history museum. Once you get into the Cold War discussion it gets very complex and suddenly you don't really find the criteria to organize it and what I like about this studio is that they all tried to organize it differently, but suddenly you get a complexity in the building where you actually leave the regular museum.

Selldorf Is this due to the Cold War because this is a complex period or, for that matter, do you have to make a decision to say: a) I ignore the site, or b) I'm happily willing to say it's as far as the project got. I would prefer, actually, not to look at your site plan, quite frankly, because it does

not deal with the environment at all. I think the premise of everything else is wonderful. But Cold War or Chinese history, it's all very complex.

Matthew Byers & Paolo Campos
Colorado College & Yale University
Cold War Museum in Berlin

The site is reformatted as an urban green surface which extends the public open space of the Lustgarten. Striations across the site are oriented north-to-south to connect the landmarks of Museum Island. The mass of the Cold War Museum is submerged below these surface striations, and swells and troughs in the surface create a variety of public pathways and experiential possibilities. The Museum exhibition provides a continuous informative experience consisting of six themes of the Cold War, which we have designated as 1) Art and Culture; 2) Propaganda; 3) Geography; 4) Military; 5) Science and Technology; and 6) Industry. The information related to each theme ranges from physical artifact to textual narrative to visual images and/or motion pictures. The gallery space therefore must allow for multiple curatorial arrangements while providing an overall organizational structure for patrons and staff.

Keith Krumweide I have questions about striation as a means of handling the landscape. I look at the site plan and it's the one project that really has the potential to begin to coordinate flows and by putting everything into the same channels, this could be anywhere. I guess that faces the Altes Museum, but I don't know that it necessarily recognizes the flow of the Lustgarten and how the Lustgarten coordinates access to the Altes and how it might begin to backflow this way – I don't know what the motivations are to moving this way across the site, or moving this way across the site, because I don't know what this is, but I also don't think the project cares.

Stefan Behnisch It's nothing.

Krumweide Well, there's a road here that goes somewhere.

Paolo Campos There's construction here…

Krumweide Okay. So there's nowhere to go here, so why do I go there, right? Why is the building set up to take me over to nothing as opposed to maybe actually channeling me…If you let the landscape actually become non-directional, because it seems to be more of a field that is defined by these points which are one way of organizing the history of the Cold War and it does allow the curator to enter into your project. When I look at the little model, there are some great lighting effects, but with the lanterns coming through these long ribs of landscape, formally it drives me batty – as opposed to penetrating something that was more of a net on the surface – that it was not so directional…but was omni-directional. You want these people in here, almost as if there are not all these level changes.

Claire Weisz Well, that's a question I had when I first looked… I mean, I really like the plans a lot and you start looking at this model and you get that sensation of when you go into Frank Gehry's Temporary Contemporary – you walk in and you're actually above a kind of warehouse space. I don't understand why there isn't a kind of tying of the landscape strategy to what's happening below so that there's an occupation of above and the way that you understand below, because those are really great spaces… I mean, right here, that's a pretty interesting landscape… Here's the pure, rolling wave strategy where no one is going to talk about

the Cold War, and then you're going to come into the tunnel and we'll all talk about it down here. That part is a little bit strange. I feel that what's so fantastic about Peter Eisenman's Memorial to the Murdered Jews of Europe is that it's all at once. You see the skateboarders on it, but it's so clear that when you see people disappearing into this volume, that it's also about something else. And this separation, so completely, of, call it content, you know? I mean, I love this project, but I find that deeply troubling.

Campos Well, I won't speak for both of us, but – and I understand your point – but some of what you're talking about in terms of [Peter] Eisenman and how people disappear and there's that polemic agenda behind the project… When we went to Berlin, I was very under-whelmed by the project, mostly because you're standing at one end of the thing, looking down a row, and you saw the street beyond and there were only a couple of points where you ever felt truly immersed in the thing.

Weisz Well, I guess the point I'm making is that you have this immersive experience below and, in a way, a non-immersive experience above. I'm just suggesting that the things that you worked so hard at below, moving this way and around and stopping, it could be equally applied to above, but different, you know?

Annabelle Selldorf Everybody agrees about how strong and powerful the diagram is. I have some questions about edge conditions as well as about the scale. I'm trying to figure out the scale of the museums throughout all of the projects and, needless to say, the last project is the most easily defined. It was a large building and there was a lot to put in that large building and now I don't know what it is. I think of it as a landscape and probably just as well accept that.

Closing Comments

Henry Cobb I'd like to go back Peter's [Eisenman] first comment this morning about contextualism, because Peter in his way, and I, in my own way, have both experienced the problem of building in Berlin in the years immediately following the destruction of the wall under the regime of [Hans] Stiemann [the director in charge of construction in Berlin's Senate] when everything had to be [uniform]…the street wall had to be 18 meters high and then had to tilt back to 22 meters. It was the reproduction of Berlin…of the Berlin block. So what is striking to me is – just to support Peter's first comment – you don't seem to have been either intimidated by or particularly concerned about the urban context here. I don't feel that it's been a major issue for you.

Stefan Behnisch That was a little bit me because, first of all, I don't like Berlin. I'm from southern Germany. Number two is: I hate Stiemann. Number three… I never understood why recreating virtually a city that was never there before…yeah? You distrust that and I thought I planned a problem with authority.

Cobb I'm glad, in a way, because you liberated the students, each one to make their own interpretation and that's quite vivid…that there have been many interpretations.

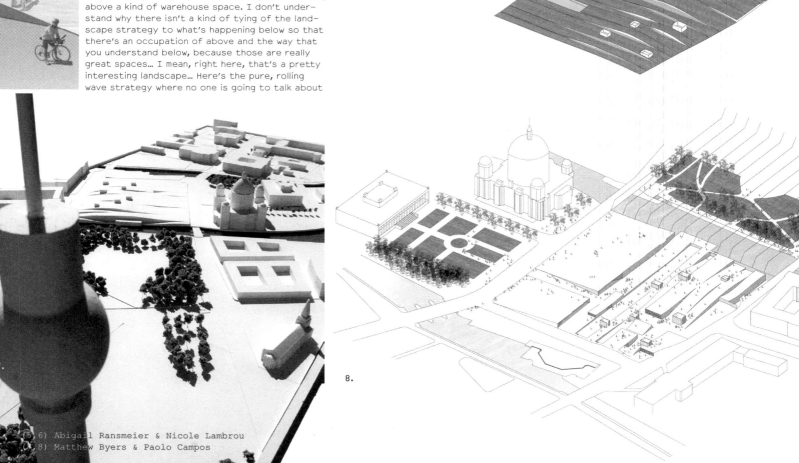

7.

8.

(5, 6) Abigail Ransmeier & Nicole Lambrou
(7, 8) Matthew Byers & Paolo Campos

Frank O. Gehry
Music Center Studio, Los Angeles
522b

with Gordon Kipping

Since the Walt Disney Concert Hall has been completed, downtown L.A. has been experiencing a potential rebirth. My office has been involved over the years in planning the Grand Avenue that joins Walt Disney Concert Hall to the Chandler and the Ahmanson theatres. We're currently working on a project across from Disney Concert Hall for hotel, residential and commercial activity. As the area starts improving it will become necessary to do something about the Chandler which is a 3200 seat theatre now used for opera, the Taper which is a 750 seat small theatre that has virtually no back of house facilities and the Ahmanson which is a 1600 seat theatre that has been recently refurbished for Broadway plays. The original planning for this complex was modeled on Lincoln Center and had nothing to do with a Southern California context. This studio proposes to undertake the renewal of the Music Center, with the opportunity for students to select portions of the project so that no single student has to design three theatres. Students would be split up into two person teams with each student on the team choosing an opera house or large theatre and communally re-planning the existing space to show the possibilities for the future. The studio will involve spending time in L.A. in early February, and as part of the trip they are invited to a conference that Richard Wurman has set up. During the travel week, students will also spend time in my office seeing how it works and getting some insights into the computer technology we're using. They will meet the other design partners in our office and we will bring in the acoustic consultant to brief them on what those issues are.

Melanie Domino
(H.I. Feldman Nominee)
Barnard College
Los Angeles Opera House

One of the initial premises of this studio was to design an opera house that would draw people from impoverished parts of downtown Los Angeles to a building that would be situated as part of a larger music center adjacent to the Disney Concert Hall. Studies of the demographics of opera-goers over the last twenty years indicate that neither the program nor a signature building would suffice in drawing large, diverse crowds. The opera house as a social venue became the starting point for this scheme as a means of attempting to dissolve the dichotomy between high and low performance arts. Glass boxes are stacked to enclose a stage that is in the round. The boxes are of varying sizes to accommodate different numbers of people. The design allows for private space but intensifies the voyeurism that has long been an integral part of attending an opera. To compensate for the lack of traditional backdrops in a round space, the floor will take on an increasingly important role; a grid of moveable platforms creates a highly flexible and customizable terrain for performances. In this scheme the theater space is the social space that is currently limited to the lobby. Access to theater is through decentralized lounges in the form of large glass boxes that extend from the seating area to the building periphery.

Sylvia Lavin I think it is a set of conflicting impulses that you on the one hand manifold the existing conventions of opera-going and yet have reproduced a centralizing, monumentalizing megastructure with a big roof and clip-on boxes. My instinct then is why is the orchestra the only thing that gets to move up and down? Why can't the boxes move all over the place? It was a very challenging thing to say when you said you wanted to return to an earlier state of the opera. To me, returning to this point is a bad idea. Looking to the past to get new ideas, that is okay, but the return ended up reproducing a very centralizing [building]...and in that sense it is like the igloo or the mega structure.

Peter Arnell If you voided out the three boxes on the right, you could almost have a proceeding stage. You could have that almost as an option. I realize that these are on different levels but if you picked up on what Sylvia [Lavin] is suggesting, maybe you can do both. Instead of consistence, you can do theater en route. You're forced to see it. You're voiding out a number of performance possibilities which if you could go to these last steps you could also embrace along with everything else.

Ernest Fleischman The interesting thing is that you can't even go back in history with a space like that. I mean how can you do a Cosi fan Tutte with two or three characters on stage at most?

Lavin Presumably they are watching it on a monitor. If you go back to the sports analogy where the stadium is like a theater, people are in the stadium, watching football in the field, watching it up on the big thing, watching it on their hand-held, all at the same time. If you use that as a contemporary diagram for the multiple forms of liveliness that you can have, monitors could work. [...] Archigram and Littlewood already took this idea further in the late 1960's. Back in the [19]60's they were introducing new technologies and new mechanics that you could do now. And then where would you go, and what kind of formal control over the system that you have put in, which basically is clip-on modules and a mega structure roof.

Greg Lynn There are two ways to go which would be the [19]70's 'it's so flexible that we can do anything' [approach] and the other would be the [Las] Vegas's 'this is a residence company for some time like the L.A. Opera or other company that does opera or experimental performances.' But there are classical or avant-garde companies that do Cirque du Soleil kind-of things that is a resident company. But it would be really hard to stage all the things you need to stage here. It would have to be an experimental theater of some kind.

Stanley Tigerman Frankly, it could be also radical as a cynical view of where we are going, between hand-helds and monitors and the variety of text. What is really going on here is how people are looking at each other, period. I mean, you are looking at them from above, from below...

Fleischman You can get more impact from a DVD if you are looking at this from anywhere but the lowest lot of seats.

Lavin If you are going to question the premise or re-inspect the premise, you need to go much further. It retains enough of the conventions that it doesn't work for the current premise and it doesn't go far enough for an inventive premise.

Frank Lupo Once again, I will support her idea. Say all of her experimentations, say they all failed, it is about the program. You particularly can say 'since you have expertise, okay it doesn't work.' But at least you can talk about program that doesn't work, unlike some of the earlier schemes where there was absolutely no program, just space.

Eeva-Liisa Pelkonen You started with this whole idea of the public. And one way to have a thesis about this is to think about how to get people, young people, to keep coming to the opera. So one road would be to look at the behavior of those people who cannot concentrate on anything for more than ten minutes.

Lavin Or, people who are able to concentrate on 40 different things at the same time.

Pelkonen Yes, at the same time, like watching the game while doing things on their Blackberry or different things. I guess I would go all the way to the marketing.

Ara Guzelimian If you projected some media on this model and lit it up at night and took a picture and said, 'I believe opera is about this glowing, crystalline, media-rich environment that has all these things' and showed us the architecture of it, [then] we would be in another space than where you show us.

Lynn I think you would have to accept that this is an opera which then there is nothing wrong with the premise. It's a media-heavy new art form – it is a new kind of theater, it is a kind of performance media-tech.

Jim Houghton As a young designer, to get the vocabulary of the project with some quick tricks, you should be talking to the problem so there is not that disconnect. If you do want to see this thing as an igloo…this is not a diagram of a program. It is what you want your architecture to be like and the program has got to be hooked up with that.

Louise Smith
University of California at Berkeley
Opera Dispersed

For the downtown Los Angeles opera house design, I pulled apart the programmatic elements of the traditionally inaccessible, intimidating, and iconic art form and scattered them on the site to create a more approachable, understandable and accessible opera and a friendly, varied urban park. The program pieces are dense at the north portion of the site – the auditorium, stage and fly tower – and disband into the support and entry elements. The landscape rises from the direction of the Disney Concert Hall to create a diverse field of structures for pedestrians to meander throughout and above a buried area for opera back-end support functions.

Sylvia Lavin I'm struck by a certain kind of formal, phenomenal vocabulary that you use. You say pulling – what is the animated force of this? What is pulling?

Eeva-Liisa Pelkonen What made you decide where these different elements are on the composition?

Louise Smith It was mostly choreographing the relationship of the boxes to each other, how they relate to the climate.

Stanley Tigerman I think you rightly emphasize the need for a side stage area. However, if you are going to have a real side-stage area, why did you not go the whole way so that you can build the set and move it sideways and take another set down? Then you might get the best feel, in this case it is possible to have five different sets waiting to come on stage at the same time by the press of a button. Why take half measures? […] If you read the whole thing as a performance, and if you look at this floor plan and care less about the particulars such as the juxtaposition or what angle they are disposed to each other, imagine that they are on a stage and that these are actors or performers – the buildings themselves. To that I am very empathetic.

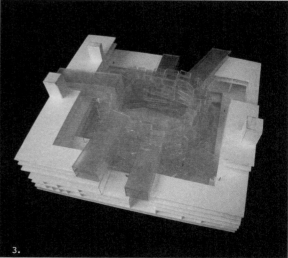

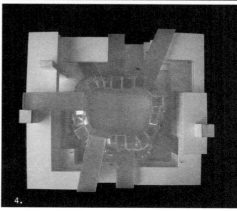

2.

3.

4.

Frank O. Gehry
(continued)

5.

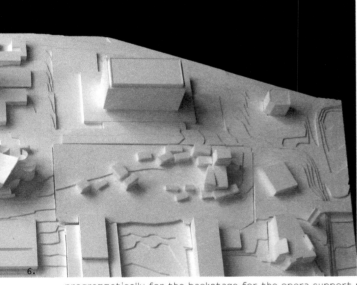

6.

programmatically for the backstage for the opera support program, and the interconnection with the rest of the support. It almost works as a topology of a hill-town scattering of these elements on the landscape, which I find interesting.

Robert A.M. Stern The thing that seems to be missing in your explanation of your hill-town is how people move. It seems to me that people are supposed to move north and south but with the landscape flow right up to your black box, [that] seems to me more like the entrance than what you say it is. You are not using the topographical arrangement, which is extremely powerful but is laying there latent, as of now.

Pelkonen I think that is exactly the problematic question. On the one hand you have the Acropolis-effect, the feel of a Greek monument like it is depicted in that perspective drawing. And then when you look at the plan, especially the underground plan, the boxes are totally non-hierarchical that you can't tell which one is the main one and you randomly come across these things. It is a very different sentiment. And then the question becomes, if you want to play both cards, there must be a moment where this duality is either experienced or contrasted in the manner that it becomes powerful. Somehow at one moment, you have to come across this duality.

Lavin The Acropolis metaphor might have been useful for you to fold in with this idea of wanting to expose parts of the whole apparatus of theater production. Back to my earlier question, what pulls you in the Acropolis is very specific, which is the Panatheneic procession. There is the whole series of things that you need to see, and wanted to see, how the story unfolds is what gets you from point A to point B and what

Then it will be in a context, it will be in a congruity about the program. The buildings are performing to some level.

Frank Lupo What is wonderful about this is that it is a strategy that works both functionally and

generates the footprint of the choreography. So if you take Bob's [Stern] point which is to take the landscape and move it in a particular direction. You could then take charge of what unfolds in a sort of classical, picturesque way, where you have to have a strategy for peeling off, opening up those corners and being very clear about what you see then. You also have these thick blank walls and it might have been interesting to pick up on the vocabulary of the Disney Concert Hall and do what it only does in the little corners, which is to peel off and let you peek in at certain moments. If you became the set designer of this procession, you could decide what view of theater production it is that you give to people by bringing them through this. Can you do it by not bringing a theater down to a popular level, but to indicate that the theater is already a completely hybrid form.

Jim Houghton It looks like you set up something almost like a teaching facility as well, to understand theater or opera, et cætera. I see where you formally enter the lobby space, and then you connect down and are never allowed to wander and that is an intentional thing. There isn't any real path.

Tigerman What if the educational entrance was brought up? Another reading of this could be a campus plan unburdened by classical precedent. There is a grid, a general structure than runs through and you've got these volumetric elements that pop up through. They are mostly rectangular except one where you go through, but that could have been played with further where other forms were juxtaposed or contradicted to enforce the column grid. I think there is a lot of reading here, instead of a reading a thing, but here there is any reading, which I think is incredible. One element of architecture of any time, classical or modern, is multiple readings – something for everyone – and you can hear commentary or critique of people bringing their own bag to the table seeing different things, which I think is great.

Timothy Campbell
Williams College
ant farm/pachinko machine

The L.A. Music Center brings spectacle back to the house of performance – erecting an animated "people billboard" at the largest scale. The opera house, medium theatre, and small theatre all share a common lobby space – a space 12' wide and 200' tall that becomes the facade for the building – an animated billboard for music performance – of people coming and going to the halls, music rooms, cafes, bars, and outdoor courtyards. From day to night the facade of the building is electrified both literally and figuratively – changing from visual electronic supergraphics to an active ant farm of theatre goers. At intermission as the theatre goers stream out into the lobby from the 3 music halls, food and drink and people are moved around the billboard/façade as the lobby becomes a giant pachinko machine – advertising the spectacle of the Music Center to the highway and all of downtown L.A.

————

Sylvia Lavin Here you made the bar into a plane in order to force people to… in order [to] reach a place, like ants, to scurry around and go everywhere, and you do produce that local spectacle I can imagine all these people walking around. Instead of worrying about the performance in the theater, you are thinking about the performance that can possibly happen all over, including the billboard. All of that seems very compelling, but I wonder if there is not a perversity in the kind of unpleasantness in walking into strangers in an eleven foot corridor? Can you choreograph the perversity of that? Like enforce a way to achieve a rush hour quality? In other words, once you put up a façade like that you can always produce all sorts of effects…some real, some not real. You don't actually have to have real people on there all the time. There are all sorts of possibilities for animating this thing and making whatever kinds of performances there are – public, classical, or experimental – to communicate through this as well.

Cesar Pelli There is nothing better than real people.

Greg Lynn What is the big garlic press thing under the main volume?

Timothy Campbell It was to make the section of the theater work so it was a nicer room.

Lynn It was a functional thing?

Campbell Yes.

Lynn You are flirting around with a sinister aesthetic, but you're not talking about it. I was just wondering if you were so indoctrinated where you went to undergraduate school that you don't see the sinister aesthetic of it, or whether you are playing with that. Because it looks kind of dark and evil… People go in one end and maybe you never see them again, or something like that. It looks like a big machine, like a people-sorting machine. I was just

equipment for sorting out four thousand people a night into all these different slots. I think that gets pretty interesting, but I think you need to go down the line and be honest about it or else you are sending these weird mixed messages. I don't believe it is about bumping into somebody in a narrow corridor, but it is about watching these people roll around in this pachinko machine like potatoes or something. And then you get the relief of being in a room where you can sit down. And that would make it very, very special to be in your seat. And then the minute you get out of your seat you feel like a potato rolling around in this agricultural thing.

Lavin I just want to say, in terms of the conversation we've been having all day, it is a very clear principle; it has an idea; it has an idea of spectacle and spectatorship, and it is using them in contemporary opera. You're basically making an argument that in these types of performance buildings a lot of the attention goes into ancillary processes. And that is where your focus is. That I think is clear and quite aggressive in the kind of things that it is trying to code. But in that case, when you have to deal with people going in and out in this very narrow bandwidth, then you actually have got to go back to look at the Colosseum and fold it. Think about the massive number of people the Roman engineers could move from one place to another through multiple entries and multiple stairwells and so forth. If that is the case, you've got to be able to come in and go up everywhere, and you've got to be able to get the bar and directions and so forth in a pattern of radical multiplicity, and you've got to figure out what the economic arguments of that would be.

[…]

Lynn Somewhere between making people go into this thing and making a lobby, there has got to be something in-between. Like Lincoln Center doing its giant elevator bringing hundreds of people up at a time from the parking garage because they know most people come from the garage and they want to make a sense of ceremony and they want to bring them up to the lobby. You can put the lobby on the twelfth floor but you have to get people there in a somewhat dignified way. You shouldn't torture them.

Lupo I don't think you are far from solving it. It is just that you don't have to have a ten foot wide corridor to get people to get that sense of looking at circulation. All your vertical circulation is up against that surface anyway. It's just that beyond that, you can relax a little bit and create gathering spaces where people can circulate. But you are always going to get the activity on that wall because you've got such a complex manner of moving up and down, up against that glass wall.

Lavin I think you can have everything you want without the corridor being eleven feet. Maybe fifteen? It can be long and narrow, but under fifteen feet. You are being an ass. There is also the issue of the billboard. There is a long tradition of the problem of the billboard in LA. I think that picking up the diagonal corner of Frank's building and transforming its geometry and continuing it along this long site is a very intelligent answer in terms of urbanism.

————

curious about the look. The entry is oppressive.

Frank Lupo But at the point when you are collecting hundreds of people coming into the building. Why does he have two pair of doors at the end of an eleven foot corridor letting people in? And why is it something that you can permeate when you filter into a grand space, and you have that grand space on the first floor, and why on earth would you choose that over being able to come inside in a more normal way, like standing upright instead of crawling?

Lynn I think if we go down the line, like, say, if you just got on a paternoster but you are a potato. You just roll into this thing, twelve at a time, you just go up on a paternoster and you get dropped on the twelfth floor or something like that. You can take this as some kind of agricultural

Sunil Bald
The World Social Forum, Sao Paolo
524b

City

Sao Paulo is the most populous metropolitan area in South America, and its richest city. A cosmopolitan and diverse city of immigrants, it contains the modern conveniences and cultural life of any European city. Sao Paulo is also the most populous metropolitan area in South America, with the greatest number of shantytown dwellers of any city in Brazil. Poverty and crime coexist with the city's hypermodernity.

Such are two sides of globalization, the results of the neo-liberalization of economies without the concurrent development of the physical and social infrastructures of developing nations, creating an imbalanced condition of opportunity and neglect, widening the gap between rich and poor.

After WWII, the United Nations solicited the participation of modern architecture to define a centralized forum for a world political body that could transcend national divisions to work on common global concerns. This studio will propose a new headquarters for the World Social Forum with its very different ambitions of de-centralizing political and economic consensus. In doing so, we will consider the utility of architecture in framing an identity for a body that claims to be "neither a group nor an organization."* We will explore the possibility of proposing a center for a body that is polymorphic and non-hierarchical. And, finally, we will propose a place for a body that seeks to "facilitate de-centralized coordination and networking"* rather than consensus.

Site

Avenida Paulista, an unusually straight avenue in a complex maze of a city, runs for almost 5km along a high Sao Paulo ridge and contains the greatest concentration of wealth of any place in South America. Home to bank headquarters and multiple financial institutions, the street is a kind of Brazilian Avenue of the Americas.

Timothy Newton
(H.I. Feldman Nominee)
University of British Columbia
Without a Center

The studio posed a central question: how does one center a decentralized organization? This proposal answers that question by proposing that one does not. Though it uses architectural space, the WSF and its affinities seem too ephemeral and temporal to require a headquarters. Rather than provide a center for an organization that wants no identifiable expression or architecture, this proposal seeks to stabilize the program by creating a downtown campus for the Universidade De São Paulo: a social forum that brings these issues to the heart of the financial district of Brazil for debate.

Will Bruder It really has a sensibility like a vertical ghetto, there's a happenstance about it that I find very appealing – it's the anti-Christ of the business suit and the towers that are everywhere else, which I think is really appealing with the program, which is as I understand it at this point. I guess the only critique that I would have is that it seems that this lateral dimension, if it was like ten to twenty percent less...it's a little bit too much space to be believable. It's too generous right now. And if this section was cut down to be something more like that, all that space between would just have a whole other energy about it. It would have another aspect of the site happen that would allow a little more of the trees and that to exist. I'm definitely glad the jungle is there. I just wish the jungle would have the street as well. You just give it that extra eight feet, maybe move the building back and just allow the jungle to have that whole left side. Nice project.

[...]

Galia Solomonoff ...I'm going to give you multiple choice. Either the building, A, looks like the model – the one in the middle. B, the building looks like a [school of] fish, and these colors plugging out of the elevations. C, it looks like it's defined by the occupants. D, none of the above. Now, which one do you think it is?

William Mitchell It's either one and two or all of the above...

Timothy Newton At the onset I would say it's like the model, but as you occupy it I think it changes. I mean, I have a problem – like other architects – with people occupying buildings – they make buildings messy.

Solomonoff [laughing]

Newton At the same level, I think that as people move things, that's what this building wants...

Solomonoff Does that produce architecture? Does the life produce architecture?

Newton I think it depends on the time frame that you're talking about. Many things are possible, but I think when it's empty, it's bad. I think when it's inhabited like this [referring to the surrounding 4th floor of the AA Building], and there are coffee cups all over the place and billboards hanging off the walls, it's a totally different animal... and it's probably a much better animal.

Leslie Gill I think the only thing...I really liked is your representation. The variety – it's very clear, very visual. The only thing I find myself wanting, though, is to know more about the module.

Newton [pointing to drawing] Right here?

Gill Yeah, those. They kind of seem like little guys whenever I look at them and in a way – I think with Marc's [Tsurumaki] comment about how they change and how larger rooms could inform – in order for me to believe in that, I want to understand more about the construction of the units or how they even get in there? There's no room for a crane – they're not coming in on a crane. How do they get in that narrow of a space?

Newton One way I was thinking about them, it might be sort of counter intuitive, that they're a vertical favela. They could be built out. Potentially, I could imagine people bringing little bits of stuff up..

Gill Right, but then that needs to be part of your architectural narrative and some index of that shown in the structure. I mean I feel that the areas where it basically falls apart are on the circulation and in the infrastructure that allows things to change.

[...]

Joel Sanders Like everybody else, I commend you on a very accomplished project as well as the narrative of your presentation, which had some very intelligent ideas guiding the project. What I find most convincing about it is when I see it as a kind of updated transformation of a kind of Bo Bardi type. Which is – how do you pronounce her name? Lina, who does that paradigm all the time – the suspended box, which is the style of Brazilian type homes...which for me it is still about, you know, inside and outside, building and non-building. For me, I almost feel like it's the skin of a [Lina] Bo Bardi typology, like a gift wrap, a piñata that's open and allows the interior concept to kind of activate the street and create this kind of urbanistic blend – it brings those things together those two worlds. The parts that I feel least convinced about are the modules. I guess for me it doesn't feel dense enough. I guess I'm hung up on this other reading that you began with the floor plates and you began to dematerialize them. But then I think you sort of fetishize it with these sorts of boxes. I appreciate the – again all those comments come to mind and I feel like we're just revisiting them now with Archigram. I'm just not convinced about the need to create these boxes – will they ever be used with all these cranes? Probably not. Also, in terms of sunscreen, again I think it's a wonderful idea, but by virtue of it being an interactive space – I mean it's a wonderful climate in Brazil, but it still gets cold and it still rains. And that really makes, for me, problematic the various

*All quotes from the World Social Forum Website: www.forumsocialmundial.org.br.

120 *Advanced Studios, Spring*

you've done is that it's this precisely designed artifact.

George Knight There's a kind of lust after motion and transformation that starts from the metaphor of the jellyfish and that kind of thing. These things don't in fact move like jellyfish – it doesn't have that particular kind of animal living in it. It has something else that's probably even more interesting, that's shown by the coral reef there. The fascinating thing about a coral reef is the fairly static infrastructure. There's all this life, all these fish zipping in and out, and appearing and disappearing – and the choreography of that is absolutely fantastic. There's no need to play with the fairly static stuff – it is transforming, it is transforming slowly. There are all these amazing appearances and disappearances and this life. And I think that's very much what you've created, in fact. Being inside this…it's like being down in a coral reef. You feel the activity, and there are people appearing and disappearing and construction going on. That's not just messiness that's going on inside your building – that's this extraordinarily powerful thing. If you were to accept

types of occupation that you're arguing are going to take place there. And then also just the fact – and this is an ongoing theme today – I think all of the projects want to try to embrace that aspect of the program that talks about a complete circuit of unplanned, contentious subversiveness, which is an idea of architects and of designers – that you can try and design spontaneity. And again, one thinks of Archigram – they really just made infrastructure. At the end of the day, part of what's so satisfying about what

the power of that, then I think it would only just strengthen your theme because it could be. With the sense of light and the sense of depth, with things appearing and disappearing, it's actually like scuba diving in the barrier reef…[laughing] just fabulous – it's a terrific scheme. I think if you just go one step further and sort of think that dynamism really comes from the people in here, it becomes even more powerful, not less.

Sunil Bald
(continued)

Brent Flemming
Clemson University
fluid institution

Ross Smith
Wesleyan University
Grass Roots Tower

While a website of the World Social Forum provides it with a consistent virtual presence, the organization's physical presence remains fluid as hundreds of thousands of people from around the world descend on, and in effect, take over a portion of a city, such as Bombay or Davos, each year. This project's urban strategy is to create an architectural object that provides an institutional identity for the WSF headquarters, while expressing the irony of its location. Programmatically, the project uses the fluid nature of the organization as a way to reconsider institutional space, where program is typically compartmentalized. Instead of overlaying program onto the site, program is invented through the interaction of landscape and a fluid spine that runs the length of the site. The fluid spine serves as a programmatic armature that breaks the institutional framework by short circuiting the larger zones.

Leslie Gill ...I appreciate the fact that you went back to the website and looked at how this organization is physically tangible at this moment, and you began to see what their own logic was and then to use that logic to start your own programming strategies. So, I'm sympathetic to the way you're developing through the project. I think that the physical model – the study models, as well as the final model – show how you're struggling to still resolve that and make it work. I think that especially in the left iteration all of your moments of interchange turn into, sort of...glorified lobbies. Where up until you're here [pointing at model] and here, the program expands and one imagines that they should have the integrity of their base program. So that if it's the book stacks, one can imagine that the book stacks actually cross the gallery. Whereas here, it feels that the book stacks are much more conventional near the auditorium, so the book stacks never actually mix with the circulation. And I may be wrong and that's not how you're conceiving it, but that's how I read the 3-D images and the plan images. I would encourage you to bring those things back in, so that one understands the reading room becomes part of the gallery and how do those surfaces and those different criteria blend through one another. How do you install security or back rooms, and begin to use those kinds of issues to help you develop the next level of architectural problems?

[...]

William Mitchell Well, you know, there's a point of technique here – this is really not directly about your project, but how you've developed it. It's very interesting actually. So, you've gone through a bunch of digital representations – right? So, you've worked very beautifully with the milling machine, and I think...I mean these are exquisite – they're gorgeous. You understand the craft of the milling machine, which is fundamentally about relief. So, you begin to understand the project in terms of relief – it's a very powerful exercise in relief. And then you use the laser cutter, which is a device about cut-out shapes that maybe twist a little bit. So you begin to understand the project in those terms. Then you use shaded images – so, you begin to understand the project as surfaces and light. What we used to know about drawing by hand is that every time you shift the representation – whether it's sketching by hand, hand drafting, drafting by scale, working with a physical modeling in cardboard, or something – each shift in representation gave you a way to carry over some of your ideas and then study new things about the building and new aspects of it. Exactly the same thing happens with digital media, I think. The craft traditions and the conventions of thinking that way about the representation, not just being something that the computer does, but the change of representation being a moment that opens up a way to understand your project in different ways – it's really important here. I start to see the beginnings of that in your project, and what I would love to see is push that much, much harder – you know, take those moments, as shifts of representation, as moments to critically think about what you carry forward, so that you don't lose the drama of the relief, for example. It's what you drop off, what you restudy, what you begin to understand differently through the digital media. This is a craft, and I think it's part of the cognitive process of digital media. You know, we used to know how to do this with drawing by hand, but we kind of lost it...I feel sort of personally responsible.

[laughing]

The World Social Forum is an anti-neoliberal organization which promotes a socially conscious alternative to globalization. The site for this organization's headquarters is along the most prominent business avenue in Sao Paulo, Brazil. The challenge of designing a headquarters for a grass roots organization along a business avenue in Sao Paulo was the focus of this project. Beginning with the typology of the corporate office building and infusing it with green space and public

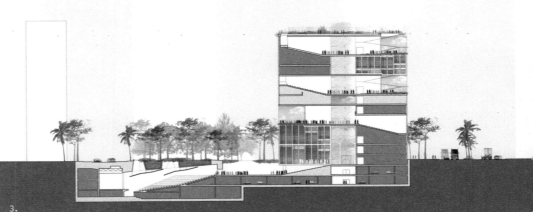

3.

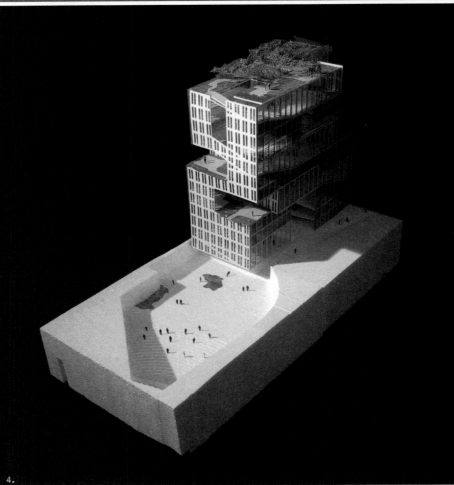

4.

programs, I produced a building which fit the context of the site while engaging with the local community and environment. The final project is similar to other corporate headquarters in size and shape, but different in its tactility and public access, setting it apart from other institutions along the avenue and making it an icon for the WSF.

Marc Tsurumaki The distinction between the primary parts of the building – I mean, I understand that there are these sort of larger public floors that are related to the broadcasting. Are all the spaces that are sort of coded in the more fine-graining private? In the sense that, are they more accessible to the public as well? Is it a question of broadcast and production? Is it a question of more privatized and secure versus more open? I'm just trying to understand what that principle distinction is.

Will Bruder I really like this project. The sectional quality, the model wins me over a lot more than the renderings. The renderings just aren't talking to me. It almost feels like the city in the renderings and then the model offers me all other possibilities. One thing, I guess, as a thought, it's rather daunting the idea of walking from the top to the bottom; it's rather magical the idea going to the top and cascading down to the bottom. Right now the diagram that you've given doesn't offer preference or possibility to that elevator really being that important. I mean, it's sort of like going to the Dutch pavilion [MVRDV] at Hannover. The idea that there is this amazing experience even though the walk there is painful; but then when you got there it gives back. And cascading down through your model in particular, I really would begrudge any partition or anything inside the building at one level, because just looking through that model and the texture of the horizontal louvering versus the vertical and the language of that is... I mean it's really a big idea that's here. But, for me, I'd like to figure out how you go up through that garden that you've driven up through it there with all that mesh and all that greenery in your model and be going on this odyssey to the top and then discover this world that you've been to the top of the jungle and then come down. It's pretty cool.

Tsurumaki I would like to follow up on that a little bit – I like your project quite a bit as well. It reminds a little

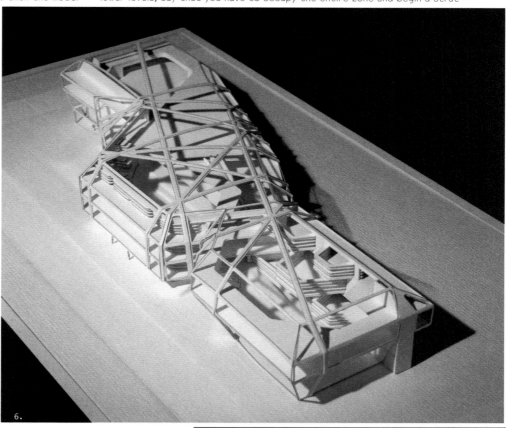

6.

bit about what George [Knight] was talking about a moment ago relevant to the other project with the typological sort of standardized. For me, your project becomes interesting when I think about it as kind of strategy where on the one hand it does actually sort of mimic the scale in almost a bureaucratic receptiveness – it's like the sort of generic office buildings that are around the site. Then it literally injects this erosive texture into it that begins to insert a greater degree of public-ness, greater degree of exteriority. It's almost like a very normative building that's being sort of pulled apart by a new set of agendas. So I admire that a bit. Somebody mentioned the Dutch Pavilion a moment ago, and this is a little bit like a celebrity death match between Diller and Scofidio's Eyebeam and the Dutch Embassy project – but I don't mean that in a pejorative way again. I think it's actually worthwhile to look into that. One of the things that I'm looking at now – having accepted those premises – on one hand, I'm curious, your building is less continuous than it seems to me to be? In other words, one can read the continuity of this public movement through the building. But in fact, maybe it's more interesting this way. You have to actually interface with others – you put these ramps here to get you across, right?

Leslie Gill My addition to that would be that I feel that what's happening underground and at grade level is less resolved architecturally. So maybe if you start with the entire lot, instead of just carving this shape from the lower levels, say that you have to occupy the entire zone and begin a strat-

5.

7.

egy of shifting and changing in the same way that you've done in other parts of the building and begin to think of your ground plane as the same thing. Once you've done that it would free you up inside the building, so you can go back through the building and to work with a similar pattern horizontally; you could begin to not only carve voids out, but also shifts. That may give you the programmatic emphasis that you didn't know were there and may resolve some of the issues that come out of coming from the top down.

Joel Sanders I agree with all of the comments. I think this is an extremely intelligent project and I think it's coming out, at least for me, at the right time of the day; which is not to diminish the power and intelligence of the earlier projects, but many of them again – and I'm sympathetic with other students who are each trying to radically reinvent a new kind of spatial typology, with all sorts of new form sensations in the space. And I think this is the first one that finds this distortion of the typology of this city in a very clever and strategic way and actually a very believable way – it fits, it's just fine. I think where it's more reticent, it has less chance of blowing the whistle. Thinking through the program, there's this local scale and it's evidently represented through technology and space by choosing that particular technology. I'm not sure I agree, because you can say what you want about simulcast, it could look exactly like what you want. But other projects are starting with an architecture and then a sort of conventional approach to the program, and I think it's a very interesting thing that you did.

Keith Krumwiede
Edgemere/Edgeville, New York City
526b

with Patrick Bellow, Jonathan Falkingham *(Urban Splash Development), and* James Axley

The studio will focus on the redevelopment of eighty-seven acres at the far edge of New York City. Edgemere is one of the largest remaining tracts of vacant urban oceanfront property along the northeast coast of the Atlantic Ocean. It is located at the eastern end of the Rockaway Peninsula in Queens. Initially developed as a seaside resort in the late 19th century with the construction of the Lancaster Hotel in 1895, the challenges of the site were made evident immediately; a storm buried the hotel beneath tons of sand the following year. The hotel reopened the next year, and many others followed, making the area a popular summer destination for New Yorkers up until the Second World War. At this point, the area began to fall into decline and in the 1960s most of the hotels and bungalows were razed in preparation for never-executed urban redevelopment schemes during the Lindsay administration.

Edgemere, largely dormant for these past 40 years, is currently the subject of a Request for Proposals by the city's Housing and Preservation Department. In responding to the RFP, as well as other documented ambitions for the site, the studio will project yet another utopia for Edgemere. This utopia will, as is stated by Lefebvre in The Right to the City, "be considered experimentally, by studying its implications and consequences in the field." As such, it must be understood as being capable of implementation now and adaptation in the future. Particular attention will be paid to ecological, economic, and social factors as they impact the site locally and bind it to global networks of influence and interaction.

Aaron Fox
(H.I. Feldman Nominee)
Wesleyan University
Urban Ecology

My approach integrates services of all users into an urban ecosystem. I began by assessing the needs of the existing residents and potential markets of newcomers. An array of independent but interrelated subsystems was identified to provide users with an overlapping network of infrastructure. When deployed, this ecosystem provides the city with a larger park and more real estate than is requested by the RFP. More importantly, users are provided with services that are spatially and operationally integrated, making the neighborhood a unique re-conception of city living.

Diana Balmori I really think that the intention that you take with open space is very good. I like the playing with the fences and all that you have done in creating a fill and using them as part of a landscape feature, to organize things and making them an important part of the design. I like the idea of an elevated boardwalk. I understand much less of the landscape between the towers, the bungalows, and the railroad, but anyway you've tried to design and tried to look at scholars into design landscape. I don't quite sense the creation of these walls on the high-rise there and the relationship with the bungalows as a conscious, clear determination. It just seems to be a little bit accidental. Again, it has some problems. Although you've solved something by moving past the continuous wall, by moving every other one out at different directions, you still have the non-stop wind problem. At any rate, my question has to do with the lack of clarity of the space between the railroad and the towers, and the towers and the bungalows. It seems they divided the whole site into strips, horizontal strips this way and making the space, therefore, feel much more linear and smaller than it really is.
[...]

Sunil Bald This project is part of the approach when one goes about filtering water. In this case, there is the landscape, and there is a series of filters. I just wonder what type of typological resistance does each of those have and if you can evaluate it. For instance, when you move through this kind of surreal cutout suburban development, does that offer more resistance than moving through a series of slabs? Does that offer more resistance than walking underneath the subway lines? Does that offer more resistance than moving through a bunch of shops? I image it would technically, but it is a little bit difficult to understand what those are right now or at least how you are thinking about it. It is more that you are using those edges in relationship to each other than using it to create alleys to some degree, whether it is at the micro-scale of the little houses or let's say between the subway line and the slabs or slabs and the developments. Rather than looking at how they stiffen individually, I was wondering with the slabs why they are exactly where they are. Why they are closer to a subway or why aren't they on the other side of it? Looking over why they are over there or like Keller [Easterling] said, 'why is the retail under?' Right now, it's just very hard to know because I cannot get a sense of what your sense on that question.

Nick Johnson You are the first person to make me smile. I commend you for that. 'Fun' and 'joy', neither of them is a four letter words. I think too often architects think in those four letter words. I think the spirit you have shown in this has been quite dramatic. I also think your presentation is incredibly clear. It's great. Obviously, your work is really strong. You are the first person to talk about what it feels like to be inside your space. When you talked about wind blocks, you are actually thinking what it feels like to be there. A lot of architects don't even consider them, but with your drawing the wind velocity convert a sense of feeling, again it is a very strong part of your presentation. You started to talk about place. You also talked about the process in nature in which the shifting sun will affect the atmosphere of the earth and the notion of the bungalows on stilts dealing with the climate and the condition here. It is very strong, so there is an awful lot to congratulate you on. I am not persuaded at all - this was a comment raised in respect to other students as well - by the blocks, particularly the orientation of the blocks. Although you made them a single aspect, it is going to animate what conditions exactly you are going to put in the back and perhaps further exacerbate the difficult condition and the constraint the site imposes. I would personally plan a much more satisfactory solution by turning these things around. I think on the whole you dreamt about the place and it might be quite a good place to be.
[...]

Michael Bell If I were you and doing this project, I wouldn't have those platforms. Without the platforms, you go from zone to zone and you have to cross between the zones. You are talking about homesteading and the model of, in a sense, division of land prior to the arrival of infrastructure that would allow passage without crossing another's property. I think it was a study done a couple years ago when someone was looking at the subdivision of property in Texas...and later on the arrival of subdivision roads, system such as bypass seizure of properties. What's most fascinating to me about the project is the way you literally would

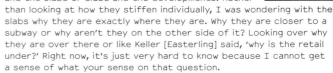

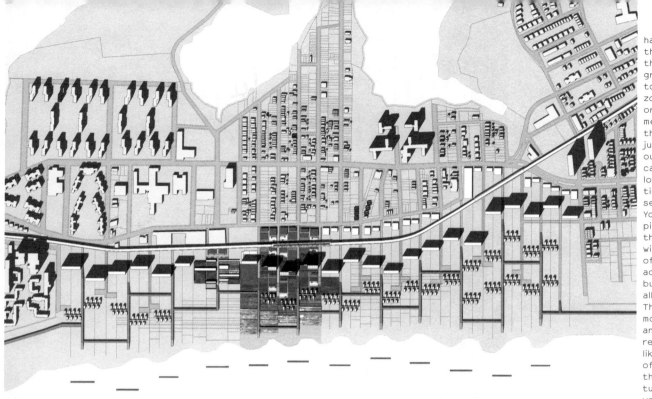

1.

have to go from that rectangle to that rectangle. It is great that you have to step out of your zone and elevated up or down, but it took me a while to get to that because I am just trying to figure out the plan. Optically, any of the plans looks like the elevation, and it has the sense of a desert. You can call it semi-pixelization. Everything is operating with the oscillation of rectangles and adjacent rectangles, but there is not really any overlapping. They don't get much more to it than rectangle shearing against rectangle, which is like the subdivision of property. I keep thinking of architectural spaces where you go from one room to another without having the ability or means to go into a hall…like Loos's Raumplan where you start to go out to a room and enter into differentiated levels. But without the references, I just think one of the things that is powerful about your project would be to read – somehow territories are never really easily mitigated – that you are crossing other people's land to get to other places.

Ayat Fadalfard
City College of New York
Ecological FlexiMesh

The design approach for this site was to project a "flexible mesh" over the entire site, one that is capable of reacting to existing site conditions and forces. This highly responsive mesh runs from the northern edge of the site down towards the beach and provides ecological services and different levels of human occupation. This system was proved, based on extensive research on dune morphologies and other ecological and environmental factors, to be most successful on this particular site. This project, as a result, suggests a new way of urban living with nature.

Keith Krumwiede
(continued)

Patrick
Bellew You
build the
dune fences

and then things happen naturally?

Ayat Fadalfard There are two types. There
are both artificial and natural dunes.

Michael Bell Are you going to talk about the
shape of the berms.

Diana Balmori They have very particular
shape because of biowind.

Bell Can we presume they are naturally
formed? Do them emerge?

Edward Mitchell Are they really shape or system?

Bell Just be very specific of this.

Fadalfard I am constructing this because
it creates a pocket…

Balmori The reason for that is just for
drainage?

Mitchell What about the sand?

Balmori I think that's great. I think it is a
great idea.

Keith Krumwiede It is shape and a system.
What is the agenda of the project? What if the
dunes are left in their state of naturalness or do
you recognize these dunes are actually operating on particular shapes that are reconstructed?
That should happen at the very beginning of the
project — seeing that through and looking for
mutation as you move through.

Balmori There are different forms for where
the winds come from the ocean and what it is in
the back. Whatever form you get, you have to
plant it very quickly so that it won't go away.
Whatever it is, it is not that shape that you have
at first. But I am assuming that it is what you
build first and then allows these shapes to happen.
This idea is a very good idea as far as being able
to take the system and see what it can do for
your design. I suspect you will be most interested
in that and that it became a passion — an organization for the whole scheme. Is that the case or
not? I am assuming. I am asking that.

Fadalfard It started with these chipboard
models as part of a series of design exercises.
I came up with this idea that flat surface on the
north side of the subway toward the beach controls the environment in intervals. This creates
a movement from north to south. There is some
form-making, but it works on this particular site.
This shows the different type of vegetations
that happen here: from tree to shrubs to grass
to mesh. I also have some ideas about dividing
the housing into 3 main
parts: circulation core,
green roof and a double
layer of skin with plantings
in the interior.

Balmori So you are
growing things in-between
the layers?

Fadalfard You have
a view toward the beach.
I was hoping to make
the berms act as a wind
protection system. From
south to west, the activities are happening in-be-
tween the berms.

Balmori You seem to
have very powerful im-
ages about this mysteri-
ous place — a place I love
to be in. From the point
of view of the images,
you've been able to captivate what you are doing and your experiments
with this interest me. It doesn't matter whether I like them or don't like
them. I really found that is something we all need to do — to be able to
take these things and apply them to the land and see if we can use them
as the bases for design. I praise you for that, but it all falls apart for
me when I get to that end over there, in which I am seeing the utopia of
the [19]50s. These are isolated pieces of ground in which these towers
are placed. They are not designed with the ground around them. They are
just absolutely isolated pieces that are found on the ground. It is a very
interesting ground, but there is no connection to the design methodology of the towers. The land does not want the towers to come down on it,
which is precisely the problem of many buildings of the [19]50s and [19]60s.
They never deal with the ground, so that is my specific problem with this
design, and I would like to hear what others think about it.

Keller Easterling I was looking at this and thinking if one were really
to divide this or if I were working for you and trying to figure out what

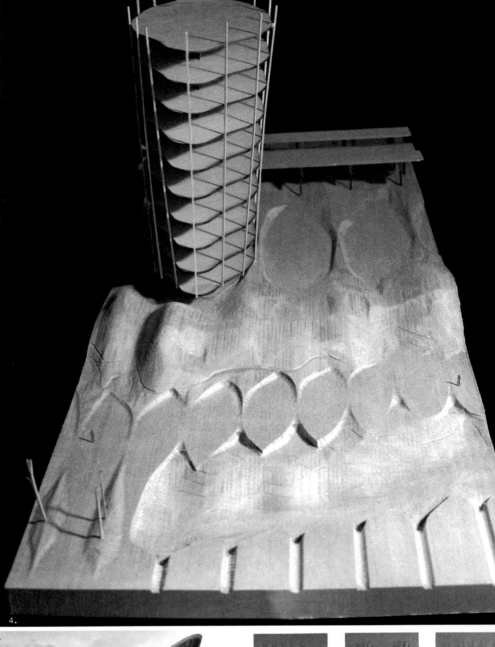

4.

5.

6.

you want somehow by looking at
this, it is exactly somewhere in
between shape and system be-
cause you don't know which one to think. The redundancy
of it means that you don't know which one would fail, so
you don't know what the eventual shape would be. That
is something quite interesting, and then you see that he
also decided to cultivate buildings here as if one would
almost cultivate vegetation and find these kinds of moments. Right now, the only thing we see is the contingency for cultivating. That might be wind, at least that
is the kind of mental look of the presentation, the visual
persuasion that is something about wind, but how great it
would be if somehow you could make some kind of argument where the quail pond, the real estate, the maniacal
green and all the contingency become something you can
treat, something you can cultivate and play with. Some
of them fail and some of them succeed.

[…]

Sunil Bald There is a fundamental contradiction in terms of your understanding of the site as mud, treating it in a messy way like your idea of the ground plane. Your tower is about engaging the site as sky and view. I think it goes back to the other comment of more tectonic basis. In that section, the disconnection between the way you treated the ground and the self-contained tower might go back to your confused aspiration for the project. What do you really value about this place? Is it really much more about the softness of the underfoot and the instability that you are kind of stabilizing, or is it about the stability of the tower that you are kind of making — where one can be safe in the tower from the surrounding while still being able to look out into the sea and the sky?

Julia McCarthy & Meaghan Smialowski
Yale University & Washington University
<u>Everything IN Between</u>

"Everything in Between" is an urbanism project which aims to encourage and support sustainable urban development economically, environmentally, and socially by using city-owned vacant land in Edgemere, Queens. In addition to the city's need for housing, we respond to the neighborhood's need for infrastructural improvement, specifically drainage control, water treatment, and roadway improvement. After evaluating the available lot conditions, our project distributes drainage/filtration beds in an effort to control and treat water. These drainage beds create and yet limit a system of available lots for development of varying densities. The project allows for slow-paced repopulation of the neighborhood with infrastructural innovations to support such growth over time.

Edward Mitchell There are a whole bunch of questions here. I think there is an aesthetic fragment. We are not sure what the measure is, like the key to the aesthetic. What is the goal of the whole system?
[...]
Diana Balmori There is an attempt to try to work out the land in a certain intelligent way, and there is a level of detail about how it is working that I really think is very, very good. I am not inspired by the images. I really want you to show me something that is really beautiful out of the result and those sort of faded out images don't do it. But the attention that you have paid to the materials, into each piece of the landscape that you are creating in which you are going to put those buildings, I think, is very good. I am not convinced that the discontinuity of infrastructure can become that way simply because it costs too much to build them piece by piece on the street, so I don't think that is very realistic. In terms of the buildings, I really think the issue of the façade is an important one and your ability to address the vision is very good.

Nick Johnson I really like what you've done. I don't understand, after twenty-five minutes of presentation, what it is all about. I really don't think you do yourself any favors at all in the way you talked about it or presented it graphically to us.

Diana Balmori I agree.

Johnson I think that is a real issue that you face and you have got to address it because there are some really strong elements [here]. The

objective of getting water into rejuvenating the quality of the waterway and the bay is a really, really strong principle. The tower at the end of this connecting piece to the beach, which is part of nature, is a really strong solution. I like the fragmenting bits of nature. I do think there is a problem with the buildings, the tall buildings. I still don't understand the scheme. You should be able to condense some of the really striking strengths of the scheme to us in ten minutes, five minutes each, both orally and graphically.

Albert Pope One of the things that makes it difficult to talk about this project is the fact that someone else brought you to develop this project and master planned it. This is part of a larger master plan, and it is hard to judge with everything we've seen today because you do not have to work with the density. Someone else brought you into their scheme to be part of their master plan. The ability to work in this scale could be great because I can see how this kind of environment might relate to this treatment of a natural garden in this sort of man-made natural system you are proposing. It could tie into a larger project, but it is hard to asset it because we know all these other actions going on around it, and it is hard to place this in the larger scheme you presented. I think it is probably integrated pretty well.
[...]
Sunil Bald It is interesting in looking at these two where you have on one side surface and the other is housing. Surface, I guess, is your problem and housing — without may be thinking housing also has surface and we also live on surfaces — also becomes a problem, especially the use of the horizontal slab over here and the vertical surface over there. I wonder if there is a way to actually consider crossing those. If building surface could be thought of as part of this system, what would be the morphological consequences that way? It is not just about, I guess, the internal habitation with the quality of light that begins to shape this thing, but if you took that set of concerns to begin to shape the housing, you might actually form a more radical proposal. And vice versa, to think about what does it mean to understand or to live with the land, is nature center, which I think is a beautiful way to actually end it. Live with the land. Does that actually mean going inside the nature center inside the building? Are there another ways to live on that surface? I want to ask about this drawing because it became the beginning or the end of how each of your concerns sits next to each other…
[...]
Michael Bell I think it is an incredibly strong project in a lot of ways. I have a lot of doubts about it. I have no idea if it would actually work. I agree with Ed [Mitchell] and I'll be looking for testing. But the reason I can go either way is that I am not positive – well, I'll be much more direct – I think you could have presented [this] in five minutes by just making some sort of claim about the role of porosity and the pore surfaces and say that the theory that pore surfaces are being applied to lots of different realms, but not to integrate either the depth of the idea or the desire to present it in a longer period of time. You have the stage and you want to use it. At the back of my head, I keep feeling that this is a kind of fraction. This proposal is dealing with drain-off and water drainage etc. That is a form of fraction. You are trying to mitigate something that can be done better, and there are some mechanics to that. But when you started going about this business about school and university within five miles – the reason I asked if you were a planner on the side there, was [because] you were touching on the equity issues that are just generally harder planning curriculums/planning ideologies for the past forty and fifty years, which is the idea that somehow urban planning is invested in mitigating these equity issues. But in the end, I feel like you started there and you moved toward the porosity thing. I would like you to try to tie a tighter knot. Are they actually going to relate? Do those more porous landscapes do anything about education? I think the project is moving in the right direction. But for example, there are no jobs out there. Of course there isn't any education. There is no retail. All of these things are missing while housing gets built. I just want to say that I guess the testing of it would be the critical thing. What would stop you from being able to do this? By addressing that, it would then further enlighten the invention, which is where you are going as well. Personally, if I looked at this from a distance, I thought … the future of this type of work [has] got to do with not so much the porosity is this or that or the rainwater is this or that, but it would have to do with some sort of focus on allowing property to breathe and addressing territory waste that is more advanced than subdivision.

8.

Thesis
599b

with Keith Krumwiede *(Thesis Coordinator),* *and* Faculty

Proposals for the Thesis option must be submitted by the beginning of the preceding fall term for review and approval by the Design and Rules Committees. Proposals must include a complete program, documentation, and project statement. Students with approved proposals can take an Independent Study with an instructor of choice in the fall term as thesis preparation.

Andrew Lyon
Brown University
Lost In Transmission: Waste America

With the American desire for privacy and commodity, comes expansive growth and enormous waste. From Cul-de-sac's to Cardboard boxes, the American landscape is being commoditized and consumed. Growing populations surrounding urban areas, once small towns are eating up their land. We are seeing a kind of Super-Size Me Urbanism. The consumption centric society is quickly meeting its limits.

What if a suburb based on expanding growth meets with these limits? This project proposes that what will fit into the expansive grid of the west is an urban form for growth and waste management. What is lost in transmission is regained in localization. The Not-in-my-backyard planning that has pushed the mechanics of growth to the outskirts of the city are contained and commoditized within.

The result is a kind of autonomous hybrid, collecting commodities and waste, and returning energy to the system. It is a growth generator.

These small fast growing nearly towns, obese with opportunity, are facing a crisis of success. This thesis is focused on looking at the conditions that have created that crisis and suggesting possible solutions that maintain the stated goal of the town.

Considering the current political and social conditions present in the United States, this thesis does not pretend to support the goal of what William McDonough calls "Eco-effectiveness." Or rather a belief that utilizing a cost efficient energy strategy does anything more than support increased demand for energy. Rather it presents a corporate scenario of eco-efficiency.

"With eco-efficiency, is being less bad being good, or is it simply being bad, just less so?"
        —William McDonough, Interview in Massive Change

Ulitmately, the question is not what changes? It is not what is the new building form or urban form? It is in a new frontier of limited land, how can we continue to let the boomburbs boom?

Allan William Martin
Yale University
Genetic Algorithms to Optimize Performace Criteria
Within Construction Constraints

This thesis makes a case for a modular, computer-based, generative design system that is not purely form-making, but resolves performance criteria with the geometric constraints of a construction method. This aims to suggest the utility of computational methods both to expand the architect's ability to explore design options while ensuring practicality.

The system has three modules: the performance evaluation engine, the parametric engine, and the algorithm. Performance can be defined in terms of acoustics, structure, lighting requirements, etc. The parametric engine is responsible for describing the possible configurations of the designed object. The algorithm resolves the requirements of the first two modules.

This thesis will explore the ability of a form-finding genetic algorithm to resolve acoustical performance (fitness) requirements of an acoustical shell within the geometric restrictions of its assembly system. Genetic algorithms have been used to optimize the designs of design concert halls and acoustic reflectors, but these examples generally do not take into account the actual construction of those halls and reflectors beyond specifying materials.

This project is a variation of the Firehouse 12 bar and recording studio in New Haven designed by Gray/Organschi Architecture. The performance criterion was to achieve an acoustically dead space with a hard (i.e. typically sound-reflective) material, in this case birch plywood. The assembly system allowed for deformations in the plywood that reduced the convergence of reflected sound waves or made convergences occur above typical human head height.

Adding a genetic algorithm to the typical analysis process effectively converts its methods used to test acoustic properties into form-generating tools. Solutions to the design problem will take the form of varied configurations of deformed plywood panels, which as a whole serve as an acoustical shell assembly. These panels will be mounted at the corners in such a way to allow each corner to be offset from non-deformed plane of the panel. The set of distances each corner is offset, combined with a scan of the resulting curvature, will serve as the data to build the genotype of the shell. Solutions will be simulated and evaluated virtually and the genetic algorithm will search for a fit solution.

Three software tools are necessary for this process, one for each module. The first is an acoustical ray-tracing environment to serve as a rudimentary acoustical analysis engine and the fitness function for the genetic algorithm. A set of scans with a non-contact 3D scanner will record the geometry of the possible configurations of a single plywood panel, and the second tool will parametrically model the assemblage. Finally, a simple genetic algorithm will be applied to test possible configurations of panels, effectively acting as a bridge between the first two tools.

The first scenario produced an acoustic shell to maximize the sound received by a single listener from a single speaker. This was a trivial case to validate the algorithm, since it should converge to an elliptical shape placing the speaker at one focus and the listener at the other.

The final scenario was between a panel of seated speakers and an audience standing behind them to maximize the acoustic performance of an acoustically deadened space, the fourth floor pit of the A+A building at Yale.

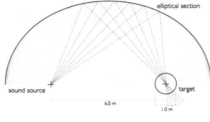

01	02	03
SCENARIO_ideal	SCENARIO_00	SC

ideal case
The first run is intended to be a simple test case to check the system. It is known that the ideal geometric way to focus sound from a single point source to a single target is through an elliptical section.

baseline
A single flat panel the equivalent size of a 2 by 6 panel assembly is placed 3m above a single source and single target, just as the first scenario.

run

results
7800.0

results
156.0

resul
49

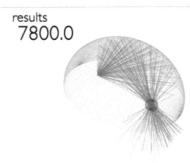

next step
Running a simple case to check if the assembly system can perform for the intended criteria at all. First, a baseline case needs to be scored.

next step
Testing the corresponding panel assembly.

next
To che
instea
scenar

MASTER OF ENVIRONMENTAL DESIGN

Eeva-Liisa Pelkonen *(coordinator)*, Peggy Deamer, Keller Easterling, Karsten Harries *(Philosophy)*, Dolores Hayden, Sandy Isenstadt *(History of Art)*, Emmanuel Petit, Alan Plattus. *Visiting critics:* Arindam Dutta *(MIT)*, Edward Eigen *(Princeton University)*, Joan Ockman *(Columbia University)*, Felicity Scott *(Columbia University)*.

2nd year students: Joy Knoblauch *(advisor: Peggy Deamer; reader: Emmanuel Petit)*, Frida Rosenberg *(advisor: Emmanuel Petit; reader: Peggy Deamer)*, Leslie Ryan *(advisor: Karsten Harries; reader: Keller Easterling)*, Sara Stevens *(advisor: Keller Easterling; reader: Alan Plattus)*.
1st year students: McLain Clutter *(advisor: Peggy Deamer)*, Britt Eversole *(advisor: Keller Easterling)*, Enrique Ramirez *(advisors: Eeva-Liisa Pelkonen and Alan Plattus)*, Molly Steenson *(advisors: Emmanuel Petit and Keller Easterling)*, Federica Vannucchi *(advisor: Karsten Harries)*.

The key word of this year's M.E.D. research was **Synergy**. *First of these was the question how architecture participates in identity construction. Rosenberg looked into changes to European, particularly Swedish, identity as it struggles to respond to multi-culturalism and European integration. Knoblauch discussed how the English architect and educator, Robin Evans, addressed individual identity formation in his teaching and writings. Ryan and Stevens shared an interest in the hidden economical and ecological forces that shape the environment, dealing, respectively with a Superfund site in Hamden, CT and with ubiquitous and ever more sophisticated retail formats discussing, for example the financial tools that gave birth, almost accidentally to now huge mini-storage industry to those that made Home Depot into a retail success story. The first year students have benefited from similar overlaps from the get-go. Eversole and Vannuchi are both dealing with post-war Italy; Ramirez and Steenson share an interest in new technologies; while Clutter, Ramirez and Vannucchi are all interested in representational strategies. The quality of the work so far pays tribute to their strong sense of community.*

McLain Clutter
Syracuse University
Imagineering New York

Conventional wisdom holds that we should not believe what we see in the movies. For the educated audience, even those films that purport to be 'documentary' or 'realistic' are fundamentally mediated texts. When it comes to filmic representations of New York City (where it has become routine, for example, to depict penniless twenty-something residents of spacious SoHo lofts), this rule seems doubly valid. However, through a close examination of the developing relationship between the planning policies that have shaped New York, and the policies and incentives invented to attract motion picture productions to the city, a different story emerges.

The conjuncture of planning, cultural policies and film-making reached a pivotal point in 1966 when, under threat of bankruptcy and crumbling urban infrastructure, New York City mayor John Lindsay signed Executive Order 10 – a measure intent on attracting film productions to New York. The effects of the policy were immediate – adding $20 million to the city economy in the second half of 1966, and enabling the film industry to grow into a $500 million dollar industry in New York by 1980. While Lindsay's policies regarding location filming in New York drew productions to the city, their contemporary urban planning policies were replete with scopophilic tendencies intent on grooming the image of New York as it might be captured on film. These tendencies are visible in planning documents such as the 1969 Plan For the City of New York; and the 1967 report The threatened city: a report on the design of the city of New York, produced by the City Planning Commission. By cross-reading urban policies during the period between 1966-81 with contemporaneous films set in New York, such as Sidney Lumet's 1973 film Serpico, or Paul Marzursky's 1976 film Next Stop Greenwich Village, the research will challenge the conventional duality between representation and reality.

Britt Eversole
Yale University
Progetto e Impero

The journal Contropiano (1968-1971) was the product of a collaboration between Alberto Asor Rosa, Massimo Cacciari, and Antonio Negri. Within its pages, a theoretical version of the operaismo project was undertaken by its contributing authors, attacking the cultural institutions of 'adversarial bourgeois class' to reveal to the workers the reality of their conditions. One of the primary targets of that critique was the built environment and the ideology that both permeates and is propped up by pianificazione. Though Contropiano was a political/cultural criticism journal, a significant portion of its contributors were intellectuals at the Istituto Universitario di Architettura Venezia, such as Cacciari, Francesco Dal Co, Manfredo Tafuri, Giorgio Ciucci, Mario Manieri-Elia, and others.

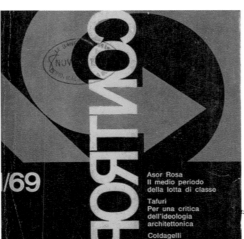

Within the United States, the Italian leftist critique of architecture and the city during the 1960s and 70s is understood primarily through a single source – Tafuri. His totalizing project – which argued that architecture is always co-opted by the dominant ideology of the class in power – still affects and afflicts the discipline's struggle to project a social and political relevance for architecture. However, Tafuri's work represents only one example of the sustained critique of cultural production conducted by a constellation of Italian intellectuals. Among the many riviste of the period, Contropiano is an extraordinary example of the diversity of positions of thinking in the 60s. This thesis proposes to return to the original essays of the journal to develop a better understanding of the broader context of the leftist thought and critical philosophy which influenced the architectural historians at the IUAV during the 1970s. Such a project will suggest new points of view on the political critique of architecture, and possibly decenter Tafuri from the position granted him by his Anglo-audience. The task of the project is to construct a field of positions, arguments, lines of thought around Contropiano, repositioning Tafuri as but one of many critics all working on a common project – the ideological critique of the built environment.

Enrique Gualberto Ramirez
University of California at Los Angeles
Operation Magic Fire (1)

This project examines an unusual series of events starting in 1942 with the testing and development of napalm at Harvard University, and culminating in 1943 when Erich Mendelsohn, Konrad Wachsmann, and Antonin Raymond, all well-known architects, were hired by the United States Chemical Warfare Service and the Standard Oil Development Corporation to design a series of "Typical German and Japanese Test Structures" at Dugway Proving Ground, a weapons testing facility in the Utah desert. These structures were full-scale models of German and Japanese apartment housing, designed to test the effect of the M69 incendiary bomb, the world's first napalm weapon, invented by Harvard chemist Louis Fieser. The three architects also enlisted the help other German immigrants in the American design community, including furniture designer Hans Knoll and landscape architect and urban planner Paul Zucker.

A.

Their research not only investigated building construction techniques in major German and Japanese cities, but also assessed the bomb-target value of housing stock in these cities. The resulting data, which included everything from an analysis of wood employed in German and Japanese home construction, to the study of the relative flammability of specific German – and Japanese – made interior furnishings, such as tatami floors and baby cribs, was used with devastating effect.

This thesis begins with an account of the National Defense Research Committee's (NRDC) wartime research into incendiary explosives. The NRDC supervised Louis Fieser's work at Harvard as well as Mendelsohn's, Wachsmann's, and Raymond's work for the Chemical Warfare Service and Standard Oil at Dugway Proving Ground. The thesis specifically focuses on the technological, political, and cultural ramifications involved in the simulated construction of Axis cities in the Utah desert, a program contributing to the wholesale destruction of cities by Allied bombers during World War II. The thesis also adds a biographical dimension to these architects' wartime work, asking the difficult question of how a group of ex-patriot designers were willing and able to develop architectures that were in fact instruments of aggression.

----

(1) "Operation Magic Fire" (unternehmen feuer-zauber) was the code name given to the deployment of aircraft in support of Nationalist forces during the Spanish Civil War. These were the same aircraft used in the bombing of Guernica in 1937 by the Nationalists. The term "Operation Magic Fire" is thus used to suggest the relationship between the scientific development of napalm and the destruction of cities during World War II.

(A) Dugway Proving Ground, German-Japanese Village, Observation Bunker, South of Stark Road, in WWII Incendiary Test Area, Dugway, Tooele County, UT, Overall View of Observation Bunker with Building T-8100 in the Background, in Historic American Buildings Survey/Historic American Engineering Record (Library of Congress), HAER UT-92-B-3.

Molly Wright Steenson
University of Wisconsin at Madison
The Excitable Crowd:
Characterizing Mobile, Social Space

We live and die by our mobile phones. We wake to their alarms, customize them to suit our personalities, express our love and frustration on them, coordinate movements and conduct business through them. Mobile technology reaches spaces where the Internet and landline telephony cannot. It also reaches people who may be excluded from these technologies: those who can't read can still use mobile phones, where other information technology proves more difficult.

Mobile and embedded technologies affect the urban framework and the living environments, not just our social interactions. They shift the nature of space by enabling a roving co-presence, generating new types of territory, and facilitating the physical delimitation of space. But these technologies also raise questions about power relationships between global technology networks and the user on the ground. How liberating are these spaces? What do they enclose that isn't readily perceivable?

"The Excitable Crowd" investigates the character of this mobile, social space. Its case studies include a group of San Francisco women using the mobile phone for urban coordination and interpersonal power plays, teenagers navigating both Tokyo and gender and age boundaries through technology, and mobile telecenters (ad hoc and situated) in the developing world. These case studies show the intersecting dimensions of mobile, social space at different scales, from the personal space of the body, to the territory of the city, to global networks and protocols governing and enabling mobile technology.

Federica Vannucchi
University degli Studi di Firenze
Superstudio: Discourses Through Images

The design collective Superstudio was formed in 1966 as an avant-garde architectural group within the University of Florence. The group was composed of Adolfo Natalini, Christiano Toraldo di Francia, Roberto Magris, Gian Piero Frassinelli, Alessandro Magris. Alessandro Poli joined the group in 1970 and stayed two years. The group emerged during a time of particularly intense intellectual debate regarding the definition of architecture and its social commitment. Superstudio produced a large and influential body of projects from 1968 to 1973 to decidedly mixed reception. Some considered Superstudio's projects a critical reaction to the dissolution of the relationship between the practice of architecture and the needs of everyday life, while others, like Manfredo Tafuri criticized the group's proposals as non-operative and confined in a cynical passivity. On the other hand, the recent retrospective exhibition of their work bore witness to the contemporary attraction to their ideas and imagery.

This thesis will contribute to this ongoing discussion by contextualizing their work within the broader Italian debates about the role of art and architecture in the social realm. One of the key figures that will be discussed in the thesis is the art critic Giulio Carlo Argan, who put forward the idea of "death of art" at the hands of the capitalist system and believed that the only way out of the dilemma was by eliminating the physical object. Members of Superstudio took this proposal to their hearts and focused their artistic production increasingly on images and films. In the end the thesis will assess whether Superstudio succeeded in this critical strategy or whether it added to nothing more than nostalgia about the paradise lost.

M.E.D.
Second Year
Thesis

Joy Ruth Knoblauch
Cornell University
Architecture and Contingent Subjectivity:
Robin Evans' Theories and Designs (1963-1982)

Almost never does the discipline of architecture under-take detailed research, informed by a rich theoretical background, on the issues of privacy and inter-subjectivity, except in the early work of one architect: Robin Evans. His early work at the Architectural Association, from 1963 to 1982, attempted to use the design of housing to foster a specific mental state which would invert the alienation of post-war public housing. In particular, his goal was to nurture an easy sociability, something he felt had been lacking in domestic life since the nineteenth century. In 1978, his well-known essay "Figures, Doors and Passages" suggested that the root of this deficiency was a nascent divided-self, the evolution of modern institutions and the advent of hallways. His theory of history was inspired by an admiration for Michel Foucault's genealogical approach and R.D. Laing's theories of the divided-self, among others. In this way, he wrote about a type of subjectivity which is contingent upon its social, historical and architectural context.

The essay is reasonably well-known but the disappearance of the design studies which preceded the essay constitutes a crucial lesson for architects. A combination of accident, local fights, the reception of the visual aspects of the work and a larger shift in the direction of architecture in the early 1980s led to Evans' abandonment of the study of domestic circulation and sociability. None of this was inevitable, but nevertheless the absence of his early work in the canon of architecture has contributed to the impoverishment of the discipline in terms of theories of contingency and the problem of housing design.

Excerpt from Chapter 3, "Design and Control"
In his undergraduate thesis, "Towards Anarchitecture", Robin Evans argued that the major motivation for technologies of control is to minimize mess. Among the most intimate of those messes, he felt that individuals favored the hallway, as an advance which prevented the accidental mixing of inner and outer selves. Among the most public of those messes, he felt that the state's desire to locate families in precise units had produced an overly bounded domestic architecture, which also used the separation of destination from route to place households in separate, manageable units. As an architect, he sought to reintroduce mess, spontaneity and conviviality into his designs and those of his students at the Architectural Association. He combined his analysis of hallway circulation as isolating with his desire to enable choice and arrived at a modified enfilade arrangement where circulation often passes through rooms.

A.

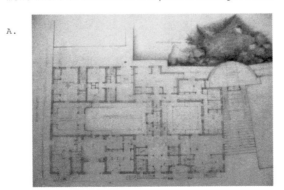

Evans' hoped that by providing multiple options for circulation a more rich and messy everyday social life would result. His archive includes drawings of such schemes including elevations and plans for mixed unit housing which would alleviate the boundedness and isolation of postwar housing. For example, the drawing above includes a unit in the upper left wherein route the occupant would pass through the main rooms as part of normal circulation. The unit in this case appears to be a studio or bedsit unit. In the lower left is a larger unit wherein circulation again passes through the major spaces of the unit, although the bedrooms are left as termination points. As the circulation passes through the living spaces it is often demarcated by columns which provide some separation but allow for spontaneous interaction between residents.

Despite the increased choice and potential social interaction that would come from mixing circulation routes, still there is a subtle balance between control and choreography. It is arguable that forcing people to walk through a main room is no different than forcing them to walk through a hallway. Some of the work seems to carefully address this problem, such as a "Large House at Notting Hill" by Dan Davis which has some hall spaces around the edges of the building and some very porous rooms such that there are many ways to move from space to space within the building. A scheme by Bill Greensmith for the City of Rooms project is perhaps the best of both worlds since it allows the walker to choose. The way that this room is designed, one could walk through the central seating space, since it is arguably the shortest path, but one could also walk around the liminal spaces at the sides. They are also plausible candidates for shortest path, thus providing the occupant with an option to avoid contact. Location in space could thus became a way to communicate one's mood regarding desire for company.

(A) Image courtesy of the Frances Loeb Library, Harvard Design School. This drawing is uncatalogued and undated.

Frida Karin Rosenberg
University of Texas
The Turning Torso: Dices of European Imposition

The high-rise Turning Torso in Malmö is a reinvention of Swedish identity, creating an image of a region between Denmark and Sweden. The Turning Torso, a 190m tall building, is located next to the sea in The Västra Hamnen [West Harbor] – a new district of Malmö that markets itself as the City of Tomorrow.(1) Malmö is Sweden's third largest city and is located on the southern tip of Sweden. By new investments, marketing and designing new neighborhoods, Malmö wants to be a cosmopolitan node – a gateway to the Baltic region.(2)

In 2000, the 18km Öresund-bridge between Malmö and Copenhagen was completed. In an attempt to expand the economic potential of the region the bridge formulated visions of structural change. Incorporating both sides of the sound, the population in the area, and the consumers, The Öresund is the 8th largest "city" in Europe. The final result as it stands is a region that is "a desperate reaction to the imposed necessities of a global economy."(3) This is, in particular an increased market economy between Sweden and the other Nordic countries. According to statistics, around 25,000 people living in one of the Nordic countries commute to work in another country everyday. Moreover, "four out of five of those live in Sweden."(4) A recent study showed that 43% of the commuters live in Malmö and daily travel over The Öresundsbron.

In 2001 the European Housing Expo Bo01 opened, a newly built permanent city district with mixed buildings, encompassing both commercial and social services together with about 500 housing units.(5) Supported by the Swedish government and the European Commission, this new development is attempting to attract an international audience. The area in the northeast corner of Bo01 is called the European Village, which was "constructed as an international single-family home development, to display how the EU building guidelines are implemented in various European countries."(6) Countries of the EU and the EFTA organization were invited to demonstrate their national architecture and construction methods appropriated to the Swedish climate and construction conditions. Building the European Village was an effort to test the application of the European Construction Products Directive (ECPD), which are the basic, common guidelines for architecture. Because of the restrained housing development, as a result of high standards, i.e. building costs and an expensive labor market, cities like Malmö and Gothenburg and especially Stockholm have a large housing shortage. It is in the Swedish Government's interest to increase the competition on the building industry, generating lower constructions and labor costs.

At the northeast tip of the Bo01 area stands The Turning Torso, Europe's tallest apartment building. The building, which is based on a sculpture by Santiago Calatrava called Twisting Torso, is designed like a body in movement. The former CEO of The Turning Torso – contractor and board chairman of the Malmö branch of the co-operative housing association HSB, Johnny Öhrbäck – saw the sculpture at an exhibition in 1999 and contacted Calatrava. He wanted to know if it was possible to build a high rise on the same principles. The building is 54 stories high and made up of nine volumes. The first two cubes, 4000m2 or twelve floors, are allocated for office space. The rest of the building, 13,500m2, contains 157, mostly rental apartments ranging from 45 to 230 square meters. External facilities, such as a sauna, private wine cellar, rooms for parties, exercise rooms and office space for rent, are included in the apartment package. The cheapest apartment, one bedroom of about 50m2, costs 7000kr ($1000).

In April last year, a weekly TV production of a political debate program on national television produced a debate on The Turning Torso. The program engaged experts and critics questioning "The Turning Torso as a symbol for the future of Malmö". Among others, the association Jagvillhabostad.nu [I want a place to live. now], was represented. The organization has formed as a critique towards a socially political problem shaped by a housing shortage for students and the lower class. Malin Norlander, a graphic designer, also took part in the program. She has brought about a lot of attention in the media through the production and selling of T-shirts with the statement: "Fucking Torso."

The T-shirt, Fucking Torso, is a result of these controversial circumstances and the fact that the cost of building The Turning Torso has more than doubled during the course of its construction. But most of all, the moral reconfiguration of the developer – organization HSB – a company that had always, up until now, built apartments for the people, was what made building The Turning Torso a sour issue. Building The Turning Torso changed the outlook of what a cooperative business in the position of HSB should be. Formed in 1924, this company currently encompasses 500,000 members that through a system of renting the apartment from HSB are in turn owners of HSB. The money that paid for The Turning Torso came from its members, yet the building was not built for its members. The Turning Torso is built for a high-income citizen.

The Öresund-region has through building The Öresundsbron and the high-rise Turning Torso, been claimed as the most potent region in Sweden, situated closest to the rest of Europe. The high-rise has also in many ways reached the goals as a symbol for Malmö through the media. Building The Turning Torso is a facelift – the former welfare state, in a condition of identity crisis, promulgating itself as somebody on the map of the European Union and beyond. But for how long will they last in the European community of competing identities? (7)

In January, two delegates from the MGM Mirage Design Group in Las Vegas visited Malmö and the Turning Torso. Two new Turning Torso's are in the planning stage in Las Vegas. The two new high-rise copies are planned to be 60m taller than the original in Malmö. Lars Danielsson, CEO of HSB commented; "there is only one original and that is in Malmö."

----

(1) www.malmo.se accessed April 8, 2006.

(2) http://home.att.net/~amcnet/bo01.html accessed April 8, 2006.

(3) Ibid.

(4) Ibid. The first conducted study on this matter ever, commissioned by The Nordic Council, showed that 25, 394 people had their largest income from another country than the one they were living in. 19, 651 of theses people were living in Sweden. The study by SCB is an analysis of one month in 2001.

(5) http://www.eaue.de/winuwd/187.htm accessed April 9, 2006.

(6) Ibid.

(7) On the Calatrava-Turning Torso site Cales Pas posted the following comment; "This building will be insignificant when the four new buildings projected by Calatrava will be built in Valencia near the city of arts and sciences. The tallest of the four buildings will be 280 meters high and the smallest will be 220 meters so they will be the tallest skyscrapers of Spain and possibly one of the tallest in Europe." November 14, 2004

Leslie Ann Ryan
(Field and Porter Prize Winner)
California Polytechnic, San Luis Obispo
Introduction: The Ecological Project

Olin's Pine Swamp in Hamden, Connecticut, is flooded swampland that has gradually become enveloped by industrial parks and older residential districts. It is a small but common example of a landscape that has been contaminated by industrial waste disposal, in this case,

as the result of years of producing weapons for wars from the Spanish-American War of 1898 to the enigmatic Cold War years. The environmental and social legacy of industry, war, and secrecy is stamped on many twenty-first century American landscapes. It's a familiar sight; the post-industrial landscape is dotted with the middens of infrastructure and sites that are no longer needed for industrial production. Piles of trash that are hundreds of feet high, water that must be carefully treated and monitored to avoid major public health problems, radioactive sludge poured into sewer lines – these are the products of accepted means of production that aren't only historical, they are also the "new" ground of many landscape remediation and restoration projects. Landscape architects, engineers, and planners are working with developers and cities to come up with technological and aesthetic design solutions for the problems, such as those of the Olin Pine Swamp, that the industrial past has left in its wake.

The swamp is a trope that begrudgingly opens a door into some of the more complex, intractable, and ubiquitous problems of what we call post-industrial. The first question is – what exactly is post- about post-industrial? A number of American cities are no longer the manufacturing centers that they were in the nineteenth, and far into the twentieth, centuries, but this has had no impact on consumption levels. We have more things, not fewer. We haven't stopped producing wastes or wasting land, and new industrial sites are constructed to replace those that are too damaged or unprofitable to persist. Those new industrial landscapes are likely to be in China and other Asian countries, along with Mexico, India, or South Africa. This particular post- is shorthand for "moving industry elsewhere so it is someone else's problem," or perhaps for "now we are depositing the wastes of production in authorized locations." Products have shadowy, companion products. While we tend to call these "by-" products, as if they can easily be shunted into the background, the products preceding and following our products occupy space as insistently as a body or a building. Where should waste products go? Who will count these by-products as neighbors?

Energy production, mining, and regulations of water have left satellite-scaled marks on the landscape--in infrastructures that string across and through the landscape, pit mines that are kilometers across, and dam projects that flood upland valleys and canyons. Landscape architect James Corner's winning competition submission for Fresh Kills Landfill in Staten Island, New York, is a high-profile example of a contemporary landscape remediation project. The fifty year old landfill will be covered with strata of impermeable membranes and soil, and then sculpted and planted to become new tidal marshes and playgrounds. (1) Another example is Peter Latz's Duisburg Nord Landscape Park in the Ruhr Valley of Germany. An abandoned steel factory was transformed into a park organized around the factory's infrastructure; contaminated land was buried, providing new ground for water retention ponds; thin soil was planted with tough pioneer species in the expectation that good soil will develop from bad. (2) Both projects are optimistic representations of the look that the post-industrial landscape might take, although as geographer David Harvey commented after viewing an exhibition of the projects, the scope of the work lacks any sense of atonement or responsibility.(3) There is little acknowledgement that there had been any strife, discord or injury in the making of the new park, only that a restoration of "friendly relationships" had occurred with the cap of gravel and synthetic membrane laid over years of waste. Optimism is a cover as well as a salve; brownfield is an optimistic designation for wasteland, as if these contaminated sites are merely dormant, and waiting to be revived as green, lush, productive fields. And the engineering exists, of course, to make these deserts bloom again.

Caught in this discussion are questions about the subjective and qualitative effects of the reshuffling of materials. What happens to the psychological and narrative aspects of water and waste? Or, the perplexing situation of water that is waste? Social theorist Ivan Illich writes that water throughout history was the "stuff of purity" that washed away the stains of life and death. It now has become H2O, "a social creation of modern times, a resource that is scarce and that calls for technical management."(4) What, as Illich asks, happens to the dream-life of water? Poetry and dreams are human things; the transformational prospects they provide are as essential for well-being as air or water. To speak of poetry in this sense concerns the ability to imagine, invent, and feel the correspondences between an inner life of dreams and the matter outside. The work of poetry is to help us "feel our surroundings as an ensemble, and to take them personally," writes poet Richard Wilbur. "It is spoken by the whole psyche."(5)

"We tell ourselves stories in order to live" writes Joan Didion, "We interpret what we see, select the most workable of the multiple choices."(6) The stories we elect to tell about ourselves shape the environment that others after us will inherit. Along with our stories, the inheritance includes a complicated array of involuntary reactions, new and unexpected products, continuing maintenance, and inevitable risks. A haunting refrain is the imperative to pay attention to the costs of our beliefs.(7) As beliefs emerge from events, and events from beliefs, they construct the quite literal foundations of our cities and landscapes. Our beliefs naturalize social and political situations. A generation of children practiced "duck and cover" in the event of atomic bomb attacks – what were they learning to believe about the world? These exercises appear especially peculiar as we discover that while Cold War fears focused on contamination emanating from foreign sources, our own radioactive waste was buried in shallow graves or, with aplomb, poured down the drain. Seeing and not-seeing, when dangers are hidden under water or behind veils of secrecy, is an aesthetic issue with deeply ethical implications. This aesthetic problem touches on an odd mixture of visual hegemony and invisible risks, uses of difficult words like nature, and social reform and the forgetful side of memory. What landscape are we inhabiting (or skirting around)? What is the story that will be engraved on the walls that the next generation will be reading, or submerged in the water that generations after us will be drinking?

The pine swamp that I found is not the one I had imagined when I began my research. Entering the swamp has led into a very literal 'miry Slough' of morality tales, social injustices, and compromised public resources. The sweet image of glacial kettles and floating bog islands, and problems such as invasive plant species, faded into the background once the history of a site conscripted for military and industrial uses began to unfold. My "walk in the park" shifted into a story of decades-long use as a site of military/industrial production, including the enigmatic Cold War years, as weapons were tested and the detritus of manufacturing was dumped in the swampy ponds. A pair of 1956 newspaper articles found in the archives of a local library illuminated a more complex and insidious history, as I learned that the corporation who owned the swamp also produced nuclear fuel from 1956-1974 at the factory a mile away. What kinds of wastes were buried along the shoreline of the ponds? This precise history had been forgotten: the secrecy demanded by military operations, fuel production, business methods and trade formulas essentially veiled the site.

Two recurring themes resonate throughout: why we should remember, and why we should be able to forget. Memories of past uses and resultant waste-products are often forgotten over time, through neglect and the desire to evade the liability and costs of remediation. Without memory's record of what happened, at what time and in what quantities, the general well-be-

ing of the public is at the mercy of decisions that are based on irresolute information. It is the public who bears the consequences of this kind of industrial forgetting, as private interests and their profits move on and what remains is polluted water, forlorn and hazardous landscapes, or parks littered with warning signs because it's too dangerous to wander from the designated path. But we also need to insist on the capacity to forget. Without the possibility of remembering and forgetting, we have no possibility of re-making ourselves or the world we inhabit. Without forgetting, we are constrained to a past, a condition that is made more prohibitive when it is toxic, polluted, and contaminated. The technological solutions that stabilize wastes for a generation or so are condemning subsequent generations to stand at attention and unyieldingly guard against change. Post-industrial remediations can rarely be left alone; they require constant chaperoning. While remembering our productions of the past is crucial to understanding how to remedy current problems, just as essential is the ability to forget. We need to be able to forget the past, to some degree, in order to invent our own time.

This ecological project owes much to the work of theorists such as Félix Guattari, Gregory Bateson and Bruno Latour. Guattari's constellation of three ecologies – the subjective, the social, and the environmental – lays the groundwork for a political discourse that emerges from an ethical and aesthetic base. The "ecological" of the ecological project begins here, in the spidery labyrinth of emotions, politics, and water. Bateson's formulation of the basic unit of survival as an interlocking of organism plus environment had inspired much of Guattari's three ecologies. Bateson's "double bind" theory is applicable to the problem of determining which information to attend to – do we believe the beautiful view or the hushed cautions to beware? Latour's call for a new Constitution that refers to things as well as persons and is open to a multitude of voices, opens up a thought-space for water and governing bodies. All three take issue with the transcendent view of a pure nature that ignores the thickets of entangling social problems or relies on technocratic proposals which boldly declare the solution is forthcoming. In the bifurcation of nature into "matters of concern" (the social place of dreams and poetry), and "matters of fact" (the rational world of abstraction and measurement), Latour tells us that "we had better believe the poet" who tells us that the world is not divided.(8)

Throughout, little will be said about the healthy functioning of ecosystems, or fragmented habitats. Olin's Pine Swamp is already an eccentric landscape of introduced species, and its "lakes" should always be read as if they were in quotes. What is most important to me is understanding the situations that allowed the swamp to become a Superfund site, why people have strong emotional reactions to this place, and how, through remembering the past, and as we look at what this one might become, we might also uncover possible means and methods of not re-producing contaminated landscapes in other places.

----

(1) Linda Pollack. "Sublime Matters: Fresh Kills." Praxis, Journal of Writing and Building. Vol. V, issue 4. 2002: (58-61).

(2) Peter Reed. Groundswell: Constructing the Contemporary Landscape. New York: Museum of Modern Art, 2005.

(3) David Harvey. Keynote Address. Groundswell: Constructing the Contemporary Landscape. Museum of Modern Art. The Cooper Union, New York. 15 April 2005.

(4) Ivan Illich. H2O and the Waters of Forgetfulness: Reflections on the Historicity of "Stuff." Dallas: The Dallas Institute of Humanities and Culture, 1985. p. 76.

(5) Richard Wilbur. "Poetry and the Landscape." Gyorgy Kepes, ed. The New Landscape in Art and Science. Chicago: Paul Theobald and Co., 1956. p. 89.

(6) Joan Didion. The White Album. New York: Simon and Schuster, 1979. p 11.

(7) Helen Mayer Harrison and Newton Harrison. The Lagoon Cycle. Ithaca: Cornell University/Herbert F. Johnson Museum of Art, 1985.

(8) Bruno Latour. "Nature at the Crossroads: A Philosophical Look at the Politics of Science." Dorothy Nelkin Lecture Series. Vanderbilt Hall. New York University School of Law, New York. 24 October 2005.

Sara Stevens
Rice University
Systems of Retail: The Bigger Box
Excerpt from "Self-Storage: Frontiers of
Real Estate Development"

One industry that seems to fly below the radar, rarely attracting the attention of urbanists concerned with the built environment, is the contemporary American self-storage industry.(1) Until recently, this industry has avoided prime real estate, choosing to locate on the edges of small towns, or near industrial areas away from new suburban development. The majority of owners are small-time entrepreneurs owning an average of only three facilities. But the largest companies, Public Storage, Shurgard, Storage USA, and U-Haul, use this industry to maneuver financial gains from real estate plays. The self-storage industry is inexorably tied to a particular brand of Wall Street financial scaffolding which has resulted in a set of building formats that maximize the tenets of real estate finance.

The most interesting facet of the early developments was the expectation that the buildings would only be temporary. Public Storage began as simply a way to make money on land while waiting for a better, more profitable use to appear. This was just an elaborate system of landbanking—what developers call ground cover. The buildings were cheap, capitalization rates were high, and if a residential development or another commercial use was determined to be more valuable, then when the short-term leases ran out, the building could be bulldozed for new development with no loss. Public Storage's early properties were located in areas relatively close to urban centers, in the projected path of new development. The self-storage concept would provide quick, short-term returns while holding land for future, grander development as the city expanded out to meet it. Under this model, it set the standard for the building type as something cheap and quick that could be dispensed with on opportunity's knock. In the meantime, though, the company realized that profits were too good to bulldoze and sell the land, much less to change anything, and the most profitable plan was to do was more of the same, minus the bulldozer.

As the industry grew, it acquired greater sophistication in profit-gathering techniques. Measures and statistics became increasingly important to gauge success, growth, and profits. Public Storage, always the largest company in the industry, spent heavily on computer technology in the mid-eighties to develop sophisticated demographic and mapping software and databases to track the success of their locations and that of their competitors. This was important information to have to present to investment groups who funded their operations. Proving that a market existed for their product in a given area, and showing that they were neither over-saturating an area nor cannibalizing their own locations meant that they could get more money to continue developing more buildings.(2) The goal was to create 'barriers to entry' for their competitors, meaning, get to a given market area first, in a prime location, to make it more difficult for your competitors to follow. To measure market saturation, figures for the square feet of self-storage per person in a given area were calculated and compared in regions across the country to justify further building and industry growth.(3) The barrier to entry concept represents a fundamental change in the industry as well. Rather than focus on building cheap buildings on cheap land at the outskirts of development, new facilities need to be placed in commercial centers, near major thoroughfares and freeways, with greater visibility to attract their desired market segment. "Mini-storage used to cater to the blue-collar, pickup-truck set," said Frank Mason,

while president of the National Mini Storage Institute. But that has changed, and those in the industry are now, "building better, more secure facilities in urban areas, so we open the market to the Mercedes set."(4)

All growth in this industry is critically linked to its investment structure. The largest self-storage companies, Public Storage, Storage USA/Extra Space, U-haul, and Shurgard, have ties to or are themselves Real Estate Investment Trusts (REITs) which supply capital needed for development, and take a cut of profits which are shared as dividends among their investors. The equity REIT involvement in the industry has, in the words of a leading business journal, taken what was once considered the "ugly duckling" of commercial buildings and turned it into "a beautiful swan" as high-yield equities.(5) Public Storage, the largest self-storage company by far, is also the second largest REIT in the country.

What is unusual about the self-storage industry's connection to REITs is that most REITs invest in higher-profile buildings like office buildings, skyscrapers, apartments, and other large, visible, high-quality projects. Pensions are especially known for investing in 'trophy properties', a category that would not likely include self-storage facilities.(6) Simply put, self-storage facilities hold a reputation that is antithetical to a typical REIT-owned property. The probable connection between the two goes back to the original scheme of Public Storage—that is, the landbanking strategy. REITs are conservative investing structures, described as carrying high-profile real estate. So REIT investment in self-storage facilities began with centrally-located facilities on land that would be valuable no matter what is built on it. Self-storage is nothing more than what developers call a 'taxpayer' – a land use that will pay the property taxes. But this 'taxpayer' is also a dividend payer, stock payer, and pension payer.

The self-storage industry is able to generate profits due to its ties to real estate investing, and almost as a sideline rents small spaces for personal and business storage. This model, though not a franchise system, is very similar to McDonalds' system, which makes profits on their franchising deals and real estate, and sells hamburgers on the side. What is new in the self-storage model is that a supporting building industry and land use type have developed and flourished as a result. Catering to shareholders and dividend payments, this industry holds a growing stake in the built environment. In Form Follows Function, Carl Willis argues that the variations in skyscraper form between New York and Chicago "can best be understood as products of standard real estate formulas that were modified by local conditions…. Distinct vernaculars of capitalism evolved in each city from this combination of economic logic and the particulars of place."(7) Like Carol Willis shows for skyscrapers, the self-storage industry has developed its own 'vernacular of capitalism' when compared to other retail sectors. In combination with the financial scaffolding provided by real estate investment trusts, the self-storage industry has turned a temporary, 'taxpayer' land use type into a formidable retail industry which exerts considerable influence on the contemporary American built environment. Whether it is storage, burgers, or skyscrapers, the money is always in the real estate.

----

(1) Keller Easterling, Enduring Innocence: Global Architecture and Its Political Masquerades (Cambridge, Mass.: MIT Press, 2005), 1.

(2) Stephanie Wilkinson, "Winning the War in the Mini-Storage Business," PC Week 4, no. 48 (1987): 64-5.

(3) Dave Cook, "Planning for the Unpredictable," Mini Storage Messenger, (2004 [accessed November 12 2005]); available from http://www.techfast.com/news_13.html.

(4) Ellen Paris, "Rent-a-Closet," Forbes 139, no. 13 (1987): 136.

(5) Toddi Gutner and Amy Dunkin, "Self-Storage: A Niche with Room to Grow," Business Week, April 22 1996, 154. Morris Newman, "Public Storage: Mini-Storage Turns Landscape Orange," Los Angeles Business Journal 12, no. 6 (1990): S40-1.

(6) Morris Newman, "Public Storage: Mini-Storage Turns Landscape Orange," Los Angeles Business Journal 12, no. 6 (1990): S40-1.

(7) Carol Willis, Form Follows Finance: Skyscrapers and Skylines in New York and Chicago, 1st ed. (New York: Princeton Architectural Press, 1995), 19.

M.E.D.
Colloquium
752b

Eeva-Liisa Pelkonen

with MED students:
Joy Knoblauch, Frida
Rosenberg, Leslie Ryan,
and Sara Stevens

This year's colloquium investigates the contemporary urban situation, framed as *Situations Not Plans*. Exploring the splinters of the metropolis through the production of subjects and urban ecologies, this course will focus on infrastructural conditions – fluctuating connections between environments that respond to social and political forces. The goal of the course is to question rather than accept the preconditions that determine fixed plans. How can urban planners and architects respond to physical and psychological relationship between humans, environment, and culture? We seek to examine theoretical foundations (and diversions) of contingent and contradictory relationships between organism, environment and society. As an alternative to plans, this course is interested in situations – infinitely layered, unobjective and messy.

Three themes will structure the components of the course: ecology, subjectivity, networks. Ten people from a variety of disciplines have been invited to speak on these three subheadings. The students will engage in an analysis of contemporary urban conditions through discussions with the speakers who have been invited to situate urbanism as an interrelated field that punctures or exceeds the urban plan.

– – – –

Thomas Blom Hansen
*Professor in Department of Anthropology,
Yale University*
– – – –

William Mitchell
*Professor in Media Lab, and Program in Media Arts
and Sciences, MIT*
– – – –

Daniel Barber
PhD candidate in architecture, Columbia University
– – – –

Keller Easterling
*Associate Professor in School of Architecture,
Yale University*
– – – –

Noa Steimatsky
*Assistant Professor of History of Art and Film
Studies, Yale University*
– – – –

Antoine Picon
*Professor of History of Architecture and Technology,
Harvard GSD*
– – – –

Benjamin Aranda
Principal Aranda/Lasch and terraswarm
– – – –

Anne Galloway
*Lecturer and PhD candidate in
Department of Sociology & Anthropology,
Carleton University, Ottawa*
– – – –

Steven Stoll
*Assistant Professor of History and American Studies,
Yale University*
– – – –

Edward Soja
Distinguished Professor of Urban Planning, UCLA
– – – –

Anne Galloway

– – – –

Leslie Ryan She [Anne Galloway] is a Ph.D. candidate in the Department of Sociology and Anthropology at Carleton University in Ottawa, where she is currently writing her dissertation on the creation of pervasive computing technology in an attempt to produce an urban context. Her research intersects with art, commerce, and academics through key studies of many ongoing projects, many of which were covered in the readings for today. She has published many papers and articles and given many talks in North America and Europe. Anne is also one of the parties responsible for the journal Space and Culture, which, if you haven't read, [it] is very, very interesting. Interesting fact about Anne...in 2005 she was nominated for "World's Hottest Urban Blogger" by gridskipper.com.

Anne Galloway What?

[laughter]

Ryan Yeah, you didn't know this?

Galloway No!

[laughter]

Ryan Well, a lot of the blogs on there were actually quite interesting.

Galloway Okay, that's good. Well, thank you for the introduction. You make me sound so interesting. So, actually I would like to start by introducing how it is I got to where I am because that is probably the single most important thing that's happened. I was originally trained as an archeologist. I practiced archeology for six years in South America. I spent every summer there. My focus was on Incan architecture and textile production, so lots of weaving, mostly lots of buildings, and always space and culture.

After finishing my masters in archeology, I thought that I didn't want to go back to school at all. I wasn't overly thrilled with academia – didn't want to be an archeologist any more – and I went into webwork; because you can [be a geek, get paid for it,] and I didn't know what else to do. I started thinking about technology in the ways that I had been taught to think about space and culture. I happened to meet my supervisor by taking one of his classes. I just noticed that he was teaching a class one fall and I took it and he convinced me do my Ph.D. That's pretty much how I ended up studying old dead people and then brand new technologies, which don't really exist. The one thing that always carried through was this interest in social and spatial organization and what it means to experience the world through that lens. In fact, my methodologies and theoretical orientations haven't changed in ten years. They've developed further, but I still have the exact same interests that I did in archeology. So it's nice to find a way to work with that again. I began by looking at precisely how people were coming together in space and time. The interest in space and time was a matter of history, community, and space, technology, and culture. So I brought all of those interests together.

When I was invited to come here, I was coincidentally working on a paper at the same time, which is probably the abstract you were given. Then I realized that the situation and plans thing were important. I have taken that work that I did on that paper and reinterpreted it entirely through a lens of situation and plans for you so that I could take this stuff and make it more relevant to what you guys were interested in.

I want to start with a little bit of research that I did. I'm a big fan of going to the Oxford Dictionary to look up words. It's how I start every research project. I make sure I know what words mean, but more importantly, I make sure I know what words used to mean and how they've changed over time. So, I looked up 'scenery.' I just thought 'let's start with what's a scene?' As it turns out, scenery was originally spelled with an A: S-C-E-N-A-R-Y. Then it later shifted to E-R-Y. This is an interesting shift because 'scenary' with an 'a' comes from the Italian for scenario. It was directly related to the sequence or organization of plot in a play. It was a performative concept. It was meant to be performed.

'Scenery' with an 'e' referred to a representation of that. It initially started as part of the landscape type scenery, the idea that it was a place where things happen. It's no longer about how things happen, but where they happen. We shifted, in fact, to a sense of mobility to a greater sense of immobility or, rather, a more static representation took over the original concept that was more performative. I became really interested in that, because there we get a shift from situation to plan. I started thinking that scenery is kind of a funny thing. We started with 'landscapes'. The word 'scape' in English was actually taken from landscape. It was shortened then and reapplied to 'cityscape', 'sound-scape', 'body-scape.' I've even heard 'object-scape'. We took this sense of 'scape' and it is attached to this sense of 'scene.' It's a matter

of unfolding, but, more importantly, it is a representation of it. The word landscape itself always originally referred to paintings. They were always representations of something. They were referring to an object in the world. It was already framed. A landscape, then, is a plan. It's not a situation. It's been fixed. It requires a certain amount of immobility in order to communicate its power. It's also one of the reasons why we've been able to engage landscapes with such nostalgia over the years. They get captured in beauty. That aesthetic quality and that quality of perfection are really important in the communication of what a landscape is, and, more importantly, what belongs there and what doesn't. A landscape, contrary to the land itself... -scaping is framing, it's excluding something in order to keep something inside.

This got me thinking about maps and plans because actually mapping, and cartography in general, shared a lot with landscape painting. Cartographers a long, long time ago, say in the 1600's, shared a lot in common with landscape painters. They often worked together and they often used the same types of perspective. The evolution of map projections – the ability to represent the world according to particular perspectives – evolved alongside landscape painting. There was this sense of being able to capture it again...to frame it and work with that.

The sense of mapping that I'm most interested in, and the one that I think refers best to this concept of plans is literally the type of maps that we're familiar in western conceptions of space and time, which would involve mostly the cardinal directions. It is not a cultural universal to go north, south, east, and west. There are many cultures who deal with it differently. There is this idea that the western intellectual, political, economic situation of the time compelled map making and this would include western all the way to Arabs because the Arabs were some of the finest cartographers the world has ever seen. What holds them all together is that, no matter what, maps and plans are artifacts of empire. It's not just directionality that's important. A map or a plan, or being able to pinpoint a precise location on the planet in terms of longitude and latitude – that idea of precision is a first crucial step in being able to plan the movement of people and goods and to control territory and resources. They, by definition and by use value, control architectures. They are meant to order the world and help the sort of structuring that allows empire to exist and be maintained. When we think about, even now, GPS technologies as the height of empire, the ability to create something like that out of a military complex, out of an industrial type organization, to get that sort of precision is entirely about controlling the flow of goods and people and about marking space. If you can make a map that says exactly where your territory is, it's also a means of exchange. By that I mean, people disagree about maps. If you've ever known of countries that have border disputes, each country will map its border differently. The countries are the same, but the maps aren't. There have been really interesting cases in particularly native Andean cultures.

I pulled back to my original research in anthropology and archeology in the Andes, because the Quechua and the Aymara have really interesting ways of dealing with space and time that are almost completely opposite to western conceptions. For example, the past is considered to be in front of you because you can see it and the future is behind you because you can't see it. Time is always cyclical. There are no fixed points of reference. Things like latitude and longitude...they require fixed points of reference and they're usually arbitrary points. When we are discussing the topographic map, bringing in the third dimension – altitude, height, whatever you want to call that third dimension – it requires using a fixed arbitrary point, usually mean sea level. That makes our fixed point of reference – fixed and external to the body – which makes it a very different way of measuring things. Andean conceptions, on the other hand, take the body as the first point of reference because the body moves through space and time and all points of reference are relative. They are never fixed.

I got thinking about what this would mean when we are trying to make sense of mapping. To take these maps and say, 'I want to control this particular space because there is something about it that I value, that I want, that I need.' And these maps don't change unless they are being used by different people.

– – – –

ELECTIVES

Fall: Neil Thomas & Aran Chadwick ***The Liquid Threshold Between Order & Chaos*** [625a]; John Jacobson & Lindsay Suter ***Architectural Product Design*** [674a]; Edward Parker ***Aluminum Design: Casting & Design*** [682a]; Claire Zimmerman ***Case Studies in Architectural Theory*** [704a]; Fred Koetter ***Issues in Architecture & Urbanism*** [717a]; Karla Britton ***The Construction of Exactitude*** [757a]; Carter Wiseman ***Writing on Architecture*** [768a]; Peter Eisenman ***Introduction to Visual Studies*** [801a]; John Blood & Kent Bloomer ***Geometry, Drawing, & Visual Inquiry*** [802a]; Sophia Gruzdys ***Drawing & Architectural Form*** [803a]; Victoria Sambunaris ***Photography for Architects*** [813a]; Mark Gage ***Form, Shape, & the Emergence of Exoticism*** [869a]; John Eberhart & Eeva-Liisa Pelkonen ***Eero Saarinen: Digital Modeling & Animation*** [870a]; Michael Weinstock ***Evolutionary Design & Digital Fabrication*** [881a]; Alexander Garvin ***Introduction to Planning & Development*** [903a].

    Spring: Tim Macfarlane & Ingalill Wahlroos-Ritter ***Exploring Glass*** [635b]; Martin Finio ***Systems Integration & Development in Design*** [639b]; Kimo Griggs & Edward Parker ***Materials & Morphology*** [661b]; Peter de Bretteville ***Furniture Design & Fabrication*** [681b]; Keith Krumwiede ***Gross Domestic Product: A Research Seminar on the House*** [748b]; Ben Pell ***Ornament & Technology*** [688b]; Emmanuel Petit ***Architectural Multiplications*** [750b]; Mario Gooden ***Critical Architecture*** [760b]; Eeva-Liisa Pelkonen ***Alvar Aalto*** [767b]; Sunil Bald ***Architecture & the (Un)Making of Nations*** [778b]; Turner Brooks ***Drawing Project*** [804b]; Philip Grausman ***Freehand Drawing*** [808b]; Paloma Pajares & Dino Marcantonio ***Classical Drawing*** [811b]; Victoria Sambunaris ***Intro & Advanced Photography for Architects*** [813b & 814b]; Mark Gage ***Atmosphere & Effect*** [828b]; Dolores Hayden ***Built Environments & the Politics of Place*** [914b].

Neil Thomas & Aran Chadwick
The Liquid Threshold Between Order & Chaos
625a

Dyrden Razook & Timothy Newton
Univeristy of Virginia
& University of British Columbia
<u>Field Column</u>

This irregular compression structure gains its strength through redundancy. It was constructed through and additive triangulation method.

Mark Davis & Jeremiah Joseph
University of Washington
& University of Kentucky
<u>Nervi Nomenclature</u>

This self-sufficient structure was asked to explain tensile and compressive force. It was produced by the suspension of a fabric coated with high-strength plaster. The fabric section is "heavy wool with canvas above and below, sewed together along a diamond grid. The hardened plaster-fabric section is extremely strong in compression, but despite the internal tension ring made naturally by the dome shape, the four corners needed further tensioning. Use of cord and standing on the corners forced failure of the material at about 500 lbs.

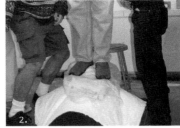

2.

3.

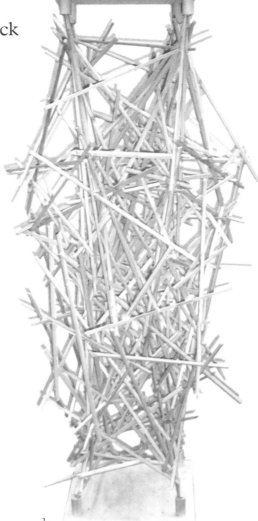

1.

John Jacobson & Lindsay Suter
Architectural Product Design
674a

4.

5.

6.

Edward Parker
Aluminum Design: Casting & Design
682a

Matthew Byers
Colorado College
<u>Meniscus</u>

The principle design strategy of the Meniscus was the desire to eliminate the need for mechanical fasteners or tools of any type for assembly. The transition between the aluminum leg and mahogany table top occurs without interruption, with the threaded stem of the table pinching the top and bottom cast aluminum pieces together, clamping the table top between them. The Meniscus is designed for use as a side table and can be easily disassembled for shipping, and reassembled in thirty seconds with no tools. A highly restrained material palette was employed, using only aluminum and ebonized mahogany.

Ashton Allan
Brown University
<u>Aluminum Guitar</u>

The modern electric guitar has been designed to be a smaller version of an acoustic guitar, and is therefore bulkier than necessary. This project looks to use the properties of cast aluminum to inverse the typical electric "bolt on neck" into a more efficient and sonically satisfying "bolt on body." The casting and walnut inserts are designed for ergonomics and weight balance on an unconventionally light instrument. The aluminum body also provides excellent grounding for the electronics, giving the plugged-in guitar an extremely quiet noise floor.

Gray Shealy
Clemson University
<u>Jetliner Window Wall</u>

This project sought to experiment with the flexibility and latent, yet untapped creative possibilities within the wall of the jetliner cabin. The cast aluminum piece becomes a new take on the window frame itself, creating a material transition between the aluminum skin on the exterior to the softer, more tactile interior. The window positions itself aerodynamically, as if it is being molded by the forces of the wind in the atmosphere. Rather than tamper with the engineering complexities of an actual airplane wall, the project becomes an unusual door or installation piece for a restaurant, hotel, or airport lounge. Much like the skin of the plane, the door positions itself within the duality of travel conditions: one side is a simple aluminum plating, as if it were the exterior of the aircraft; the other side is not unlike an aircraft interior, with vacu-formed plexiglass tiles on CNC-milled foam that take their fluid surface form from the impact of the heavier, more prominent window frames.

7.

8.

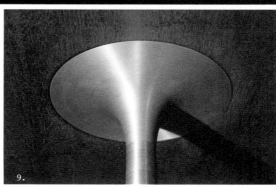

9.

10.

11.

12.

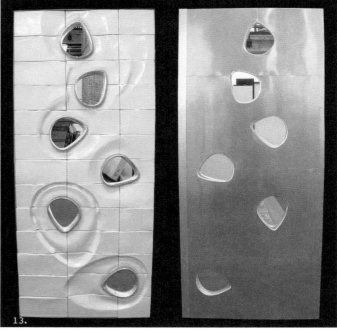

13.

Claire Zimmerman
Case Studies in Architectural Theory
704a

YoungJin Lee
Seoul National University, Korea
Eastlight

In the 1930's when Korea began to be urbanized, The poet Kim Kwang-Kyun(1) depicted his sensational solitude standing in front of urban high-rise buildings:

"Gaslight "
A gaslight is hanging in the desolate sky
It says I should go somewhere alone
The long-lasting summer is folding its oars
A line of high-rise building is covered by dusk like a pale gravestone
Fascinating night scene is tangled like a weed
Any thought became mute and loses its sound.
The dark is touching my skin
A strange shout on the street
Makes me cry without reason
Mingling within a hollow crowd
Where this huge sadness stays inside me
The lengthened shadow seems too dark
A sad sign telling me where and how to go
A gaslight is hanging in the desolate sky.

The narrative feels like a shadow moving between high-rise buildings that stand like pale gravestones. When the space where we can cast shadows, and the streets where we can walk begin to disappear in the night, the city becomes a spectacle, which Guy Debord introduces in his book, "Society of the spectacle." Devoid of form, it changes itself into an enormous empty showcase of sound. People themselves become empty showcases, dependent on the gas light for their form, for their shadow.

Through her book, "Privacy and Publicity", Beatriz Colomina analyzes modern architecture as a form of media, and asserts that architecture is filled with media – defining modern characteristics. From her standpoint we could understand that architecture doesn't reside in people's living space but in media. Similar to Debord, her urban architecture is much less about form than it is about people.

The typical space for spectacle could be showcases. The people in the city make themselves into spectacle, gazing at others and being gazed at by others.

The showcases are where spectacle begins, and allow for only visual perception. They admit the primary power of vision. Even though the sands of a summer beach and a rolling wave are displayed, we cannot feel the rough texture of the sands and red-hot summer sun. What we have is just simulation. The transparent glass of showcases literally creates a condition of alienation in modern society. Unfortunately people can enter modern society only through this transparency.

Dadaist and Surrealist Marcel Duchamp's work "The Bride Stripped Bare by Her Bachelors" comes to mind. The naked bride above keeps taking off her clothes, while short and poor bachelors in loose jackets seem to be moving with showing her a sense of their frustration. The glass blocks their meeting. As seen this work, showcases creates space of unsatisfied desire .

We should ask ourselves a few questions: what did this society of the spectacle transform people's living space into? Is urban space no more than a site that we parade along, without perceiving each other's real existence? What relationship with society can the spectacular individual define? Under these circumstances of alienation what contribution did architecture make in order to bring people together? How have architects tried to restore a lost humanity and identity?

These questions are ones modern architects and urban theorists took great pains to answer. They introduced the concept of place which is different from modern space, or a site. It has a premise that a certain event or activity will take place.

----
(1) Korean Modernist poet. Famous for synesthesia technique, urban image, and spatial formative technique.

Fred Koetter
Issues in Architecture & Urbanism
717a

Andrei Harwell
Carnigie Mellon University
Bounding the Japanese City

While to the foreign visitor, the modern Japanese city may appear to have been modeled largely on Western paradigms, it has at its core a set of values which are different from Western ones. These core values constitute, in the words of Japanese architect and theorist Kisho Kurokawa, an "invisible city," comprised of the "religion, philosophy, esthetic sensibilities, lifestyles, customs, psychological backgrounds, sensitivities, and awareness of traditional orders" of the nation.

Japanese cities are touted by western visitors as modern and efficient, even sustainable; indeed, a perfunctory review of their physical conditions by western eyes reveals cities which are lively, exciting, and in which mixed-use and mixed density dominate. But a deeper look reveals that their forms are bound up in social conventions which are different and perhaps even in opposition to those of the West: an emphasis in Japanese life on gender roles, hierarchy, disconnection with natural processes, and historical discontinuity. Nowhere can these be better observed than in the physical boundary conditions which contain and separate the day-to-day activities of the typical Japanese citizen. These physical boundaries mirror the conditions of life, the separation of work and family, of husband and wife, and differ widely from their American counterparts.

This study focuses on the two major cities of the Kansai region, Osaka and Kobe, and Hanshin, the suburban corridor that stretches between them. With 17 million inhabitants, this is the second largest metropolitan region in Japan and the 6th largest in the world (Tokyo - Yokohama is the largest in the world with an astounding 33 million inhabitants). Osaka forms the main commercial center of the region, and its satellite communities spread out in a linear pattern along commuter rail lines towards Kobe.

To discover the nature of Hanshin's invisible city, we must first begin by separating those urban effects that are caused by more universal constrictions, specifically geography. The Japanese's ability to inhabit their land is severely restricted by the geography of their island nation: 70% of the core of the country is covered by volcanic mountains with steep slopes and dense forests. Cities are generally pinned between these mountain slopes and the ocean. Hanshin is a microcosm of this tendency (figure 5). The region's boundaries on the north and south describe the great driving force in the Japanese need for density: the city is hemmed in by topography.

Though the Japanese city may appear to have characteristics of the western city, it is in fact quite different. An "invisible city" of social conventions and shared beliefs imprint the Japanese city with urban qualities unlike the west. Geography and economics have led to the physical striation of space between uses - the wealthy, the middle class, and industry. Social conditions have lead to the separation of work and home, the walling of houses, and the creation of domestic downtown spaces to serve the needs of workers. Philosophical and religious views have led to an easy reconciliation of new and old, historic and a-historic.

In the United States, our views of the city carry with them their own load of social, historical, and philosophical baggage. Perhaps through the examination of other urban conditions, we may be able to find ways to improve our own cities, and better understand our own urban condition.

Karla Britton
The Construction of Exactitude
757a

Britt Eversole
Yale University
The Limit of Morality: Cesare Cattaneo's Como
L'Unione Lavoratori dell'Industria

While working for Terragni, Cattaneo collaborated with Mario Radice on a fountain just outside of Como, built in 1936. The design featured a sculptural element comprised of a series of circles and spheres stacked atop one another. The circles are linked by the spheres, floating above the ground by means of a dynamic cantilever. Additional circles embedded in the ground or rotated perpendicular to the ground repeat the geometric motif to which the designer's chose to limit themselves. The fountain is a play on the plastic potential of pure geometries in a dynamic composition. Cattaneo and Radice needed only the most ideal geometry – the circle – and the most ideal platonic form – the sphere – to create a modern design. Once the simplest gesture possible was selected, the design demonstrated how many structural and spatial variations could be achieved without introducing a new element.

Yet it should be noted that the sculpture completely conceals its construction. The entire design is a steel space frame, encased in a smooth stucco finish. The cast concrete fountain and embedded circles are also finished in stucco such that all the elements appear homogenous, pure and identical. The continuity of the design's appearance was thus paramount over all other considerations. It was important to maintain the purity of the expression to match the purity of the gesture – and the purity of the geometry. From the exterior, the repeated motif suggests a cylinder articulated as a cage with no top, no bottom and no scale. It is incomplete and indeterminate, as if it could continue ad infinitum, and its only purpose is to give shape to the air passing through it. Rephrased, when seen from without, the circular frame contains and refers to nothing but itself as the repetition of primal geometric form. Once under the suspended circles, one looks up through the repetition of rings and sees the sky framed – the body is elevated through the voided center toward the heavens. When the body is absent, the sculpture is a pure intellectual gesture where the unity of the design

is produced through repetition, relation, and restraint; but with a body, it is transformed into a metaphysical event. We should be clear that Cattaneo and Radice are not rehashing the Enlightenment geometries of Ledoux. There is no object here, nor is there a purity of single isolated geometric form as a representation of ration. Rather, there is a purity of the system – a unity of similar yet different parts in relation to one another, which achieve their greatest synthesis with the introduction of a body. And yet the system is suspended and cantilevered – it resists gravity and the ground. Here again, we have a structural frame in tension with the ground – but instead of reacting to the earth with apathy, as in the Palazzo dei Congressi, the sculpture hesitates and floats over the ground, refusing to touch it.

In later projects, the circular frame never again emerges. But in the fountain, his projects with Terragni, and his early design studies, we see Cattaneo's nascent interest in the theme of the structural lattice that was to emerge in his work in the late 30s. Not all of his projects feature structural grids. The Giuseppe Garbagnati Kindergarten at Asnago (1935–37) has no structural frame, nor does his House for a Christian Family or his church designs from the early 40s. All are one story buildings outside of the city – there is need neither for height nor for density. Yet where Cattaneo could have generated an object in the landscape or an expressionist form, he returns either to geometric forms (circles and spheres for the church) or to the grid as an order of the ground plane (in the house for a Christian family). In almost all of Cattaneo's projects, he returns to a literal graphic or structural expression of order, be it cosmic spiritual order or mental Cartesian order – and for Cattaneo, it would appear that these are not separate considerations but intimately linked ideas, working together to achieve a unity, mediated by self-imposed restraint.

Carter Wiseman
Writing on Architecture
768a

Benjamin Smoot
University of Virginia
Four Times Square: Defining the Green Trend

Previously reserved for owner-occupied houses, small public projects, and the buildings of organizations with direct connections to environmental concerns, green building in the U.S. had never been associated with large-scale, profit-driven development.(1) For those pushing environmentally sensitive design, this convention had long been the great hurdle, for investors waiting it out on the sidelines, the great risk. With the emergence of the first green high-rise in the country, however, the debate was finally set to play itself out. Whether they saw it as the herald of a new age of commercial design, or simply a trendy glitch in the real estate traditions of the city, those who followed the rise of this tower agreed on one thing: with the fate of 4 Times Square, so went the future of green design […]

The 4 Times Square project called for 1.6 million square feet of office space to be squeezed into just one acre of real estate.(2) Previous green buildings in the U.S. had not gone beyond 50,000 square feet,(3) and nowhere in the world were the current advances in sustainable technologies being tested in a structure of this size. It was a five hundred million dollar job with no precedents.(4) The Dursts and their development team were striking out on their own, optimistic that the tower would be a trend setter, but mindful of the extra effort and cost required in discarding conventional practice […]

Perhaps most difficult of all was the existing tenant/developer relationship.(5) In a 1997 article, project architect Daniel Kaplan noted the "Byzantine line of contractual responsibilities"(6) that each proposed building approach had to survive. Seemingly simple decisions had to pass from architect to developer to tenant to interior architect and so on. With the standard separation of core-and-shell (developer) from interior fit-outs (tenant) in place, designing the tower as a coordinated system would be impossible without a buy-in on the part of those who were to occupy the building. And with so little hard data available to influence bottom-line thinkers, the architects resorted

to, in Kaplan's words, "leading, cajoling, educating and pushing the tenants,"(7) to incorporate the proposed green strategies […]

The real distinction for the Conde Nast building, however, remains its ecological efforts. In truth, all of the work that went into greening the high-rise did not result in a fully effective, energy-neutral tower. Not by a long shot. But the symbolic value of a large, green, and for-profit development in New York City's unforgiving real estate world was immense. It was a challenge aimed at the developers who watched from the periphery; the efficient, intelligent skyscraper had become a realized concept and it was sitting right there on Manhattan bedrock. Suddenly, to exclude high performance design from new buildings was to risk becoming obsolete […]

----

(1) Anne B. Frej (ed.), Green Office Buildings A Practical Guide to Development (Washington, DC: Urban Land Institute, 2005), 9–11.

(2) Alexanra de Blas, Radio Interview with Robert Fox (transcript), Radio National, http://www.abc.net.au/rn/science/earth/stories/s317459.htm (accessed October 24, 2005).

(3) Michael A. Rivlin, "Skyscrapers.alt," Gotham Gazette, http://www.gothamgazette.com/commentary/comm.14.shtml (accessed October 10, 2005).

(4) Phil Storey, "Casting a Long Shadow," Green@Work Magazine, http://www.greenatworkmag.com/gwsubaccess/05summer/cover.html (accessed November 6, 2005).

(5) Daniel Kaplan, "Manhattan's Green Giant," Environmental Design and Construction, Sept , (1997). Via Clean Air Counts, http://www.cleanaircounts.org/Resource%20Package/A%20Book/EStar%20Buildings/Manhattan's%20Green%20Giant.htm (accessed November 6, 2005).

(6) Ibid.

(7) Ibid.

Peter Eisenman
Introduction to Visual Studies
801a

This course introduces a way of seeing, reading and thinking about architecture through history and drawing. It is not so much a course in how to draw, but how to draw critically, and what that implies. If the buildings we are looking at in the course are critical, what makes them so? Criticality is a commentary on what existed at some moment in time. The purpose of the weekly drawing assignment is to see if students can visualize in drawing what they have been thinking about.

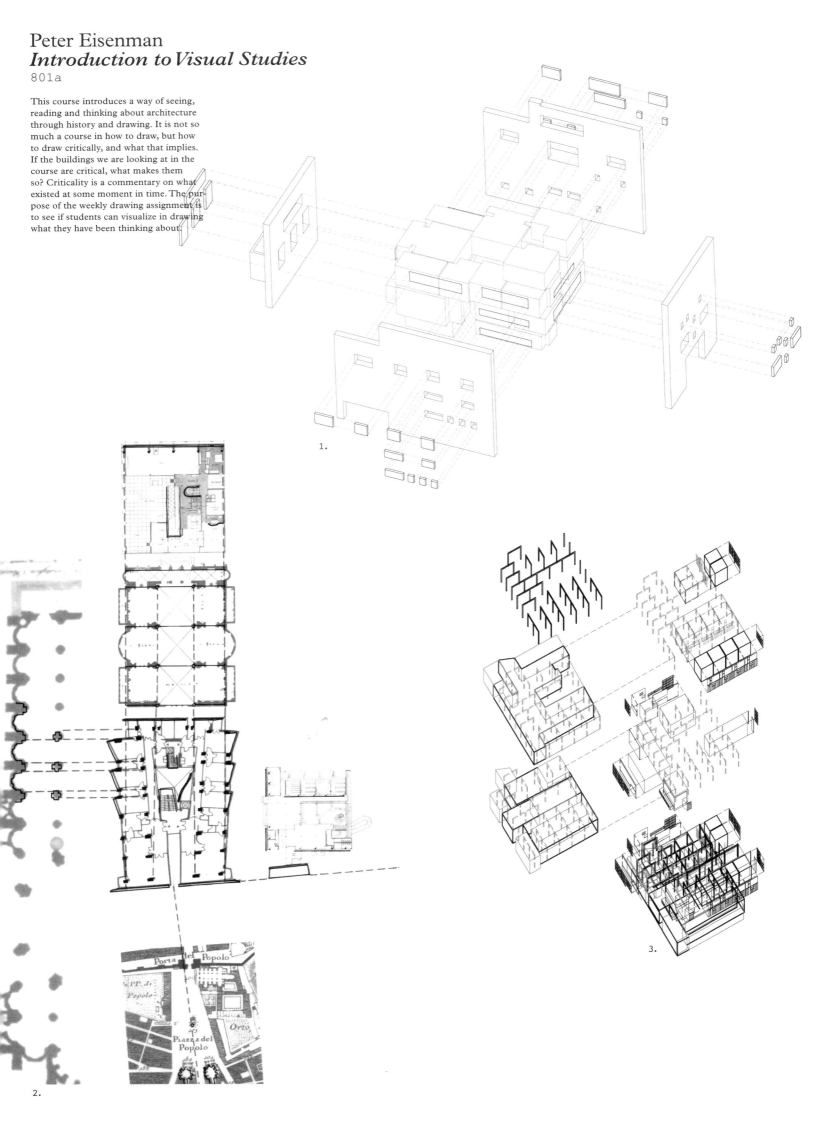

1.

2.

3.

John Blood & Kent Bloomer
Geometry, Drawing, & Visual Inquiry
802a

Ji-eun Cha
Ewha Womans University
<u>Geometry & Nature:</u>
<u>Golden Section</u>

The objective of this exercise was to heighten awareness of geometry occurring in nature through analyzing natural objects. I selected Nautilus which is well-known as an example of golden section and tried to draw nautilus in relation to a geometric lattice. The scaffold getting from nautilus was almost corresponded to golden section rectangles.

Michael Krop
University of Virginia
<u>Imaginary Section</u>

This drawing explores the transparencies and unexpected geometries that result from overlaying two separate tiling systems. It took on an unplanned life of its own as the original geometric patterning became secondary to areas of in-between and overlap
----

Gabrielle Ho
University of California at Berkeley
<u>3D Tiling: Close-packing,</u>
<u>Duality, Operations of</u>
<u>Transformation</u>
An exploration in the geometric properties present in a close-pack/dualed transformation. An articulation of a gradual change from one discreet polyhedron to another. A 3D lattice is first constructed by freehand, and through line weight variation the sense of depth is defined.

Isaac Strackbein
University of Colorado at Boulder
<u>Linear Handed Undulation</u>

A pair of three dimensional objects was designed such that the first object could be mirrored but not rotated to create the second object. A three dimensional cubic lattice was used to arrange the objects in space. A connection rule was established as to their arrangement within the lattice: Left, Left, Right, Right connections, head to tail, arranged linearly. The cubic lattice and page were laid out in AutoCAD, the handed objects were drawn in on two separate sheets of trace paper. These were then scanned in and the composition was put together and color gradients were added using Photoshop.

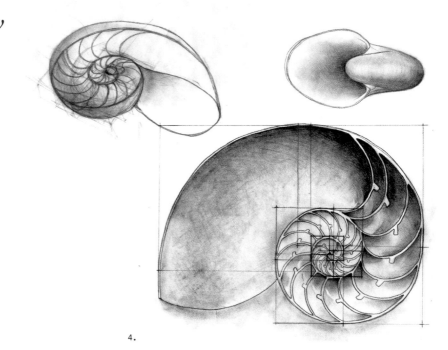

4.

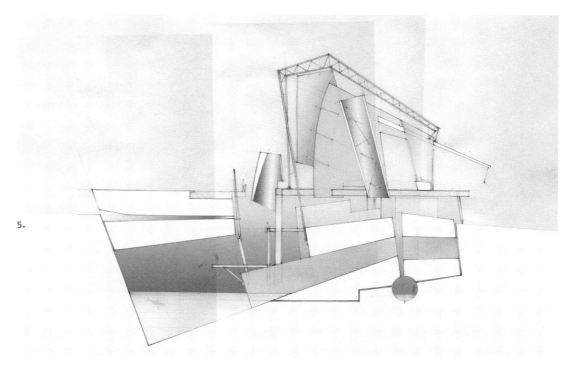

5.

6.

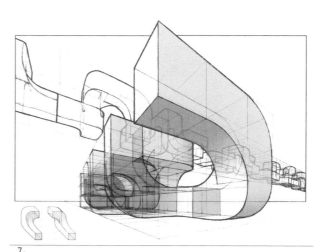

7.

(1) Benjamin Smoot
(2) Stephen Nielson
(3) Erica Schroeder
(4) Ji-eun Cha
(5) Michael Krop
(6) Gabrielle Ho
(7) Isaac Strackbein

Sophia Gruzdys
Drawing & Architectural Form
803a

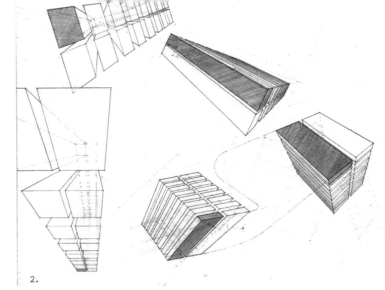

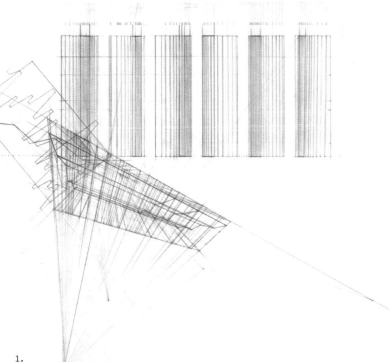

1.

2.

3.

Victoria Sambunaris
Photography for Architects
813a

Mark Gage
Form, Shape, & the Emergence of Exoticism
869a

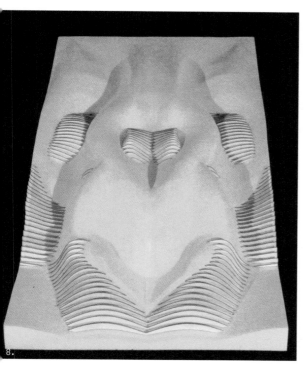

8.

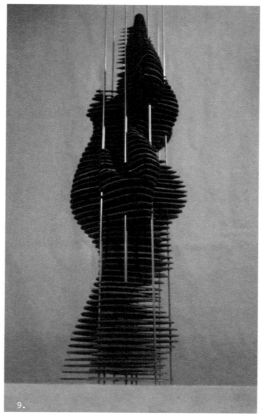

9.

10.

John Eberhart & Eeva-Liisa Pelkonen
Eero Saarinen: Digital Modeling & Animation
870a

The goal and objective of the course was to use digital media to study Eero Saarinen's architecture. Qualities of buildings that can be best rendered through digital representation, such as construction and design process, formal and spatial qualities, and structural systems were given special focus. The course was organized around three components: lectures, archival research and digital workshops. The students will be using material from the Eero Saarinen Papers at the Manuscript and Archives at Sterling Memorial Library as their source material.

11.

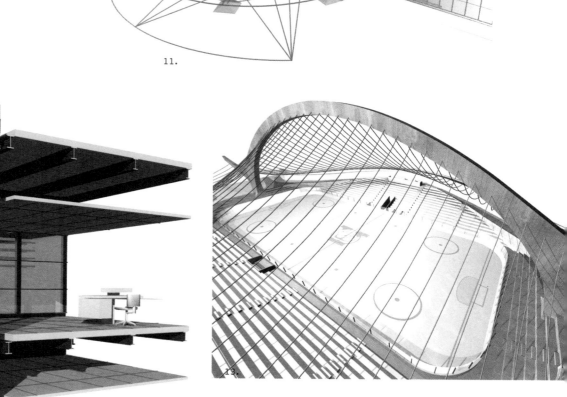

12.

13.

(1) Nicole
(2) Allen S
145 (3) Julia Suh

Xinghua Zhao
Marisa Kurtzman
at Fadaifard

(9) Jason deBoer
(10) Timothy Kirkby
(11) Karl Mascarenhas

(12) Kathryn Stutts
(13) Andrew Steffen

Michael Weinstock
Evolutionary Design & Digital Fabrication
881a

Abigail Coover & Nathan Hume
University of Virginia
& Ohio State University
<u>Honeycomb Pavilion</u>

This semester long investigation of emergent design processes resulted in a dynamic trajectory of experimentation where the final result is, like emergent design, irreducible to its parts. The proposed installation for the vacant lot adjacent to the A+A is the accumulation of not simply evolutionary design techniques, but also a successive evolutionary design process. The original goal of the project was to integrate multiple surfaces into a single complex structural system. This goal remained the primary objective of the semester's experiments as well as the final project. As the semester progressed, a secondary goal emerged. Almost all of the projects shown to us in class as well as in the writings on evolutionary design use form-finding as well as the proliferation of organic patterns to create surfaces that provide structural integrity, but typically limited spatial transformations. Thus the secondary goal of the project was to use emergent forms and patterns as a means of both structural and spatial invention.

1.

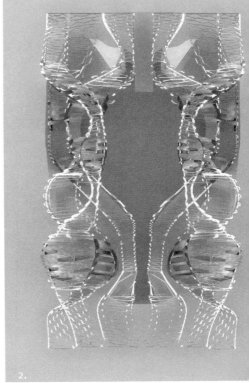

2.

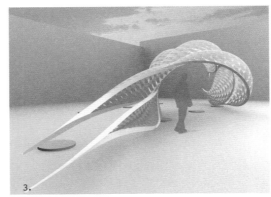

3.

Alexander Garvin
Introduction to Planning & Development
903a

This course demonstrates the ways in which financial and political feasibility determine the design of buildings and the character of the built environment. Students propose projects and then adjust them to the conflicting interests of financial institutions, real estate developers, civic organizations, community groups, public officials, and a widest variety of participants in the planning process. Subjects covered include housing, commercial development, zoning, historic preservation, parks and public open space, suburban subdivisions, planned communities, and comprehensive plans.

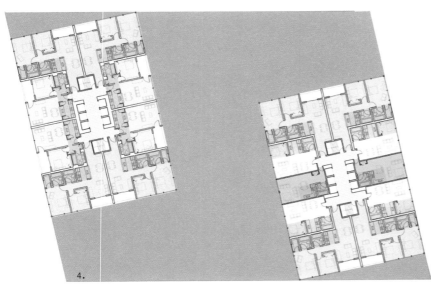

4.

LIBERTY CORNER

5.

Tim Macfarlane & Ingalill Wahlroos-Ritter
Exploring Glass
635b

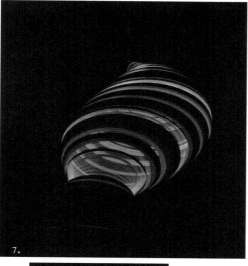

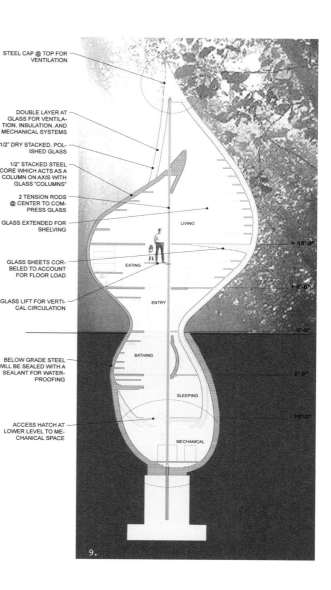

STEEL CAP @ TOP FOR VENTILATION

DOUBLE LAYER AT GLASS FOR VENTILA-TION, INSULATION, AND MECHANICAL SYSTEMS

1/2" DRY STACKED, POL-ISHED GLASS

1/2" STACKED STEEL CORE WHICH ACTS AS A COLUMN ON AXIS WITH GLASS "COLUMNS"

2 TENSION RODS @ CENTER TO COM-PRESS GLASS

GLASS EXTENDED FOR SHELVING

GLASS SHEETS COR-BELED TO ACCOUNT FOR FLOOR LOAD

GLASS LIFT FOR VERTI-CAL CIRCULATION

BELOW GRADE STEEL WILL BE SEALED WITH A SEALANT FOR WATER-PROOFING

ACCESS HATCH AT LOWER LEVEL TO ME-CHANICAL SPACE

LIVING
EATING
ENTRY
BATHING
SLEEPING
MECHANICAL

+ 18'-9"
+ 9'-0"
0'-0"
- 9'-0"
- 18'-0"

Martin Finio
Systems Integration & Development in Design
648b

with Vincent Chang, Peter Chow, Fiona Cousins, Kenneth Gibble, Erleen Hatfield, Robert Haughney, John Jacobson, Sarah Sachs, Edward Stanley, Paul Stoller, *and* Barry Svigals

This course is an integrated workshop and lecture series in which students develop the technical systems of preliminary design proposals from earlier studio work. The careful advancement of structural form and detail, environmental systems, and envelope design, as well as an under-standing of the constructive processes from which a building emerges, are all approached systematically, as elements of design used not only to achieve technical and performance goals but also to reinforce and re-inform the conceptual origins of the work. The workshop is complemented by a series of lectures from leading structural, environmental, and envelope consultants. Detailed technical drawings and analyses are required.

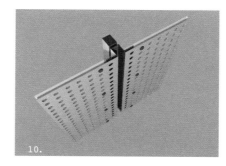

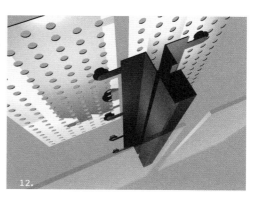

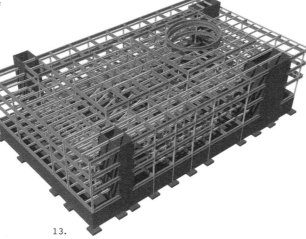

(1,2) N. Hume & A. Coover
(3) Burke, Dial, & Graham
(4,5) Corbett, Lawson, Reidel, & Van Brocklin
(6-9) Sallie R. Hambright
(10-12) Fung, McBride, Richards
(13) Knox, Lee, Lui, Namgoong

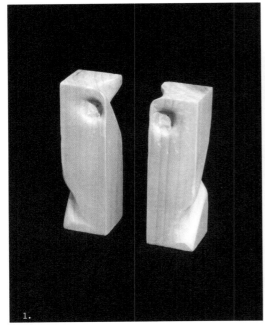

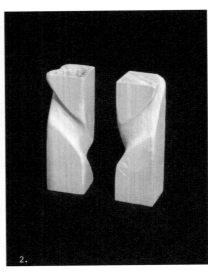

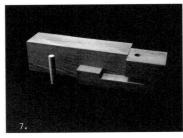

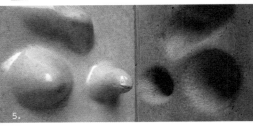

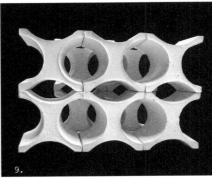

Peter de Bretteville
Furniture Design & Fabrication
681b

10.

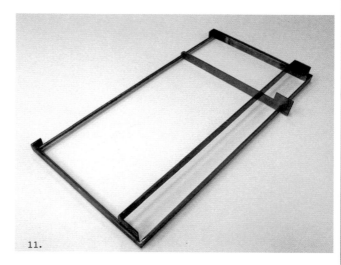

11.

12.

Keith Krumwiede
Gross Domestic Product:
A Research Seminar on the House
748b

This research seminar investigates and reports on the state of the contemporary, speculative, single-family American house. While cognizant of the larger networks within which the house resides, this seminar focuses its research on the house itself and its immediate environment, the subdivision. The class collectively produces a graphic document that not only charts the historical development of the American single-family home, but also, more critically, reports on its current status, as well as trends for the future. Each student is responsible for a particular research territory that may include changing design directions, construction techniques (the ubiquitous platform frame), marketing strategies, subdivision development trends, financing methods, material transformations, the arrival of "smart" houses, and the boom in shelter magazines. Lectures by invited speakers and field trips supplement individual research that uses national databases, builder Web sites and plan catalogs, mortgage finance materials, shelter magazines, and personal interviews.

Plan Strategy 1: Site Lines
Focus Views to Front and Back Yards to Enable Other Homes to Built on Sides

Plan Strategy 2: Marking Ownership
Some Home Owners Prefer Gap versus Party Wall to Establish Ownership.

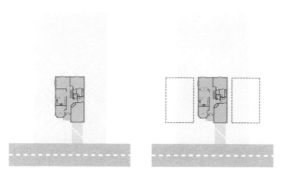

Sources: Floor Plan based on Google Image search of term "Simple Floor Plan"

13.

Plan Strategy 3: Stretch and Double
Increase Square Footage by Stretching and Increasing Floors

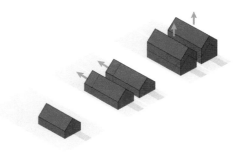

Plan Strategy 4: Pump Up the Volume
If Lot Size is LImited then Add Floors to Increase Square Footage

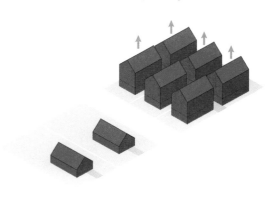

(1,2) Ji-eun Cha
(3) I. Garcia & I. Strackbein
(4-5) S. Nielson & J. Cielo
(6-7) Todd Fenton
(8) C. Corbett & R. d'Cruz
(9) M. Krop & B. Smoot
(10) Timothy Campbell
(11,12) Emily Youhna Rhee
(13) Sini Kamppari

Ben Pell
Ornament & Technology
688b

Khai Fung & Christopher Lee
University of Michigan at Ann Arbor &
University of California at Berkeley
Cloud Cover

Our project began with an interest in the wallpaper case studies presented in the class through the semester, especially Tord Boontje and Charles Voysey's work. Boontje brings forth functional uses to patterns, and Voysey usually has a specific repetition of elements, and sometimes has a "piece" that protrudes from the established pattern.The project developed into "3-dimensional wallpaper" that would begin to define space, and create effect. Its function would be a screen that goes in front of a picture window. With the laser cutter, we produced pattern, repetition and overlaps to create points of congruence, and took into consideration its ability to reproduce tiles quickly. The laser also provided accuracy which allowed us to develop "puzzle clouds" that acted as interlocking pieces between tiles.

Frank Melendez
University of Arizona
Translucent-Transparent Screen

This project explores CNC milling techniques as a contemporary tool to investigate the subject of ornamentation in architecture. Stemming from Bernard Cache's surface investigations of the early 90's, this project opens up new possibilities of ornamentation through lamination and CNC milling sequences. The material choice of acrylic provides an opportunity to study various effects produced by the CNC machine while allowing for transparent and translucent surfaces. Functionally, the acrylic panels can be configured to form a screen with various levels of transparency. By rotating the panels prior to lamination, unexpected patterns and shapes emerge.

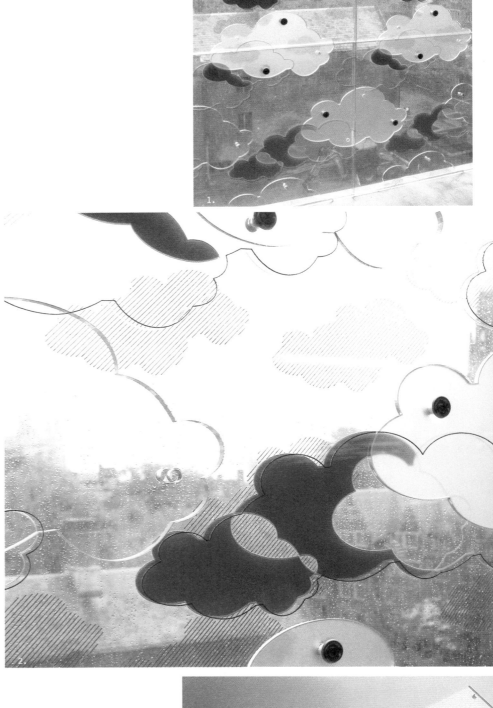

1.

2.

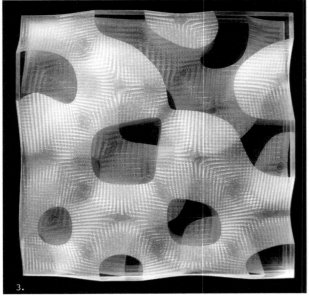

3.

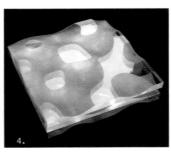

4.

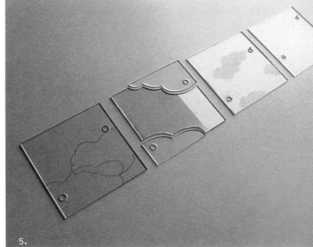

5.

(1,2,5) Khai Fung & Christopher Lee
(3,4) Frank Melendez

Emmanuel Petit
Architectural Multiplications
750b

Vincent Wan
University of Hong Kong, Hong Kong

Foa's Phylogenesis Ark: Biological Analogy and Taxonomy in architecture classification

----

This paper delves into the Phylogenetic tree of Foreign Office Architects, a collective 'biological' auto-bibliography of their work, which revived the dormant conundrum of how architecture should be taxonomized. Originating from Durand's novel typological categorization in Precis des Lecons d'Architecture, inspired by Cuvier, subsequently architects have categorized architecture in different ways, e.g. Wittkower's Palladian Villa analysis, Rossi's typological scrutiny, or Koolhaas' S,M,L,XL. By differentiating the two versions of phylogeny, phenetics [Michener1957] versus cladistics [Hennig1966], it is illustrated how FOA transcends architecture taxonomy from a typological to populational paradigm incorporating the temporal criteria. While all the aforesaid based its categorization on geometrical and formal characteristics, resulting in a homeostatic categorization frozen in time, phylogenetic categorization surpasses distinguishing architecture on mere formal basis and uses surface operations along its evolutionary history as a differentiation methodology. It is the operations inherent in the evolutionary process that induce the final characteristics being most substantial, not merely the characteristics itself.

However phylogeny also has its constraints, possessing a regressive tendency because it is an a posteriori classification emerging from a population. It is a hypothesis of relationships between species and does not represent absolute truth – subjecting to falsification and modification as new evidences are found – proven by the alterations in FOA's Phylogenetic tree since its first appearance in 1996. Moreover, it is clearly an arborescent model – extremely hierarchical with centers of significance and subjectification, implying stratification and linear thinking.

In addition, it is important to note that FOA have not used the phylogenesis paradigm to its full potential. They only use the phylogram as a self-analytical retrospective and not as an instrument to predict or facilitate the emergence of new species. It is a one-way equation, from the phylogram one can deduce along the line what characteristics is inherent in that particular project, but a building with all the characteristics will not necessary result in the same piece of architecture. In biological science, ultimately the spirit and objective of phylogenetic categorization is to predict the distribution of new characteristics and distill what characters led to the survival of certain species. When FOA applied the biological model to architecture, the projectile operativity of the phylogram is latent in their mode of production, but it has not yet matured into a methodology where the species can evolve under the system rather than just get invented and then categorized.

Phylogeny is undoubtedly a progeny of Darwinism and its significance is that it subverts Aristotelian teleological concept of science, vis-a-vis a natural selection mechanism based on environmental factors. The crux faced by FOA is similar to the paradox between teleological thinking and philosophical naturalism. Viewing phylogeney as a mere taxonomical effort leads to stagnancy, ossification without progress. Towards the other extreme, using it as a pure autopoeitic code or generative algorithm (like Karl Chu and William Mitchell), can lead to excessive proliferation of species that is exhaustive and irrelevant. FOA needs a balance of both. In devising a DNA system for the practice, FOA can eventually become the demiurge of the phylogenetic kingdom; at the meantime it requires the negative feedback from the analytical results of the taxonomy to achieve equilibrium in a projective momentum. Thus FOA is navigating towards the right track: only by further exasperating the potential of the entropic reaction of inconsistency/consistency and repetition/differentiation, a combination of top-down and bottom-up approach, then the phylogenetic system will achieve its maximal potential and the resultant species will sustain a symbiotic relationship between the endogenous development of a consistent architectural logic for the office and the exogenous influences exerted by the ecological and socio-economical factors.

Mario Gooden
Critical Architecture
760b

Sung Ik Cho
Seoul National University, Korea

Revised Modernism: The method of critiquing in OMA's works

'Critique' and 'revision' of modern architecture constitutes an important strategy in the design method of OMA's 'critical architecture'. Through the strategy of revision, his architecture could absorb the accomplishment of modern architecture as it is located in the extension of modern context. Simultaneously he could create new values in process of critique.

Maison Bordeaux of Rem Koolhaas could be compared with Villa Savoye of Le Corbusier. The primary concept of Maison Bordeaux is a floating concrete box above the excavated spaces in the hill, which is conceptually similar to the composition of Savoye. Other than the conceptual similarity as a floating box, Maison Bordeaux refers to Corbusier's Villa Savoye, which is a realization of 'The Five Points of a New Architecture' (1929) in diverse aspects. For example, Maison Bordeaux is a maximization of the 'free façade'. At first glance, the oculus windows seem very randomly arranged on the façade so that there is no regulation in elevation. But actually, the seemingly random gesture is based on the consideration of the location and eye-level of occupants. They suppose various heights of users, like adult, children and handicapper. It could be compared with the Savoye's window which is based on the assumption of 'modular' man. Le Corbusier supposed the cinematic view from inside toward the landscape. The cinematic view could be provided by a standardized level of horizontal line. The particular height is derived from the concept of a single idealized body, so the generalized height is applied everywhere. In Maison Bordeaux, a tension cable and cylindrical core of staircase displace the regularity of Savoye's pilotis. A piston-driven elevator platform for the handicapper displaces the sequential space experience of 'architectural promenade'

Modern architecture is the ingredient for Rem Koolhaas, and the criticism of Modern architecture is his architectural generator. The method of critique in his works could be categorized: displacement, rescale, transplant, indeterminacy, specification. What is important in his critique is that he did not depart from negation of modern architecture, but revises the modern to optimize the hidden potential of it. The idealized conception of modern architecture is displaced by the program-oriented and client-oriented solution, on the basis of a specific social and cultural situation.

"My work is deliberately not utopian: it is consciously trying to operate within the prevalent conditions without the suffering, disagreeing, or whatever other kind of narcissism we have, all of which may be merely a complex series of alibis to justify certain interior failings. So it is certainly critical of that kind of utopian modernism. But it still remains aligned with the force of modernization and the inevitable transformations that are engendered by this project which has been operating for 300 years. In other words, for me the important thing is to align and find an articulation for those forces, again without the kind of purity of a utopian project. In that sense my work is positive vis-à-vis modernization but critical vis-à-vis modernism as an artistic movement."(1)

Toward the revised modernism, he displaces order with disorder, function with detailed program. He specifies the general solution and customizes the standardized elements. Though most new architectural stream has been evolved from the criticism of the previous architecture, what is remarkable in Rem Koolhaas' works is that he optimizes the hidden values of the precedents to disclose their contradictions.

----

(1) Rem Koolhaas, Conversation with Students, 1996

Eeva-Liisa Pelkonen
Alvar Aalto
767b

The seminar was organized around themes that connect Aalto Aalto to a larger discursive framework within the Modern Movement: function, materiality, regionalism, urbanism, organicism, typology and Finland. The seminar concluded with Demetri Porphyrios reminescensing about his time in Aalto's office and his dissertation research, which led to the publishing of the book Sources of Modern Eclecticism. Studies on Alvar Aalto, some twenty years ago. To the question why did he chose to study Aalto in the mid-1970s when everybody else in Princeton around him was obsessed about Le Corbusier, Porphyrios responded: "Because he is the best!" As their final project students could opt to do either a research paper or analytical drawings.

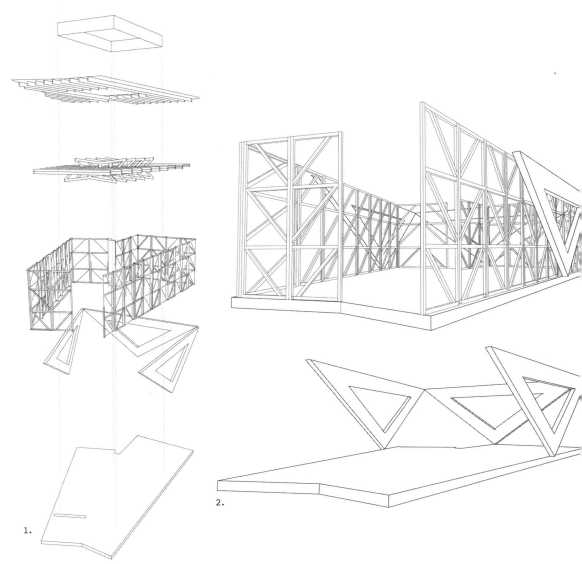

1.

2.

Sunil Bald
Architecture & the (Un)Making of Nations
778b

David Nam
Cornell University
The Conflict of Iconography & the EU Supra-Nation

In Rem Koolhaas' essay "€-conography, How to undo Europe's iconographic deficit?", Koolhaas begins by acknowledging the necessary clandestine nature of the processes that preceded the official formation of the EU, however he is critical of the absence of any strong visual representations to support the EU in the following period. He writes, "...the seemingly charming ineptness of Europe's representation is proving to be a serious political liability that erodes internal support and unnecessarily weakens external performance."

Citing a growing apathy regarding attachment to the EU, and the diminishing popularity of the image of the European Union amongst its citizenry, Koolhaas and other proponents for a more definitive image for the European Union attribute this growing trend to an absence of positive, identifiable iconography. In addition to the continuation of the habits of secrecy necessary for the processes leading up to the EU, Koolhaas also blames an ingrained "traumatiz[ation]" resulting from the memory of the "efficiency of Nazi and Soviet Propaganda."

The exhibition "The Image of Europe," as well as his proposal for a new EU flag, a colored barcode that can be augmented with the colored stripes of newly acceded Member States, both attempt to offer a new visual presence for the EU. With branding tactics, Koolhaas has identified, with his signature irony, the primary unifying element of the EU: its economy. Entry into the EU translates to market accessibility, and Koolhaas bluntly promotes that, conceiving of the EU as a client in need of a stronger public image, so that it can better promote its aims. In the symposium accompanying the "The Image of Europe," Romano Prodi acknowledged that, "The reality is that Europe is more a commercial and economic reality than a political one... We needed 40 years to have the Euro; we shall need 40 years at least to have a common foreign policy."

[...]

The competition for the European Central Bank Headquarters addresses the problems of representing the European Union. In his essay, "Euro Space, a State of Mind, Combine and Conquer," Mark Leonard identifies the strengths of the EU as a policy making body, by contrasting its absence of a singular identity to the more overt strategies of American foreign policy. What many critics cite as "weaknesses" of the governing body of the European Union – its decentralization and distribution of power amongst many leaders, and it's lack of presence – Leonard contends to be its power, "it is a foil to the pyrotechnic might of the US military machine."

What the EU offers, that the US is incapable of doing, are the promises and subsequent privileges of inclusion; to date these privileges primarily concern market accessibility. The borders of the EU are not static, rather their explicit elastic nature offers the would-be Member States incentive to amend their internal policies towards those promoted by the EU. As a result, Turkey has revoked the death penalty, the UK has amended its ban on gays in the military, etc. Leonard contrasts this to US foreign policy that operates on a short-term and temporary basis through predominantly military means.

If US strategies are characterized by presence in the most physical sense, the virtue of EU policy is the absence of this. Like other proponents of networked organizations, Leonard recognizes the benefits of "stealth," at times "invisible," strategies of polycentric organizations: "Europe's invisibility allows it to spread it's influence without provocation. Put bluntly, even if there were people angry enough to want to fly planes into European buildings, there is no World Trade Center to target."

The flip side of this argument is typified in Kissinger's much quoted statement: "What telephone number do you dial to reach Europe?" What has been seen as Europe's operational strength has been equally criticized as it's representational weakness. In 2004, "The Image of Europe," an event held in Brussels to mark the Dutch EU presidency (one that rotates every six months), an exhibition designed by Rem Koolhaas and AMO presented a visual history of Europe. The exhibition addressed what has been acknowledged as Europe's image deficiency through a panoramic representation of the history of the European Continent for the past 3000 years.

Turner Brooks
Drawing Project
804b

4.

5.

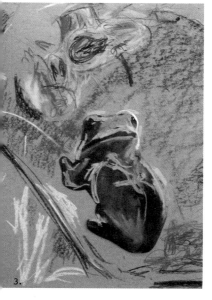

3.

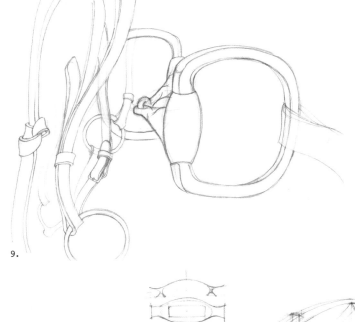

6.

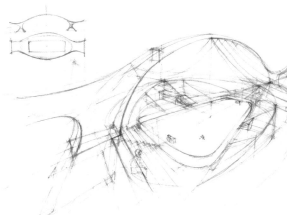

7.

Philip Grausman
Freehand Drawing
808b

8.

9.

10.

11.

1.

IONIC ORDER OF WACHOVIA

YALE UNIVERSITY OF ARCHITECTURE, SPRING 2006
JEJON YEUNG   PROF. D.MARCANTONIO, P.PAJARES

2.

IONIC TEMPLE

SAM ROCHE
MMVI

3.

4.

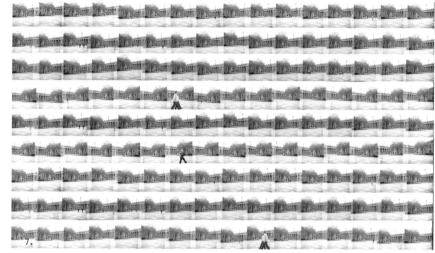

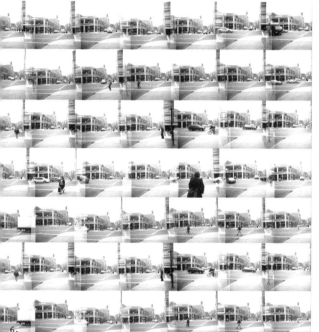

(1) Mario Cruzate
(2,4) M. Jejon Yeung
(3) Sam Roche

(5,8) Audrey Vuong
(6,7) Abigail Coover
(9-11) Matthew Byers

Mark Gage
Atmosphere & Effect
828b

This seminar tracks the movement in architecture away from the modern notions of space, volume, and firmness toward the sensibilities of effect, atmosphere, and the ephemerally fashionable. The seminar begins with a historical survey of architectural effects covering over two thousand years of visual architectural innovation, providing the basis for inquiry into various contemporary sensibilities of atmosphere, such as new experiments in color, gradient effects, opalescence, luminescence, aggregate gradation, translucency, 3-D pattern, and visual and physical texture. Case studies are explored concerning practitioners, OMA, Jun Aoki, Kazuyo Sejima, and others as well as similar sensibilities currently found in art, motion pictures, motion graphics, the fashion industry, and product design.

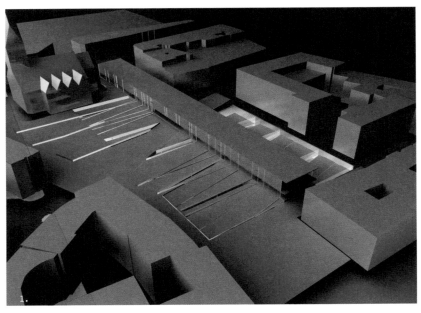

1.

2.

Dolores Hayden
Built Environments & the Politics of Place
914b

Nicole Lambrou
Binhampton University, SUNY
The Berlin Wall: Case Study of a Character
Unfolding Along Bernauer Strasse

Whereas a wall is conventionally conceived of as a neutral architectural element that distinguishes spaces, it is the purpose of this research endeavor to provide evidence for understanding the wall as an active participant in its given context; specifically, the Berlin Wall exaggerated the difference between Eastern and Western ideologies and, in that act of separation, precipitated its eventual demise.

By absorbing social narratives over time, ones that are even literally etched onto its surface, the Wall served to continually reinforce, extend, and even mirror those ideologies back to the urban realm it was situated in. Whether in the form of a barbed wire fence or as the accumulation of seven strips of physical surveillance, the Wall did not divide the citizens of Berlin passively; instead, it shaped both their individual and collective personas. While notions of boundary and threshold immediately trigger corresponding impressions of bifurcations, the Wall's function inevitably extended beyond the mere representation of a political dichotomy.

"Berlin!," exclaims Marion, the trapeze artist in the film Wings of Desire, "Here I'm a foreigner, yet it's all so familiar. Anyway I can't get lost. You always end up at the Wall." The Wall is ubiquitous. It does not simply encircle the boundaries of the city but, having obliterated a horizon line and an impression of perspective beyond, it is exactly what orients in this urban scene. Queues are now given by the path and dimension of the Wall, replacing the more conventional orienting qualities of an urban setting that include means of gathering and dispersal, densities of streets, and iconic locales.

Ashley Klein
Emory University
Dalston Theatre + Historic Picture House

Hypothetically, the Theatre would not be in threat of demolition if its restoration was deemed plausible by the Hackney Council. Though the Dalston Theatre entrance was recently described by English Heritage as an "attractive and architecturally distinctive frontage", the organization was unable to list the theatre as a historic building because of the deterioration of the interior. Hackney Council claimed that the buildings should be demolished because of asbestos, structural damage, drug users and squatters. However, OPEN (Organization for Promotion of Environmental Needs Limited) recently commissioned a structural engineer, Brian A. Morton MBE C.Eng MICE Dip Conservation (AA) IHBC of the Morton Partnership to assess the feasibility of the Theatre's repair. In his survey, Morton confirmed that it is feasible to restore the Theatre's facades.

Should Morton's survey be accurate, it would be proven that the destruction of the buildings on Dalston Lane would be primarily to serve the interest of its developers. As Bill Parry-Davies, the director of OPEN commented, "The building's potential for regeneration of the wider area is being dismissed in the name of 'best value' and the scramble for short term financial gain."(1) The new development to be imposed on Dalston Lane could potentially destroy the neighborhood's social culture, but should the Theatre be preserved and transformed, both the present and future community of Dalston would benefit from its presence. Since the Theatre was opened in 1886, it has reflected the social and cultural history of Dalston and simultaneously has symbolized the district's contemporary life. Any facility that could replace the Theatre, while even if as flexible, will hold in it no account of history. It is the memory of a place that inspires its growth, and the Theatre, as a malleable form of history, is able to both remind its patrons of the past and provide a place for new visions to materialize.

----

(1) http://opendalston.blogspot.com/2005_12_01_opendalston_archive.html

----

UNDERGRADUATE STUDIOS

The purpose of the undergraduate major is to include the study of architecture within the broader context of a liberal arts education. The curriculum includes work in design, in architectural history, theory, and criticism, and in urban studies, leading to a bachelor of arts degree. Students are prepared for
157   *advanced study in architecture, art, history of art, city planning and development, environmental studies, the social sciences, or public affairs.*

Emmanuel Petit
The Analytical Model
249a

Christian Nakarado
Silliman College
Formal Analysis of Steven Holl's
Oceanic Retreat, Kauai

Steven Holl began this project for a private residence with a signature scientific metaphor, this time relating to the geological significance of the site. The overt themes of shifting tectonic plates and erosion of solid forms are included through several blatant and inelegant moves. But geometric and tectonic analysis revealed many more subtleties in the project that proved it to be quite thorough in its pursuit of Holl's geological conceit. Programmatic analysis yielded a much different reading of the home, which was well thought out in providing for its residents' needs, yet unable to relate directly to the conceptual concerns that really drove the design of the house.

Laura Cheung
Branford College
Architectural narrative in the
Vanna Venturi House

Robert Venturi's references to architectural precedent, ranging from modernism to the vernacular, suggested a narrative between the iconic house and an antagonist chimney. Looming behind the elevation's split arch and gable, the chimney collides with the central staircase and the diagonals of the plan. The fragments of the stair remain as artifacts of the collision, while secondary entrances at each corner undermine the interior volume. Yet, the apparent aggressor also emerges as the hearth and column of organization for the program, setting into motion the reclamation of the broken ideal: the split arch, expanding through the section and arriving at the rear elevation, finally reinstates itself as a complete Palladian window.

Claire Matthews
Davenport College
Gwathmey, 1970

This Steel Residence is one of a pair designed by Charles Gwathmey in Bridgehampton, NY, in 1970. Plan studies made obvious Gwathmey's precise geometric overlaps and intersections. Section studies demonstrated consistency of certain horizontal lines throughout the house, whether as the bottom of a window or setback in the chimney. Subsequent models studied spatial relationships, circulation, tectonics, light and density. The tectonics of a rectangular shell of walls intersected by a semicircular wall contrasted an interior tectonic element, the solid mass of the chimney and a closely aligned furniture piece. Circulation, light and density are strongly correlated and create a gradient from narrow, dark areas with defined movement to freer light-flooded areas.

1.

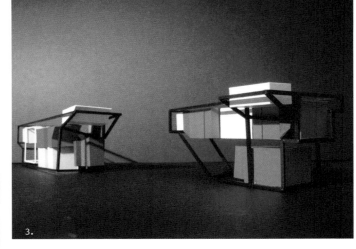

2.

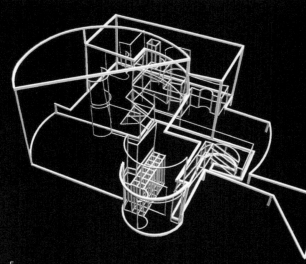

3.

4.

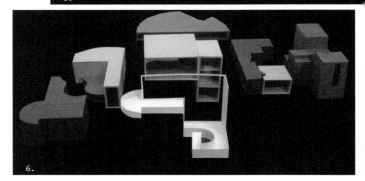

5.

6.

Aleksandr Bierig
Branford College
Discrete Indiscretions

Beginning with an archetypal rectangular pavilion, interior programmatic and exterior contextual pressures generate formal deviations which define this project. Determining the minimum programmatic elements to constitute a farmers' market: a table for vendors, access for shipping, storage, and lavatories; the building allows the remaining space to be programmatically undefined, while remaining spatially articulated. The box is skewed towards the edge of the site and the roof plane is rotated off axis. Through these shifts, each face reacts to its respective context: a slower pedestrian route, a plaza opposite a prominent park, and a stretched storefront on a commercial strip. One gesture satisfies all three conditions; the whole generates the parts.

Seema Kairam
Silliman College
An Inhabitable Framework

The farmer's market that I designed for small park near Wooster Square is a place of transition between commercial and residential zones, agricultural and urban regions, ethnic boundaries, and signifies a progression through the seasons. The long awkward site became a continuous spectrum of space signified by the patterns of overlapping gradients in the stone paving throughout the park. The "market stall," is simply a two dimensional boundary or frame that defines a discrete unit of space within the continuous spectrum. Through this intervention the park that was previously skirted around by neighborhood residents, now is divided into inhabitable spaces that can serve the neighborhood in as many ways as they can imagine, from a playground, to a piece of public art to a structure that can be converted into a farmer's market on a sunny Saturday morning.

Robin Swartout
Calhoun College
Depalma CT Enclosure

The site on which this project is located is most commonly used as a pedestrian passageway between the wooster square park and the restaurants and shops of wooster street; yet once a week it is transformed into a farmer's market. This project aims to accommodate both of these activities and to hopefully bridge the gap between the site's role as an interstitial space and also as a destination in its own right. The permanent structure's fluid form is largely transparent in order to maintain the site's role as a passageway, yet punctuated with bench elements to encourage static use of the site.

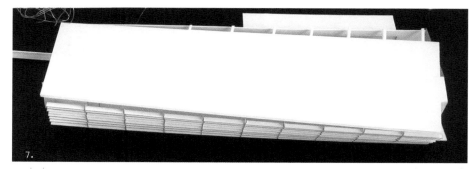

7.

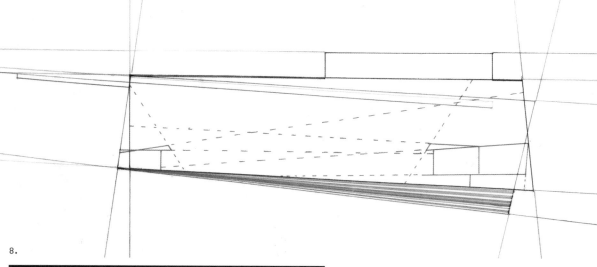

8.

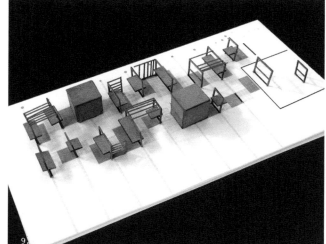

9.

10.

11.

(1,3) Christian Nakarado
(2,4) Laura Cheung
(5,6) Claire Matthews

(7,8) Aleksandr Bierig
(9,10) Seema Kairam
(11) Robin Swartout

Steven Harris
Senior Studio
450a

with Bimal Mendis

Victoria Wolcott
Pierson College
Tulare Blend: Agricultural and Automotive Landscapes
————

This project attempts to provide visitors with a unique rest stop experience on Route 99 in Central Valley, California. The landscape brings together the built and natural environments by overlaying the two systems of organization. From these systems, new patterns emerge, allowing for the 'blend' of concrete and grass, sun and shade, indoor and outdoor, etc. In addition, the project aims to comply with LEED Gold Standards for New Construction – solar energy powers the buildings, reed beds recycle gray water for on-site use, and signs about sustainability and the local landscape educate every visitor.

————

Carl D'Apolito-Dworkin
Timothy Dwight College
The Bold and the Fearful
————

Description: The project was to design a rest stop. Some visitors to a rest stop are scared to seek interaction with others. There is an attitude behind each parking configuration and an undercurrent of fear, curiosity, or desire vibrates across every space. Lights and trees form rooms for cars and trucks. Spots accommodate different types of interaction in both night and day. Every visitor plays his/her ideal part. Large areas are dominated by interaction of the community or by individual behavior, by comfort and safety or by excitement or even fear. At area edges lurk another type of world. Edges are varied and are governed by thresholds that shield, entice, or boast. At night the bathroom becomes an anonymous stage for the rest stop with shadows criss-crossing in the night. Visitors are able not only to take their place in the dance of trucks and cars but to see this place as it relates to the whole drama. This dance is created by rearranging the standard elements necessary for a rest stop and the elements which make the rest stop ecological.

————

Frances Edelman
Silliman College
Parallel Park[ing]
————

The California Department of Transportation (CALTRANS) and The Great Valley Center announced a competition for a self-sustainable and "off the grid" roadside GreenStop. This is a unique opportunity to create a "green" rest area that can serve as a model for current and future rest stops within the state system, with the ability to be customized so as to be regionally relevant for each location. The site for purposes of the competition is the Tipton rest area site along Route 99 in Tulare County, San Joaquin Valley, CA. While the design is required to address the larger sustainability and interpretive issues, it is also required to provide an image and identity reflecting this region of California's Central Valley.

I saw the rest stop as an opportunity to create a landscape experience influenced by the local environment. A series of systems mediate that experience. The natural landscape serves as a filtration system for the site: waste water is filtered through various types of grasses/reeds on gently sloped surfaces. It relates to the landscape of the surrounding site and requires no maintenance. Constructed, occupiable corridors of manicured lawn mediate between the natural landscape and the vehicles by dictating pedestrian access into the built and natural environment. These corridors allow for interaction between the freeway and the rest stop: pedestrians can view the freeway up close and at eye-level. A self-sustaining water cycle supports the manicured landscape by recycling the waste water from the restrooms. The paving becomes turf pavers whenever possible to reduce the amount of impervious surfaces. The parking grid of offset and separated cars and trucks becomes the grid for the whole site. The trucks frame the landscape on one side and on the other side of the site, trees frame the freeway. The trees, mirroring local orchard organization, become the marker of the rest stop. Located in the middle of the site, the restrooms are a place of interaction between the cars and the trucks. The restrooms activate and integrate into the landscape: they are embedded into the ground to allow for the landscape to be continuous.

————

Nathan Elchert
Silliman College
Inhabitable Green Billboards
————

My scheme calls for the atomization of rest stop amenities into distinct units, arranged so they can be read as a series of billboards from the road. The functional spaces are enclosed with topiary walls that are sustained by the processed wastewater of visitors. The verdancy of these walls provides a visual registration of the human contribution to and impact on the site. Since most users of Route 99 are simply passing through, the rest stop is a unique opportunity to impress travelers with the identity the Great Central Valley. Instead of relying on nostalgia for the pastoral landscape, my design emphasizes a legible commitment to sustainability.

————

1.

4.

2.

3.

5.

6.

7.

8.

(1,5) Victoria Wolcott
(2,3) Carl D'Apolito-Dworkin
161 (4,7) Frances Edelman   (6,8) Nathan Elchert

Senior Travel

Senior Thesis

Gabriel Smedresman
Branford College
Alphabetic Architects: Geofroy Tory and the Renaissance Reconstruction of the Roman Capital Alphabet
----

The designer of this woodcut, the Parisian scholar and printer Geofroy Tory, intended it as an illustration of the choice between virtue and vice. He wrote, explaining its significance:

> To give you more clearly to understand this divine Pythagorean letter Ypsilon, I have drawn it for you once more. Imagine that the upright and broadest limb is the road of Adolescence, the broader of the two arms is the road of Pleasure, and the narrower arm the road of memory and virtuous contemplation.

Geofroy Tory was one in a series of scholars, architects and artists, who, in the late fifteenth and early sixteenth centuries, invented the capital letter as we know it today. The serif capital letter was based on Roman inscriptions from the first century AD, which Renaissance antiquarians believed to be aesthetically superior to the scripts they were using at the time, a combination of medieval blackletter and a curving script from the ninth century called the Carolingian. But, as we can already see from Tory's bizarre conception of the letter Y, the Renaissance reconstruction of this antique form was no straightforward imitation. By the time the form had solidified in the calligraphy, architecture, literary criticism, biblical exegesis, mnemonic aids, Platonic philosophy, and Pythagorean number symbolism all played an essential role in its birth.

Many Renaissance scholars were tight-lipped about the sources of their thoughts, preferring to preserve the aura of mystery and awe surrounding the antique. But Tory, a Frenchman outside of the direct academic circles of Italy, in his enthusiasm to explain the perfection of these letters, reveals much about the thoughts behind the construction. And while what historian Stanley Morison called Tory's "cabalistic abracadabra" may have quickly faded to obscurity, Tory's work lives on through his student, Claude Garamond, whose self-titled typeface is still frequently used today.

The work of Tory and his fellow alphabetic architects is also significant for its role in the great advances of art and architecture made during the Italian Renaissance. Early Renaissance architecture and its relationship to the rediscovery of classical literature and Roman architecture and statuary that characterized Italian humanism has been well documented. It is a complex story of brilliant designs and enigmatic writings, subject to constant re-interpretation. But the return of artistic lettering to classical forms is a subcurrent in the fifteenth century humanist revival of antiquity that has been infrequently studied. The reconstruction of the Roman capital letter unfolds in the same scholarly circles that develop the rest of Renaissance architecture, artistic content, and technique, and its invention is a lens through which we can see the Renaissance fantasy of the antique, coupled with a fundamental shift of artistic emphasis towards reconnecting content and form.

Tory, Geofroy. Champfleury. New York: Dover Publication, 1967, p.153

Urban Design Workshop
2005/2006

Alan Plattus, *Director*

Surry Schlabs, *Project Manager*

Student Fellows 2005-2006:
Timothy Applebee, Elizabeth Barry, Gabrielle Brainard, Michael Grogan, Andrew Lyon, Nicholas McDermott, *and* Jacob Reidel

1.

Founded in 1992 by Alan Plattus, then Associate Dean and Professor at the Yale School of Architecture, the Yale Urban Design Workshop (YUDW) is a community design center based at the School of Architecture. Since its founding, the YUDW has worked with communities all across the state of Connecticut, providing planning and design assistance on projects ranging from comprehensive plans, economic development strategies and community visions to the design of public spaces, streetscapes and individual community facilities. Clients include small towns, city neighborhoods, planning departments, Chambers of Commerce, community development corporations, citizen groups, and private developers. The YUDW also worked with Yale University over a three-year period, developing a comprehensive campus analysis leading to a campus master planning process, for which YUDW served as a consultant. After a number of years on the Yale campus, the YUDW is currently located in a storefront space on Chapel Street in New Haven's Dwight neighborhood, two blocks from the School of Architecture.

In all its work, the YUDW is committed to an inclusive, community-based process, grounded in broad citizen participation and a vision of the design process as a tool for community organizing, empowerment, and capacity-building. A typical YUDW project may include design charrettes, focus groups, and town meetings, as well as more conventional means of program and project development. These projects are staffed mainly by current graduate professional students at the Yale School of Architecture supervised by faculty of the School, but often also include Yale College undergraduates, recent graduates of the School as full-time staff, faculty and students from Yale's other professional schools (including the Law School, the School of Forestry and Environmental Science, the School of Management, the School of Public Health and the School of Art), as well as outside consultants and other local professionals.

Recent and current projects undertaken by the YUDW include downtown and neighborhood plans for the Connecticut towns of Bridgeport, New Britain, and North Branford, a Route 1 Corridor Study for the town of Old Saybrook, and a planning/development study for an old airport in the town of Bethany.

Additionally, the summer of 2006 will mark the completion of the new Greater Dwight Daycare Center and office building, developed by the Greater Dwight Development Corporation and designed in collaboration with New Haven's Thompson | Edwards Architects.

3.

4.

5.

6.

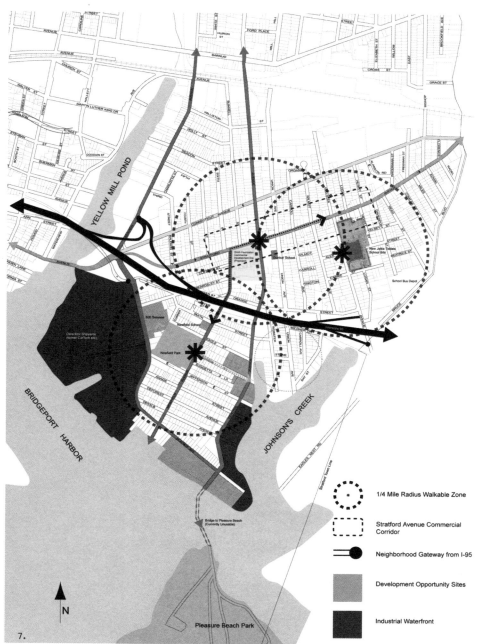

7.

1/4 Mile Radius Walkable Zone

Stratford Avenue Commercial Corridor

Neighborhood Gateway from I-95

Development Opportunity Sites

Industrial Waterfront

YELLOW MILL POND

BRIDGEPORT HARBOR

JOHNSON'S CREEK

N

Pleasure Beach Park

bethanyairport
hangar renovation

The Building Interior
accommodates a large,
multi-purpose space, as
well as several smaller
rooms, including a kitchen,
foyer/gallery, restrooms,
and a conference room.

Schematic 3-D Model

8.

(1-6) Greater Dwight Daycare Center
(7) Preliminary Analysis of the East End neighborhood, Bridgeport, CT
165 (8) Bethany Airport Reuse Proposal

Travel Fellowships
2005/2006

*David M. Schwarz/Architectural Services Summer Internship
and Traveling Fellowship, 2005*

- - - -

Marisa Kurtzman
Wesleyan University
Constructed Identities: Modern Architecture
in Mexico and Cuba, 1920-1960

- - - -

In the Fall of 2005, I conducted an independent study of the origins and development of modern architecture in Mexico and Cuba between 1920 and 1960. As part of the project, I traveled to both countries to photograph what remains of those built landscapes. These are the results.

Modern architecture's presence in Latin America is difficult to address without first acknowledging that the concept of a singular "Latin America" is an imaginary construct born out of the region's colonial heritage. While many Latin American nations share commonalities like history and language, it is important to recognize the uniqueness of each country's social, cultural, and ethnic heritage.

Mexico and Cuba are an interesting focus because they offer examples of how modern architecture developed from different Latin American architectural traditions. They also demonstrate how that development varied according to the prevailing political and cultural conditions of the day. In Mexico, a succession of governments embraced modern architecture to affirm an independent national identity that was both rooted in local history and adhered to European and North American

1.

3.

cultural ideologies. In Cuba, modern architecture had a more conflicted relationship with national identity. Before the 1959 Revolution, it was touted for its striking expression of lo cubano. Afterwards, it was disparaged for its associations with the pre-Castro bourgeoisie.

The buildings I photographed do not represent a complete survey of modern architecture in either Mexico or Cuba. Restricted access, building alteration or deterioration, and my own time constraints limited the scope of my work. I hope, however, that the material I gathered can serve as a preliminary guide for learning more about an often overlooked aspect of modern architecture's global dissemination, and provide insight into how modern architecture had a very real impact upon the formation of the two distinct national identities expressed in Mexico and Cuba's built environments.

- - - -

George Nelson Traveling Fellowship, 2005

- - - -

Naomi Darling
Princeton University
A Journey into the Chinese Garden

- - - -

The Chinese garden is "a four-dimensional time-space presentation. Beholders gradually become aware of these dimensions while moving in sequential spaces, following planned touring routes, over a period of time. This cumulative visual presentation leads to a dramatic effect on the viewer through mobile viewing, which cannot be compared to ordinary static viewing experiences." (1)

My interest in Chinese Gardens came about indirectly from an interest in English Picturesque gardens and Japanese strolling gardens. A common trait shared by these gardens is a choreographing of movement through space and time – a feature that has long characterized the Chinese garden. Realizing that both the English and Japanese Garden were influenced and inspired by the Chinese Garden, I felt compelled to delve deeper into the Chinese Garden and experience for myself the source. While in China, I focused specifically on the relationship between interior architectural space and exterior landscape as experienced by a visitor to the gardens.

2.

There are three main types of Chinese gardens: private gardens of the nobility in the south of China, temple gardens, often high in the mountains and inhabited by monks, and imperial gardens of the emperors in the north of China. The private gardens of the south, with a concentration in Suzhou, are first experienced as disorienting and expansive despite their small area. Windows peer into adjacent spaces that can not be reached directly, movement is non-linear, and a layering of indoor and outdoor spaces seamlessly integrate the interior architectural space and exterior garden space. As part of my research of temple gardens, I visited the four sacred Buddhist mountains of the north, south, east and west. In all cases, temple complexes are scattered over the mountains, connected to each other by pathways and thousands of stone steps. The temple complexes are built in such a way that the courtyards, gardens, and temples integrate indoor and outdoor spaces, and orient to the views and topography of the site allowing their layout to break free of more traditional axial temple planning. The imperial gardens in the north are on the scale of royal gardens and public parks. Due to their sheer size, the imperial gardens often incorporate aspects of both private gardens, temple gardens, and more formal axial planning with spatial hierarchies.

For this exhibition, I have installed windows that offer views into eight gardens: four private gardens in the south, two sacred Buddhist mountains and two imperial gardens. I invite you to partake in an experience of the Chinese Garden.

Ya-Sing Tsu, Frances. Landscape Design in Chinese Gardens. New York: McGraw-Hill Book Co., 1987, p.175

Takenaka Corporation Summer Internship, 2005

Andrei Harwell
Carnegie Mellon
Bounding the Japanese City

Every summer since 1987, the Yale School of Architecture has selected one student to participate in a summer internship at the Takenaka Corporation in Osaka,

4.

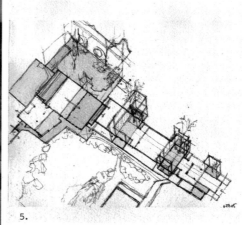

5.

together and managed the dormitory together, fostering a sense of social cohesion within the class. Having unrestricted access to my Japanese peers through the dormitory allowed me develop an inside perspective on Japanese corporate life which I would not have been able to develop otherwise. They were gracious hosts, and willing to answer the strange and endless questions I posed to them.

I worked at Takenaka's main office in downtown Osaka. Assigned to the medical design group, I was given a series of small projects to develop initial schematic designs for. Working under the direct supervision of a project manager and group leader, I was given criticism weekly, and asked to produce sketches, models, and drawings for presentation of each project to the client.

During evenings, I was engaged with my research on urbanism – visiting many of the neighborhoods of Osaka and Kobe and studying their urban and architectural qualities. On weekends I traveled to other cities via train. I recorded my impressions in a sketchbook and spent significant time trying to capture what I saw through photography. Upon returning to Yale, I condensed my thoughts into a research paper entitled "Bounding the Japanese City," attempting to correlate a cultural narrative with the Japanese urban environ-

Japan. The Takenaka Corporation is Japan's fifth largest construc-

6.

7.

tion company, with an award-winning design department. The company is still family owned, and began in the 16th Century as temple builders.

As the 2005 Takenaka Intern, I had three goals: to participate in the life of Takenaka's main office, to research the nature of Japanese Urbanism and its relationship to Japanese culture, and to travel and look at a variety of Japanese cities, landscapes, and buildings.

The core of the Takenaka Internship is participation in an abridged version of Takenaka's training program. Each freshman employee is required to participate in this program, living as a class in Takenaka's Fukae dormitory, and rotating through four different departments in the Corporation. I lived at the dormitory from May to August, along with one-hundred seven incoming freshman. A mix of to-be professionals was represented there: construction managers, architects, marketers, and administrators. We took meals together, trained

ment in which I had lived. The intent of the paper was to uncover some of the "invisible" cultural codes which structure Japanese cities – cities which superficially seem like Western ones, but are really quite different.

Living in Japan and working at Takenaka has influenced my thinking about the condition of both American and foreign cities, and has greatly expanded my world view. I am grateful to the Yale School of Architecture and to the Takenaka Corporation for giving me this opportunity.

Stephen Harby & Alexander Purves
Rome: Continuity & Change
792c

This intensive four-week summer workshop takes place in Rome and is designed to provide a broad overview of that city's major architectural sites, topography, and systems of urban organization. Examples from antiquity to the twentieth century are studied as part of the context of an ever-changing city with its sequence of layered accretions. The seminar examines historical continuity and change as well as the ways in which and the reasons why some elements and approaches were maintained over time and others abandoned. Drawing is used as a primary tool of discovery during explorations of buildings, landscapes, and gardens, both within and outside the city. Students devote the final week to an intensive independent analysis of a building or place.

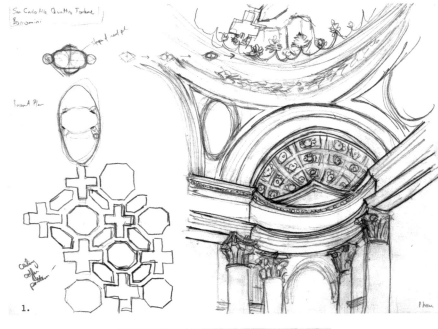

1.

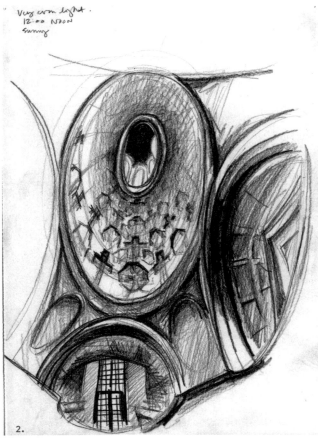

2.

3.

4.

5.

7.

6.

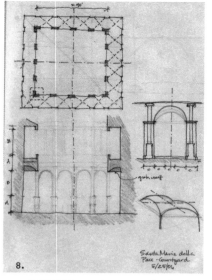

8.

Santa Maria della
Pace - Courtyard
5/25/04

9.

11.

10.

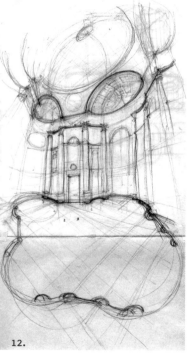

12.

Lectures
Fall 2005

Chip Lord & Curtis Schreier
Ant Farm: 1968-1978
   Thursday, September 8

Jeanne Gang, *Louis I. Kahn Visiting Assistant Professor*
Through Material
   Monday, September 12

Esther da Costa Meyer
The Raw and the Cooked: Lina Bo Bardi
(Brendan Gill Lecture)
   Thursday, September 15

Building Project 2005 Open House
   Thursday, September 22

Massimiliano Fuksas
Four Projects: Lost in Translation
(Paul Rudolph Lecture)
   Monday, September 26

Kurt Forster, *Vincent Scully Visiting Professor*
Surface Tension in Contemporary Architecture
   Monday, October 10

Ada Karmi-Melamede
Recent Work
   Monday, October 24

Brigitte Shim, *Eero Saarinen Visiting Professor*
Site Unseen
   Thursday, October 27

Charles Jencks
The Iconic Building: The Power of Enigma
   Monday, October 31

Glenn Murcutt, *Davenport Visiting Professor*
Sustainability: A Copout for Good Design?
   Thursday, November 3

Neil Denari
Formagraphics
(Myriam Bellazoug Memorial Lecture)
   Monday, November 7

Michael Maltzan
Oblique Actions
   Monday, November 14

Massimiliano Fuksas
Four Projects: Lost in Translation

Bruno Zevi asked, 'What are you planning for the next 10 years?' It was the first time that my old professor was winning me, against me, because I was much more hard, much more radical. He asked me what am I doing... After we said goodbye, I walked a lot [and thought], 'What am I doing in the next 10 years?' For three months I was quite obsessed with this idea of 'what am I doing in ten years?'... And the Biennale, three or five years after, was the result of this question...and what I wanted to do in [that] event was not only this – I said to not make only building – but to do something else for the life. To be an architect, it's a project of the life. It's my project to only do beautiful things. Our project is a project of life. We are part critics, and we are part of the architecture of the world. This comes in part from [Michel] Foucault. The second one is not [from an] architect, but mostly Hitchcock and Kubrick.

   Another thing I will tell you. I didn't want to be an architect. I wanted to be an artist. And after a few years of art, I discovered architecture...when I was [in] my second or third year in architecture, I discovered we [architects] can do a lot of things...and the students of architecture, they are not used to going outside of Italy. I said I have to go outside to Copenhagen and other countries. Then I saw one fantastic, [really] fantastic lecture, the work of Jorn Utzon in Potsdammer Platz Royal Academy. He was so charming– he was real charming. It was so good that I offered to work in his office the day after. 'Why?' he said. I said, 'I don't know.' He said, 'But I don't want students in my office, students are a real pain. You know why? They are pretentious. And secondly, they don't do anything.'

Michael Maltzan
Oblique Actions

Thinking about issues of that kind of space – the space of cities like Los Angeles, contemporary cities – in the beginning of my work was made a lot more complex given that such a large proportion of those types of cities are made not really public in any kind of traditional way, but are often made up of a carpet of single family houses with disconnected and very often internalized lives. And in the beginning, because most of the projects I received were houses, I was looking for ways of thinking about the city in them, and I think I have continued to approach those projects as really distillations or microcosms of a larger and more complex social organization. Many of the projects are trying to demonstrate the intention to create a more fluid overlapping between normally discrete programmatic spaces and roles, with an effort to look at ways that distinctions between public and private coexist or can coexist within the same intervention. At times, reproducing hierarchies and mechanisms is usually associated more with urban typologies than with the house.
   [...]
   I was looking at a different way of the relationship between this exterior form and the interior form. And I got very interested in an idea – which is a game that mathematicians play, I guess amongst themselves over coffee or something – called geometric dissecting – in which you can take a shape, very often a pure shape, and by looking at different ways of dissecting that geometrically, you can begin to create other shapes. In this case, a series of irregular sided figures. What was interesting to me about that was that in a sense the exterior shape and the interior shape shared an almost geometric memory of each other, but it meant that the exterior form did not depend on a typical way of generating that form. It had, for instance, a heptagon. In our case or in these dissections, it has no real center, but it is much more about potentially a kind of graining of the space – not so much a center that you look through or occupy, but that you potentially look across.

Lectures
Spring 2006

7.

8.

9.

10.

11.

Stuart Lipton, *Edward P. Bass Distinguished Visiting Architecture Fellow*
Does Real Estate Development Have a Social Function?
> Monday, January 9
> ----

Against Type
Panel Discussion in conjunction with the exhibition Transcending Type
Suzanne Stephens *(moderator)*; Sulan Kolatan, Hadrian Predock, John Frane, Jesse Reiser, Jeanne Gang, George Yu, Paul Lewis and Marc Tsurumaki *(participants)*
> Thursday, January 12
> ----

Sunil Bald, *Louis I. Kahn Visiting Assistant Professor*
Fold, Crease, & Tear along Perforation
> Thursday, January 19
> ----

Mirka Benes
Meaning through Transposition in Landscape/Architecture: The Case of Baroque Rome
(Timothy J. Lenahan Lecture)
> Monday, January 23
> ----

Sam Jacob
Everything you Can Eat
(Myriam Bellazoug Lecture)
> Thursday, January 26
> ----

Keller Easterling
Reception & discussion to celebrate the release of the book: Enduring Innocence
(Labyrinth Books, 290 York Street, 6 pm)
> Tuesday, January 31
> ----

Tony Fretton
Buildings & their Territories
(Paul Rudolph Lecture)
> Monday, February 6
> ----

Wendy Steiner
What is Aesthetic Conservatism?
(Brendan Gill Lecture)
> Thursday, February 9
> ----

Amanda Burden
Shaping the City: A Strategic Blueprint for New York's Future
(Eero Saarinen Lecture)
> Monday, February 13
> ----

Craig Dykers
A way of thinking, a way of working, and the works of Snohetta
> Monday, February 20
> ----

Stephen Johnson
The Urban Web
(Roth Symonds Lecture)
> Monday, March 27
> ----

Hon. Joseph Riley
The Mayor As Urban Designer
Keynote, Connecticut Mayor's Institute, co-sponsored by School of Management and Regional Plan Association
> Thursday, March 30
> ----

Werner Sobek
Archi-neering the Future
(Gordon Smith Lecture)
> Monday, April 3
> ----

Greg Lynn, *William B. and Charlotte Shepherd Davenport Professor*
Families of Form
> Thursday, April 6
> ----

Frank Gehry & Paul Goldberger
"A Conversation"
> Friday, April 7
> ----

Yale Women in Architecture
Panel Discussion
> Monday, April 17
> ----

Mirka Benes
Meaning Through Transposition in Landscape/Architecture: The Case of Baroque Rome

In conclusion, I would like to say [that] the larger scheme of the professional disciplines of landscape architecture, current design courses, and professional practice, focus meaningfully on material, structures, sciences, technologies, brownfields, and soil. Moving now to the contemporary issues, focusing on sites and infrastructure and the formal, the functional, the aesthetic and the outright philosophical issues involved – these issues stem from a configuration of concerns, from concrete to spiritual. They form the map and the matrix in which the design profession carves [out] its territory. The questions of 'what is that configuration?' and 'how is the territory carved?' are of general interest for designers. And a good way to take conscience of its structural quality is to study how those issues operated in a different place or time. Thereby, for example, involving the student of design, in the professional design school, in the matter of translation from one situation to another in the historical situation not as a model, but as a way of synthetic thinking. This is my view, that history as a subject matter is one of the key roles in the design curriculum. Such a translation involves, in fact, the rehearsal of the act of synthetic thinking, which is how you conceptualize the landscape architectural dialectic in design.

Today the three professional practices, architecture, landscape architecture, and urban design and planning are separate ones. In Baroque Rome, they were one. Today science has a logical and abstract structure. In 17th century Rome, in the time of Galileo Galilei, science was severely subject to religious dogma and oscillated in a tension between studying [the] beauty of external forms and surfaces in nature and the move to investigate the internal structure of nature in logical and abstract thought. Today many materials are synthetic or artificial. At that time the range was great between artificial ones, like stucco and mortar, to marbles and travertine. In focusing on Baroque Rome – a period of exceptional innovations in architecture, in relation to the kinds of development, social and scientific – we have talked about the social and landscape architectural ones and on figures such as the [Antonio] Rinaldi and [Francesco] Borromini as test cases in landscape architectural design. We can address such issues and tensions.

> ----

Craig Dykers
A Way of Thinking, a Way of Working, and the Works of Snohetta
> ----

Many of you will probably have an image of a glowing orb in the heavens – this is sort of my view of the sun – but if you open your mind long enough, as the sun moves through the sky, it creates a sort of beautiful arch over the space above us. And as the days change and as the seasons change this creates a kind of golden dome of light above us, which in many ways is a more beautiful way of understanding the sun in time. In a sense, we believe we exist in moments of time, but the time that we exist in cannot be so readily defined. The same is true in reverse if you take a fluid or moving object and freeze it for a moment – it has a way of describing the moment in a more clear and comprehensive way. Probably our sense of time then distorts our understanding of history. Most of us like to separate history into moments of time: the past, the future, the present, but in some way this is too simplistic and has created a sort of collision of histories. We like to, therefore, describe architecture in clearly defined ways. We call some architecture modern, some classical. I prefer to use the terminology the avant-garde and the derriere-garde. Everyone knows that the derriere-garde is just as important as the avant-garde. Somebody has to care for what has happened before us. So in a way, none of these definitions define any one thing as being better than the other – it simply describes to us that some things are familiar and some things are unfamiliar.

> ----

(1) Esther da Costa Meyer
(2) Massimiliano Fuksas
(3) Kurt Forster
(4) Charles Jencks
(5) Glenn Murcutt
(6) Michael Maltzan
(7) Stuart Lipton
(8) Mirka Benes
(9) Tony Fretton
(10) Craig Dykers
(11) Werner Sobek

Symposia
2005/2006

1.

2.

3.

4.

5.

Philip Johnson and the Constancy of Change
Thursday, February 16 - Saturday, February 18
––––

Presented in cooperation with the Museum of Modern Art, Philip Johnson and the Constancy of Change traced the life and legacy of this complex powerbroker of twentieth century architecture. The sessions examined the architect's eclectic relationship with history, Johnson's endorsement of a series of Modernisms, his skilled use of the visual and written media, and his politics of patronage and the inference of his persona, all capped by a keynote address by Vincent Scully.
––––

Thursday, February 16, MoMA
––––

Terence Riley, *MoMA*
Portrait of the Curator as a Young Man

Film Screening
This is Philip Johnson
directed by Merrill Brockway
––––

Jeffrey Kipnis, *Ohio State University*
The Very Picture of Architecture
––––

Friday, February 17, YSoA
––––

Roaming Through History
––––

Introductory Remarks
Emmanuel Petit, *Yale University*
––––

Kurt Forster, *Yale University*
The Autobiographical House
––––

Charles Jencks
The Truths About Johnson
––––

Mark Jarzombek, *M.I.T.*
Producing Johnson
––––

Response
Alan Plattus, *Yale University*
––––

Keynote Address
Vincent Scully, *Yale University*
Philip Johnson: Art & Irony
––––

Saturday Morning, February 18, YSoA
––––

Reckoning with Modernism
––––

Phyllis Lambert, *Canadian Centre for Architecture*
Breaking with Modernism
––––

Stanislaus von Moos, *University of Zurich*
Playboy Architecture Then & Now
––––

Mark Wigley, *Columbia University*
Reaction Design
––––

Response
Sandy Isenstadt, *Yale University*
––––

Rhetoric and Media
––––

Ujjval Vyas
Philip Johnson & Rhetoric of the New
––––

Beatriz Colomina, *Princeton University*
Johnson on TV
––––

Detlef Mertins, *University of Pennsylvania*
A Taste of Modern
––––

Response
Emmanuel Petit, *Yale University*
––––

Politics of Patronage
––––

Joan Ockman, *Columbia University*
The Figurehead
––––

Reinhold Martin, *Columbia University* ·
"Liquidity", Architecture & Oil
––––

Michael Sorkin, *The College of the City of New York*
The Plot Against Architecture
––––

Kazys Varnelis, *University of Limerick, Ireland*
Johnson's Empire
––––

Response
Peggy Deamer, *Yale University*
––––

Concluding Remarks
Peter Eisenman, *Yale University*
Modern Architecture: Romanticism & Disintegration
––––

Vincent Scully
Philip Johnson: Art and Irony
––––

The subtitle of this talk really doesn't mean anything. They demanded a subtitle and I gave them that. It should probably just be called 'Philip Johnson', and in comparison with the other talks on the program for this symposium, which are specialized studies which will undoubtedly break new ground, I though it best to be more general and, therefore, perhaps more self-evident.

For example, I ask you, how about Saarinen and Johnson? How could they be fit into a course on Modern Architecture? I thought it's probably like this, [Eero] Saarinen first, and [then] Johnson, in that order. And described in the syllabus as 'Eero Saarinen: Americaniza-tion of the International Style, corporate architec-ture, the style for the job. Philip Johnson: the Inter-national Style and its collapse, history, postmodernism, neo-modernism, and expressionism.' Those two descrip-tions seem fair enough, but they seem bloodless and categorical. Especially in the case of Johnson, whom I knew much better than I did Saarinen, and whose unique presence on the architecture scene was hardly confined to his work as a practicing architect.

He was a special kind of cultural presence, like Frank Lloyd Wright — whose successor perhaps in a more sociological than architectural way and, above all, in the popular mind, he almost was. But the times were dif-ferent. Wright remained a turn-of-the-century radical throughout his whole life while, later in the century, Johnson became a kind of powerbroker on the archi-tectural scene. Still, despite the obvious differences between them, they had much in common. Both of them were American confidence men, adept at self-promo-tion and the flattery of clients. One was surely a great architect, the other, perhaps not. But at the very beginning of his career, and probably outdoing anything he was to accomplish later, he somehow managed to build — and what may well turn out to be — the most concep-tually important house of the century. When he visited Taliesin back in those days, [Frank Lloyd] Wright said 'the prince is visiting the king.'

But this was the occasion in 1955 when Wright, grumbling about not having been met at the train sta-tion, came up on Johnson at the obligatory cocktail party in Hendrie Hall and said, first of all, 'Why Philip, I thought you were dead.' And then, still grumbling, he turned back toward Philip, now abashed and trying to hide across the room, and in a centurion voice which rang throughout the hall, he cried out 'why Philip, little Phil, all grown up, building buildings and leaving them out in the rain.' Then later that night, Johnson, giving Wright the finest introduction I've ever heard describing the ritual procession through Taliesin West and coming at last to the fire burning in the heart of the desert, said, 'I wept.' Johnson often wept for art — never for him-self, and rarely for mankind.

His services — like those of most architects, and for which he called himself a whore — were for the rich, not the poor. It was all 'Acropolis' for him — never re-ally 'the town'. For his complex problems, his attention span was too short and his impatience too demanding. Community was not for him. He was fundamentally lonely — the existential individual on guard in the world. And here he is on the left…old [referring to slide of Johnson in his New Canaan gatehouse]. Just about the same age Wright was over here. And what a difference between them. Wright all aglow with nineteenth century self-sat-isfaction…approval. Johnson — fragile, vulnerable, worn down physically, and perhaps spiritually, from the many transformations of his life — standing near the end of it in the mournful shadows of a cavernous building directly inspired by the work of much younger men.
––––

On the Waterfront
     Friday, March 31 - Saturday, April 1

On the Waterfront examined the enormity of the task of large scale waterfront planning in three very different mega cities: Toronto, London and New York. This topic is one of the most important concerns of today's architect, urban planners, developers and politicians. These three cities are chosen not because they are representative cities; rather, they serve as exemplary cities. Although the scope and the time frame of the projects to be done in these three cities are largely different from each other, they all face the problems and possibilities that confront modern urbanism.

     Friday, March 31, 2006

     Opening Remarks
     Robert A.M Stern, *Yale School of Architecture*

     Introduction
     Alexander Garvin, *Yale School of Architecture*

     Keynote Address
     Robert Bruegmann, *School of Architecture and the Program in Urban Planning and Policy, University of Illinois at Chicago*
     Urban Cinderella: The Working Waterfront

     Saturday Morning, April 1

Toronto

     Moderator
     Alan Plattus, *Yale School of Architecture*

     Christopher Glaisek, *Toronto Waterfront Revitalization Corporation*
     Planning the Redevelopment of Toronto's Waterfront

     Bruce Kuwabara, *Kuwabara Payne McKenna Blumberg Architects*
     The Architecture of the Toronto Waterfront

     Alan Vihant, *Concord Adex*
     Developing the Toronto Waterfront

London

     Moderator
     Keith Krumwiede, *Yale School of Architecture*

     Stuart Lipton, *Yale School of Architecture*
     Development on the Thames River Waterfront

     Richard Burdett, *London School of Economics*
     The Changing Thames River Waterfront

     Saturday Afternoon, April 1

New York City

     Moderator
     Edward Mitchell, *Yale School of Architecture*

     Joseph B. Rose, *Georgetown Partners; New York City Planning Commission*
     Queens West: The Changing Waterfront of Long Island City
          ----
     Thom Mayne, *Morphosis*
     The Future of the Olympic Village at Queens West

     Henry Elghanayan, *Rockrose Development Corporation*
     Developing Queens West

Robert Bruegmann
Urban Cinderella: The Working Waterfront

This talk is a set of reflections – it is a really fascinating thing. One of the things that I thought I would focus on here is the fact that since the 1960's there has been an absolute explosion in the number of these port and waterfront regeneration schemes. As you see from the images here they span every continent, and it has really happened in lightning speed considering how slowly things tend to evolve in the city. There has been remarkable quick change. That change is usually ascribed to two places in the United States: Boston and Baltimore – the big bang, if you will, of urban waterfront regeneration.

Now the story as it is usually told is a simple, triumphant Cinderella story. The city develops, the waterfront develops, it booms, but with little regard to the environment and almost no regard for waterfront as amenity. These areas tended to be industrial zones. So Baltimore in 1875, just as Baltimore in 1935 in a way, turns it back on the harbor. What sticks out in the harbor is strictly things that are there for business reasons, and it actually walls the city off from the water. Then the next chapter is that the city and the harbor tend to go into decline. The harbor declines because there are bigger ships and there are newer port facilities, and the port goes into a downwind spiral. This happens in many American cities after WWII. The ports are troubled in the interwar years, but also right after WWII it begins to radically go into decline. In the case of Baltimore, here is a city that in 1953 was likely to go into bankruptcy if [it] didn't do anything. The population had plummeted, the economic base of the city plummeted, and so on. So chapter three, the port, in turn, rejuvenates itself. There is a major private public attempt to recreate the port as something else. It is remade as public space with a lot of recreational uses, it caters to a great many tourists, and lastly these new institutions – like for example Camden Yards and the Aquarium – crown it.

As far as architects are concerned, the really wonderful thing is when it is crowned by significant pieces of architecture, that the euphoria generated by the Baltimore model has taken abroad, and major architects go to work on them. As a result, we have things like Genoa and Bilbao. Now the typical ending to this story, in many of the books published by the Urban Land Institute and others, is '… and everyone lived happily ever after.' But of course, as you would expect from a historian, I think the story is, as it gets older, more complicated and even more conflicted. Let me tell you a little about this complication, even with the examples that we just seen, in the case of Baltimore and Bilbao, these are cities that are still struggling. Many people think that the attention to the waterfront has probably taken away the attention that should have been spent towards the rest of the city. In Genoa – this was for the exhibition in 1992 – it wasn't finished on time and it was a financial disaster. The mayor was booted out of the office because of some shenanigans in connection with it – so all is not really rosy. Nevertheless, it is clear that this whole movement has taken the world by storm.

So let's go back a little bit and look at the story. I want to look at it particularly in the light of the larger urban history. The thing I find most interesting about the waterfront is that it is part of a much larger urban pattern of decentralization. Waterfronts were typically adjacent to downtown, then they got bigger and more industrial and moved out. And in doing this, it is the same that has happened with the population and much of the jobs of most cities. What happens when people move out is that it creates something of a vacuum in the center. So we see over and over again a process of gentrification at the core as the flip side of decentralization going to the edge. You can see this, for example, very clearly in the case of Paris in the 1930s.

Ant Farm: 1968-1978
August 29, 2005 - November 4, 2005

Ant Farm was founded as an architecture and design group in 1968 by Doug Michels and Chip Lord, who were soon joined by Curtis Schreier, Hudson Marquez, and W. Douglas Hurr. Other members came and went over the years. The collective, whose base shifted between San Francisco and Houston, saw themselves as part of the cultural underground. A friend compared them to a toy Ant Farm, where frenetic activity takes place below the surface and collectivity is a way of life. The name stuck.

In the early years of their collaboration, Ant Farm set out to create a new architecture suited to an alternative, nomadic lifestyle. They concentrated on developing giant inflatable structures, easy and cheap to build and transport and symbolic of their opposition to mainstream Brutalist architecture. Ant Farm completed several successful architectural commissions, including their award-winning House of the Century in Texas. But their wide-ranging and imaginative interests could not be satisfied within a single discipline, and from the beginning Ant Farm explored the expressive potential of video and performance. Media Burn, a spectacular performance and later a widely distributed videotape, was a literal collision of two American icons: the car and the television set. On July 4, 1975, in the parking lot of San Francisco's Cow Palace, Schreier and Michels drove the Phantom Dream Car, a customized 1959 Cadillac Biarritz, full speed through a pyramid of flaming TVs.

Ant Farm also worked with T.R. Uthco, San Francisco artists Doug Hall, Diane Andrews Hall, and Jody Procter, to create The Eternal Frame. This 1975 videotaped reenactment of the Kennedy assassination is a quintessential comment of the replacement of real experience and memory with a mass-media version etched into the collective consciousness.

1.

Ant Farm's 1974 public sculpture Cadillac Ranch is that rare artwork that has achieved the status of icon. Commissioned by Stanley Marsh 3, Ant Farm members Lord, Michels, and Marquez partially buried ten Cadillacs nose down in a wheat field on Marsh's ranch in Amarillo, Texas. The work is both a celebration of the evolution of the tailfin (1949-1963) and a critique of Detroit's practice of planned obsolescence.

Ant Farm disbanded officially in 1978 after a fire in their San Francisco studio destroyed much of their work. This exhibition comprises a timeline designed by the artists that, together with drawings, collages, posters, photographs, mail art, objects, and video-works, tells the story of Ant Farm's activities during the ten years of their collaboration.

The exhibition is dedicated to Ant Farm founder and member Doug Michels, a 1967 graduate of the Yale School of Architecture, who died in an accident in June 2003.

Transcending Type
November 14 - February 3, 2006
Architecture & Vision

New ideas often lie dormant in the mundane or the too familiar. Art and architecture can correct this myopic state, clarifying our vision and energizing the objects and buildings before us.

Such was the challenge for the participants in the U.S. Pavilion of the 2004 Venice Architecture Biennale, for which the Bureau of Educational and Cultural Affairs of the U.S. Department of State chose Architectural Record as curator. The pavilion is part of the 9th International Architecture Exhibition of the Venice Biennale, whose theme, "Metamorph," signals critical transformations in architecture over the past 50 years.

Entitled Transcending Type, the U.S. exhibition, developed by the editors of the magazine, features six American architects in the vanguard of contemporary design. The participants are KOL/MAC LLC,

Lewis.Tsurumaki.Lewis, Predock_Frane Architects, Reiser+Umemoto, Studio/Gang/Architects, and George Yu Architects. Each solution explores new forms and uses for iconic modern building types, providing a fresh perspective on structures that have been stereotyped and replicated globally. Drawings, digital media, and three-dimensional installations present a 21st-century vision for familiar project categories, including the shopping center, apartment tower, sports stadium, parking garage, spiritual space, and highway interchange.

This exhibition, now reassembled at the Yale School of Architecture Gallery, suggests architecture's transformative power, whether reached through tectonics, scientific exploration, or sheer imagination.
- Robert A. Ivy, *FAIA, editor-in-chief, Architectural Record*

Prairie Skyscraper: Frank Lloyd Wright's Price Tower
February 13, 2006 - May 5, 2006

The Architect: Frank Lloyd Wright (1867-1959) is considered the most influential American architect of the 20th century. Wright made paramount contributions to architecture not only in terms of innovative structural systems, architectural space, and ornamentation, but also in emphasizing the relationship of architecture to its natural site and the place of architecture in art and life. Wright's architecture built new and modern lifestyles.

Wright's relevance in American architecture initially emerged as he sought the expression of democracy through the concept of organic architecture. Organic architecture's principle insisted that buildings grow naturally from their environment, be harmonious with their materials, and respond to the needs of their inhabitants. These principles would allow form and function to be integrated into a unified whole.

During the years of his practice Wright contributed Prairie and Usonian house designs to American residential architecture while

2.

3.

he also designed commercial and civic buildings. The Prairie houses (1900—1914) blended with the landscape, and shifted traditional domestic architecture with its boxed-in rooms to open, flowering spaces. The open floor plan was also present in the Usonian house, which Wright began developing in the late 1930s. He believed Usonian houses would serve Americans by providing livable, well-designed, tasteful dwellings which the middle class could afford. These economical and technologically innovative houses used inexpensive materials such as wood, brick and glass and were based on standardized layouts with modular grids. Aspects of these houses have been incorporated in mainstream American home design since.

Later in his career, Wright's non-residential architecture maintained a dialogue with nature through the union of site and structure. The tree became the metaphor for his only built skyscraper, the Price Tower, in Bartlesville, Oklahoma. This exhibit explores the Price Tower's architectural form determined by its particular function environment, patron, and the materials used in its structure, façades and interiors.

The Client: Harold C. Price, Sr. (1888—1962) founded the H.C. Price Company in 1921 as a pipeline construction and pipe coating firm which eventually became an international construction enterprise. At

into an organic architectural and urban whole and Harold C. Price Sr.'s entrepreneurial ability and commitment to Bartlesville, Oklahoma.

Prairie Skyscraper: Frank Lloyd Wright's Price Tower is organized by Price Tower Arts Center, Bartlesville, Oklahoma, in cooperation with The Frank Lloyd Wright Foundation Archives, Scottsdale, Arizona. The exhibition, its tour and publication are made possible in part by the Henry Luce Foundation, the Buell Family of Bartlesville, the Oklahoma Tourism and Recreation Department, and the Oklahoma Arts Council.

The exhibition installation has been designed by Zaha Hadid and Zaha Hadid Architects, London, and is co-produced by Price Tower Arts Center and Yale University School of Architecture Gallery.

– – – –

Year End Exhibition of Student Work
May 19, 2006 - July 28, 2006

– – – –

This exhibition is a partial record of a year's research undertaken at the Yale School of Architecture; research into what is possible and what is desirable, into what a student architect can discover about the self, the world and the art of architecture. On the walls of the gallery lie compelling evidence of possibilities and paths open to architects today. Here we can see the fruits of serious investigation, the diversity of stylistic expression, of scale and type of work undertaken; the diversity of media available to help study, express and realize ideas. What is accomplished in architecture school is important for the individual student; but it also plays a very real part in determining how our built

the suggestion of his sons Harold Jr. and Joe, both of whom had been influenced by noted architect Bruce Goff while attending the University of Oklahoma, Price arrived at Taliesin in the autumn of 1952 expecting Wright to design a modest low-rise. He left with the plan to build a nineteen-story mixed residential, retail and office tower. Construction began in 1953 and was completed in February 1956.

On its fiftieth anniversary, Price Tower stands as a testament to Frank Lloyd Wright's ideas of design, ornament and purpose integrated

world will develop and evolve. As the open-ended, never-ending process of education confronts beginning architects, realities that will be true for them will always come into sharp focus; work can always be improved; what is designed is almost never completely satisfying for the designer; optimism is essential, the architecture project is never really finished.

– – – –

Perspecta 37 "Famous"
The Yale Architectural Journal

- - - -

Edited by Brendan Lee, DaeWha Kang, Justin Kwok
and Robert McClure
Designed by Jeffrey Lai

February 2006
ISBN 0-262-61205-4
9 x 12, 120 pp., 160 illus., 30 color
$20.00/£12.95 (PAPER)

Does fame empower architecture or undermine it? Does the star power or cult status of an architect enhance the art or dilute it? This issue of *Perspecta* – the oldest and most distinguished student-edited, university-based American architecture journal – examines the inner workings of fame as it relates to architecture though media and culture. It looks at how the commodification of architecture affects the design process – whether fame emphasizes all the wrong aspects of architecture or provides the only way an architect can produce truly ambitious projects. How does architecture generate fame? And how does fame generate architecture?

Celebrity permeates all levels of contemporary society; architecture, academia, the architectural press, and the mainstream media all play a role in promoting the mystique of the designer genius. The tradition of learning through apprenticeship and the struggle to have projects commissioned and built perpetuate the importance of the famous architect. Does this serve architecture or only the architectural star? The contributors to *Perspecta* examine both sides of the argument: Architecture moves forward through a process of innovation; fame provides the architect with the leverage needed to accomplish innovation. Or is it that fame, because of its relationship to the media and popular tastes, inevitably dilutes the quality of the architecture? Does "famous" architecture glorify only itself and neglect the people, the values, and the functions that it must serve?

- - - -

Perspecta 38: Architecture After All
The Yale Architectural Journal

- - - -

Edited by Forth Bagley, Ceren Bingol, Marcus Carter
and Christopher Marcinkoski
Designed by Danielle Aubert & Willy Wong

April 2006
ISBN 0-262-52452-X
9 x 12, 112 pp., 30 color illus.
100 duotone illustrations.
$20.00/£12.95 (PAPER)

The profession of architecture is increasingly characterized by divergent architectural ideas and divergent political, social, technological, and economic agendas. Much of current practice focuses on the process of architecture (its how) rather than its meaning, effect, or reason for being (its why). This issue of *Perspecta* – the oldest and most distinguished student-edited architectural journal – explores the practice of architecture after the breakdown of consensus. Designers, theoreticians, and scholars investigate an architectural landscape devoid of a dominant ideology or ethos. Their essays take specific points of departure – globalization, urbanism, pedagogy, irony, as well as form, theory, and ideology – to address broader questions about the social, economic, and political fallout from these modes of practice, considering whether the lack of an overriding ethos in architecture is liberating or limiting for the profession. And, after all, is it conceivable, or desirable, to return to an architecture derived from a single, dominant mode of operation?

- - - -

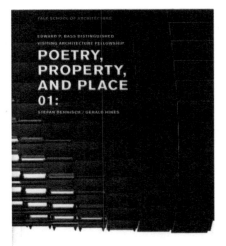

Poetry, Property, and Place, 01
Stefan Behnisch & Gerald Hines

September 2006
ISBN 0-393-73220-7
192 pp.
$35.00 (Paper)

Poetry, Property, and Place, 01: Stefan Behnisch / Gerald Hines is the first in a series of books from the Yale School of Architecture, which studies the collaborative process between architects and developers made possible by the Edward P. Bass Distinguished Visiting Architecture Fellowship. In a Yale advanced studio, students designed projects that would transform Garibaldi Repubblica, a neglected site in central Milan, into a vital urban place. The book includes interviews with Bass Distinguished Visiting Fellow Gerald D. Hines; Saarinen Visiting Professor Stefan Behnisch; as well as those who participated in the studio research process. The book is distributed by W. W. Norton & Company and is available internationally.

- - - -